Maṇḍalas and Yantras in the Hindu Traditions

Maṇḍalas and Yantras in the Hindu Traditions

by

Gudrun Bühnemann

with contributions by H. Brunner,
M.W. Meister, A. Padoux, M. Rastelli
and J. Törzsök

D.K.Printworld (P) Ltd.
New Delhi

Cataloging in Publication Data — DK
[Courtesy: D.K. Agencies (P) Ltd. <docinfo@dkagencies.com>]

Bühnemann, Gudrun, 1955-
Maṇḍalas and Yantras in the Hindu traditions / Gudrun Bühnemann.
xvii, 304 p., 25 cm.
Includes bibliographical references (p.)
Includes index.
ISBN 8124603979

1. Mandala. 2. Yantras. 3. Hindu symbolism. 4. Hinduism — Rituals. I. Title.

DDC 294.537 22

ISBN 81-246-0397-9 (Hardbound)
ISBN 81-246-0398-7 (Paperback)
First published in Leiden, The Netherlands in 2003
Revised edition published in India in 2007

Published and printed by:
D.K. Printworld (P) Ltd.
Regd. office : *'Sri Kunj'*, F-52, Bali Nagar
New Delhi - 110 015
***Phones* : (011) 2545-3975; 2546-6019; *Fax* : (011) 2546-5926**
***E-mail*: dkprintworld@vsnl.net**
***Web*: www.dkprintworld.com**

CONTENTS

NOTES ON CONTRIBUTORS

HÉLÈNE BRUNNER [-LACHAUX] was a member of the Centre national de la recherche scientifique (Section of Oriental Studies), Paris, from 1963 to 1985. She retired in 1985, but continued working in her field, that is Āgamic (Saiddhāntika) Śaivism, as represented in mediaeval texts, Āgamas or *paddhatis*. She passed away on March 27, 2005. Her major publications include an edition and French translation of the Somaśambhupaddhati (four volumes, Pondichéry: Institut Français d'Indologie 1963–1998) and a French translation of the *kriyāpāda* and *caryāpāda* of the Mṛgendrāgama (Pondichéry: Institut Français d'Indologie, 1985).

GUDRUN BÜHNEMANN is a Professor at the Department of Languages and Cultures of Asia of the University of Wisconsin-Madison. Her major publications include *Budha-Kauśika's Rāmarakṣāstotra: A Contribution to the Study of Sanskrit Devotional Poetry* (Vienna: Institut für Indologie, Universität Wien, 1983); *Pūjā: A Study in Smārta Ritual* (Vienna: Institut für Indologie, Universität Wien, 1988); *The Worship of Mahāgaṇapati according to the Nityotsava* (Wichtrach: Institut für Indologie, 1988); *Forms of Gaṇeśa: A Study based on the Vidyārṇavatantra* (Wichtrach: Institut für Indologie, 1989); and *The Iconography of Hindu Tantric Deities.* Volume I: *The Pantheon of the Mantramahodadhi.* Volume II: *The Pantheons of the Prapañcasāra and the Śāradātilaka* (Groningen: Egbert Forsten, 2000–2001).

MICHAEL W. MEISTER holds the W. Norman Brown Chair of South Asian Studies at the University of Pennsylvania. He has edited the *Encyclopædia of Indian Temple Architecture*, *Discourses on Śiva*, *Making Things in South Asia*, Coomaraswamy's *Essays in Early Indian Architecture* and *Essays in Architectural Theory*, *Cooking for the Gods* and *Ethnography and Personhood.*

ANDRÉ PADOUX is Directeur de recherche honoraire at the Centre national de la recherche scientifique, Paris. His publications include *Vāc. The Concept of the Word in Selected Hindu Tantras* (Albany, New York: State University of New York Press, 1990); *Le cœur de la Yoginī. Yoginīhṛdaya, avec le commentaire Dīpikā d'Amṛtānanda* (Paris: De Boccard, 1994); and (with Lilian Silburn) *Abhinavagupta. La lumière sur les tantras, chapitres 1 à 5 du Tantrāloka, traduits et commentés* (Paris: De Boccard, 1998).

MARION RASTELLI received her Ph.D. in Classical Indian Studies (Indology) in 1998 from the University of Vienna. She is presently a research fellow at the Institute for the Cultural and Intellectual History of Asia of the Austrian Academy of Sciences, Vienna. Her research focuses on the teachings and ritual of Pāñcarātra. Her most important publications are: *Philosophisch-theologische Grundanschauungen der Jayākhyasaṃhitā. Mit einer Darstellung des täglichen Rituals* (Wien: Verlag der Österreichischen Akademie der Wissenschaften, 1999) and *The Religious Practice of the* Sādhaka *According to the Jayākhyasaṃhitā* (Indo-Iranian Journal 43, 2000: 319–395).

JUDIT TÖRZSÖK is Lecturer ('Maître de conférences') in Sanskrit at the Université Charles-de-Gaulle-Lille 3 (France). She completed her D.Phil. thesis in Oxford in 1999 on a Tantra entitled the Siddhayogeśvarīmata, belonging to the tradition of the Trika. Her research focuses on the early Śaiva Tantric traditions. Since 2001 she has been contributing to the Hindu Tantric Dictionary (Tāntrikābhidhānakośa) and participates in the Skanda-Purāṇa project (Groningen, the Netherlands).

LIST OF ILLUSTRATIONS

Illustrations to "Maṇḍala, Yantra and Cakra: Some Observations" by Gudrun Bühnemann:

1. A yantra for attraction (*ākarṣaṇayantra*), described in Mantramahodadhi 20.84cd–85; reproduced from the Mantramahodadhi (edited by R. Prasāda, Lucknow: Smarahiṃsakadatta Press, 1872, appendix). The name Devadatta (to be replaced with the intended person's name) appears in the centre of the pericarp of the lotus, and the *krodhabīja* (that is, the syllable *hūṃ*) in the four lotus petals. The yantra should be drawn on a leaf of birch-bark using a mixture of red sandalwood paste and one's own blood. After the *pūjā* the yantra is normally soaked in ghee.

2. A supporting maṇḍala for the *vardhanī* vessel in Tantric *pūjā*; reproduced from Bühnemann 1988b, Illustration 36.

3. A ca. 17th-century yantra with the Rāmarakṣāstotra inscribed on textile (33 x 34 cm); photograph by G. Bühnemann. In 1979 this yantra was part of the collection of Sarabhai Nawab (Ahmedabad).

4. A yantra assigned to stanza 55 of the Saundaryalaharī; reproduced from Saundaryalaharī 1957: 87. The syllable *yaṃ* (which is usually the seed [*bīja*] syllable of the element wind) is inscribed thrice in the yantra. According to the instructions (*prayoga*), the yantra should be drawn on a golden plate or on fish-bone. One should repeat the stanza 20,000 times a day for 45 days to secure freedom from bondage.

5. A yantra for subjugating one's master, described in Dāmodara's Yantracintāmaṇi 3.20–26 (Türstig 1988: 21); reproduced from Türstig 1988, appendix, yantra no. 3. The name Devadatta (to be replaced with the intended person's name) appears in the centre of the pericarp of the lotus prefixed by the syllables *oṃ śrīṃ* and suffixed by *śrīṃ oṃ*. On the lotus petals the syllables *śrīṃ* and *kṣaḥ* alternate. The yantra should be drawn on a leaf of birch-bark using yellow pigment. It should then be placed into a vessel and burnt, and its ashes consumed.

6. A *pūjāyantra* of Mahāgaṇapati, reproduced and adapted from Bühnemann 1988b, Illustration 40. The yantra features a downward-pointing triangle inside a hexagram, surrounded by an eight-petalled lotus and a square with four gates.

Illustrations to "Maṇḍalas and Yantras in Smārta Ritual" by Gudrun Bühnemann:

Part I. Selected Maṇḍala-like Structures, Maṇḍalas and Yantras

Following a common South Asian tradition of depicting maṇḍala-like structures, the east (and not the north) is shown on top of the diagrams.

1. A diagram showing the deities of the *baliharaṇacakra*, or *baliharaṇamaṇḍala*, reproduced from Kane 1968–1977, volume 2: 747. With minor variations, this diagram is found in a number of contemporary texts, such as the Ṛgvedīyabrahmakarmasamuccaya.
2. A table showing the arrangement of the five deities in (domestic) *pañcāyatana* shrines as prescribed by Bopadeva.
3. A maṇḍala of the heavenly bodies (*grahadevatāmaṇḍala* or *navagrahamaṇḍala*); a contemporary print reproduced from the ritual manual Ṛgvedīyabrahmakarmasamuccaya.
4. The *(durgā)saptaśatīmahāyantra*; a contemporary print reproduced from the manual Ṛgvedīyabrahmakarmasamuccaya.
5. The *rudrapīṭhamahāyantra*; a contemporary print reproduced from the manual Ṛgvedīyabrahmakarmasamuccaya.

Part II. Bhadramaṇḍalas

Table: Constituent Parts of the Bhadramaṇḍalas.

Black and White Prints of Maṇḍalas

The black and white prints of maṇḍalas which are listed below are reproduced from the Bhadramārtaṇḍa (BM) edition. The edition does not illustrate all maṇḍalas described in the BM. In addition, some maṇḍala drawings are incomplete and have not been reproduced here. Since the original numbers of the illustrations as printed in the BM have been retained, some numbers are missing.[1] A complete list of maṇḍalas described in the BM is provided in the appendix to the article. The diagrams use the following scheme to indicate colours other than black and white: one dot in the centre of a square – yellow; two dots – red; and three dots – green.

[1] These are the numbers 24–25, 36, 38–40, 50–51 and 53–65.

Illustration to "The Use of Maṇḍalas and Yantras in the Pāñcarātra Tradition" by Marion Rastelli:

1. Ca. 17th-century bronze statue of the 16-armed Sudarśana-cakrapuruṣa in the Śrī-Kālamekaperumāl Temple, Tirumohur, Madurai District; photo courtesy of the Institut Français de Pondichéry/École Française d'Extrême-Orient.

Illustration to "Maṇḍala and Yantra in the Siddhānta School of Śaivism: Definitions, Description and Ritual Use" by Hélène Brunner:

1. The *sarvatobhadramaṇḍala* reconstructed according to Śāradātilaka 3.106–131ab and Rāghavabhaṭṭa's commentary.

Illustration to "Icons of Inclusivism: Maṇḍalas in Some Early Śaiva Tantras" by Judit Törzsök:

1. The outline and construction of the *śrīmaṇḍala* according to the Netratantra with an illustration of some technical terms (see Appendix 1 for a description); drawing by Paul Coatalen.

(In the illustration the bottom is the western direction, for the disciple would enter and see the maṇḍala from the west, facing the auspicious eastern direction.)

Illustrations to "Maṇḍalas in Abhinavagupta's Tantrāloka" by André Padoux:

1. Outline of the maṇḍala of the three tridents and (seven) lotuses (*tritriśūlābjamaṇḍala*) prescribed by the Trikasadbhāvatantra; see Tantrāloka 31.10–41b; drawn by and reproduced with the kind permission of Stephanie Sanderson.

2. Outline of the maṇḍala of the trident and lotuses (*triśūlābjamaṇḍala*) prescribed by Mālinīvijayottaratantra 9.6–31 (= Tantrāloka 31.62–85b); drawn by and reproduced with the kind permission of Stephanie Sanderson.

3. The maṇḍala throne and the three goddesses enthroned upon it, as visualized along the axis of internal sensation during internal worship; see Tantrāloka 15.295c–328b; drawn by and reproduced with the kind permission of Stephanie Sanderson.

Illustrations to "The Śrīcakra according to the First Chapter of the Yoginīhṛdaya" by André Padoux:

1. The *śrīcakra*, reconstructed and drawn by Gérard Huet and reproduced with his kind permission.

2. The bodily cakras according to the first chapter of Amṛtānanda's commentary on the Yoginīhṛdaya; adapted from Padoux 1994: 126.

Illustrations to "Vāstupuruṣamaṇḍalas: Planning in the Image of Man" by Michael W. Meister:

1. The geometric construction of a cardinally oriented square locating an altar as defined in Śulba-Sūtra texts of the third-fourth centuries B.C.

2. Vāstupuruṣamaṇḍala of 81 squares, as described in the Bṛhat-Saṃhitā (Apte/Supekar 1983: VPM-4).

3. Ground plans and constructing maṇḍalas:

A. Bharateśvara temple, Bhubaneshwar, Orissa, ca. 600–650 century A.D. The walls, in thickness, are half the breadth of the sanctum. Entries project beyond the square maṇḍala (*karṇavyāsa* system).

B. Śiva temple no. 2, Mahuā, Madhya Pradesh, ca. 650–675 A.D. Measurements at the hoof-moulding of the *vedībandha* demonstrate that projections on the walls directly express the inner space of the sanctum and the central 'place for Brahman' (*brahmasthāna*) of the *vāstumaṇḍala*.

C. Mahādeva temple, Amrol, Madhya Pradesh, ca. 700 A.D. Diagram to demonstrate extension of the *brahmasthāna* and sanctum to demarcate the central offsets of the outer walls.

D. Naktimātā temple, Bhavanipur, Rajasthan, ca. 875 A.D. In the ninth century, the maṇḍala diagram is used in a different way, still demarcating the central offsets, but pulling them within the constructing grid (*bhadravyāsa* system).

4. Bṛhadīśvara temple, Gaṅgaikōṇḍacōḻapuram, Tamilnadu, ca. 1035 A.D. Plan with odd-numbered grid (after Pichard 1995: 47).

Colour Plates

6. A *rāmaliṅgatobhadra* with 26 *rāmamudrās* and 28 *liṅgas*; painting preserved in the S.R.C. Museum of Indology, Jaipur; photograph by G. Bühnemann.

7. A *caturmudrārāmaliṅgatobhadra* with 4 *rāmamudrās* and 8 *liṅgas* and a *sarvatobhadra* in the centre; painting from Rājasthān reproduced from Stadtner 1998: 350, no. 353, with the kind permission of Robert Clark, Barcelona. This *bhadra* corresponds to the *bhadra* reproduced as Illustration 42 from the Bhadramārtaṇḍa (see Illustrations to "Maṇḍalas and Yantras in Smārta Ritual" [Part II. Bhadramaṇḍalas] by Gudrun Bühnemann).

8. A *gaṇeśabhadra* with five icons of Gaṇeśa reprinted from Gaṇeśkoś (edited by A. Gāḍgīḷ, Puṇe: Śrīrām Book Agency, 1981 [in Marāṭhī]): 477.

9. A *gaṇeśabhadra* with 21 icons of Gaṇeśa; painting preserved in the Bhandarkar Oriental Research Institute, Puṇe, Mahārāṣṭra.

10. A *sūryabhadra* with 12 icons of the sun; painting from Rājasthān reproduced from Stadtner 1998: 350, no. 352, with the kind permission of Robert Clark, Barcelona. This *bhadra* corresponds to the *bhadra* reproduced as Illustration 67 from the Bhadramārtaṇḍa (see Illustrations to "Maṇḍalas and Yantras in Smārta Ritual" [Part II. Bhadramaṇḍalas] by Gudrun Bühnemann).

11. The construction of a *dvādaśaliṅgatobhadra* with a *sarvatobhadra* in the centre; photographed by G. Bühnemann in Puṇe, Mahārāṣṭra.

12. The invocation of deities into areca nuts placed on a *sarvatobhadra* during a *vratodyāpana* rite; photographed by G. Bühnemann in Puṇe, Mahārāṣṭra.

13. A vessel of plenty placed on a *sarvatobhadra* during a *vratodyāpana* rite; photographed by G. Bühnemann in Puṇe, Mahārāṣṭra.

14. The *cakrābjamaṇḍala* reproduced from the colour print inserted in the back of volume 1 of Padmanabhan's edition of the Pādma-Saṃhitā.

15. The *navapadmamaṇḍala* reproduced from the colour print prefixed to the foreword of the first edition of the Jayākhya-Saṃhitā by Krishnamacharya (1931). Apte 1973: 505 points to the fact that the drawing is not in accordance with the textual description in every detail. The nine lotuses should have the same size and should be adjacent to one another.

INTRODUCTION

Gudrun Bühnemann

General Remarks

In recent years maṇḍalas have attracted much interest among a wider public. The main focus of such interest has been directed toward Tibetan maṇḍalas, specimens of which have been included in numerous publications. But maṇḍalas are found across a wide spectrum of South Asian religious traditions, including those of the Hindus and Jains. Maṇḍalas are also part of East Asian Buddhist traditions.

In South Asia, maṇḍalas have been used mainly in occasional rites of worship. In these rites deities are invoked into maṇḍalas with the aid of mantras. The construction of a maṇḍala is specially important in Tantric initiation (*dīkṣā*) rites. In esoteric teaching, a maṇḍala may be visualized as present in the practitioner's body by correlating the cosmic symbolism of the maṇḍala with the practitioner's body parts. Maṇḍala patterns have had other far-reaching influences. They have, for example, had an impact on ancient town-planning. The use of maṇḍalas is also documented in alchemy.[1]

The South Asian tradition of preparing and worshipping maṇḍalas and yantras continues up to the present. On the level of folk art the *kohbar* maṇḍalas, which decorate the walls of the nuptial chamber in the Mithilā region of north Bihar (India) and Nepal, are a good example of this. So are the auspicious floor designs prepared with rice flour or coloured powders and regionally known as *rāṅgoḷī*, *ālpanā*, *muggulu* or *kolam*, which have been influenced by maṇḍala and yantra patterns.

Yantras have been employed especially in rites of magic. Their use has been recommended in astrology and, to some extent, in Āyur-Veda. The yantra of a deity is customarily placed under the deity's statue at the time of its installation in a temple. Patterns of

---

[1] For a detailed examination of the use of mantras, yantras and maṇḍalas in Āyur-Veda and in alchemy, see Roşu 1986a and 1986b.

yantras, like those of maṇḍalas, have had widespread influence. In the *citrabandha* compositions in Sanskrit, for example, text can be arranged in yantra-like shapes.[2]

Like maṇḍalas, yantras continue to be worshipped in South Asia. The *śrīcakra* or *śrīyantra*, which is a configuration of a central point and sets of triangles surrounded by lotus petals, circles and a square, is widely worshipped in contemporary India and Nepal. It is installed and worshipped, among other places, in the Śṛṅgeri *maṭha*, which claims to uphold Śaṃkara's tradition. In Nepal, it decorates roofs of shrines. The *śrīcakra* is now also sold as a pendant to be worn around the neck, and is printed on popular wall calendars. A numerical yantra, the *visoyantra*,[3] is currently worshipped in Ambāji, Gujarāt.[4] Popular books promote yantras for miscellaneous mundane purposes, including safe driving. Copper yantras from India can easily be purchased over the Internet for similar purposes.

Patterns typical of maṇḍalas and yantras have inspired modern Indian architecture, art and dance. The Mumbai-based contemporary architect Charles Correa has been guided by maṇḍala designs in his layout of buildings, such as the new State Assembly (Vidhan Bhavan) in Bhopal. Inspired by a *navagrahamaṇḍala* pattern, Correa designed the Jawahar Kala Kendra, a cultural centre in Jaipur. Correa's Surya Kund in Delhi is said to be based on a maṇḍala plan featuring the *śrīcakra* in its centre.[5] Inspired mainly by the *śrīcakra*, the 20th-century Indian artist Nirad Majumdar created his ink drawing *Yantra*.[6] The contemporary dancer Chandralekha acknow-

---

[2] Some authorities do not recognize these compositions as poetry. For an exhaustive treatment of this topic, see Rudradev Tripāṭhī's study, Saṃskṛt-sāhitya meṃ śabdālaṅkār (Dillī: Śrīlālbahāduraśāstrī Kendrīya Saṃskṛt Vidyāpīṭh, 1972 [in Hindī]).

[3] This yantra is reproduced in Bunce 2001: 53, who labels it erroneously 'Amba Matta Yantra' instead of 'Ambā Mātā Yantra.' It is also known as *bīsonyantra* (Pranavananda <1977>: 52), while Chawdhri 1992: 53, 202–211 classifies it as *beesiyantra*.

[4] For contemporary yantra worship in Gujarāt, see the discussion in Padmaja 1985.

[5] For pictures of the Vidhan Bhavan, see Khan 1987: 134–139; for the Jawahar Kala Kendra, see Khan 1987: 142–143 and for the Surya Kund, see Khan 1987: 105, 159.

[6] Nirad Majumdar's *Yantra* is reproduced in Chakravorty Spivak 1999: 193, Figure 2. Numerous modern maṇḍalas have been created by both Asian and Western artists: see, for example, the oil painting by the Nepali artist Sharda Man Shrestha (reproduced in Singh 2000: 85, Plate XI) and the maṇḍalas by the German artist Lore Bert (reproduced in Singh 2000: 87, Plate XII).

ledges the influence of the Saundaryalaharī attributed to Śaṃkara on her dance piece 'Yantra: Dance Diagrams,' a work in which geometrical figures are created by dancers.

Some Problems

While a body of literature is growing in which maṇḍala-like structures of different cultures are compared with one another and their use in therapy is explored, not much solid research has been done on maṇḍalas in the Hindu traditions, and indeed no systematic study has as yet emerged. Descriptions of maṇḍalas in ancient texts are barely studied, and usually left untranslated. Descriptions of them in popular books often appear to be confused, since many authors apply the same terminology to what appear to be somewhat similar structures without differentiating between traditions. Psychoanalysts and psychologists endeavour to interpret the maṇḍala by applying their own categories. These approaches are of limited value for an understanding of the structures and functions of maṇḍalas in the context of South Asian traditions. Since maṇḍalas are not objects of art *per se* but are embedded in a ritual context, a purely art-historical approach to the subject will not do justice to them either.

Thanks to advances in the study of Tantric texts over the past decades and the increased availability of objects from South Asia, new materials have become available which put us in a better position than previous scholars to carry out research on maṇḍalas and yantras. But museums are usually not the places to look for maṇḍalas and yantras, since the latter are ritual rather than art objects, and so executed by craftsmen rather than artists. An exception is the collection of about 60 copper yantras from Bengal in the Museum für indische Kunst, Berlin. The private collection of yantras and maṇḍalas of Robert Clark, Barcelona, is documented in Stadtner 1998.

Drawings of yantras are often found in South Asian manuscripts and printed books dealing with magical and Tantric rituals, and in art catalogues as well.[7] The yantra designs found in these sources are

---

[7] See, for example, Sotheby's London: Catalogue of Islamic, Indian, Tibetan, Nepalese and South-East Asian Decorative and Other Works of Art, also Antiquities. Days of Sale: Monday, 16th February 1981, 2 pm, Tuesday, 17th February 1981, 10.30 am and 2 pm.

often repetitive. One problem is the authenticity of maṇḍala and yantra designs. Yantras are frequently executed on copperplates as ordered by a practitioner. They are copied from drawings in manuscripts, sketchbooks (Nepal) or printed books. Their structures and the mantras inscribed in them often contain errors that go unnoticed due to the ignorance of craftsmen, copyists and practitioners. Pranavananda <1977>: 75–79 examines nearly 200 *śrīcakras* from various parts of India and concludes that most of them show major or minor flaws in their designs or other irregularities, and so do not tally with the descriptions in ancient texts. According to this author (Pranavananda <1977>: 4, 109), certain changes were made to the structure of the *śrīcakra* early on and these errors have been perpetuated blindly by tradition. Artists in popular tourist spots in Rājasthān and Nepal paint mostly for the tourist industry. They freely mix elements from different traditions and copy designs from books and museum catalogues printed in the West. Their products often do not represent a continuation of ancient traditions. During a recent visit to Bhaktapur in Nepal I interviewed a painter about the use of the *sarvatobhadras* and *liṅgatobhadras* in his country. He had not seen these maṇḍalas, and indeed eagerly photocopied my diagrams. I would not be surprised if painted *bhadramaṇḍalas* are soon being sold in the shops of Bhaktapur as traditional Nepalese maṇḍalas. Customers will then use them as wall decorations, although such maṇḍalas were never intended to be hung on the wall but were traditionally prepared on the ground from powders or grains as supports for deities invoked into them. The Indigo Gallery in Kāṭhmāṇḍu was already recently displaying a painted *liṅgatobhadra* which, along with another maṇḍala, had been copied from Madhu Khanna's book 'Yantra: The Tantric Symbol of Cosmic Unity.'

Previous Scholarship on Hindu Maṇḍalas and Yantras

Among the early studies of maṇḍalas and yantras the works of H. Zimmer and P.H. Pott should be mentioned. Based on works by Sir J. Woodroffe (alias A. Avalon) (1865–1936) and his collaborators,[8] H. Zimmer (1890–1943) published his influential book 'Kunstform und Yoga im indischen Kultbild' in 1926. The work contains two

[8] For recent research on J. Woodroffe and his team of collaborators, see Taylor 2001: 203ff.

large sections, dealing with maṇḍalas and yantras, which influenced C.G. Jung (1875–1961), the originator of analytical psychology, in his interpretation of the maṇḍala.[9] Zimmer's book, which did not target an academic readership, endeavours to interpret maṇḍalas and yantras based on both Hindu and Buddhist texts and monuments. Zimmer argues that icons of deities or 'figurative sacred images' (*pratimā*) can be subsumed under the category yantra, and in fact are essentially and functionally identical with yantras, cakras and maṇḍalas (1984: 28–29). P.H. Pott's 'Yoga and Yantra' (1946) takes a different approach. Even though he recurs to his predecessors J. Woodroffe and H. Zimmer, Pott's goal is to explain the function yantras have within the context of Tantric Yoga. Like Zimmer, Pott refers to both Buddhist and Hindu texts throughout his work. A classic work is G. Tucci's 'The Theory and Practice of the Maṇḍala, *With Special Reference to the Modern Psychology of the Subconscious*,' published in 1949 in Italian but translated into English only in 1961. The book's main emphasis is on the symbolism of Buddhist maṇḍalas, although the *śrīcakra* and Hindu parallels are considered.

Comparatively recent publications for a general readership include the book on yantras by M. Khanna entitled 'Yantra: The Tantric Symbol of Cosmic Unity,' published in 1979, and S.K.R. Rao's small work 'The Yantras,' which appeared in 1988. Rao also authored a two-volume book on maṇḍalas entitled 'Maṇḍalas in Temple Worship' (1988–1990).

In 1986 A. Padoux edited 'Mantras et diagrammes rituels dans l'hindouisme,' which is a collection of scholarly articles on mantras, maṇḍalas and yantras employed in the Hindu traditions. The contributions are based on lectures presented at the conference 'L'Hindouisme—textes, doctrines, pratiques' of the research team no. 249 of the Centre national de la recherche scientifique (CNRS) organized by A. Padoux in Paris in June 1984. These lectures—some of which have been abbreviated or thoroughly revised—are published along with a summary of the discussion that followed their presentation.[10]

---

[9] C.G. Jung's remarks and observations on the symbolism of the maṇḍala appear in several sections of his Collected Works; see, for example, Jung 1950 and Jung 1964.

[10] Padoux's volume contains the following papers that specifically focus on maṇḍalas and yantras: 'Maṇḍala et yantra dans le śivaïsme āgamique. Définition,

Several authors have studied individual maṇḍalas and yantras. Kramrisch 1946, volume 1: 46–63 was the first scholar to analyze two main types of the *vāstupuruṣamaṇḍala*,[11] a maṇḍala employed in the construction of buildings. She was followed by others,[12] including Apte/Supekar 1983 and Apte 1986 and 1987. Apte also conducts research on maṇḍalas in the Pāñcarātra tradition. Apte 1973 focuses on maṇḍalas described in the Jayākhya-Saṃhitā. In the introduction to his edition and translation of the Pauṣkara-Saṃhitā (Part 1, 1991), the same author analyzes one of four sets of maṇḍalas described in this Saṃhitā. This set comprises 25 maṇḍalas, which Apte attempts to reconstruct.[13] The well-known *śrīcakra*, which is employed in the ritual worship of Tripurasundarī, is the subject of several publications.[14]

Bunce's recent volume on yantras (2001) examines the relationship between numbers and yantras. The book is based on secondary materials, with Johari 1986 as one major source.

---

description, usage' (H. Brunner) [the revised and enlarged version of this article appears in this volume in English translation]; 'Quelques remarques sur l'usage du maṇḍala et du yantra dans la vallée de Kathmandu, Népal' (A. Vergati); 'Pañjara et yantra: le diagramme de l'image sacrée' (B. Bäumer); 'De l'efficience psychagogique des *mantras* et des *yantras*' (F. Chenet); 'La vision de la divinité dans les diagrammes selon le vishnouisme vaikhānasa' (G. Colas); 'Les diagrammes cosmogoniques selon le Svacchandatantra: Perspectives philosophiques' (C. Conio); '*Mantra* et *yantra* en médecine et alchimie indiennes' (A. Roşu); 'Le śrī-cakra dans la Saundarya-Laharī' (T. Michael); 'Maṇḍala and Āgamic Identity in the Trika of Kashmir' (A. Sanderson).

[11] For an assessment of Kramrisch's work on the *vāstupuruṣamaṇḍala*, see Bafna 2000: 30–31.

[12] See, for example, Kulkarni 1979; see also the interpretation of the *vāstupuruṣamaṇḍala* given in Daniélou 1977: 28–35 (2001: 39–41). The relationship of the *vāstupuruṣamaṇḍala* to architecture is the topic of Meister's contribution to this volume.

[13] Apte's set of reconstructed maṇḍalas is reproduced in colour in: Prakṛti: The Integral Vision (Volume 3: The Āgamic Tradition and the Arts, edited by B. Bäumer, New Delhi: D.K. Printworld (P) Ltd., 1995): 193+, 'Illustrations P.P. Apte 1.1–1.25.' However, due to an error, the plates are appended to another article by Apte included in this volume. Black and white drawings of the same set of maṇḍalas are included in Apte's edition and translation of the Pauṣkara-Saṃhitā (Part 1), appendix, pp. i–xxi.

[14] See, for example, Rao 1914–1916, volume 1: 330–332, Zimmer (1926) 1984: 158–180, Pott (1946) 1966: 40–44, Bolton/Macleod 1977, Pranavananda <1977>, Kulaichev 1984, Michael 1986, Fonseca 1986, Khanna 1986, Kulaichev/Ramendic 1989, Rao 1990, Brooks 1992: 115–146, 189–199, Rao 1998 and Wilke 2005.

The Scope of this Book

My interest in maṇḍalas goes back to a period in the 1980s when I conducted research in Puṇe, Mahārāṣṭra. The plan to publish a book on maṇḍalas and yantras in the Hindu traditions took shape over time as I observed the growing popular interest in Tibetan Buddhist maṇḍalas. Unlike the many Tibetan maṇḍalas which include pictorial representations of multiple deities, most published maṇḍalas in the Hindu traditions appear to be simpler and more abstract in design. However, Hindu maṇḍalas, especially from Nepal and Rājasthān, often include painted images of deities.[15] Complex maṇḍalas are also described in texts, and the practitioner is instructed to visualize multiple deities in the maṇḍalas, although these deities may not be represented. This volume reproduces several maṇḍala designs, some of which have been reconstructed from texts. Since texts often do not specify all details of the maṇḍalas, such reconstructions necessarily remain tentative.

With the exception of the *śrīcakra*, which has attracted considerable interest, adequate attention has not been devoted to maṇḍalas and yantras in the Hindu traditions and their multiple uses. Unlike the approaches of earlier books, which indiscriminately deal with Buddhist and Hindu maṇḍalas and which often arrive at generalized conclusions, this book attempts to clarify important aspects of maṇḍalas and yantras in specific Hindu traditions through investigations by specialists. In the present state of research it is best to avoid generalizations and broad comparisons across traditions that rarely take into account existing differences, and often turn out on closer examination to be inaccurate. The complex Buddhist maṇḍalas for their part merit a separate study. Nevertheless I hope that this book will indirectly contribute to a better understanding of the maṇḍala in other South Asian traditions, and will lay the foundation for future inquiries.

The essays in this book explore some aspects of maṇḍalas and yantras in the Smārta, Pāñcarātra, Śaiva and Śākta traditions. An essay on the *vāstupuruṣamaṇḍala* and its relationship to architecture is also included. It would have been useful to have essays on the use

[15] In Nepal, even the *śrīcakra* occasionally includes painted images of deities; see, for example, Illustration 43 in Kreijger 1999: 110–111. For a 19th-century maṇḍala from Rājasthān with icons of goddesses, see, for example, Pal 1997: 215, 337.

of yantras in Indian medical systems, astrology or folk traditions, or on geographical space as a maṇḍala. It was, however, not possible to find qualified authors who could write these essays within the given time frame. Thus this book is a contribution to the study of an area of South Asian culture which has hardly been researched, but it is not an exhaustive treatment. This would have been an unrealistic goal, given the extant mass of material on the topic.

In secondary sources, maṇḍalas (and yantras) have been described too uniformly as aids to meditation or visualization.[16] While they certainly function as meditational devices in some traditions (as, for instance, the *śrīcakra* frequently does), this use of maṇḍalas is but one aspect of a larger picture. In this regard H. Brunner's paper in this volume is significant, since she sets out to examine some popular notions about maṇḍalas critically and to emphasize other uses of maṇḍalas in ritual. In architecture, the notion of an 'all-governing maṇḍala' of symbolically significant dimensions which underlies all buildings is frequently met with in the literature, and has recently been challenged by Bafna 2000: 42–43.[17]

The first essay in this book is designed as an introduction to the topic. Referring to H. Brunner and others, I discuss the meanings of maṇḍala, yantra and cakra, and suggest distinctions among these terms. This is followed by a treatment of different categories of maṇḍalas, yantras and cakras and their constituent parts.

In the next essay, I focus on maṇḍala-like structures and actual maṇḍalas and yantras currently employed in the ritual practice in Mahārāṣṭra. In its first part, I discuss maṇḍala-like arrangements, such as the *baliharaṇacakra* and *pañcāyatana* shrines, along with the *navagrahamaṇḍala* as an example of a maṇḍala with a lotus design. A description of two yantra structures follows. Together with the previous essay, this section is intended to introduce the reader to basic concepts and maṇḍala designs in the Hindu traditions. The second part of the essay focuses on a specific category of maṇḍala called *bhadramaṇḍala*s. These are square-shaped maṇḍalas employed mainly in concluding ceremonies of religious observances (*vrata*).

---

[16] For a critical examination of the claim that maṇḍalas in Shingon Buddhism are aids or 'supports' for visualization practices, see Sharf 2001.

[17] See M. Meister's paper in this volume for a critical assessment of Bafna's position.

Marion Rastelli's essay focuses on the use of maṇḍalas and yantras in the Vaiṣṇava Pāñcarātra tradition as based on original passages from the Saṃhitās. It describes the selection, purification and ritual acquisition of the maṇḍala site, guidelines and materials used for drawing maṇḍalas, and the types of maṇḍalas found in the texts. She then discusses the multiple functions of maṇḍalas in Pāñcarātra rituals. The choice of a maṇḍala for a rite is guided by the desire to achieve specific results. It depends on the suitability of a maṇḍala for a certain rite and the main deity worshipped in it. The use of maṇḍalas in initiations (*dīkṣā*) is treated elaborately. Some details of the ritual, such as the casting of a flower onto a maṇḍala by the blindfolded initiand, have parallels in Buddhist Tantric initiation rituals.[18] The deity is made to be present in a maṇḍala by imposing the deity's mantras on the maṇḍala structure. Two important maṇḍalas in the Pāñcarātra tradition are the *cakrābjamaṇḍala* and the *navapadmamaṇḍala*. The Pāñcarātra Saṃhitās consider the maṇḍala a representation of the deity's body, and of the universe as well. According to some Saṃhitās, emancipation is only possible through maṇḍala worship. Rastelli further discusses the significance of yantras in the Pāñcarātra tradition. She focuses especially on the *saudarśanayantra*[19] which is considered so powerful that the person who wears it requires another yantra, the 'yantra of the wearer' (*dhārakayantra*), to keep its power in check. As in the case of maṇḍalas, the material from which yantras are made is considered essential for the efficacy of the rite. Different materials are believed to produce different results. (The texts of the Śaiva Siddhānta that Brunner examines emphasize the varying efficacy of the materials from which maṇḍalas are constructed, from precious stones on downwards.)

The three following essays deal with aspects of the Śaiva traditions. Hélène Brunner has been researching Śaivāgamas for more than thirty years. Most of her work is written in French and therefore accessible to a more limited readership. For this volume, her French paper, originally published in Padoux's edited volume, 'Mantras et diagrammes rituels dans l'hindouisme,' (1986: 11–35), was translated into English by R. Prévèreau, M.A., and completely

[18] This topic has been dealt with repeatedly; for a description of the disciple's entrance into the maṇḍala and his casting of a flower, see, for example, Wayman 1974. For an early Śaiva parallel, see J. Törzsök's paper (187–189) in this volume.

[19] The *saudarśanayantra* appears to be identical with the *sudarśanayantra* (see section 2.3.3 of the following essay).

revised and enlarged. Brunner's essay is divided into two parts. The first part attempts to clarify the meaning and use of the terms maṇḍala, yantra and cakra. Her classification of different types of maṇḍalas based on their ritual application is of special interest. (I have taken up Brunner's discussion of the different types of maṇḍalas in the following essay [section 1.2], as has Törzsök in her own.) The second part describes the use of maṇḍalas in the ritual worship of Śiva. Brunner reconstructs the *sarvatobhadramaṇḍala* described in chapter 3 of the Śāradātilaka, which is used in an initiation (*dīkṣā*) ritual, and analyzes its structure in detail. Finally, she discusses the significance of maṇḍalas in the Siddhānta School.

Judit Törzsök examines pre-11th-century Śaiva maṇḍalas as icons which express a relationship between certain branches of Śaivism and between Śaiva and non-Śaiva groups. In the first part of her paper she deals with the uses of the terms maṇḍala and cakra, a topic also taken up by Brunner. This leads into a discussion on how the circles (*cakra*) of deities are present in a maṇḍala. Törzsök then focuses on two kinds of maṇḍalas: maṇḍalas used in initiations (*dīkṣā*) and maṇḍalas (and yantras) for the acquisition of supernatural powers (*siddhi*). Giving examples from the Svacchandatantra, she shows how maṇḍalas can visually represent doctrines of other Śaiva groups and teachings of non-Śaivas. Törzsök specifies three major strategies (specialization, expansion and substitution) which are employed to adapt maṇḍalas to a specific purpose, such as the acquisition of supernatural powers. In the Appendices, Törzsök attempts to reconstruct four maṇḍalas from textual descriptions. The reconstruction of two maṇḍalas (see Colour Plates 18–19) is tentative and does not show the outer boundaries that are characteristic of maṇḍala designs. These boundaries are not specifically mentioned in the texts, but are likely to have been assumed.

André Padoux's first essay in this volume examines descriptions of maṇḍalas and their use in Abhinavagupta's Tantrāloka (early 11th century). Basing himself mainly on material from various sections of the text, Padoux portrays the uses of such maṇḍalas as the *triśūlābja-maṇḍala* and *tritriśūlābjamaṇḍala* in rites, including the different forms of the initiation (*dīkṣā*) and the practitioner's daily ritual worship, in which the maṇḍala is visualized as being present in his body.

André Padoux's second essay deals with the *śrīcakra* as described in the first chapter of the (most likely) 11th-century Yoginīhṛdaya.

This chapter offers a description of the 'descent' (*avatāra*) of the *śrīcakra* as a cosmic process and manifestation of divine power, which the practitioner visualizes and experiences in his body. The *cakra* is portrayed here as a cosmic rather than a ritual diagram, whose contemplation has a visual/spatial as well as a phonic/mantric dimension and leads to an identification of the Yogin with the supreme level of the word (*vāc*).

Michael W. Meister measured a large number of ancient temples in the course of extensive research in India. His drawings of ground-plans of temples show how the *vāstupuruṣamaṇḍala* was used in practice. Meister's contribution to this volume is concerned with the *vāstumaṇḍala* as described in Varāhamihira's Bṛhat-Saṃhitā and its application in temple architecture.

This book contains only one bibliography, in order to avoid repetition of references and to allow the interested reader to find relevant literature on maṇḍalas, yantras and cakras in one place.

The title of this volume contains the much-debated word Hindu, which has been the focus of some controversy. I will not discuss the problems associated with this term here.[20] I have decided, for pragmatic reasons, to use it rather than choices such as 'Brahmanical,' a word which would indicate to some that the subject matter is concerned only with the Brahmin community. The equally problematic terms Tantrism and Tantric[21] are also used in this book for practical reasons and without further discussion.

Remarks on the Transliteration

It is difficult to avoid inconsistencies when transliterating words from different Indian languages. For the names of many places and temples, popular transliterations are already in circulation which may not conform to scholarly standards. I have in many instances retained the popular transliteration of such words in order to avoid burdening the reader with unusual spellings of names. The transliteration of words from Nevārī poses its own problems, since there is often more than one current spelling of a word. I am aware of minor inconsisten-

[20] For a discussion of the problems associated with the term Hinduism, see, for instance, Smith 1987.

[21] Padoux 1987b, Verardi 1994: 52–53 and Urban 1999, among others, have discussed these problematic terms.

cies in spellings of words from Indian languages used by the different authors, and also their divergent treatment of parentheses. It is difficult to avoid such inconsistencies without interfering too much with the style of the individual contributions.

Acknowledgements

My research for the volume extended over a prolonged period of time. I would like to thank the University of Wisconsin-Madison and the Lumbini International Research Institute for support at different stages of my research. I am indebted to Professor K.S. Arjunwadkar and Dr. R.P. Goswami for valuable suggestions on earlier drafts of my chapters in this book. I am also grateful to G. Mevissen, M.A., for some bibliographical references; to R.S. Green, M.A., M.W. Dennis, M.A., and S. Weier for help with computer-related issues; to T. Cowall and P. Radder of E.J. Brill Publishers for editorial support, and to Professor J. Bronkhorst for including this volume in *Brill's Indological Library*. I would like to express my thanks to P. Pierce, M.A., for editing my contributions for style. Finally I thank R. Prévèreau, M.A., for preparing the translation of H. Brunner's paper from the French.

Remarks on the South Asian Edition of This Book

This edition is in large part a reissue of the book published in 2003 by E.J. Brill Publishers, with minor corrections and updated information worked into the text. I wish to thank Professor H. Isaacson for corrections he suggested in his review in *Nagoya Studies in Indian Culture and Buddhism (Saṃbhāṣā)* 24 (2004: 153–158), most of which have been incorporated. The drawings of the maṇḍalas on pp. 88–118 and the diagram on p. 250 have been improved. In addition, the captions in Devanāgarī script on pp. 88–118 have been composed anew to make them more legible.

Sadly, H. Brunner, who contributed to this volume, passed away on March 27, 2005, before this edition could be published.

MAṆḌALA, YANTRA AND CAKRA: SOME OBSERVATIONS

Gudrun Bühnemann

1 *Maṇḍala*

1.1 *The Term Maṇḍala*

In its most general use, the word maṇḍala refers to something that is round or circular, such as a ring or circle, further, a region, terrestrial division, domain, assembly or a group.[1] The term is used in Kauṭilya's Arthaśāstra, book 6, in the sense of a spatial configuration of neighbouring states from the viewpoint of a king. In Tantric traditions, the term maṇḍala often refers to a space with a special structure that is enclosed and delimited by a circumferential line and into which a deity or deities are invited by means of mantras. This space is often a circle, but may also appear as a square, a triangle or another shape.[2] The various shapes and structures of maṇḍalas are based on the traditions of the different schools, ritual applications, the deities worshipped and the practitioner's qualification and goal. Maṇḍalas themselves are prepared from various materials, including

---

[1] For a discussion of the uncertain etymology of the word maṇḍala, see Mayrhofer 1986–2001, volume 2: 294. A religious etymology of the word appears in Kulārṇava-Tantra 17.59:

maṅgalatvāc ca ḍākinyā yoginīgaṇasaṃśrayāt /
lalitatvāc ca deveśi maṇḍalaṃ parikīrtitam //

"O mistress of the gods, it is called maṇḍala because it is auspicious (*maṅgalatva*), because it is the abode of the group of Yoginīs of the Ḍākinī, and because of (its) beauty (*lalitatva*)."

For an etymology of the word maṇḍala, which divides the word into the components *maṇḍa* (explained as *sāra* [essence]) and *la* (from the verbal root *lā* [to take]), see Tantrāloka 37.21 with Jayaratha's commentary, referred to in Padoux, p. 227); Buddhist texts also divide the word maṇḍala into these two components, but different interpretations are given to them; cf. the discussions in Wayman 1999, Lessing/Wayman 1978: 270, note 1, Toganoo 1971: 150–160, Rambelli 1991: 9–13 and Tribe 1994: 127.

[2] Brunner, p. 157, note 5 and Törzsök, p. 208 also refer to semi-circular maṇḍalas and maṇḍalas having the (triangular) shape of a vulva (*yoni*), among others.

coloured powders, precious stones, fruits and leaves, and fragrant substances.[3] It must be emphasized, however, that the maṇḍala is not merely a physical structure with a specific design. A maṇḍala is the place in which the practitioner beholds the deities who have been invoked into it and so have become an integral part of the structure.[4] Maṇḍalas figure among the places into which deities can be invoked. These include statues, vessels and fire.[5]

Maṇḍalas are required in occasional (not daily) rituals, such as festivals or religious observances (*vrata*) and more importantly Tantric initiation (*dīkṣā*) rites, in which latter the viewing of the maṇḍala is an essential element.[6] At the time of initiation the maṇḍala structure functions as a place in which the deities become visible to the initiate for the first time, thereby confirming the initiate's new identity (Törzsök, pp. 183–184, 189, 190). The maṇḍala structure can function as an important device for representing the pantheon of deities in a system or school, and expressing the hierarchy of deities within the system. This hierarchy can even include deities of other systems as part of a 'lower revelation,' and can indicate a cosmic order as well (Törzsök, p. 196). Further, maṇḍalas, like yantras, are used in rituals leading to the attainment of supernatural powers (*siddhi*).[7]

While most maṇḍalas follow the common pattern of a concentric arrangement of deities in order to express a hierarchy, the trident maṇḍala of the Trika also features a vertical ascent. The maṇḍala's trident is seen as rising three-dimensionally from a central lotus, as if coming out of the maṇḍala's surface (Törzsök, p. 196). We do not know whether three-dimensional maṇḍalas were actually constructed. Such maṇḍalas are known from Buddhist texts and traditions. The Viṣṇu-Saṃhitā (cf. Rastelli, p. 123) instructs the practitioner to make the lines of a maṇḍala in varying thicknesses, with the centre

[3] For materials listed in the Pāñcarātra Saṃhitās, see Rastelli, p. 123; for maṇḍalas made from fragrant substances (*gandhamaṇḍala*), see Padoux, p. 226.

[4] See the discussion in Törzsök, pp. 183–184 for more details.

[5] Rastelli, p. 126 discusses the worship of the deity in four places (*catuḥsthāna*) attested to in the younger Pāñcarātra Saṃhitās. These places are a maṇḍala, a vessel, fire and a statue. Törzsök, p. 193, note 60, quoting the Tantrāloka, lists 11 supports of external worship, including a rosary, manuscript and mirror.

[6] Cf. Rastelli, pp. 130ff., Törzsök, pp. 185ff. and Padoux, pp. 227ff. for this aspect of maṇḍalas.

[7] See Törzsök, pp. 201–209 for a description of such use of maṇḍalas in early Śaiva Tantras.

of the maṇḍala its most elevated part, which could be taken to presuppose the concept of three-dimensionality. Three-dimensional yantras are not uncommon in the Hindu traditions, and are described below in section 2.1.

Different theological interpretations have been applied to maṇḍalas, the structural parts and deities being correlated with doctrines of different systems. Interpretations are extremely varied, and even one text may provide more than one interpretation of the parts of a maṇḍala.

Patterns exhibited by maṇḍalas have had widespread influence. Maṇḍala patterns of cities have frequently been described.[8] However, it often remains unclear what the connection between a maṇḍala and a city or temple really means, as Bafna 2000: 26 notes. Problems arise when one attempts to correlate maṇḍala structures and actual building plans. Gutschow 1982: 179, 185 argues that contemporary drawings of maṇḍalas of cities, such as the maṇḍala of the city of Bhaktapur in Nepal, usually do not reflect ancient guidelines for town-planning but rather represent a specific interpretation of existing urban conditions. A maṇḍala pattern is thus projected onto the city by establishing connections between already existing buildings. These connections may not be immediately intelligible to the outside observer, and are indeed open to interpretation.

The terms cakra and yantra are sometimes used as synonyms for maṇḍala, and all three terms are often translated indiscriminately as '(mystical) diagrams.' The fact that the geometric designs of maṇḍalas, yantras and cakras are similar contributes to confusion among the three. Not only Western authors confuse the terms, even later Sanskrit texts often use 'maṇḍala' and 'yantra' rather loosely as synonyms. Occasionally metrical considerations and constraints may have played a role in the choice of a word, as when a text uses the word *pura* ('city'), for example, as a synonym for maṇḍala.[9] Other

---

[8] See, for example, Gutschow/Kölver 1975, where the authors describe the layout of the city of Bhaktapur in Nepal; see also Zanen 1986: 148–150, relating to the Nevār town Sankhu. For a critical approach to a maṇḍala as a concept said to underlie town-planning, see Roy 1977, who discusses the layout of Jaipur, and Tillotson 1987: 81–83, who focuses on the palaces of Bundelkhand.

[9] For the use of the word *pura* ('city') as a synonym for maṇḍala, see the discussion among T. Goudriaan, H. Brunner and P. Filliozat reproduced in Padoux 1986: 32, and also Rastelli 2000b: 375, note 57.

synonyms of maṇḍala found in the literature are *yāga*,[10] *bhavana/bhuvana*, *veśman* and, in a metaphoric sense, *pīṭha*.[11]

Various definitions of the term maṇḍala have been proposed. Kramrisch 1946, volume 1: 11 defines 'maṇḍala' as a yantra when she writes about the *vāstupuruṣamaṇḍala*: "The Vāstupuruṣamaṇḍala, the diagram of the temple, is a Yantra...." Liebert 1976: 168 does the same when she defines the word as the name "of a kind of *yantra*."[12] Similarly, Renou/Filliozat 1947–1953, volume 1: 568 state that yantras in which a more or less decorated circle predominates are called cakra or maṇḍala. In addition, some authors assume that yantras are the counterparts of maṇḍalas in the Hindu traditions. This erroneously implies that maṇḍalas are rarely part of the Hindu traditions and that yantras are not found in the Buddhist traditions.[13] Thus Tucci (1949) 1961: 46 states: "in Hinduism, however, *yantras*, purely linear designs expressing the same principles, are usually substituted for maṇḍalas ...;"[14] and Eliade 1969: 219 writes: "The simplest maṇḍala is the *yantra*, employed by Hinduism...."

Several scholars have attempted to establish semantic distinctions among the three terms maṇḍala, yantra and cakra.[15] One approach attempts to establish distinctions on the basis of the structure and constituent parts of these objects. Rao 1914–1916, volume 1: 330 states that a cakra "is defined in the Tantras as a figure consisting of

---

[10] Rastelli, p. 119, note 1, reports that the Pauṣkara-Saṃhitā uses the word *yāga* synonymously with maṇḍala.

[11] For a discussion of the terms *bhavana/bhuvana*, *veśman* and *pīṭha* as synonyms for maṇḍala, see Törzsök, p. 182.

[12] A similar statement is found in Bernier 1979: 120: "Every maṇḍala is essentially a *yantra*...."

[13] Bizot 1981 describes Buddhist yantras in South-east Asia, especially Cambodia and Thailand. Yantra are also described in Buddhist Sanskrit texts, such as the Vimalaprabhā commentary on the Kālacakratantra, chapter 3 (Vimalaprabhāṭīkā of Kalkin Śrīpuṇḍarīka on Śrīlaghukālacakratantrarāja by Śrīmañjuśrīyaśas, volume 2, edited by V. Dwivedi/S.S. Bahulkar, Sarnath, Varanasi: Central Institute of Higher Tibetan Studies, 1994): 19, 15ff.

[14] See also Renou/Filliozat 1947–1953, volume 1: 568 for a similar statement.

[15] The following statement by Hoens (in Gupta/Hoens/Goudriaan 1979: 113) illustrates the confusion surrounding the terms maṇḍala and yantra: "In the existing literature yantra and maṇḍala are often considered to be synonyms. This is not correct, because yantra in general means an instrument, an implement. The yantra is often three-dimensional whereas the maṇḍala always is two-dimensional. Maṇḍala and yantra often have the same geometrical forms, but the yantra may also have different forms.... The yantra is more worshipped than meditated upon. As far as the aims are concerned one can say that the yantra is more used for worldly purposes than for liberation, whereas the maṇḍala is used for both purposes."

angles and petal-like parts; that which consists of angles alone is called a yantra." It is unclear which text Rao cites here, but this statement can be identified in a quotation in the commentary Saubhāgyabhāskara by Bhāskararāya (18th century) on the Lalitāsahasranāma, p. 171, 4–7. In this quotation the word angle (*asra*) is synonymous with the Sanskrit word corner (*koṇa*) as used in the terms triangle (*trikoṇa*) or hexagram (*ṣaṭkoṇa*). The expression 'petal-like parts' renders the Sanskrit word *patra*. The above distinction between cakra and yantra, however, appears to be purely theoretical and may be applicable only in a specific tradition. It does not account for the many yantras which are commonly described as consisting of petal-like parts. Zimmer (1926) 1984: 28–29 translates the three terms cakra, maṇḍala and yantra as 'circle-shape' designs (*cakra*), 'ring-shaped' designs (*maṇḍala*) and linear figures (*yantra*). It is not explained, however, exactly what is meant by these terms and what the differences between the 'circle-shaped' and 'ring-shaped' designs would be. Gaeffke 1987: 155 notes that "it has become customary to call the simpler designs for daily worship *yantras*, and to reserve the term *maṇḍala* for the larger ones in public ceremonies where the whole cosmos has to be present." Another approach attempts to establish distinctions between maṇḍalas, yantras and cakras on the basis of the deities invoked into these objects. Woodroffe 1914, volume 2: 285, note 13 makes a very generalized statement, which is applicable only to few maṇḍalas, when he asserts that the "difference between a Maṇḍala and a Yantra is that the former is used in the case of any Devatā, whereas a Yantra is appropriate to a specific Devatā only."[16] The following formulation by Shankaranarayanan 1970: 9 is a variation of Woodroffe's statement, and is equally problematic: "The Mandala is used in the case of any deity while the Chakra is specifically intended for a particular deity." Shankaranarayanan apparently replaced the word yantra in Woodroffe's definition with the word cakra. Schneider 1988: 100 attempts to make a distinction between maṇḍala and yantra on the basis of the number of deities invoked. He suggests that a maṇḍala represents the microcosm and accommodates a pantheon of deities who are positioned in it according to rank. A yantra, on the other hand, is the domain of a single deity, but may include that deity's retinue. This distinction

[16] The same, apparently widespread, definition also appears in Jhavery 1944: 71, Woodroffe 1956: 91, note 2 and in Kane 1968–1977, volume 5: 1135.

appears to be based on a statement by Pott (1946) 1966: 71, who describes "a maṇḍala as a *cosmic configuration* in the centre of which is an image or symbolic substitute of a prominent god surrounded by those of a number of deities of lower rank ordered hierarchically both among themselves and in relation to the chief figures, which configuration may be used as an *aid to meditation* and in ritual as a *receptacle for the gods*." He adds that a maṇḍala is "distinguished from a yantra by a more graphic representation of the deities or of their symbols and by a richer elaboration of the details." This last statement by Pott also takes the structure of maṇḍalas and yantras into consideration and is somewhat more satisfactory than the definitions of his predecessors.

Yet another approach looks at the ritual use of maṇḍalas and yantras. Thus Vergati 1986: 37, 44–45 observes that maṇḍalas are used in secret as well as public ceremonies of the Hindus and Buddhists in Nepal, whereas the yantras, which always represent the goddess, have more restricted uses. It has also been noted that maṇḍalas are usually objects for temporary ritual use. The deities are invoked into them and dismissed at the end of the ritual, after which the maṇḍala is dismantled. Yantras made of permanent materials into which a deity has been invoked are usually kept in the temple or shrine for continued worship (Sharma 1994: 423–424). It must be added, however, that many yantras are made for temporary use, like maṇḍalas. Rastelli, p. 144 notes yet another feature that sets maṇḍalas and yantras apart in the Pāñcarātra tradition. She states that mantras are already inscribed on yantras at the time of manufacturing the yantra. The drawing of the lines of the structure and the writing of the mantras are a single process, which may indicate that a yantra represents one integrated unit in which the deity is worshipped. Maṇḍalas, however, are constructed first and the deities are invoked into them with mantras only later. It must be added, however, that later texts enjoin that yantras be first prepared and then infused with life in a special ritual, the *prāṇapratiṣṭhā*, with the help of mantras. It is not possible to summarize all attempts at defining 'maṇḍala,' 'yantra' and 'cakra' in the literature. The use and functions of these terms are complex and it will be impossible to arrive at a universally valid definition. An in-depth study of the use of the terms in texts of different religious systems and time periods would be required to determine how the terms have been employed by different authors and how the use of these terms has changed over time.

1.2 *Types of Maṇḍalas according to H. Brunner*

H. Brunner's contribution to this book describes uses of the word maṇḍala based on her study of pre-13th-century Śaiva manuals. Even though she confines herself to an analysis of the texts of the Siddhānta School of Śaivism, her observations on the use of the terms maṇḍala, yantra and cakra appear to have a somewhat wider application. Brunner takes the term maṇḍala to signify a limited, not necessarily round, surface, and distinguishes four basic types of maṇḍalas:

Type 1: Limited surfaces without a clear structure, which are commonly employed as seats for divinities, men or objects during ritual, such as maṇḍalas of cow-dung smeared on the ground. They can be called 'seat-maṇḍalas.'

Type 2: Limited surfaces with geometrical designs prepared from coloured powders, which serve as supports for the regular or occasional worship of deities. These maṇḍalas are for temporary use, being destroyed after the ritual. They are constructed in a ritual, with close adherence to directional orientation. Commonly three, four or five different colours are employed. These maṇḍalas, often called 'powder maṇḍalas' (*rajomaṇḍala*), may be large-sized and so allow for the priest to enter through the doors and move around in 'streets.' According to Brunner, such maṇḍalas are temporarily constructed divine icons and can be called 'image-maṇḍalas' (the term is not used in any texts).

Type 3: Limited surfaces divided into a certain number of squares or units called *pada*s, domains into which divine or demonic powers are invoked to receive food offerings (*bali*). Their construction usually does not involve the use of colours. The best known maṇḍala in this category is the *vāstumaṇḍala*. Brunner also includes in this category geometrical figures divided into boxes among which objects are distributed. She refers to the maṇḍalas in this category as 'distributive diagrams.'

Type 4: The term maṇḍala is also used to designate the symbolic shapes of the five elements and the spheres/orbs of the sun. moon and fire. The shapes of the elements are visualized, for example, in the Tantric rite of purification of the elements (*bhūtaśuddhi*) of the performer's body. Since the shapes of the elements and the spheres of the sun, moon and fire are neither concrete material objects nor supports for worship in the way that the previously discussed maṇḍalas are, they do not really fit the present context and are therefore excluded from further discussion.

Concerning Brunner's first category of maṇḍalas, I would like to add that in other traditions 'seat-maṇḍala' appears to be more commonly used for ritual objects than for persons. The function of these maṇḍalas is to protect ritual objects placed *on* them. Such supports, made of various materials, may feature simple geometric patterns, and can be referred to as maṇḍalas or 'yantras for (establishing) a foundation' (*sthāpanayantra*) (see 2.2.1).

The name of the second category, 'image-maṇḍala,' may be somewhat misleading, since it suggests the presence of a pictorial representation of the deity in the maṇḍala—which is not intended. What is meant is that the entire maṇḍala is the principal support for worship and is present as an image/icon for the duration of the ritual. These maṇḍalas are also called 'powder maṇḍalas' (*rajomaṇḍala*) (but they may also be made from other materials, such as grains) and can be characterized as supports *into* which deities are invited in order to receive worship.

Brunner's classification of types of maṇḍalas and their ritual use in the Śaiva tradition is valuable. In all attempts at classification, however, we need to be aware of the fact that in both texts and ritual practice the distinction among the types of maṇḍalas is not always that clear. Any classification can therefore only be of limited practical value, and is often applicable only within one particular system.

1.3 *Some Structural Elements of Maṇḍalas*

Maṇḍalas display different shapes and patterns, and are made up of various constituent parts, depending on the tradition they come from. In the following I will describe two basic structural elements of maṇḍalas, the lotus design and square grid. In the next essay, I will provide concrete examples of these structures from the Smārta tradition of Mahārāṣṭra. Geometric figures like the triangle and hexagram, which occasionally also appear in maṇḍalas, will be described in section 2.3 in connection with yantras. In the following I will look at maṇḍala patterns of different periods and traditions simultaneously, without attempting to treat the topic historically.

1.3.1 Lotus Designs

Lotus designs appear commonly in Indian art as well as in maṇḍalas and in yantras. The lotus is a common South Asian symbol of creation, purity, transcendence and the sphere of the absolute,[17] but is especially known as a symbol of the female reproductive organ. It has also been connected with water symbolism since ancient times, as already indicated by a statement in Śatapatha-Brāhmaṇa 7.4.1.8: "The lotus is the waters." Indeed, in descriptions of the symbolic shapes (*maṇḍala*) of the elements (*bhūta*)[18] the lotus represents the element water.[19]

In maṇḍalas and yantras of lotus design, the central deity is positioned in the pericarp (*karṇikā*), and the emanations or subordinate deities in the petals.[20] A lotus design may have one ring or several concentric rings of petals. The petals of an eight-petalled lotus ideally point in the cardinal and intermediate directions, but we find numerous specimens in books and coins in which it is the spaces between two petals that are oriented to the points of the compass. This orientation may be due to the ignorance of the craftsmen who prepared the yantras. Bunce 2001: 28 explains that this latter orientation signifies power and the feminine element, but I am doubtful whether it is described in ancient texts. The eight-petalled lotus whose petals do the pointing is a shape which is well suited for positioning deities in their respective directions. This purpose is not served when two petals point in each of the cardinal directions and none in the intermediate directions. The relationship between directions and lotus petals is borne out by a statement in Maitrāyaṇīya-

[17] For a recent and detailed discussion of the symbolism of the lotus, see Garzilli 2000; for the lotus motive in architecture, see Gutschow 1997: 248ff.

[18] The symbolic shapes of the elements are classified as maṇḍalas of type 4 in Brunner's aforementioned classification of maṇḍalas (see section 1.2).

[19] See, for example, Śāradātilaka 1.23–24, where a lotus with a half moon represents water.

[20] For a description of the construction of the various shapes of petals, see Bunce 2001: 26.

Upaniṣad 6.2 which identifies the lotus (of the heart) with space (*ākāśa*), and its eight petals with the four cardinal and intermediate directions. Eight-petalled lotus designs commonly appear in the centre of Buddhist maṇḍalas, such as in the maṇḍalas of the eight great Bodhisattvas.[21] They are also found on Nepalese coins of the Malla period[22] and on Indian[23] coins. An eight-pointed star[24] can serve the same ritual function as the eight-petalled lotus, but is less common.

In addition to eight-petalled lotuses, lotuses with two, four, 10, 12, 16, 24, 32, 100, 1000 or more petals appear in maṇḍalas and yantras. The number of petals is mostly even, but yantras with an odd number of petals (for example, five) are also found, in which case their directional orientation may not be of any obvious relevance. A special kind of six-petalled lotus is the *vajra*-lotus described in the Kubjikāmata-Tantra. This is an eight-petalled lotus from which two petals have been removed. Its shape resembles a *vajra* with three peaks on either side.[25] Nepalese coins of the Malla period also depict four-petalled,[26] five-petalled[27] and six-petalled[28] lotuses.

Some texts prescribe that the lotus petals should have different shapes depending on the purpose of the associated rite. Thus the petals may be curved along their edges, and with or without pointed tips, and so forth (Törzsök, p. 207).

The lotus pattern is commonly found in current ritual practice, for example, in Mahārāṣṭra. An eight-petalled (*aṣṭadala*) lotus, prepared from grains or coloured powders, frequently functions as a support for ritual vessels. Atop the vessel is 'a dish filled (with grains)' (*pūrṇapātra*), especially uncooked rice, that serves as the seat of the main deity of the rite. In Nepal, lotus designs can also be found on stones

---

[21] See, for example, Leidy/Thurman 1997: 26–28.

[22] See Rhodes/Gabrisch/† della Rocchetta 1989, Plate 16, nos. 281–285, 289–297, Plate 17, nos. 298–299, 303–304, 313–318, 327–329, 338–344, Plate 18, nos. 345–346, 361, etc.

[23] See Sircar 1968, Plate xxiii, nos. 9 and 10 rev.

[24] See Rhodes/Gabrisch/† della Rocchetta 1989, Plate 29, no. 596 rev., Plate 30, no. 656 rev., Plate 33, no. 825 rev., Plate 35, no. 936 rev., Plate 36, no. 978 rev.

[25] For a description and a drawing of the *vajra*-lotus, see Heilijgers-Seelen 1994: 131–132.

[26] See Rhodes/Gabrisch/† della Rocchetta 1989, Plate 23, nos. 450 rev., 459–465 obv., Plate 24, nos. 466–467 obv.

[27] See Rhodes/Gabrisch/† della Rocchetta 1989, Plate 22, nos. 438 rev., 444 rev.

[28] See Rhodes/Gabrisch/† della Rocchetta 1989, Plate 21, no. 418 rev., Plate 22, nos. 445 obv., 446 obv., Plate 35, no. 953 rev.

near thresholds, on roads or in public places. These stones, which have been termed 'lotus stones' by some authors (Auer/Gutschow 1974: 29, 32, 33, 124), serve special functions in the Nevār religious tradition.[29]

A pattern of nine lotuses arranged in groups of three placed one above the other appears in several important maṇḍalas. These include the Pāñcarātra *navapadmamaṇḍala* (see Colour Plate 15), the Śaiva *navanābhamaṇḍala* (Colour Plate 18) and several versions of the Buddhist *vajradhātumaṇḍala.*[30]

In the context of specific maṇḍalas and yantras, different interpretations of the lotus design and the lotus petals are given. The (most likely seventh-century) Gaṇeśapūrvatāpanīya-Upaniṣad, section 3 gives an interpretation of the constituent parts of a yantra of Gaṇeśa. The yantra's innermost ring of eight lotus petals is taken to represent the eight-syllabled *gāyatrī*; the adjacent ring of 12 petals, the 12 Ādityas and the vowels; and the following ring of 16 petals, the *puruṣa* who consists of 16 parts (*kalā*), and the consonants. Miśra 1959: 482–483 interprets an unidentified Śākta yantra as representing the process of creation, and takes the eight petals of its lotus to signify the five elements, *manas*, *buddhi* and *ahaṃkāra*. Some

---

[29] We know of several types of stones with engraved lotus designs. One type is described as a guardian stone (Nevārī *pikhālakhu*, sometimes considered synonymous with Nevārī *chetrapāla*) in front of thresholds (Gutschow/Kölver/Shresthacarya 1987: 35, 54–55, 92, 120 and Kölver/Shresthacarya 1994: 101, 209). According to Toffin 1999: 42, the *pikhālakhu* protective stone is considered the abode of the deity Pikhālakhudyaḥ, whom both Buddhists and Hindus identify with Kumāra/Skanda. This stone reportedly has different functions in ritual: offerings are deposited on it; it receives worship as part of the marriage ceremony, at which time it may be smeared with cow-dung; or else a diagram may be drawn on it (Toffin 1999: 43). For a photograph of one such stone, see Gutschow/Kölver/Shresthacarya 1987: 120, no. 121. Another type of stone is called *chvāsa* (Gutschow/Kölver/Shresthacarya 1987: 35 and Kölver/Shresthacarya 1994: 105). This is a deified stone found at crossroads on which ritually impure (*ucchiṣṭa*) objects are discarded (Gutschow 1982: 105). The grandmother-goddess (*ajimā*) is propitiated there. For a photograph, see Gutschow/Kölver/Shresthacarya 1987: 92, no. 14. A third type of stone is called *mandaḥ/maṃdaḥ* (Nevārī) because of its maṇḍala-like design (Gutschow/Kölver/Shresthacarya 1987: 65, 120 and Kölver/Shresthacarya 1994: 258). This stone may be covered with brass. For a photograph, see Gutschow/Kölver/Shresthacarya 1987: 120, no. 122.

[30] See, for example, the central part of the 12th-century *vajradhātumaṇḍala* from Alchi, Ladakh (Leidy/Thurman 1997: 40, Figure 36). The ninefold structure is already seen in the maṇḍala of the eight great Bodhisattvas in Cave 12 in Ellora, Mahārāṣtra (late seventh to early eighth century) (see Figure 21 in Leidy/Thurman 1997: 31).

Pāñcarātra texts identify the maṇḍala with the deity's body and its constituent parts with the deity's body parts. Thus the Sātvata-Saṃhitā (Rastelli, p. 139) takes the lotus to represent the deity's intellect (*dhī* = *buddhi*). The Viṣṇu-Saṃhitā provides yet another interpretation of the lotus, equating it with the deity's heart.

The central lotuses in maṇḍalas or yantras often have triangles and hexagrams inscribed in their pericarps. In a two-dimensional structure, the lotuses are usually surrounded by a square enclosure, often termed a seat or throne (*pīṭha*), adjacent to which may be a corridor or passage (*vīthī*) for circumambulation (*pradakṣiṇā*). In a three-dimensional structure, the *pīṭha* would be the support of the lotus and project beyond it. Between one and three concentric circles and a square (with often three nested lines) frequently surround the central lotus on the outside. These geometrical structures will be discussed separately in section 2.3 in the context of yantras. In maṇḍala designs, lotuses also appear in combination with Śiva's trident(s).[31] A central lotus in a maṇḍala may be replaced by a wheel (*cakra*).[32] The deities are then assigned to the hub and the spokes of the wheel. A wheel can also appear in combination with a lotus design.[33]

1.3.2 The Square Grid

A common structural device of certain maṇḍalas is the square grid, which may incorporate a lotus design (made of squares) in its centre. Examples of this structure are the *bhadramaṇḍalas* employed in Smārta ritual, which are analyzed in the next essay. The square grid is obtained by drawing a certain number of vertical and horizontal base lines to form squares on a surface. The squares, called *pada* or *koṣṭha*, are assembled into different shapes and parts by filling them with coloured powders or grains. The constituent parts of the *sarva-*

---

[31] See the maṇḍala of the trident and lotuses (*triśūlābjamaṇḍala*) and the maṇḍala of the three tridents and (seven) lotuses (*tritriśūlābjamaṇḍala*) in Sanderson 1986 and Padoux, pp. 225ff. (with Illustrations 1–2) and the trident maṇḍala reconstructed in Törzsök, Appendix 3 (with Colour Plate 19). The trident of the Trika has been interpreted as representing the universe (Törzsök, p. 195).

[32] In descriptions of maṇḍala-like structures, words denoting parts of a lotus are sometimes treated as interchangeable with words denoting parts of a wheel; see Törzsök, p. 181.

[33] For a combination of a lotus and a wheel in maṇḍalas, see, for example, the *cakrābjamaṇḍala* (*bhadrakamaṇḍala*) described in Rastelli, p. 124 and the maṇḍala of Svacchandabhairava described in Törzsök, pp. 201–203.

tobhadra include (see Table, p. 87): a 'well' (*vāpī*), an 'offset' design (*bhadra*),[34] a 'creeper' (*vallī*), a 'chain' (*śṛṅkhalā*) and a 'crescent moon' (*khaṇḍendu*). In the centre is usually a lotus with a pericarp (*karṇikā*), and on the outside of the maṇḍala a square with three nested lines, coloured white, red and black. The three lines are identified with *sattva*, *rajas* and *tamas* [35] and coloured white, red and black respectively from the inside to the outside.[36] In addition to these parts, the *liṅgatobhadras* contain one or more phallic symbols (*liṅga*) of Śiva, which are themselves called Rudra or Śiva. Some *liṅgatobhadras* contain additional parts, such as a corridor or passage (*vīthī*) for circumambulation which surrounds a throne (*pīṭha*) and miniature creepers (*laghuvallī*) and miniature chains (*laghuśṛṅkhalā*). The characteristic element of the *rāmatobhadras* is the 'seal' of Rāma, which usually consists of the inscribed words *rājā rāma*. The *gaṇeśa-* and *sūryabhadras* feature images of Gaṇeśa and the sun respectively.

1.3.3 Other Designs

The *sarvatobhadra* reconstructed by Brunner in this book belongs to a different maṇḍala tradition from the aforementioned *sarvatobhadra*, and consists of different constituents. Structurally, the maṇḍala represents a combination of the square grid seen in the *bhadra-maṇḍalas* and a rounded lotus shape on a throne in the centre. The lotus consists of the pericarp (*karṇikā*), filaments (*kesara*), petals (*patra*, *dala*) and the tips of the petals (*dalāgra*). The throne (*pīṭha*) has four 'feet' (*pāda*) and four 'limbs' or 'bodies'(*gātra*), that is, side parts in the form of the bodies of men and animals (Brunner, pp. 167–168). There is a corridor or passage (*vīthī*) for circumambulation (*pradakṣiṇā*) and an outer enclosure consisting of entry and exit passages (*dvāra*). In addition, we find parts called *śobhā* and *upaśobhā* [37] and 'corners' (*koṇa*). Other maṇḍalas, such as the

[34] In architectural terminology, the term *bhadra* designates an offset projection common to North Indian temple plans.

[35] This interpretation is also given to maṇḍalas of the Pāñcarātra tradition (see Rastelli, p. 139).

[36] For the outer square as part of yantras, see section 2.3.8.

[37] These terms are also written *śobha/upaśobha* in the Pauṣkara-Saṃhitā (cf. Rastelli, p. 139). For an explanation of these terms, see Appendix 2 to Törzsök's contribution. Brunner, p. 169 interprets *śobhā* as a 'door' or 'entrance pavilion of the first enclosure of a palace or temple' and *upaśobhā* as possibly signifying a 'pavilion

śrīmaṇḍala and the *navanābhamaṇḍala* reconstructed in Törzsök (see her Appendices 1–2 and Colour Plates 16 and 18), feature additional constituent parts. These include door segments termed *kaṇṭha* (the upper part of a door) and *upakaṇṭha* (the lower part of a door). The *upakaṇṭha* is also called *kapola* in some texts.

Different interpretations are given to the constituent parts of these maṇḍalas. The *śrīmaṇḍala* reconstructed by Törzsök (see her Appendix 1 and Colour Plates 16–17) is surrounded by a square with five nested lines coloured transparent, yellow, black, red and white from the inside to the outside. These five lines are identified with the five *kalās* which constitute the Śaiva universe. In the Pāñcarātra tradition the maṇḍala is sometimes identified with the deity's body. Interpreting one of these maṇḍalas, the Sātvata-Saṃhitā equates the *śobhās* with the deity's organs of action (*karaṇa*), the *upaśobhās* with the subtle elements (*tanmātra*), and the corners and gates with the deity's sense organs (cf. Rastelli, p. 139). In the Pāñcarātra tradition the maṇḍala also becomes a representation of the universe, when its constituent parts are equated with cosmic principles and divine powers. Thus the Viṣṇu-Saṃhitā, for example, identifies the five colours used in the maṇḍala with the five elements (see Rastelli, p. 141).

1.4 *The Question of the Origin and Date of Maṇḍalas*

Several scholars have suggested that Tantric maṇḍalas are rooted in Vedic traditions. The layout of Vedic altars is taken as indicative of an early interest in geometric designs endowed with cosmological symbolism (Gaeffke 1987: 153). The method of determining the lines of the compass for the construction of sacrificial altars, the consecration of bricks on the surface of a *cayana* altar by means of mantras and the locating of deities on those bricks are essential features of Vedic rituals (Apte 1926: 2–3), and aspects of these rituals recur in the practice of constructing maṇḍalas and invoking deities into their parts. The sacred space of maṇḍalas and yantras can be seen as a continuation of the Vedic sacrificial site (Schneider

---

on top of a secondary door.' The translation 'offset design' for *śobhā* and 'recess design' for *upaśobhā* is used by P.P. Apte in the introduction to his edition and translation of the Pauṣkara-Saṃhitā (Part 1), p. xii. For drawings of these parts, see Törzsök's Illustration 1 and also Hikita 1991: 319.

1988: 100), and the square enclosure of Tantric maṇḍalas in particular as an analogue of the sacred fire altar (Gupta 1988: 39–41). But the similarities between the two traditions appear to end here. Authors like Mitra 1958: 112[38] are going too far when they assume that patterns displayed by yantras and maṇḍalas can be traced back to the Śulba-Sūtras of the Vedāṅgas (which prescribe the way to construct sacrificial altar diagrams), since the patterns displayed by Tantric maṇḍalas are distinctly different. So are the mantras and the deities invoked into maṇḍalas and the details of the rites. The problem of the similarities and differences between Vedic and Tantric traditions is complex and needs to be explored in greater detail in a separate study. Such an investigation would have to trace the influences of other traditions on maṇḍalas as well.

The oldest Hindu maṇḍalas may date back to before the sixth century A.D. Among the oldest maṇḍalas that can be dated are two types of *vāstupuruṣamaṇḍala*s described in Varāhamihira's Bṛhat-Saṃhitā. This text is commonly placed in the middle of the sixth century. The two *vāstupuruṣamaṇḍala*s are described in chapter 53, but were obviously not created by Varāhamihira but rather incorporated from older unidentified sources. Apte 1987: 141 notes that the first type of *vāstupuruṣamaṇḍala* is described in the Pauṣkara-Saṃhitā of the Pāñcarātra, which he dates to ca. 400 A.D. (Apte 1986: 3, 1999: 18) or at least 450 A.D. (Apte 1987), while Matsubara 1994: 34 assigns the Pauṣkara to 500 A.D. However, these early dates are highly speculative, the upper limit for the composition of the Pauṣkara-Saṃhitā being only the tenth century. Moreover, dating a Saṃhitā as a whole is problematic, since these texts were constantly revised and reworked by redactors. Sanderson 2001: 38, note 50 states that he found evidence that the Pauṣkara-Saṃhitā (along with the Jayākhya-Saṃhitā and the Sātvata-Saṃhitā) were influenced by Tantric Śaiva systems. At this time the complex descriptions of maṇḍalas found in the Pauṣkara-Saṃhitā cannot be dated with certainty. We do not have clear evidence for establishing dates for the development of yantras either. Brooks 1992: 34 considers the possibility that the most famous of yantras, the *śrīcakra/śrīyantra*, developed before the sixth century.

---

[38] Chattopadhyaya 1978: 80, too, suggests a connection between yantras and shapes of sacrificial diagrams used in the Vedic tradition.

2 *Yantra*

2.1 *General Remarks*

The word yantra designates an instrument, machine,[39] mechanical device or appliance (especially one used in warfare), and also a magic diagram. It is derived from the verbal root *yam*, 'to control.'[40]

---

[39] For this meaning of 'yantra,' see, for example, Bhagavadgītā 18.61. Mechanical appliances and machines called yantras are described in chapter 31 of the Samarāṅgaṇa-Sūtradhāra, a work on architecture ascribed to Bhoja, which was studied by Raghavan 1956: 21–31. See also the overview in Shukla 1967: 30–52. For different astronomical instruments called yantras for use in observatories, see Volwahsen 2001: 40ff.

[40] Mayrhofer 1986–2001, volume 2: 398 explains the word yantra as an instrument for fastening. Kramrisch 1946, volume 1: 11–12, who apparently does not differentiate between the terms maṇḍala and yantra, defines 'yantra' as follows: "A Yantra is a geometrical contrivance by which any aspect of the Supreme Principle may be bound (yantr, to bind; from the root 'yam') to any spot for the purpose of worship. It is an artifice in which the ground (bhūmi) is converted into the extent of the manifested universe." For two religious etymologies of the word yantra, see the following verses from two different chapters of the Kulārṇava-Tantra. The first verse derives the word yantra from the verbal root *yam* with the prefix *ni*, meaning 'to restrain, prevent, tame.'

kāmakrodhādidoṣotthasarvaduḥkhaniyantraṇāt /
yantram ity āhur etasmin devaḥ prīṇāti pūjitaḥ // 6.86

"Because it restrains all suffering arising from the defects (in the form) of desire, anger and so forth they call it yantra. The god who is worshipped in it graces (the practitioner)."

yamabhūtādisarvebhyo bhayebhyo 'pi kuleśvari /
trāyate satataṃ caiva tasmād yantram itīritam // 17.61

"O mistress of the *kula*, because it protects always from absolutely all dangers, such as Yama and (evil) spirits (*bhūta*), therefore it is called yantra."

Pūrṇānanda's Śrītattvacintāmaṇi 17.2 explains the word yantra in a similar way:

yamayaty akhilaṃ pāpaṃ trāyate mahato bhayāt /
sādhakaṃ pūjanād dhyānāt tasmād yantraḥ prakīrtyate //

"It subdues all evil, it protects the practitioner from great danger when worshipped (and) visualized (*dhyāna*); therefore it is called yantra."

(The masculine gender of yantra here is rather unusual, but see also the citation from the Kālīvilāsa-Tantra below.)

Rāghavabhaṭṭa's commentary, pp. 519, 6–7 on Śāradātilaka 24.1 quotes the following etymology of the word yantra from an unspecified Saṃhitā:

manorathākṣarāṇy atra niyantryante tapodhanāḥ /

"In this the letters of (= conveying) desires are affixed, O ascetics."

He continues with a line reminiscent of Kulārṇava-Tantra 6.86 cited above:

kāmakrodhādidoṣān vā (correct to *°doṣotthadī°*) *dīrghaduḥkhaniyantraṇāt* //
yantram ity āhuḥ / *iti*

"They call it yantra because it restrains prolonged suffering arising from defects (in the form) of desire, anger and so forth."

A general characteristic of yantras is that they are small in size. In contrast, maṇḍalas vary in size and can be large enough to allow for priests or initiands to enter them through doors and to walk around in them, for example, during an initiation (*dīkṣā*). With the exception of yantras placed below temple statues at the time of their consecration and yantras installed permanently for worship in *maṭhas* or temples, and a few other cases,[41] yantras are generally mobile, whereas maṇḍalas are not. While maṇḍalas can employ different colour schemes, the use of colour is less common if not indeed irrelevant in the case of most yantras. Texts may prescribe that the lines of a yantra be traced with a specific colour, for example, with turmeric or blood, but the space inside a yantra is never filled with colours as it is in the case of maṇḍalas. And while pictorial representations of deities can appear in maṇḍalas, such images are generally not found in yantras.[42] Like maṇḍalas, yantras are believed to be effective only when worshipped. However, some texts claim that the act of merely viewing a maṇḍala[43] or drawing or recollecting a yantra[44] brings about beneficial results. However, according to Kālīvilāsa-Tantra 7.9cd–10ab and 27.21ab, worship of a deity in a yantra is *not* recommended in the present *kali* era.

Based on an analysis of texts of the Trika School of Kashmir, Brunner, p. 162 briefly defines a yantra as a linear representation on a specific surface, such as birch-bark. She adds that yantras almost inevitably have letters, seed (*bīja*) syllables or mantras inscribed in them. Since mantras frequently employ verbs in the imperative to express an order, Brunner suggests the translation 'coercive diagrams' for yantras. Similarly, Rastelli, p. 142 concludes from her study of the Pāñcarātra texts that yantras have inscribed mantras.

Another etymology of 'yantra' is found in Kālīvilāsa-Tantra 33.1:
bījānāṃ koṇavijñānaṃ yatnatas trāyate yataḥ /
tena yantra iti khyāta īśānamukhaniḥsṛtaḥ //
"Because it with effort protects the knowledge of the angles/corners (of the drawing) (reserved) for the seed (syllables), which (knowledge) came forth from Īśāna's (that is, Śiva's) mouth, therefore it is called yantra."

(The form °*sṛtaḥ*—the text reads erroneously °*smṛtaḥ*—can be explained as an example of case attraction; °*sṛtam* is the expected form.)

[41] See Rastelli, p. 143 for yantras described in the Aniruddha-Saṃhitā, which are drawn and then worshipped on a platform and are therefore not mobile.

[42] The *saudarśanayantra* (see Rastelli, pp. 148–150), which is a combination of a yantra and a figure of Viṣṇu, is an exceptional case.

[43] See the Suprabheda quoted in Brunner, p. 175, note 53.

[44] See the description in Rastelli, p. 146.

Authors such as Kṣemarāja[45] consider it characteristic of certain yantras that mantras are inscribed in them. But at least in later texts and in modern practice mantras or syllables are not necessarily part of yantras (see sections 2.2.1 and 2.2.2).

Brunner concludes that yantras, like some maṇḍalas, are used for worship in desire-oriented (*kāmya*) rites, but their main purpose is magical. She asserts that maṇḍalas are employed in rituals to obtain the deity's favour, but without the presence of a magical element. This may be true of the limited group of texts Brunner analyzes, but it is not the complete picture, for Törzsök, pp. 201–209 discusses maṇḍalas described in the Bhairava-Tantras which are used in rituals leading to the attainment of supernatural powers (*siddhi*).

Yantras can be two- or three-dimensional. Two-dimensional yantras are designs on paper, textiles and other materials. Three-dimensional yantras are raised structures usually made of metal. The well-known *śrīyantra* or *śrīcakra* can be represented either two- or three-dimensionally. Three-dimensional *śrīcakras* are classified differently, depending on the author's use of terminology.[46]

---

[45] See Kṣemarāja's statement quoted by Sanderson in Padoux 1986: 33.

[46] Khanna 1986: 101 lists the following kinds of three-dimensional *śrīcakras*:

1) *bhūprastāra* – engraved or embossed on a flat metal surface;
2) *meruprastāra* – pyramid-shaped, with either two, three or nine elevations rising one above the other; and
3) *kailāśaprastāra* (for *kailāsa°*), having a slightly raised surface.

For information on *meruprastāra*-, *bhūprastāra*- and *kailāsaprastāra-śrīcakras*, see Rao 1990: 116–117 and Shankaranarayanan 1970: 92–94. According to Khanna, the *bhūprastāra* type of *śrīcakra* features slightly raised shapes on a flat surface. Other authors assert that the *bhūprastāra* (also called *bhūpṛṣṭha*) form of the *śrīcakra* has a completely flat surface and is two-dimensional.

Two kinds of *bhūprastāra* (called *bhūpṛṣṭha*) yantras are referred to in Chawdhri 1990: 2 and Chawdhri 1992: 8. This author lists the following kinds of yantras:

1) '*bhoo prishth* (= *bhūpṛṣṭha*) yantras' – yantras from materials that indicate the use of earth; they are further subdivided into raised yantras and carved yantras;
2) '*meru prishth* (= *merupṛṣṭha*) yantras' – raised yantras which are shaped like mountains;
3) '*patal* (for *pātāla*) yantras' – carved yantras shaped like inverted mountains;
4) '*meru prastar* (= *meruprastāra*) yantras' – cut yantras, and
5) '*ruram prishth* (misprint for *kūrmapṛṣṭha*?) yantras' – yantras that have the shape of a rectangle at their base and that of the back of a tortoise above their base.

Finer distinctions among these categories are not provided. Chawdhri's classification has been adopted by Beckman 1996: 50–52. A somewhat similar classification appears in Johari 1986: 58:

"1) Bhu-Prashtha Yantra: engraved or drawn on a flat surface.

2.2 *Types of Yantras*

Attempts to establish a distinction between maṇḍalas and yantras have already been discussed in section 1.1. This section will discuss attempts to classify yantras. Renou/Filliozat 1947–1953, volume 1: 568 attempt to distinguish between two types of yantras. The first type of yantra is supposed to be purely linear-geometric, and to be employed in temples for purposes of permanent worship. The second type reportedly features a linear design with iconic representations and is used in temporary and individual worship rites. No examples or further details are given, and in the absence of explanations and textual evidence this unusual distinction remains unclear.

In a book on yantras written for a general readership, S.K.R. Rao 1988: 14–15 distinguishes the following three types of yantras:

1. yantras for worship or for actualizing a deity (*pūjanayantra*),
2. yantras for magical protection (*rakṣāyantra*) and

---

2) Meru-Prashtha Yantra: three-dimensional form composed of metal or stone or gem-stones and shaped like a pyramid, having a broad base and narrowing gradually toward the top like a mountain (*meru*).
3) Patal Yantra: deeply engraved—exactly the reverse of the pyramid yantra.
4) Meru-Prastar Yantra: composed of pieces that are glued or welded to each other instead of being one solid piece."

Metal *śrīcakras* supported by a tortoise pedestal are commercially sold in India as *kūrmapṛṣṭha-śrīcakras*. Brooks 1990: 107 lists only the two-dimensional *bhūprastāra* ('spreading over the earth') *śrīcakra* as a category along with the fully three-dimensional *meru* or *sumeru* form and the more flattened, elongated *kailāsa* form. Rao 1990: 118 refers to a classification of *śrīcakras* into *bhūpṛṣṭha*, *kacchapapṛṣṭha* and *merupṛṣṭha* When a cakra is drawn on a flat surface, it is called *bhūpṛṣṭha*. When "supported by a dwarf pedestal, raised like the back of a tortoise" it is referred to as *kacchapapṛṣṭha*. When the cakra has the form of a mountain with different elevations it is known as *merupṛṣṭha*. Umānandanātha in his Nityotsava (written in 1745 A.D.), p. 65, 4–9, lists one type of *bhūprastāra-śrīcakra* in which the lines of the cakra are elevated, and three types of *meruprastāra-śrīcakras* in which specific parts of the structure are elevated. Pranavananda <1977>: 35–39 classifies *śrīcakras* into the following three categories:

1) *bhūprastāra* or *bhūkrama*;
2) *kūrmaprastāra* or *kūrmapṛṣṭha* and
3) *merukrama*, *meruprastāra* or *merupṛṣṭha*.

According to this author, the first kind is a *śrīcakra* whose complete design is engraved or embossed. The *śrīcakras* of the second type all feature nine triangles in a slightly elevated position. Such a cakra may also be placed on the back of a tortoise (and hence the name *kūrmaprastāra* or *kūrmapṛṣṭha*). The third type of *śrīcakra* has all its triangles raised like a mountain.

3. yantras which are also called maṇḍalas; they are defined as surfaces on which ritual objects are placed.

In the same book (Rao 1988: 19) the author introduces yet another threefold classification of yantras:

1. yantras for magical purposes, generally called protective yantras (*rakṣāyantra*),
2. yantras for actualizing divinities (*devatāyantra*) and
3. yantras that facilitate meditation (*dhyānayantra*).

The items in the first two categories in both lists are identical, even if their sequence differs. The third type of yantra in the first list will be discussed below. The third category in the second list appears to refer to certain Buddhist maṇḍalas (Rao 1988: 27). Even though descriptive details are missing and the categories are presented in a somewhat unsystematic way, Rao's classification is helpful, but clearly not sufficient. Rao has pointed the reader in the right direction by taking the ritual function of yantras into consideration when attempting to classify them.

Building on Brunner's and Rao's work as well as on the basis of my study of Tantric texts of the later period, I would like to suggest the following tentative classification of yantras as a guideline. This classification, according to the distinctive features and ritual use of yantras, is not intended to be exhaustive and may not be applicable to all South Asian Tantric traditions.

1. Yantras which function as supports for ritual implements during a worship ritual, being referred to as 'yantras for (establishing) a foundation' (*sthāpanayantra*),
2. yantras employed in a practitioner's *regular* Tantric worship of a deity, often referred to as 'yantras (which are supports) for worship' (*pūjāyantra, pūjādhārayantra*) and named for their presiding deity, for example, 'yantra for the worship of Gaṇapati' (*gaṇapatipūjāyantra*), and
3. yantras employed in optional *desire-oriented* rites, which are performed on special occasions. Yantras used in a special ritual for a certain deity are included here as well as yantras which are prepared for specific magical rites, and which are often named for these rites, for example, 'yantra for attraction' (*ākarṣaṇa-*

> *yantra*) (Illustration 1). After the ritual is complete, the instructions may recommend that these yantras consecrated for magical purposes be made into amulets and worn on the body (*dhāraṇa-yantra*) in order to obtain the desired results, such as protection or the acquisition of power and wealth. Among these yantras, the yantras for protection (*rakṣāyantra*) figure prominently in texts. In the category of yantras for desire-oriented rites I also include magic (number) squares.[47] These are diagrams with numbers inscribed, the sum of which remains the same, regardless of the direction in which one adds them up.

These three categories are detailed below.

2.2.1 Type 1: Yantras for Establishing a Foundation

These yantras feature simple geometric shapes, such as a triangle or a circle. They function as supports for ritual implements, such as lamps or vessels, in special desire-oriented (*kāmya*) or magical rites. Such supports also figure in the regular Tantric *pūjā*, in which they appear to be referred to as maṇḍalas (see Illustration 2).[48] Their function can be compared to that of the 'seat-maṇḍalas' in Brunner's maṇḍala classification (section 1.2); however, Brunner's 'seat-maṇḍalas,' which are made of cow-dung and similar materials, are without any clearly recognizable structure.

2.2.2 Type 2: Yantras Employed in Regular Worship

Yantras of this type usually feature common geometric shapes, but generally do not have mantras inscribed, at least according to the later Tantric texts that I have studied. However, the deity and her/his emanations are invoked into the yantra with mantras. A few yantras have the names of these emanations or surrounding deities inscribed following the expression 'salutation to' (*namaḥ*). Regardless of whether the mantras are only used to invoke the deity or whether they are also inscribed in the yantra, they are of utmost importance. It is for this reason that the Kulārṇava-Tantra states that a yantra

---

[47] For magic (number) squares, see, for example, the illustrations in Abbott 1932: 515–521 and the discussion in Cammann 1969.

[48] The maṇḍala in Illustration 2 serves as a support for the *vardhinī/ vardhanī* vessel in a Tantric *pūjā*.

consists of the deity's mantra.[49] Yantras employed in regular worship are often made of durable materials, such as copper.

In this category of yantras I would also include the *śrīcakra*, also called *śrīyantra*. In addition to being worshipped in ritual, this cakra is also visualized and experienced in the practitioner's body as a manifestation of the cosmic process of creation and resorption with spatial and mantric aspects, as Padoux explains in his contribution to this book.

2.2.3 Type 3: Yantras Employed in Optional Desire-Oriented Rites

The third category of yantras is required for the performance of optional rites, such as specific magical rites, and they are often made of perishable materials, such as birch-bark or paper. These yantras are drawn, according to the instructions, with special writing materials and substances, such as animal or human blood or ashes from a cremation ground. Johari 1986: 63 reports that such yantras may be made from wheat flower, rice paste, beans or (grains of) rice.[50] They may also be incised on more permanent materials, such as metal plates. Discussions of the various styluses used and the materials on which protective yantras can be written are commonly found in texts. The materials are considered extremely important for the success of the ritual, and correspond to the nature of the rite performed. Thus cruel rites require repulsive materials, and the yantra used in the rite of liquidation (*māraṇa*) as described in Mahīdhara's 16th-century Mantramahodadhi 25.56ab and 25.59ab should be written on human bone with certain poisonous substances.

General instructions for drawing yantras for different purposes, including reducing fever, keeping snakes away and countering the effects of poison, can be found in various texts, such as chapter 24 of Lakṣmaṇadeśika's Śāradātilaka (10th-11th century), which is based

---

[49] Cf. Kulārṇava-Tantra 6.85ab and 6.87:

yantraṃ mantramayaṃ proktaṃ devatā mantrarūpiṇī / 6.85ab
śarīram iva jīvasya dīpasya snehavat priye /
sarveṣām api devānāṃ tathā yantraṃ pratiṣṭhitam // 6.87

See also the similar quotation from the Kaulāvalīya-Tantra in Woodroffe 1956: 93, note 2:

yantraṃ mantramayaṃ proktaṃ mantrātmā devataiva hi /
dehātmanor yathābhedo yantradevatayos tathā //

[50] Two yantras made from beans, rice and coloured stones are reproduced in Plate 2 of his book.

on chapter 34 of the Prapañcasāra (ca. 10th century), and in chapter 20 of the Mantramahodadhi. Yantras for magical purposes (for example, Illustration 5) are described in detail in Dāmodara's 17th-century Yantracintāmaṇi, also known as the Kalpacintāmaṇi. The applications include the six rites of magic (*abhicāra*), namely, appeasement (*śānti*), subjugation (*vaśīkaraṇa*), immobilization (*stambhana*), enmity (*vidveṣaṇa*), eradication (*uccāṭana*) and liquidation (*māraṇa*). Depending on their purpose, these yantras are named 'yantras for subjugation' (*vaśyakarayantra*), 'yantras for attraction' (*ākarṣaṇayantra*) (Illustration 1), and so on. The use of yantras in rites of magic, which has been documented by previous scholars,[51] continues up to the present day and can be observed even in modern Indian cities. Yantras featuring Hanumat are sold in India for the safety of one's vehicle (*vāhanasurakṣāyantra*). Other yantras are used for curing diseases at the recommendation of astrologers.[52]

Yantras used in magical rites may be ritually destroyed after their use, inserted into a statue of a deity that will then undergo burial, or be crushed and eaten, tied to a tree or concealed in the intended person's home, depending on the instructions. They may be enclosed in an amulet container, such as a tube or a locket,[53] sealed and then worn around the neck, on the head, in one's headgear,[54] in a tuft of

[51] See, for example, the list of yantras popular in South India published in Thurston 1912: 185–187 and references in Abbott 1932, s.v. yantra.

[52] See, for example, the numerous yantras in Chawdhri 1990, Shubhakaran 1992, Beckman 1996 and Khurrana 2000, and the section on yantras ('*jantra*') in Dietrich 1998: 172–175.

[53] For yantras preserved in container amulets, see Untracht 1997: 132.

[54] Amulets hidden in hats, turbans and other headgear are documented in Untracht 1997: 89. In his popular books on yantras, Chawdhri (1990: 6, 1992: 10) refers to a category of yantra which is kept under one's cap or turban or in one's pocket. He calls them '*chhatar*' (vernacular form for *chatra* [umbrella]) yantras. This category has been borrowed by Beckman 1996: 52. Chawdhri (1990: 4–6, 1992: 9–11 [cf. Beckman 1996: 51–53]) includes '*chhatar*' yantras as category 6 in his following classification of yantras, which is also summarized in Bunce 2001: xv:

1) '*sharir*' (= *śarīra*) yantras – the yantra designs in the cakras of the human body;
2) '*dharan*' (= *dhāraṇa*) yantras – yantras worn on the body;
3) '*aasan*' (= *āsana*) yantras – yantras kept under one's seat (*āsana*) during worship or under the foundation of houses, temples or a statue of a deity;
4) '*mandal*' (= maṇḍala) yantras – yantras formed by nine individuals, one of them seated in the centre and the others in the eight directions; the person in the centre performs the worship of the '*ishat*' (= *iṣṭa*) yantra (that is, any particular yantra), while the others recite certain mantras;
5) '*pooja*' (= *pūjā*) yantras – yantras installed in houses or temples for worship;

hair, on the arm, under the armpit, on the wrist or a finger and so forth.[55] A yantra which is to be inserted into a locket is first drawn on a piece of paper or similar material and consecrated in a worship ritual by a specialist. These lockets can be attached to the necks of animals, such as cows, for their protection. Yantras may also be attached to protective dolls hung near the entrance to a home or be placed above a door.

Yantras employed in desire-oriented rites may be similar in design to the yantras for establishing a foundation (type 1), but they often have mantras inscribed. The mantras can be seed syllables (*bīja*) combined with verbs in the second person singular imperative, such as 'subjugate' (*vaśīkuru*), which ask the deity to carry out the magical effects of a rite on its recipient. The centre of the yantra is frequently inscribed with the name of the person to be influenced, termed the recipient or intended person (*sādhya*). The place in which the person's name is to be written is often indicated by the name Devadatta. The recipient's name is either surrounded by, or its syllables are intertwined with, the syllables of the mantra.

Yantras may also contain longer mantras[56] or even well-known hymns (*stotra, stuti*). The composition and ritual use of hymns or devotional poems in praise of deities has a long history in South Asia. Such hymns are found in the Purāṇa literature and the Tantras, and in independent collections attributed to sages or seers as well. To reinforce the efficacy of hymn-recitation in bringing about the promised material benefits, the practice arose of reciting hymns a given number of times. This practice is modelled on that of repeating powerful mantras. In time, hymns came to be regarded as powerful magical formulas. Whereas the shorter mantras may be repeated millions of times to achieve a particular result, hymns are recited at most hundreds or thousands of times. Hymns employed for such purposes include hymns for protection. These hymns often include in their titles such terms as 'armour' (*kavaca*), 'protection' (*rakṣā*), or 'cage' (*pañjara*). In these hymns the deity is asked to protect each

---

6) '*chhatar*' (= *chatra*) yantras – see above; and

7) '*darshan*' (= *darśana*) yantras – yantras which the devotee beholds in the morning for the sake of auspiciousness.

[55] Rastelli, p. 146 also refers to yantras hidden between the breasts of women.

[56] Compare the practice of inscribing *dhāraṇīs* in maṇḍala-like structures in a Buddhist context, which is documented, for example, in Drège 1999–2000, Figures 1–9.

part of the practitioner's body. The different parts, from head to feet, are systematically enumerated. For each part of the body, the practitioner addresses the deity using a different descriptive epithet, which is often connected with the respective body part. The deity's names are assigned to and 'deposited' on the body parts of the practitioner, and are believed to protect him like divine armour. As well as being recited, these hymns can be arranged in the form of yantras. For those who cannot themselves recite the hymn, a yantra with the hymn inscribed in it is thought to bring about the same beneficial effects as recitation. An example of a yantra in this category is the *rāmarakṣāyantra*, which represents in a graphic mode the Rāmarakṣāstotra ascribed to Budhakauśika. In my study of the Rāmarakṣāstotra I reproduce two yantras in which the Rāmarakṣā-stotra is inscribed (Bühnemann 1983: 93 and 107). Another, yet unpublished *rāmarakṣāyantra* is included here as Illustration 3. The yantra consists of a hexagram with a drawing of Rāma and different seed (*bīja*) syllables in the centre. The hexagram is surrounded by concentric circles and by squares, the first of which has elaborate gate structures which open in the four cardinal directions. The innermost square contains the text of a version of the Rāmarakṣā-stotra.[57]

In addition to yantras containing the text of entire hymns, there are also yantras which are associated with individual stanzas of hymns of praise. Well-known examples are the yantras associated with the Saundaryalaharī and the Bhaktāmarastotra. The Saundarya-laharī is a hymn to the Tantric goddess Tripurasundarī in 100 (sometimes 103) stanzas. It is traditionally ascribed to Śaṃkarācārya, identified with the Advaitin Śaṃkara. The Bhaktāmarastotra by the Jain poet Mānatuṅga is a hymn to the first Jina Ṛṣabha in 44 stanzas according to the Śvetāmbara version, or 48 stanzas in the Digambara version. Each verse of the Saundaryalaharī became associated with a specific seed (*bīja*) syllable, which is inscribed in a yantra shape, such as a square, a hexagram, a triangle, a lotus, and so forth (for example, Illustration 4). Only one of these yantras has the name of the intended person (*sādhya*) of the rite inscribed on it, and only one

[57] Different versions of the hymn are presented and dicussed in Bühnemann 1983. The text inscribed in the *rāmarakṣāyantra* reproduced in Illustration 3 contains an introductory section with miscellaneous verses and verses 2–15 (cf. Bühnemann 1983: 26–27) of the *stotra*, which latter request Rāma to protect the practitioner's body parts.

yantra contains a verb in the second person singular imperative. These yantras are worshipped, and the seed syllables inscribed in them are recited a large number of times, for the attainment of desired, usually mundane, benefits. Each individual stanza of the Bhaktāmarastotra is associated with a mantra addressing not the Jina Ṛṣabha but goddesses, Yakṣas and gods, and each mantra is prefixed by seed syllables. The mantras often contain second person singular imperative verbs. In a similar fashion individual yantras are also associated with the 47 stanzas of the Jain Kalyāṇamandirastotra. The yantras associated with the stanzas of these three hymns were obviously created later, their connection with the stanzas not being evident from the text itself.[58]

The general instructions require that yantras be infused with life in the rite of *prāṇapratiṣṭhā*, which is also performed on statues of deities. According to Rāghavabhaṭṭa's 15th-century commentary on the Śāradātilaka and texts such as the Mantramahodadhi, the *prāṇapratiṣṭhā* rite entails that certain mantras are inscribed in the yantras. These mantras can be seen in some yantras which are prepared on permanent materials, such as metal plates. The two *rāmarakṣāyantra*s reproduced in Bühnemann 1983: 93 and 107 also contain them. The mantras include the syllable *hsauḥ*, which represents the soul (*jīva*) of the yantra; the syllables *haṃsaḥ so 'haṃ* ("I am that goose"), which represent its life breath (*prāṇa*); the vowels *i*/*ī*, which represent the yantra's eyes, and the syllables *u*/*ū*, which represent its ears; and the seed syllables *laṃ raṃ maṃ kṣaṃ vaṃ yaṃ saṃ haṃ hrīṃ āṃ* of the ten directional guardians, beginning with Indra in the east, which represent the heart (*hṛdaya*) of the yantra. In addition to the *prāṇapratiṣṭhāmantra*, the following *yantragāyatrī*, an imitation of the well-known *gāyatrī* (*sāvitrī*) mantra, found in Ṛg-Veda 3.62.10, is inscribed in circular form:

yantrarājāya vidmahe varapradāya dhīmahi /
tan no yantraḥ pracodayāt //[59]

---

[58] Regarding the connection between the yantras and the stanzas of the Saundaryalaharī, Anantakṛṣṇa Śāstrī comments: "There seems to be some mystical connection between each sloka and its Bījākshara. But it is not intelligible; nor has any of the Prayoga Kartas explained the same" (introduction to his translation of the Saundaryalaharī, 1957: 13).

[59] Cf. Rāghavabhaṭṭa's commentary, p. 519, 33–34 on Śāradātilaka 24.2. The *yantragāyatrī* appears with minor variants in many texts. Brahmānandagiri's Śāktānandataraṅgiṇī, p. 257, 13–14 gives the following version:

oṃ yantrarājāya vidmahe mahāyantrāya dhīmahi /

"We know the king of the yantra; we think of the bestower of boons. Therefore may the yantra inspire us."

Texts such as Brahmānandagiri's 16th-century Śāktānanda-taraṅgiṇī, pp. 264, 6ff. also enjoin that certain purificatory rites (*saṃskāra*) be performed on yantras, just as they are performed to purify mantras.

In this section I have suggested a classification of yantras into three types: 1 yantras for establishing a foundation, functioning as supports for ritual implements; 2 yantras employed in regular Tantric worship; 3 yantras employed in optional desire-oriented rites. The three types of yantras can be distinguished according to their ritual functions. The first and second types have similar geometric designs but usually no mantras inscribed. Yantras of type 2 usually consist of more complex geometric designs than type 1 yantras. Both types differ in ritual function. The first type is used as a support for objects in rituals, while the second type is the main object of worship. Yantras of type 1 are similar in function to the aforementioned 'seat-maṇḍalas' (see Brunner's category 1 described in section 1.2) and are occasionally also referred to as maṇḍalas (see 2.2.1). But they differ from Brunner's 'seat-maṇḍalas' of cow-dung and similar materials which have no clearly recognizable structure. Yantras of type 3 are used in desire-oriented magical rites, usually have inscribed mantras and may have unusual designs.

2.3 *Some Constituent Parts of Yantras*

Yantra and maṇḍala designs commonly feature a triangle and/or a hexagram, inscribed in one or several lotuses (*padma*) of four, eight, 10, 12, 16, 100, 1000 or more petals (*dala*). The lotus petals are often surrounded by one circle or three concentric circles (*vṛtta*) and a square (*caturasra*) with sometimes three nested lines. In yantras of the Śaiva and Śākta traditions the lines of triangles or a square may be formed by tridents whose prongs project beyond the lines of these shapes (see Colour Plate 1).

The main deity is worshipped in the centre of the yantra at a 'point' (*bindu*) which may be visible or remain invisible/unmanifest, while his/her retinue is worshipped in various parts of the structure (see Illustration 6). These parts include the angles (*asra*) or corners

---

tan no yantraḥ pracodayāt //

(*koṇa*) of a triangle or hexagram, the points of intersection (*saṃdhi*) of two triangles,[60] the lotus petals (*dala*) and the tips of lotus petals (*dalāgra*). The most important surrounding deities or emanations are invoked into the parts of the yantra closest to the centre. One obvious advantage of a yantra compared to an icon is that a yantra allows for the deities who surround the main deity in enclosures (*āvaraṇa, āvṛti,* literally 'covering' or 'veil') to be worshipped in it as well.

The structural elements of yantras vary, as do the interpretations given to these elements. Some important constituent parts are described in the following, together with examples of interpretations from texts. Most descriptions and interpretations of the constituent parts of yantras found in the literature concern the *śrīyantra* or *śrīcakra*, the most important and influential of yantras.[61]

Preliminary studies of the constituent parts of yantras are found in the works by A. Daniélou. The author's 'Hindu Polytheism,' 1964: 351–354 contains an enlarged and revised version of the section on yantras printed in Daniélou's older French edition of the book, 'Le polythéisme hindou,' 1960: 525–539. Daniélou does not indicate the sources of his interpretations of the yantra designs clearly, but it can be inferred that he draws on articles in Hindī.[62] In his later work on the Hindu temple (Daniélou 1977: 26–28 [2001: 37–38]), the author takes up the discussion of the constituent parts of yantras once again. Daniélou's interpretations of yantra constituents continue to be

---

[60] Special terminology is used in connection with the *śrīcakra*. The three circles outside of the overlapping triangles are referred to as three girdles or belts (*valaya*); a point of intersection between two lines is called *saṃdhi*; a point of intersection between three lines is known as *marman* ('vital point'), and a point of intersection between a *saṃdhi* and *marman* is termed *granthi* ('knot'); see Bhāskararāya's Setubandha, p. 31, 9 and Umānandanātha's Nityotsava, p. 64, 4–5.

[61] Detailed notes on different interpretations that have been given to the constituents of the *śrīcakra* and a critical evaluation of these interpretations are provided by Pranavananda <1977>.

[62] Devarāj Vidyāvācaspati's article entitled 'Tantra meṃ yantra aur mantra,' printed in the magazine Kalyāṇ, published by the Gītā Press (Gorakhpur), Śakti *aṅka*, 1934: 387–397, is cited in Daniélou 1964: 353. The original article does not indicate the sources on which Devarāj Vidyāvācaspati's interpretations are based. Daniélou 1977: 26 (2001: 37) refers to an article by Ḍabrāl, entitled 'Śrīyantra kā svarūp,' printed in Śakti *aṅka*, 1934, p. 592–609. Daniélou erroneously refers to the author as 'Kalika-prasāda Dabrāl' and specifies the page number as 591. However, the author's name is Lalitāprasād Ḍabrāl and the article is found on pp. 592–609. As the title indicates, Ḍabrāl's interpretation is concerned with the constituents of the *śrīyantra*.

influential and are partially adopted and summarized in Johari 1986: 52 and Bunce 2001: 27–29.

2.3.1 The Point (*bindu*)

The point (*bindu*) is located in the centre of the yantra and may be visible or remain invisible. It is often interpreted as the principle from which all form and creation radiates (for example, Shankaranarayanan 1970: 29). Verses 11–12 of the first chapter of the Yoginīhṛdaya describe the point as "throbbing consciousness whose supreme nature is light and which is united with the flashing flow [of divine power], the seat (*baindavāsana*) which is the [birth]place of the flow made up of the three *mātṛkās*" (Padoux, p. 241). According to Daniélou 1964: 351, the point represents the element ether. The most likely seventh-century Gaṇeśapūrvatāpa-nīya-Upaniṣad, section 3 equates the central point with the void of space.

2.3.2 The Triangle (*trikoṇa*, *tryasra*)

The triangle is a common constituent of yantras. It can be either downward-oriented or upward-oriented, and less frequently oriented toward the right or left sides.[63] The downward-pointing or inverted triangle is known as a symbol of the female pubic triangle and the female sex-organ or womb (*yoni*, *bhaga*).[64] The letter *e* is identified with it because of its triangular shape (in certain Indian scripts).[65] This triangle is known as a symbol of the feminine in other cultures as well. In Buddhist Tantric texts the downward-pointing triangle is referred to as the *dharmodaya*/*dharmodayā*, 'the origin of existents (*dharma*).'[66] This triangle is visualized in *sādhanas* as the place in which everything originates. The downward-pointing triangle also symbolizes water.[67] This symbolic significance is known from other

---

[63] Bunce 2001: 28 considers triangles whose apexes point to the left or right sides as constituent parts of yantras.

[64] See, for example, Jayaratha's commentary on Tantrāloka 3.94. Cf. also Buddhist texts quoted in Wayman 1973: 172.

[65] B. Bhattacharyya has discussed this issue in more detail in his foreword to the second edition of the Jayākhya-Saṃhitā (1967: 30) Because of its shape the *e* is called the 'womb of the world' (*jagadyoni*) and is referred to as a triangle (*tryasra*); cf. also ibid., Figure 1, p. 34+.

[66] For some remarks on the *dharmodaya*/*dharmodayā*, see Bahulkar 1979.

[67] See, for example, the Vāstusūtra-Upaniṣad, cited in Bäumer 1986: 56.

cultures as well, for which the downward-pointing apex suggests the direction of falling rain. Daniélou 1977: 26 (2001: 37) further explains the downward-pointing triangle as a symbol of Viṣṇu.

Tantric texts commonly describe the reverse triangle, that is, a triangle sitting on its base with its apex upwards, as the symbolic shape of the element fire.[68] The apex of the upward-pointing triangle indicates the direction of the flame. In Nepal, upward-pointing equilateral or isosceles triangles cut into stone or metal are frequently seen in shrines and temples. The triangular hole[69] is considered a symbol of the Nevār god of music, dance and drama, Nāsaḥdyaḥ, who is sometimes identified with Narteśvara or Nṛtyanātha.

In connection with the *śrīcakra*, authors such as Bhāskararāya[70] refer to the downward-pointing (*adhomukha*) triangles as Śakti triangles and the upward-pointing (*ūrdhvamukha*) triangles as fire (*vahni*) or Śiva triangles. The inverted triangle is also taken as representing *prakṛti*; the upright triangle, *puruṣa* (Daniélou 1964: 352). Both types of triangles are intertwined in the hexagram (see 2.3.3). In yantras of Kālī, five triangles appear in the centre. In other traditions, triangles are represented with a protruding 'gate' on each side.[71] These gates are identical in shape with the T-shaped gates of the outer square of yantras (see section 2.3.8).

The triangle is naturally connected with the symbolism of the number three. Its three lines are usually interpreted as tripartite units (most commonly, metaphysical concepts). Thus Shankaranarayanan interprets the lines of the central or primary (*mūla*) triangle (when understood as the *kāmakalā*[72]) in the *śrīcakra* as representing the powers (*śakti*) of will (*icchā*), cognition (*jñāna*) and activity (*kriyā*) (1970: 37), following an interpretation already attested, for instance, in Jayaratha's commentary on Tantrāloka 3.94. In another context Shankaranarayanan 1970: 38 interprets the lines of the triangle as

---

[68] Cf., for example, Śāradātilaka 1.23cd, where a triangle with *svastikas* represents fire.

[69] For more information and illustrations of the triangular *nāsaḥ* holes, see Wegner 1992: 126, Figure 1 and Kölver 1992a: 214, Illustration 1.

[70] Cf. Bhāskararāya's commentary Setubandha, p. 31, 2–3 (composed in 1741 A.D.) on Nityāṣoḍaśikārṇava 1.31 (the text is considered to be a part of the Vāmakeśvara-Tantra) and Umānandanātha's Nityotsava (1745 A.D.), p. 64, 6.

[71] Cf. the yantra of Chinnamastā described in Kubjikā-Upaniṣad 17.5.

[72] For a recent discussion of this term and possible translations, see White 1998: 176ff.

representing the three *guṇa*s or the three states, waking (*jāgrat*), dream (*svapna*) and deep sleep (*suṣupti*) (1970: 38). The Gaṇeśa-pūrvatāpanīya-Upaniṣad, section 3 interprets the lines of the central downward-pointing triangle in a yantra of Gaṇeśa as the three worlds and the three Vedas.

D. Chattopadhyaya 1973: 300–301 asserts that not only the triangle inside of yantras but the yantra in general represents the female reproductive organ when he writes: "A Tantrika, when he really confides in you, will frankly confess that these diagrams are but representations of the female organ." In support of this statement, he cites Bhandarkar 1965: 140, who makes the following remark about the ritual worship (*pūjā*) of the *śrīcakra*: "[The Cakrapūjā] consists in the worship of a picture of the female organ drawn in the centre of another consisting of a representation of nine such organs, the whole of which forms the Śrīcakra." In a somewhat generalized statement D. Chattopadhyaya 1973: 301 adds that "there are in Tantrism various yantras... bearing different names... but the essential feature in all of them is the same. It consists in the representation of the female organ either by the picture of a lotus (*padma*) or by the diagram of a triangle, usually by both." This author is correct when he observes that both the triangle and the lotus are symbols of the female reproductive organ, and that both are important constituent elements of yantras. But he goes too far when he takes *every* yantra as a representation of the female organ. This claim has rightly been challenged by S. Chattopadhyaya 1978: 81, who emphasizes the fact that not all yantras contain triangles.

2.3.3 The Hexagram (*ṣaṭkoṇa*, *ṣaḍara*, *tāra*[73])

The hexagram consists of two equilateral triangles with the same centre but pointing in opposite directions, usually upwards and downwards. The apexes of the two triangles of the hexagram can also be oriented to the right and left sides.[74] The triangles are shown either lying one on the other or intertwined with one another. The downward-pointing and upward-pointing triangles (see also 2.3.2) symbolize the sexual union of the female and male principles, of

[73] The word 'star' (*tārā*) appears as a synonym for *ṣaṭkoṇa* in Ahirbudhnya-Saṃhitā 26.5 and Pārameśvara-Saṃhitā 23.29, as Begley 1973: 85 notes.

[74] For two illustrations, see, for example, Encyclopaedia Judaica (New York: Macmillan Company, 1971), volume 11: 690, Figure 2; and 693, Figure 10.

Śakti and Śiva, of water and fire.[75] In Buddhist Tantrism, the word *evaṃ* is thought to be represented by two intertwined triangles, symbolizing the union of 'insight' (*prajñā*) and 'means' (*upāya*). The triangular shapes of *e* and *va* in certain Indian scripts lend themselves to such an interpretation.[76] In descriptions of the symbolic shapes (*maṇḍala*) of the elements (*bhūta*), the hexagram represents the element wind.[77]

In the hexagram the deities are often worshipped at the points of intersection of the two triangles, while in the eight-petalled lotus they are worshipped in the petals, which ideally face in the cardinal and intermediate directions. Occasionally a six-pointed star[78] or a six-petalled lotus, such as the *vajra*-lotus, can replace the hexagram in rituals (Heilijgers-Seelen 1994: 131). Like these objects, the hexagram is equated with sextuple concepts and groups. Thus Gaṇeśapūrvatāpanīya-Upaniṣad, section 3 interprets the hexagram in a yantra of Gaṇeśa as representing the six worlds and seasons.[79]

The hexagram has been used for decorative purposes or as a magical sign in many civilizations around the world. It is also

[75] In section 2.3.2 the symbolism of the two triangles is explained: the downward-pointing triangle symbolizes the female principle and water, while the upward-pointing triangle symbolizes the male principle and fire. In alchemy, the two triangles of the hexagram also represent the union of fire and water. For the symbolism of the water and fire triangles in the Tantric *agnihotra* ritual of Nepal, see Witzel 1992: 788.

[76] Cf. Saṃpuṭa-Tantra, chapter 4 (= Elder 1978: 109 [text], 189 [translation]); cf. also Wayman 1973: 172–173, who discusses three meanings of *evaṃ*, and Kölver 1992b. Kölver discusses the shapes of the letters *e* and the *va*, which were reminiscent of downward-pointing and upward-pointing triangles around the sixth century A.D., and were visualized as intertwined to form a hexagram. The nasal of *evaṃ* corresponds to the central point (*bindu*) inside the hexagram. When Vajrayoginī is described as situated 'in *evaṃ*' this means that she is visualized inside a hexagram. In addition, the syllable *va* is the seed syllable of the word *vajra*, which can signify the penis (English 2002: 150).

[77] The symbolic shapes of the other elements are according to Śāradātilaka 1.23–24: a square with thunderbolts (*vajra*) – the earth element; a lotus with a half moon – water; a triangle with *svastikas* – fire; a circle with six dots, that is, a hexagram – wind; and a circle – ether.

[78] For Nepalese coins of the Malla period showing the six-pointed star, see Rhodes/Gabrisch/† della Rocchetta 1989, Plate 31, no. 724 rev., Plate 33, no. 826 rev.

[79] For interpretations of the *ṣaṭkoṇa* current in Nepal, see Joshi 1981 and Deep 1993: 98–100. Joshi summarizes various interpretations which identify the hexagram with well-known groups of six, such as the six systems of philosophy (*darśana*).

known, for example, as Magen David, the 'Shield of David' or as the 'Seal of Solomon.'[80] It appears on the inside of Hindu yantras and is also seen in Buddhist maṇḍalas of Vajravārāhī/Vajrayoginī.[81] The hexagram is a decorative motif in Islamic monuments of North India. Its centre features a point (*bindu*), a lotus or a dancing peacock (Nath 1975–1976: 74–75).[82]

In Nepal, the hexagram is frequently represented and considered an auspicious symbol of the goddess by both Buddhists and Hindus.[83] It is sometimes found superimposed on the latticework of windows of temples or shrine rooms.[84] The point (*bindu*) in its centre often bears an image of the deity worshipped in the temple or shrine. The hexagram also appears in mediaeval coins of India[85] and, along with other geometrical designs, on Nepalese coins of the Malla period.[86] Auer/Gutschow 1974: 106 report that the hexagram is also called *śrīmaṇḍala* in Nepal. It is considered a symbol of education, science and of the goddess Sarasvatī, and therefore became the logo of Tribhuvan University, colleges and other educational institutions.

---

[80] For information on the hexagram in mediaeval Europe and the Near East, see Encyclopaedia Judaica (New York: Macmillan Company, 1971), volume 11: 687–697.

[81] For a 13th-century Tibetan maṇḍala depicting the goddess Vajravārāhī standing inside a hexagram, see Béguin 1990: 173; other examples from Tibet are found in Rhie/Thurman 1999: 118 and 440, Kossak/Singer 1998: 97 and Leidy/Thurman 1997: 105. For a photograph of a hexagram representing Vajrayoginī in Tibet, see Stoddard 1999, Figure 30. The question needs to be examined whether the hexagram in maṇḍalas of Vajravārāhī/Vajrayoginī indicates the maṇḍala's Śaiva origins. While the hexagram is commonly found in Hindu maṇḍalas and yantras, with intersecting upward-pointing and downward-pointing triangles already appearing in the *śrīcakra*, in Buddhist traditions they appear especially in maṇḍalas of Vajravārāhī/Vajrayoginī. The name Vajravārāhī itself indicates a Buddhist version of the Brahmanical goddess Vārāhī.

[82] According to Nath 1975–1976: 78, the hexagram is also found in Indian temples, especially in Rājasthān, where it is believed to have been associated with the worship of Śiva and Śakti.

[83] Bangdel 1999: 464 writes that : "[s]pecifically, the double-triangled *yantra* in the Tantric tradition is a universal symbol for the goddess's generative and destructive powers ..." and 1999: 540, note 118 that: "[t]he *yantra* symbolizes the seat/presence of the goddess...." Gutschow 1982: 97, Plate 105 assumes that the hexagram represents Tripurasundarī.

[84] For photographs, see, for example, Bernier 1978: 259, Plate 11 and Gutschow/Kölver/Shresthacarya 1987: 203, no. 416.

[85] See, for example, Sircar 1968, Plate xxiii, no. 7 obv., Coomaraswamy (1927) 1985: 45 and Smith 1972, volume 1, Plate xxx, no. 14 rev.

[86] See Rhodes/Gabrisch/† della Rocchetta 1989, Plate 20, nos. 382–384 rev., Plate 21, nos. 412–417 rev., etc.

It is found on the king's headgear and on Nepalese orders, decorations and medals. Bernier 1978: 252 assumes that this design has been borrowed from the Islamic tradition of North India, but Begley 1973: 84 considers it most likely that the hexagram was already an important Tantric symbol before the Islamic hexagram became widely circulated in India. More research would be necessary to trace the history of this important motif. The hexagram is an important motif in the later Tantric iconography of the Sudarśanacakra, Viṣṇu's *sudarśana* wheel, which often has a yantra-like structure inscribed on it.[87] This structure consists of a hexagram surrounded by one or more rings of lotus petals. The personification of Viṣṇu's wheel, the Sudarśanacakrapuruṣa, is shown inside (or standing against) the structure.[88] The reverse side of these icons often depicts Narasiṃha. If combined with a representation of the Sudarśanacakra, this deity may be represented inside an upward-pointing triangle.[89]

2.3.4 The Pentagram (*pañcakoṇa*)

The five-pointed star, the pentagram, pentacle or Star of Solomon, is less commonly found in yantras. It is known as a symbol also in other civilizations. The pentagram is a constituent part of some yantras of Guhyakālī (see Colour Plate 1), since the number five has special significance for the goddess Kālī. It is again found on Nepalese coins of the Malla period,[90] as well as being the logo of some educational institutions in modern Nepal. Daniélou 1977: 28 (2001: 38) equates the pentagram with Śiva as 'the destroyer of love and lust' (*smarahara*). This interpretation is not compatible with another statement by the same author (Daniélou 1964: 353) according to which the pentagram signifies love and lust and the power of disintegration.

---

[87] Details on the multi-armed Sudarśana icons can be found in Begley 1973: 84–92.

[88] See Begley 1973: 90 (with Figure 70) for a ca. 17th-century bronze statue of the 16-armed Sudarśanacakrapuruṣa in the Śrī-Kālamekaperumāl Temple, Tirumohur, Madurai District. The deity is standing against a hexagram which is surrounded by rings of eight, 16, 32 and 64 lotus petals. These lotuses are supported by an eight-petalled lotus (see also Illustration 1 in Rastelli's contribution).

[89] See Begley 1973: 88–89 and Figures 67 and 69.

2.3.5 The Octagon (*aṣṭakoṇa, aṣṭāra*)

The octagon appears less frequently as a constituent part of yantras and can be formed in several ways. A common method to obtain an octagon is to draw two crossed or intersecting squares. The two overlapping squares appear as a symbol in various civilizations.[91] The symbolism of the octagon, like that of the eight-petalled lotus, is connected with the eight directions. The octagon appears on Indian[92] coins and on Malla coins of Nepal.[93] It also decorates a window in a religious building of the Tripureśvara temple complex in Kāṭhmāṇḍu.[94]

2.3.6 The Lotus

The symbolism of the lotus is discussed in section 1.3.1 in connection with maṇḍalas.

2.3.7 The Circle

One circle or three concentric circles frequently surround the inner structure of yantras. According to Daniélou 1964: 352, the yantra's outer circle, given its revolving tendency, characterizes manifestation. Among the symbolic shapes (*maṇḍala*) of the elements (*bhūta*), the circle represents ether.[95]

2.3.8 The Outer Square

The circle or circles in a yantra are usually surrounded by an outer square which often consists of three nested lines. The square, which also appears on the outer part of maṇḍalas, is called 'earth house' (*bhūgṛha*), 'earth city' or 'earth citadel' (*bhūpura*),[96] since the square

---

[90] See Rhodes/Gabrisch/† della Rocchetta 1989, Plate 21, nos. 406–409 rev., Plate 28, nos. 566–567 obv.

[91] See, for example, Encyclopaedia Judaica (New York: Macmillan Company, 1971), volume 11: 689–690, Figure 3, for this design as used in 13th-century Germany.

[92] See Sircar 1968, Plate XIX, no. 11.

[93] See Rhodes/Gabrisch/† della Rocchetta 1989, Plate 15, nos. 274–275; Plate 20, nos. 391–392, 396, Plate 21, no. 400, etc.

[94] For an illustration, see Gail 1984–1988, volume 2, Plate XVI, no. 2 and p. 97, and Gutschow/Kölver/Shresthacarya 1987: 203, no. 417. The temple is currently being renovated.

[95] See, for example, the description in Śāradātilaka 1.23–24.

[96] For a description of the different stages of constructing a *bhūpura*, see Bunce 2001: 20–22; for variations in the shapes of *bhūpuras*, see Bunce 2001: 23–25.

is a symbol of the earth. Among the symbolic shapes of the elements, a (yellow) square represents the earth.[97] The symbolism of the square is connected with that of the number four and the four cardinal directions. The square has a T-shaped gate (*dvāra*) in the cardinal directions. Like the sides of a square, the gates are equated with groups of four, as in Miśra's interpretation of an unidentified Śākta yantra (1959: 482–483) in which they are taken to represent the four Vedas. Pāñcarātra Saṃhitās interpret the three nested lines of the outermost square as representative of the three constituents (*guṇa*) of primary matter (*prakṛti*) in the Sāṃkhya system, namely *sattva*, *rajas* and *tamas*. This interpretation is also attested for the three nested lines of the outer square of the *bhadramaṇḍala*s of the Smārta tradition, which are white, red and dark and symbolize respectively *sattva*, *rajas* and *tamas*.[98] The square also appears on Nepalese coins of the Malla period.[99]

Influenced by C.G. Jung, Dehejia 1986: 42 would have us recognize the mediaeval alchemists' motif of the 'squaring of the circle' (*quadratura circuli*) in South Asian maṇḍalas and yantras which feature a circle surrounded by a square. Such an interpretation does not find support in the South Asian traditions. Moreover, in mediaeval European drawings of this motif the square always touches the circle. In contrast, South Asian maṇḍalas and yantras show a significant gap between the circle and the square that surrounds it.

Gupta 1988: 39–41 offers the hypothesis that the square enclosure of maṇḍalas represents a Tantric analogue to the sacred fire altar and thus has Vedic origins (see section 1.4).

2.3.9 Other Structural Elements

It is not possible to survey all constituent elements of yantras, which include shapes such as the heptagon.[100] One unusual design is found in a yantra of Guhyakālī from Nepal (see Colour Plate 1). This

---

[97] See, for example, Śāradātilaka 1.24ab, where a square with thunderbolts (*vajra*) represents the earth element.

[98] The symbolism of these three colours is frequently referred to; for more information, see Goudriaan 1978: 166–175 and the Suprabheda, quoted in Brunner, p. 173, note 49.

[99] See Rhodes/Gabrisch/† della Rocchetta 1989, Plate 20, nos. 382–383 obv., 390 rev., Plate 22, no. 446 obv.

[100] Some additional shapes are described in Bunce 2001: 27–29.

complex yantra features a pentagram (see 2.3.4) in the centre, surrounded by a shape with nine corners (*navakoṇa*). The nine-angled shape is situated within two overlapping squares (see 2.3.5), which in turn are surrounded by a lotus design with rings of eight, 12 and 16 lotus petals. Outside of this is a square whose four sides are made up of tridents (*triśūla*) surrounded by skulls. Four enclosures surround this structure, which feature (from the inside to the outside): (1) water (here representing the Ocean of Blood [*śoṇitoda*]), (2) the eight cremation grounds (*śmaśāna*), (3) skulls (*muṇḍa*) and (4) flames (*vahnijvālā*).[101] A circle of flames is also known to surround Tibetan Buddhist maṇḍalas, some of which include a circle representing cremation grounds. According to Macdonald/Vergati Stahl 1979: 91, cremation grounds (*śmaśāna*)[102] have been part of Buddhist as well as Hindu maṇḍalas and yantras in Nepal since the 15th century.[103]

3 *Cakra*

The term cakra, 'circle' or 'wheel,' has several primary and secondary meanings.[104]

---

[101] The Sanskrit terms are taken from a description of Guhyakālī's yantra in Puraścaryārṇava, pp. 1149, 22 – 1150, 8. The Puraścaryārṇava quotes the Mahākāla-Saṃhitā, a basic work advocating the worship of Guhyakālī, which was most likely written in Mithilā (Michaels 1996: 319).

The outer enclosures of Guhyakālī's yantra also appear in other Nevār Hindu yantras. The *paścimakarmayantra*, included in the 'Book of Pictures Containing Images and Yantras,' preserved in the Bhārat Kalā Bhavan, Vārāṇasī, no. 10054, and dated 1764/65 A.D. (see negative 3–12 of the American Institute of Indian Studies, Gurgaon), features enclosures with (1) a floral design (?), (2) a water design, (3) skulls and (4) flames.

[102] For a study of cremation grounds, see Meisezahl 1974 and Pott (1946) 1966: 76–101 ("The Sacred Cemeteries of Nepal") and the discussion in English 2002: 136–143. For the cult of *śmaśānas*, see Tsuda 1990. Tsuda 1990: 98 notes that the eight cremation grounds appear on the outer structure of maṇḍalas of the Saṃvara class of Tantras, which dates back to the end of the eighth century A.D. De Mallmann 1986: 42 refers to cremation grounds in the maṇḍalas of Heruka/Hevajra, Saṃvara and Vajravārāhī.

[103] Pal 1974–1978, part 2: 93 is of the opinion "that generally no scenes of cemeteries are included in Hindu mandalas."

[104] For a discussion of the term cakra, see also Brunner, p. 163; Törzsök, pp. 180–183 contrasts the terms cakra and maṇḍala.

1. 'Cakra' can refer to a wheel as the central part of a maṇḍala structure, to whose hub and spokes deities are assigned. In this function, the wheel can either substitute for a lotus or appear in combination with it (cf. section 1.3.1).
2. The term cakra can refer to a group or circle of deities invoked into a maṇḍala or yantra structure.
3. Some later authors appear to use 'cakra' synonymously with 'yantra' and 'maṇḍala.'[105]
4. The word cakra also refers to a diagram/tabular device employed in ritual.
5. A well-known use of the word cakra is with reference to the 'wheels' or 'lotuses' believed to be located in the human body.

In the following, only the meanings 2, 4 and 5 are discussed.

3.1 *Cakra as a Circle of Deities*

The term cakra refers to a group of deities invoked into a maṇḍala or yantra.[106] At the same time, the term also denotes the support for these deities in the form of a specific surface.[107] This is most likely the reason why the word cakra appears synonymously with yantra and maṇḍala in later texts—a use of the term that requires further investigation. It also explains why the parts of the *śrīcakra*, which consist of a variety of shapes such as triangles and lotus petals, are referred to as the nine cakras.

---

[105] See Brunner, p. 163 and Padoux 1987a: 4. Törzsök, p. 181 expresses some reservation about the interchangeability of the terms cakra and maṇḍala in early Śaiva texts. The Śrīvidyā's synonymous use of the terms cakra and yantra in the *śrīcakra/śrīyantra* indicates a looser use of these terms (cf. Sanderson's remark in Padoux 1986: 33). The *baliharaṇacakra* described in the next article is also called *baliharaṇamaṇḍala* in some texts.

[106] Cf. A. Sanderson's remark reproduced in Padoux 1986: 33: "... the *maṇḍala* is the *ādhāraḥ* (locus) and the *cakra* (of deities/mantras) the *ādheyam* (located)...." Snellgrove 1959, part 1: 135 defines 'cakra' similarly as a "circle of divine forms of which the *maṇḍala* consists."

[107] Heilijgers-Seelen 1994: 37 gives several instances from the Kubjikāmata-Tantra, where 'cakra' refers to the seat of a deity.

3.2 *Cakra as a Ritual Diagram/Tabular Device*

The word cakra also refers to diagrams containing specific arrangements of letters of the alphabet or of numbers. Diagrams such as the *akathahacakra*, the *akaḍamacakra*, the *nakṣatracakra* and the *rāśicakra*, which are used to determine whether a mantra suits a candidate, fall under this category.[108] Unlike the 'distributive diagrams', namely, maṇḍalas of type 3 in Brunner's classification (see section 1.2), which are ritual diagrams divided into squares into which divine or demonic beings are invoked to receive food offerings, these diagrams are simply tabular devices, into which no deity is invoked.

3.3 *Cakra as a 'Wheel' or 'Lotus' in the Body*

The word cakra is used with reference to the currently rather popular Tantric concept of the 'energy centres' or 'power centres' which are believed to be located in the body. They are referred to either as 'wheels' (*cakra*) or as 'lotuses' (*padma*).[109] In some systems these cakras have lotus shapes and are populated by deities. The lotuses may also have inscribed geometric figures (triangle, hexagram). The number of cakras and their location in the body varies according to traditions. Some systems assume sets of four, five, six, nine, 12, 16, 24, 27, 32 or more cakras.

The system of six 'wheels' or 'lotuses' is particularly well known and listed below according to Śāradātilaka 5.131cd–136 and 20.66cd–67.

Lotus	Number of Petals	Syllables	Deity	Goddess
mūlādhāra	4	*va-sa*	Brahmā	Ḍākinī
svādhiṣṭhāna	6	*ba-la*	Viṣṇu	Rākiṇī
maṇipūra	10	*ḍa-pha*	Rudra	Lākinī
anāhata	12	*ka-ṭha*	Īśvara	Śākinī
viśuddhi	16	16 vowels	Sadāśiva	Kākinī
ājñā	2	*ha* and *kṣa*	Śiva	Hākinī

[108] For an extensive treatment of these diagrams, see Bühnemann 1992.

[109] As in the case of a wheel combined with or in place of a lotus in the centre of a maṇḍala (cf. section 1.3.1), the terminologies denoting parts of a 'lotus' and parts of a 'wheel' in the body are often used interchangeably.

The *mūlādhāra* or *ādhāra* is located at the bottom of the spine between the anus and the penis. The *svādhiṣṭhāna* is at the root of the penis. The *maṇipūra* is located at the base of the navel, and the *anāhata* in the heart. The *viśuddhi* is situated in the throat, and the *ājñā* in between the eyebrows. The thousand-petalled lotus (*sahasradalapadma*), also called the thousand-spoked wheel (*sahasrāracakra*), being located at the top of the head, is added to the six cakras, but is usually not counted as one of them.

Since these cakras are associated with the process of creation, they are connected with the five elements (*bhūta*) and the mind (*manas*), and with the syllables of the Sanskrit alphabet. Specific syllables are inscribed on each lotus, one syllable per petal. Each lotus is presided over by a specific deity and associated with a goddess.

This system of the Śāradātilaka differs from earlier stages of development, which are preserved in sections of the 10th-century Kubjikāmata-Tantra.[110] In one section of the Tantra the cakras are assumed to be five circles of goddesses, located below the navel, in the belly, the heart, the throat and at the top of the head or the *brahmarandhra*.[111] These circles are called the *devīcakra*, *dūtīcakra*, *mātṛcakra*, *yoginīcakra* and *khecarīcakra*, and are believed to be populated by a larger number of goddesses. In another section of the text, the cakras, with the exception of the *anāhata*, are not viewed as 'lotuses' with varying number of petals and geometric figures inscribed in the petals. Instead of the term cakra, the word *pada* is used (Heilijgers-Seelen 1994: 38).

---

[110] See Heilijgers-Seelen 1990: 59 for details on cakra systems taught in sections of the Kubjikāmata-Tantra. The author discusses one system of five cakras as reflected in the Kubjikāmata and two systems (namely, the *uttara* and *dakṣiṇa* varieties) of six cakras.

[111] See Heilijgers-Seelen 1994: 18 for more details.

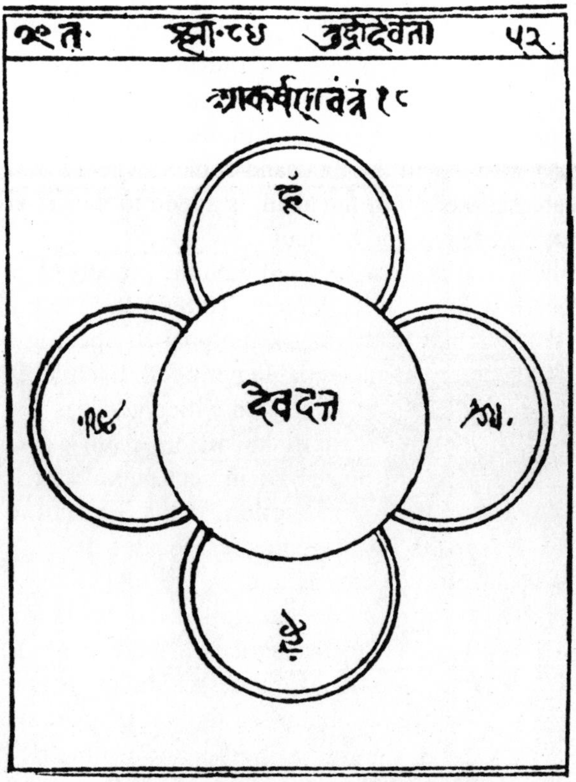

1. A yantra for attraction *(ākarṣaṇayantra)*

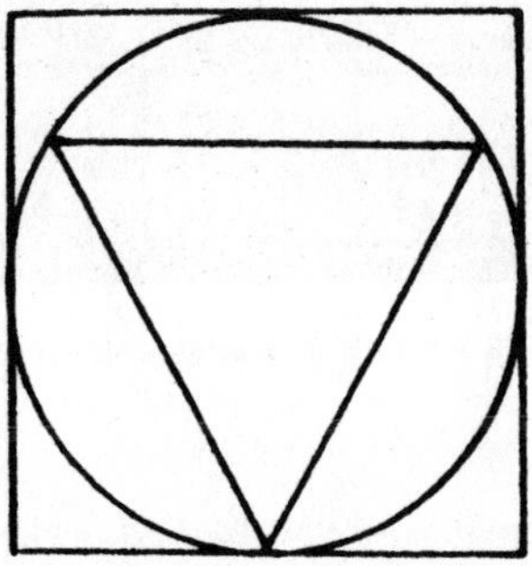

2. A supporting maṇḍala for the *vardhanī vessel*

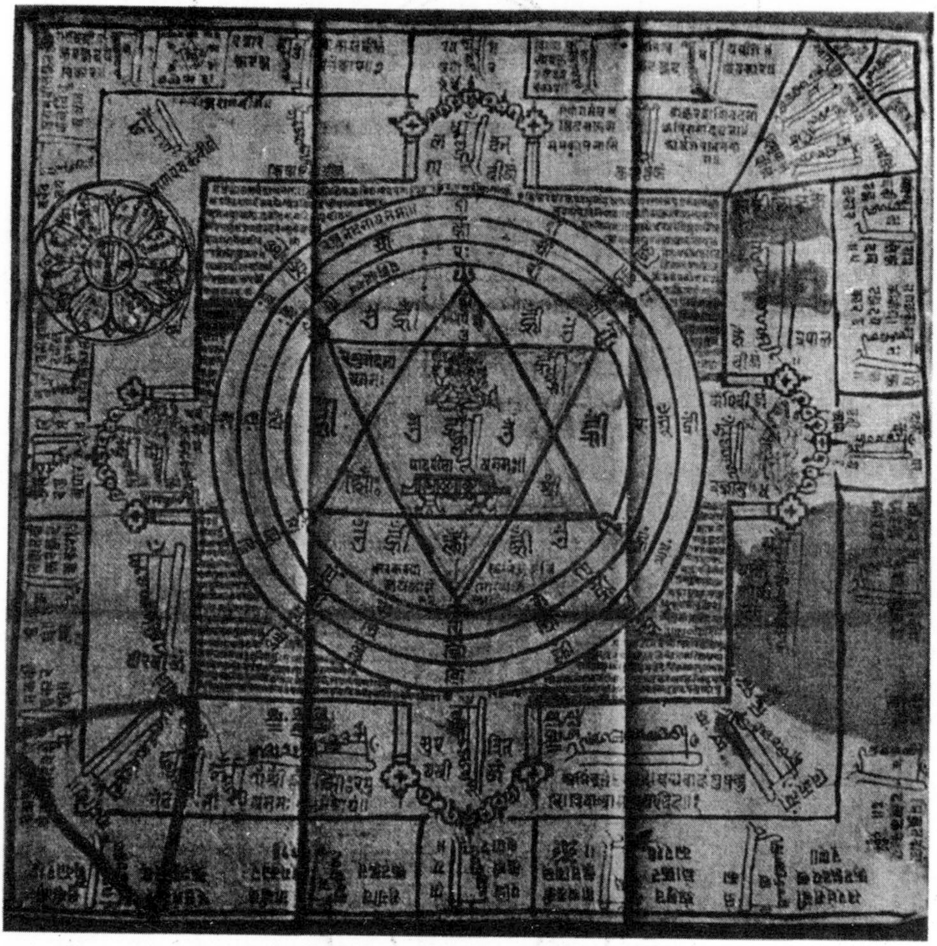

3. A yantra with the Rāmarakṣāstotra inscribed

4. A yantra assigned to stanza 55 of the Saundaryalaharī

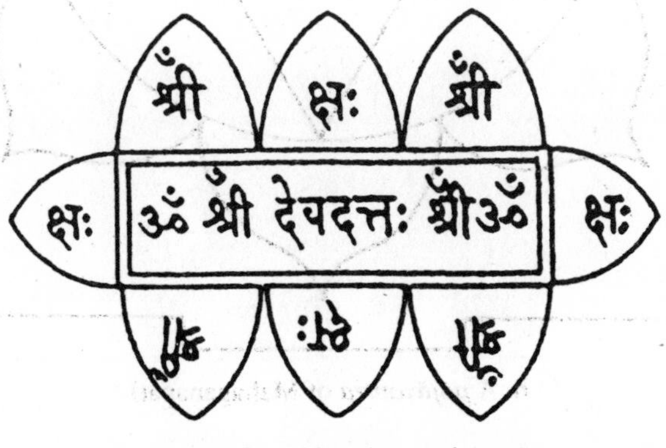

5. A yantra for subjugating one's master

6. A *pūjāyantra* of Mahāgaṇapati

MAṆḌALAS AND YANTRAS IN SMĀRTA RITUAL

Gudrun Bühnemann

PART I. SELECTED MAṆḌALA-LIKE STRUCTURES, MAṆḌALAS AND YANTRAS

1 *Introduction*

This essay describes some maṇḍalas, maṇḍala-like structures and yantras that are currently used in the ritual practices of Smārta Brahmins in Mahārāṣṭra. It draws on my observation of rituals in that part of India as well as on the study of ritual manuals. This paper is divided into two parts. Part one is designed to introduce the reader to common structures of maṇḍalas and yantras in the Smārta tradition. As an example of an early maṇḍala-like structure, the *baliharaṇa-cakra* of the *vaiśvadeva* rite is described. This opens the discussion on the directional orientation and basic designs of maṇḍalas. Describing specific maṇḍalas and yantras currently used by Smārta Brahmins, I analyze the *navagrahamaṇḍala*, the *saptaśatīmahāyantra* (which originally belonged to the Śākta tradition) and the *rudrapīṭha-mahāyantra*. Part two of this paper describes a category of maṇḍalas called *bhadramaṇḍalas*.

Initially a brief explanation of the word Smārta may be in order. Smārta is a rather loosely used term which refers to a Brahmin who is an 'adherent of the Smṛti' and of the tradition which is 'based on the Smṛti.' The Smārta tradition considers itself to be based on the Vedic heritage and the ancient orthodox texts in the Vedic tradition, such as the Dharmaśāstras and the Smṛtis. It claims to be neither exclusively Śiva-oriented (Śaiva) nor exclusively Viṣṇu-oriented (Vaiṣṇava), and often combines the worship of five deities.[1] Despite the rejection of Tantric elements in rituals by some Smārta

[1] For a discussion of the term Smārta and of the Smārta tradition, see Bühnemann 2005.

authorities,[2] the Smārta tradition has incorporated such elements, including yantras.

2 *The Maṇḍala-like Arrangement in the Baliharaṇacakra*

The *baliharaṇacakra*[3] or *baliharaṇamaṇḍala* appears to be among the earliest maṇḍala-like arrangements of the Smārtas. In current ritual practice of Mahārāṣṭrian Ṛg-Vedins, it is a circular arrangement formed by food offerings (*bali*) (see Colour Plate 2) placed on the ground in the *bhūtayajña*, *pitṛyajña* and *manuṣyayajña* rites. These three rites are variously considered parts of, or appendices to, the *vaiśvadeva* [4] rite. The *vaiśvadeva,* which is a ritual offering of cooked food before eating, is prescribed twice daily, in the morning and in the evening. There is little difference between these two ritual procedures. In current Mahārāṣṭrian practice, the cooked food, usually rice, is divided into three portions. The offerings from the first portion of food are made to the sacred domestic fire to deities as part of the sacrificial worship of deities (*devayajña*) of the *vaiśvadeva* rite. The offerings of the second and third portions of food are *bali*s, that is, offerings made outside the sacred fire. They are placed, strewn or thrown on the ground. Bali offerings are made to deities and other beings as part of the sacrificial worship of beings (*bhūtayajña*), and to the ancestors as part of the sacrificial worship of ancestors (*pitṛyajña*). The final offering forms part of the honouring of guests (*manuṣyayajña*). The ten deities worshipped as part of the *devayajña* are identical with the first ten of the group of 32 deities,[5]

---

[2] The *nyāsa* rite, for example, which forms part of the current Smārta *pūjā*, is rejected by some as Tantric; see Bühnemann 1988a: 121.

[3] In the previous essay the terms maṇḍala, yantra and cakra are discussed. Section 3 deals especially with the meanings of the word cakra. The term cakra in the compound *baliharaṇacakra* appears to refer both to the circular layout of the offerings of rice which are placed on the ground and to the group of deities and other beings who are invoked while setting down the offerings. In some texts the term *baliharaṇamaṇḍala* is used synonymously with *baliharaṇacakra* but is more appropriate in the context of the Yajur-Veda tradition in Mahārāṣṭra, where its layout is square. In that tradition fewer deities are invoked and some of their names vary.

[4] For details on the *vaiśvadeva* ritual as it is described in ancient texts, see Kane 1968–1977, volume 2: 741–748, and Gonda 1980: 417–418.

[5] I follow here the text printed in Ṛgvedīyabrahmakarmasamuccaya, fols. 29a.10–30b.3. The number and names of beings differ slightly from those listed in the ancient texts, such as Manu-Smṛti 3.84–86. Some of these differences are

beings and ancestors who receive offerings made as part of the *bhūtayajña*. The 32 deities and beings who receive offerings made in the *baliharaṇacakra* of the Ṛg-Vedins (see Illustration 1) are the following:

(as part of the *bhūtayajña*, in a circle, beginning from the east:)
(1) Sūrya,[6] (2) Prajāpati, (3) Soma and Vanaspati, (4) Agni and Soma, (5) Indra and Agni, (6) heaven and earth, (7) Dhanvantari, (8) Indra, (9) the ViśveDevas, (10) Brahmā,[7] (11) the waters, (12) herbs and plants, (13) house, (14) deities of the house, (15) deities of the site (*vāstu*); (outside the circle, in the cardinal directions, in groups of two) (16) Indra, (17) Indra's men, (18) Yama, (19) Yama's men, (20) Varuṇa, (21) Varuṇa's men, (22) Soma, (23) Soma's men; (inside the circle, in the cardinal directions, beginning from the north) (24) Brahmā, (25) Brahmā's men, (26) the ViśveDevas, (27) all beings that move by day;[8] (outside the circle, in the intermediate directions, beginning from the north-east:) (28) Rakṣasas;
(as part of the *pitṛyajña*:)
(29) Svadhāpitṛs, (30) Śyāma, (31) Śabala;
(as part of the *manuṣyayajña*:)
(32) Sanaka and other humans.

The practitioner presses together a small number of rice grains between the fingers and the thumb of his right hand. Invoking the deities and other beings, he first places the offerings so that they form of a circle. He then places some offerings inside and outside the circle, always proceeding in a clockwise direction. This clockwise movement represents the usual order of movement in rituals, counter-clockwise movement being used, for example, in rites for the dead.

In the maṇḍala-like structure of the *baliharaṇacakra*, offerings are placed in a circle, attention being paid to directional orientation. However, there is no single deity in the centre. This arrangement differs from later maṇḍala structures which follow the concentric

discussed in Kane 1968–1977, volume 2: 741ff. The diagram in Bourquin 1884: 86 includes 36 deities and other beings.

[6] In the evening ritual, Agni is invoked instead of Sūrya.

[7] Brahmā appears again in 24.

[8] In the evening ritual, the beings that move by night are invoked instead.

pattern in which one central deity is surrounded by other entities on the outside.

3 *The Maṇḍala-like Arrangement in Pañcāyatana Worship*

A maṇḍala-like pattern with one central deity surrounded by four other deities in the *intermediate* directions or corners appears in the Smārta *pañcāyatana* worship. The *pañcāyatana* worship focuses on the icons or aniconic representations of five deities, and became popular in the mediaeval period. In modern times, the five deities are the Vedic sun god Sūrya; the goddess called Devī or Durgā; Viṣṇu; the elephant-headed Gaṇeśa (Gaṇapati); and Śiva (Maheśvara). In earlier sources we find evidence for the worship of Brahmā instead of Durgā or Gaṇeśa. Worshipping these five deities is referred to as the five-fold worship (*pañcopāsanā*), or the *pūjā* of the five shrines (*pañcāyatanapūjā*). The concept of the five-fold worship is also reflected in temple architecture. Pañcāyatana temples in North India[9] place the main deity in the central shrine and four subordinate deities in smaller shrines at the corners of the square. In domestic worship, the positions of the four other deities vary with the central deity[10] (see Illustration 2). A contemporary *śivapañcāyatana* in a Mahārāṣṭrian home, for example, may feature a *śivaliṅga* in the centre and the icons of Bālakṛṣṇa (representing Viṣṇu), the sun, Gaṇapati (a red stone) and the goddess (a 'metallic' stone) respectively in the north-east, south-east, south-west and north-west (see Colour Plate 3). When Gaṇeśa occupies the centre, Viṣṇu, Śiva, Sūrya and the goddess will be placed respectively in the north-east, south-east, south-west and north-west.

It is remarkable that in this pattern one deity is positioned in the centre and the four others in the intermediate rather than the cardinal directions, as is commonly seen in maṇḍala-like structures. Perhaps the practitioner wanted to be able to face all the deities at the time of worship. One should keep in mind that the four deities who are worshipped along with the central deity are not considered to be

---

[9] For a study of *pañcāyatana* temples in North India, see Reitz 1998.

[10] The arrangement of the deities in domestic worship follows patterns prescribed in a stanza which has been attributed to Bopadeva's Yamalaprakāśa and is cited in many texts, such as Mitramiśra's Pūjāprakāśa, Kamalākarabhaṭṭa's Nirṇayasindhu and contemporary ritual manuals. For details, see Bühnemann 1988a: 50–51.

manifestations of the latter, even though their position at the time of worship is clearly subordinate.

4 *Lotus Designs and the Navagrahamaṇḍala*

A different directional orientation is followed in lotus designs, which often form the core of maṇḍala and yantra structures. The lotus pattern and the symbolism of the lotus have already been described in section 1.3.1 of the previous essay. In this structure, the main deity is positioned in the centre and the surrounding (*āvaraṇa*) deities are placed on the petals, and sometimes also on the filaments of the lotus. The surrounding deities are positioned in the four cardinal and intermediate directions, and occasionally they are also placed at the zenith and nadir of the maṇḍala. The zenith and nadir are then indicated by special markings placed near two of the intermediate directions in the maṇḍalas. The surrounding deities may form one or several circles around the central deity, following the common concentric pattern. Frequently the deities are not invoked into icons but into areca nuts (*pūgīphala*), which are readily available and can be used repeatedly.

A commonly employed maṇḍala with an interior lotus design in the contemporary Mahārāṣṭrian Smārta tradition is the *navagraha-maṇḍala*, which features the nine heavenly bodies. The *navagraha-maṇḍala* is constructed and worshipped to propitiate the evil constellations of heavenly bodies and to remove obstacles. It is employed in the *grahamakha* or *grahayajña*, the 'sacrificial worship of the heavenly bodies,' a preparatory rite preceding major rituals, such as the *vāstuśānti* or the life-cyle rituals (*saṃskāra*).[11]

In this maṇḍala, each heavenly body (*graha*) is typically represented by a specific symbolic shape and is prepared from grains or coloured powders. The grains used for each shape may be a different colour. The *graha*s (listed in the order of the weekdays) with their symbolic shapes, colours and associated directions are usually:

[11] For the *navagrahaśānti* and the worship of the nine heavenly bodies, see Kane 1968–1977, volume 5: 749–755. For descriptions of the *grahayajña* compiled from different Sanskrit texts, see Dharmakośa: Saṃskārakāṇḍa (edited by Laxmanshastri Joshi, volume 3, part 3, Wai: Prājña Press, 1981): 1554–1639.

Heavenly Body	Shape	Colour	Direction
sun	circle	red	centre
moon	square	white	south-east
Mars	triangle	red	south
Mercury	arrow	yellow	north-east
Jupiter	rectangle	yellow	north
Venus	pentagram	white	east
Saturn	bow	dark	west
Rāhu	winnowing fan	dark	south-west
Ketu	banner	smoke-coloured	north-west

The sun is positioned in the centre of the maṇḍala, which contains another lotus. In Illustration 3 a circle drawn outside the central lotus contains instructions for the sequence and placement of the heavenly bodies. Here each heavenly body is accompanied by one deity on either side. The Vedic sun god Savitṛ appears in the centre with Agni and Rudra on either side. The moon is accompanied by the waters and Umā; Mars by the earth and Skanda; Mercury by Viṣṇu and Nārāyaṇa; Jupiter by Indra and Brahmā; Venus by Indra and Indrāṇī; Saturn by Prajāpati and Yama; Rāhu by snakes and Kāla; and Ketu by Brahmā and Citragupta.[12]

The maṇḍala is surrounded by a square called the 'earth city' or 'earth house' (*bhūpura, bhūgṛha*), already described in section 2.3.8 of the previous essay. The square has four protruding gates in the cardinal directions. Inside the gates and in the four corners of the square, the eight directional guardians (*dikpāla*) are invoked:

Directional Guardian	Direction
Indra	east
Agni	south-east
Yama	south
Nirṛti	south-west
Varuṇa	west
Vāyu	north-west
Soma (= Kubera)	north
Īśāna	north-east

[12] The description of the maṇḍala's deities is found in Ṛgvedīyabrahmakarma-samuccaya, fols. 132a.2–137a.9 (this description is said to be based on an unspecified 'Pariśiṣṭa').

The *navagrahamaṇḍala* is a good example of the lotus pattern commonly seen in maṇḍalas and yantras which use a concentric arrangement of deities. The eight-petalled lotus with its petals pointing in the directions is especially well suited for placing the deities in their respective directions. The group of eight (and sometimes ten) directional guardians is also invoked into parts of the outer structures of other yantras, such as the two yantras described below.

5 *Yantra Structures*

I will now address the structure of two yantras, the *saptaśatīmahāyantra* and the *rudrapīṭhamahāyantra*, in some detail. Both yantras belong to the category of yantras which are employed in optional desire-oriented rituals (see type 3 described in section 2.2.3 of the previous essay).

5.1 *The Saptaśatīmahāyantra*

The *durgāsaptaśatīmahāyantra*, abbreviated *saptaśatīmahāyantra*, is a yantra which originally was exclusive to the Śākta tradition. It is comparatively well known in Mahārāṣṭra and is printed in the Ṛg-vedīyabrahmakarmasamuccaya, the manual commonly used by priests in the Ṛg-Vedic tradition (Illustration 4).[13] The yantra became increasingly important as the popularity of the Durgāsaptaśatī (also called Devīmāhātmya or Caṇḍī) grew. This text eulogizes the deeds of Durgā in approximately 700 stanzas. It dates back to ca. 500–600 A.D. and is attributed to the Mārkaṇḍeya-Purāṇa. The yantra is employed in the ritual worship of the goddess known as *caṇḍīyāga*, especially for Durgā worship during the Navarātri festival.

Although used by Smārtas, the yantra shows typical Tantric elements both in its structure and in the use of the seed (*bīja*) syllables inscribed in it. As noted in section 2.2.3 of the preceding essay, yantras employed in optional desire-oriented rites often contain seed syllables. These are one-syllabled mantras frequently derived from the first letter of a deity's name to which a nasal sound, the *anusvāra* or *anunāsika*, is added. A total of 85 deities are invoked

[13] For a simpler version of the yantra, cf. Coburn 1991: 115 (Figure 5.3) and 138–139.

into the yantra.[14] In the centre, a downward-pointing triangle (*trikoṇa*) is found containing salutations to the three principal emanations of the goddess, namely, Mahākālī (1), Mahālakṣmī (2) and Mahāsarasvatī (3), along with the goddesses' respective seed syllables, *aiṃ*, *hrīṃ* and *klīṃ*. This triangle is located inside a hexagram (*ṣaṭkoṇa*) in whose six corners the names of two groups of deities are inscribed. Group 1: Sarasvatī and Brahmā (4), Gaurī and Rudra (5), Lakṣmī and Hṛṣīkeśa (6), Aṣṭādaśabhujā (7), Daśānanā (8), Aṣṭabhujā (9); group 2: Nandajā (10), Raktadantikā (11), Śākambharī (12), Durgā (13), Bhīmā (14) and Bhrāmarī (15). Group 1 consists of Brahmā, Śiva and Viṣṇu with their consorts and the three great manifestations of the goddess in the Devīmāhātmya, namely, Aṣṭādaśabhujā ('the Eighteen-Armed One,' that is, Mahālakṣmī), Daśānanā ('the Ten-Faced One,' that is, Mahākālī) and Aṣṭabhujā ('the Eight-Armed One,' that is, Mahāsarasvatī). Group 2 consists of special manifestations of the goddess described in Devīmāhātmya 11.42–55. Jayā (16), Vijayā (17), Jayantī (18), Aparājitā (19) and the two vehicles of the goddess, the lion (*siṃha*) (20) and buffalo (*mahiṣa*) (21), are invoked into the points in which the sides of the two triangles forming the hexagram intersect. The hexagram is inside a lotus into whose eight petals again two groups of deities are invoked. The first group consists of the mother goddesses (*mātṛkā*): Brāhmī (22), Māheśvarī (23), Kaumārī (24), Vaiṣṇavī (25), Vārāhī (26), Nārasiṃhī (27), Aindrī (28) and Cāmuṇḍā (29).[15] The second group consists of the eight Bhairavas: Asitāṅgabhairava (30), Rurubhairava (31), Caṇḍabhairava (32), Krodhabhairava (33), Unmattabhairava (34), Kapālabhairava (35), Bhīṣaṇabhairava (36) and Saṃhārabhairava (37). Outside the eight-petalled lotus, a lotus with 24 petals is found. In it the following *śaktis* are invoked: Viṣṇumāyā (38), Cetanā (39), Buddhi (40), Nidrā (41), Kṣudhā (42), Chāyā (43), Śakti (44), Tṛṣṇā (45), Kṣānti (46), Jāti (47), Lajjā (48), Śānti (49), Śraddhā (50), Kānti (51), Lakṣmī (52), Dhṛti (53), Vṛtti (54), Smṛti (55), Dayā (56), Tuṣṭi (57), Puṣṭi (58), Mātṛ (59), Bhrānti (60) and Citi (61). Outside this lotus is a square (*bhūpura*, *bhūgṛha*) with four protruding gates. Into the

[14] For a text listing almost the same names as those inscribed in the yantra sketch, see Ṛgvedīyabrahmakarmasamuccaya, fols. 349a.12–350b.8.

[15] The names differ slightly from those in the *rudrapīṭhamahāyantra*. In that yantra, Caṇḍikā replaces Nārasiṃhī and the sequence of the last three names in the list differs.

corners of the square and the four gates two groups of deities are invoked. The first group consists of the ten directional guardians (*dikpāla*), who are invoked into their respective directions beginning from the east:[16] Indra (62), Agni (63), Yama (64), Nirṛti (65), Varuṇa (66), Vāyu (67), Soma (= Kubera) (68) and Rudra (Īśāna) (69). Brahmā (70) is assigned to the zenith, which is located between the north-east and east in the yantra. Śeṣa (71) is assigned to the nadir, which is located between the south-west and west. The second group consists of the attributes (*āyudha*) of the directional guardians, which are assigned in the same sequence (cf. also the *rudrayantra* described below): the thunderbolt (*vajra*) (72; east), the spear (*śakti*) (73; south-east), the staff (*daṇḍa*) (74; south), the sword (*khaḍga*) (75; south-west), the noose (*pāśa*) (76; west), the goad (*aṅkuśa*) (77; north-west), the mace (*gadā*) (78; north), the trident (*triśūla*) (79; north-east), the lotus (*padma*) (80; assigned to the zenith) and the wheel (*cakra*) (81; assigned to the nadir). Outside the gates Gaṇapati (82), Kṣetrapāla (83), Baṭuka (84) and the 'Yoginīs' (85) are found.

Even though the number of deities invoked into this yantra is rather large, its design is common: a downward-pointing female triangle inside a hexagram which is in the pericarp of an eight-petalled lotus. The lotus is surrounded by another lotus and a square with four gates. In addition to specific deities connected with Durgā, groups of deities appear which are often found in other yantras. They are the group of eight mothers, the Bhairavas, the ten directional guardians and behind the latter their attributes.

5.2 *The Rudrapīṭhamahāyantra*

The *rudrapīṭhamahāyantra* ('great yantra of Rudra's seat'), or simply *rudrapīṭha*/*rudrayantra* (see Illustration 5), is employed in connection with the recitation of the Rudrādhyāya of Taittirīya-Saṃhitā 4.5.1–11 of the Yajur-Veda. The Ṛgvedīyabrahmakarmasamuccaya ascribes this yantra to the Skanda-Purāṇa[17] and prescribes it for all rituals worshipping Rudra. After the deities are invoked into the yantra, a vessel (*kalaśa*) is placed on it to serve as the seat for Śiva, the principal deity of the ritual (see Colour Plate 4).

---

[16] The names of the directional guardians and their directions are listed in section 4 in connection with the *navagrahamaṇḍala*.

[17] See Ṛgvedīyabrahmakarmasamuccaya, fols. 315a.1–318a.8 for the description.

The yantra consists of a lotus pattern with five rings of petals that contain five major groups (divided into subgroups) of surrounding deities. Outside the petals is a square (*bhūpura*) with three nested lines and four protruding gates. The lines of the square are coloured, from inside to out, white, red and black. They are called *sattva*, *rajas* and *tamas* and identified with the three constituents (*guṇa*) of primary matter (*prakṛti*) in the Sāṃkhya system.[18] Outside the gates are depicted the eight great snakes. In this yantra, a total of 141 deities are invoked (the diagram numbers them only up to 121), generally beginning in the west. The five-faced Rudra (1) is invoked into the pericarp of the lotus and worshipped with the mantras corresponding to his five aspects, Sadyojāta, Vāmadeva, Aghora, Tatpuruṣa and Īśāna. The first group of surrounding deities is assigned to the innermost ring of eight petals: Nandin (2), Mahākāla (3), Gaṇeśvara (4) Vṛṣabha (5), Bhṛṅgiriṭi[19] (6), Skanda (7), Umā (8) and Caṇḍīśvara (9). In the adjacent ring of 16 lotus petals the following aspects of Śiva are invoked: Ananta (10), Sūkṣma (11), Śiva (12), Ekapāt (13), Ekarudra (14), Trimūrti (15), Śrīkaṇṭha (16), Vāmadeva (17), Jyeṣṭha (18), Śreṣṭha (19), Rudra (20), Kāla (21), Kalavikaraṇa (22), Balavikaraṇa (23), Bala (24) and Balapramathana (25). The third group of deities is positioned in the next ring of 24 lotus petals. This group consists of three subgroups: the supernatural powers (*siddhi*), the mother goddesses (*mātṛkā*) and the Bhairavas. The eight supernatural powers[20] are: atomization (*aṇiman*) (26), magnification (*mahiman*) (27), levitation (*laghiman*) (28) heaviness (*gariman*) (29), extension (*prāpti*) (30), efficacy/non-obstruction of desire (*prākāmya*) (31), sovereignty (*īśitā*) (32) and mastery (*vaśitā*) (33). The eight mother goddesses are Brāhmī (34), Māheśvarī (35), Kaumārī (36), Vaiṣṇavī (37), Vārāhī (38), Aindrī (39), Cāmuṇḍā (40) and Caṇḍikā (41).[21] The eight Bhairavas (42–49) are identical with the ones listed above for the *saptaśatīmahāyantra*, namely Asitāṅga-bhairava and the others. To the fourth ring of 32 lotus petals are assigned several subgroups of deities. The first subgroup consists of

---

[18] See also my remarks in section 2.3.8 of the previous essay for these three lines.

[19] I.e., the two attendants of Śiva.

[20] These supernatural powers are explained in Vyāsa's commentary on Yogasūtra 3.45.

[21] The names differ somewhat from those in the earlier list for the *saptaśatīmahāyantra*. In that yantra, Nārasiṃhī appears in place of Caṇḍikā and the sequence of the last three names in the list differs.

the eight manifestations (*mūrti*) of Śiva: Bhava (50), Śarva (51), Īśāna (52), Paśupati (53), Rudra (54), Ugra (55), Bhīma (56) and Mahat (57). The second subgroup consists of the eight great serpents: Śeṣa (58), Ananta (59), Vāsuki (60), Takṣaka (61), Kulīra (62), Karkoṭaka (63), Śaṅkhapāla (64) and Kambalāśvatara (64). The third subgroup consists of the kings:[22] Vainya (66), Pṛthu (67), Haihaya (58), Arjuna (69), Śākuntaleya (70), Bharata (71), Nala (72) and Rāma (73). The fourth subgroup consists of the eight principal mountain ranges (*kulācala*): Himavat (74), Niṣadha (75), Vindhya (76), Mālyavat (77), Pāriyātraka (78), Malaya (79), Hemakūṭa (80) and Gandhamādana (81). The fifth ring has 40 lotus petals with the following five subgroups of divine beings: the eight directional guardians, their consorts, the guardians' attributes, the guardians' vehicles and the directional elephants. The eight directional guardians are—as in the *navagrahamaṇḍala* and the *saptaśatīmahāyantra*—Indra (82), Agni (83), Yama (84), Nirṛti (85), Varuṇa, (86), Vāyu (87), Kubera (88) and Īśāna (89). Their eight consorts are: Śacī (90), Svāhā (91), Vārāhī (92), Khaḍginī (93), Vāruṇī (94), Vāyavī (95), Kauberī (96) and Īśānī (97). The eight guardians' attributes are as in the *saptaśatīmahāyantra*: the thunderbolt (*vajra*) (98), the spear (*śakti*) (99), the staff (*daṇḍa*) (100), the sword (*khaḍga*) (101), the noose (*pāśa*) (102), the goad (*aṅkuśa*) (103), the mace (*gadā*) (104) and the trident (*triśūla*) (105). The guardians' vehicles (*vāhana*) are Indra's elephant Airāvata (106), the ram (*meṣa*) (107), the buffalo (*mahiṣa*) (108), the corpse (*preta*) (109), the sea-monster (*makara*) (110), the deer (*hariṇa*) (111), the man (*nara*) (112) and the bull (*vṛṣabha*) (113). The directional elephants (*diggaja*) are specified as

---

[22] These names appear to have been taken from the following verse which is traditionally recited by Mahārāṣṭrian Brahmins upon rising in the morning. This verse, which is believed to secure wealth and victory, is printed in texts such as the Bhaktimārgadīp (edited by G.N. Dāṇḍekar, Mumbaī: Majestic Book Stall, 1978 [third edition]): 2:

vainyaṃ pṛthuṃ haihayam arjunaṃ ca
śākuntaleyaṃ bharataṃ nalaṃ ca /
rāmaṃ ca yo vai smarati prabhāte
tasyārthalābho vijayaś ca haste //

Actually, the verse lists only the names of five kings: Pṛthu, the son of King Vena (also spelled Veṇa); Arjuna (Kārtavīrya) of the Haihaya family; Bharata, the son of Śakuntalā; Nala and Rāma. In the yantra, the names are clearly interpreted as eight separate names. The individual who first assigned the names to the yantra did not realize that three of the epithets (*vainya*, *haihaya* and *śākuntaleya*) are adjectives that modify three of the names (Pṛthu, Arjuna and Bharata).

Airāvata (114), Puṇḍarīka (115), Vāmana (116), Kumuda (117), Añjana (118), Puṣpadanta (119), Sārvabhauma (120) and Supratīka (121). In the gates of the square outside the lotuses, the eight directional guardians (122–129) appear for the second time in the yantra. Four additional deities, who represent forms of Śiva, are invoked into the intermediate directions: Virūpākṣa (130) (south-east), Viśvarūpa (131) (south-west), Paśupati (132) (north-west) and Ūrdhvaliṅga (133) (north-east). The eight great serpents outside the square are: Śeṣa (134), Takṣaka (135), Ananta (136), Vāsuki (137), Śaṅkhapāla (138), Mahāpadma (139), Kambala (140) and Karkoṭaka (141). They appear here for the second time with variants for some of their names.

This yantra features a lotus design with five rings of petals, surrounded by a square with three nested lines. Among the deities invoked are special groups associated with Rudra/Śiva. In addition, common groups of deities who are also assigned to other yantras appear. These are the mother goddesses, the Bhairavas, the eight great serpents, the directional guardians, their consorts and their attributes. The groups of directional guardians and great serpents appear twice in the yantra, each time in a different part of the yantra, which is not unusual.

The second part of this paper introduces a structure quite different from the lotus designs described here. It deals with types of *bhadramaṇḍalas*, all of which share the square grid.

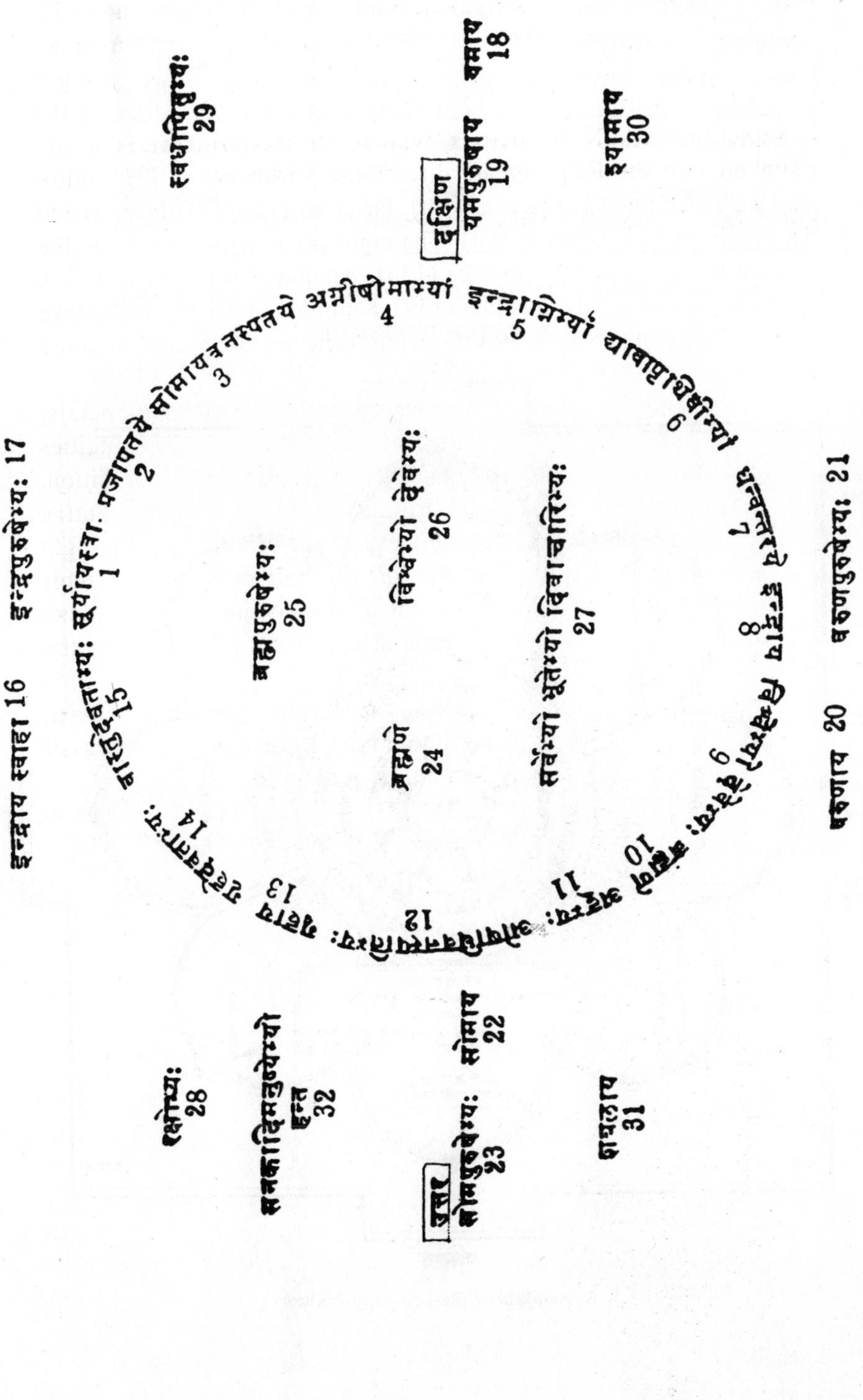

1. A diagram showing the deities of the *baliharaṇacakra*

NE EAST SE NORTH SOUTH NW WEST SW	**Śivapañcāyatana** Viṣṇu (2) Sūrya (3) Śiva (1) Devī (5) Gaṇeśa (4)	**Viṣṇupañcāyatana** Śiva (2) Gaṇeśa (3) Viṣṇu (1) Devī (5) Sūrya (4)
Sūryapañcāyatana Śiva (2) Gaṇeśa (3) Sūrya (1) Devī (5) Viṣṇu (4)	**Devīpañcāyatana** Viṣṇu (2) Śiva (3) Devī (1) Sūrya (5) Gaṇeśa (4)	**Gaṇeśapañcāyatana** Viṣṇu (2) Śiva (3) Gaṇeśa (1) Devī (5) Sūrya (4)

2. The arrangement of the five deities in (domestic) *pañcāyatana* shrines

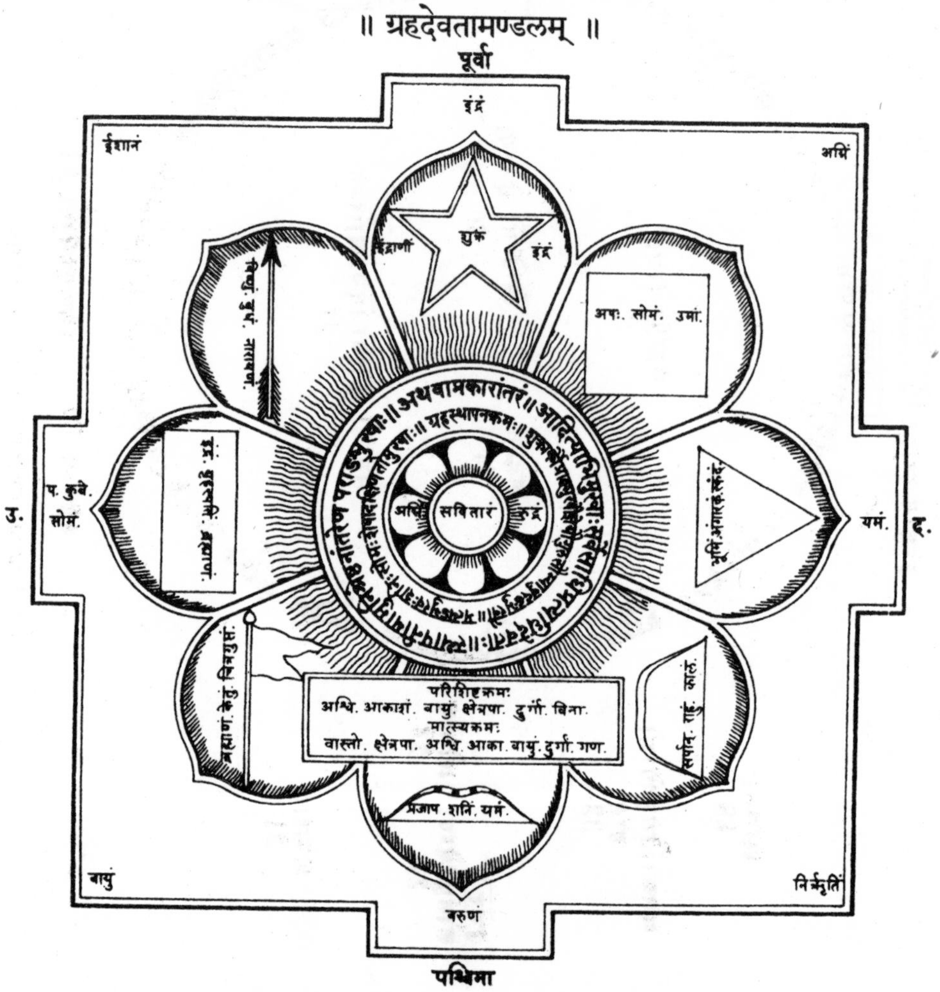

3. A maṇḍala of the heavenly bodies

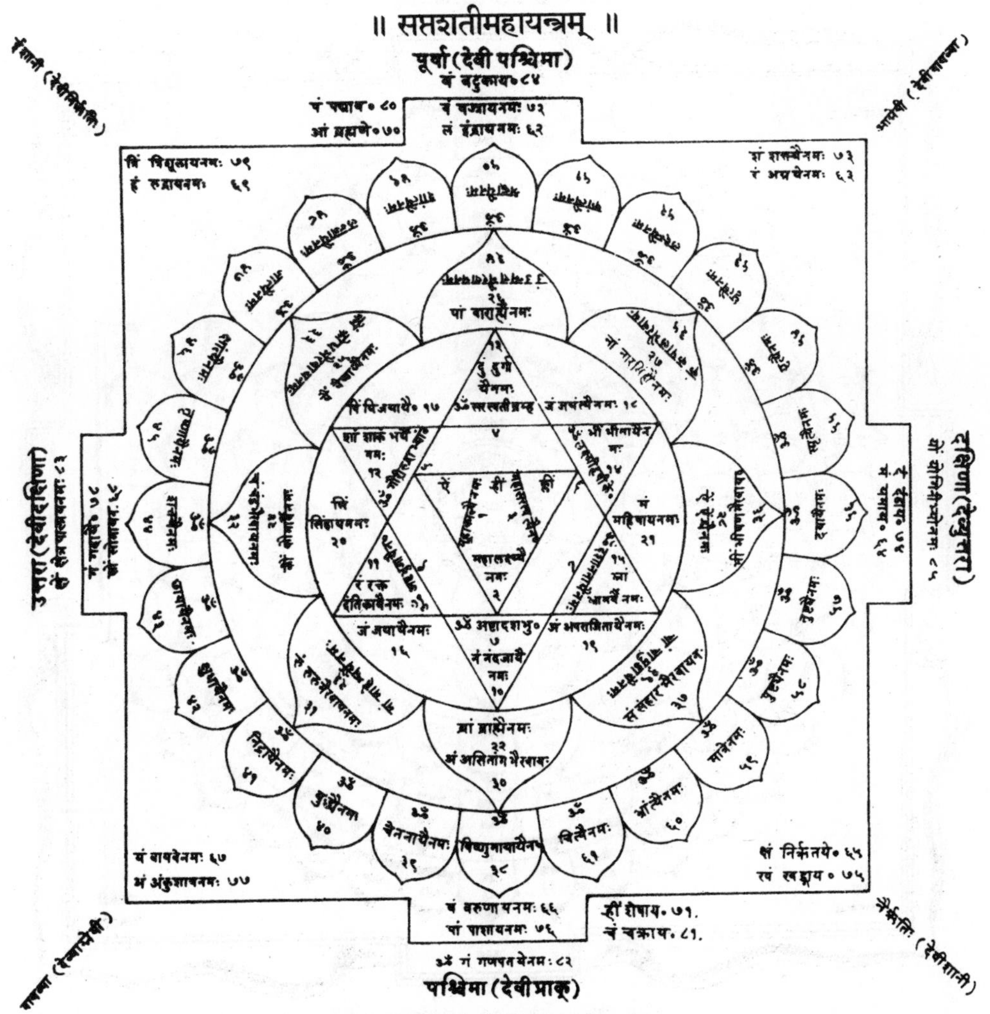

4. The *(durgā)saptaśatīmahāyantra*

॥ रुद्रपीठमहायन्त्रम् ॥

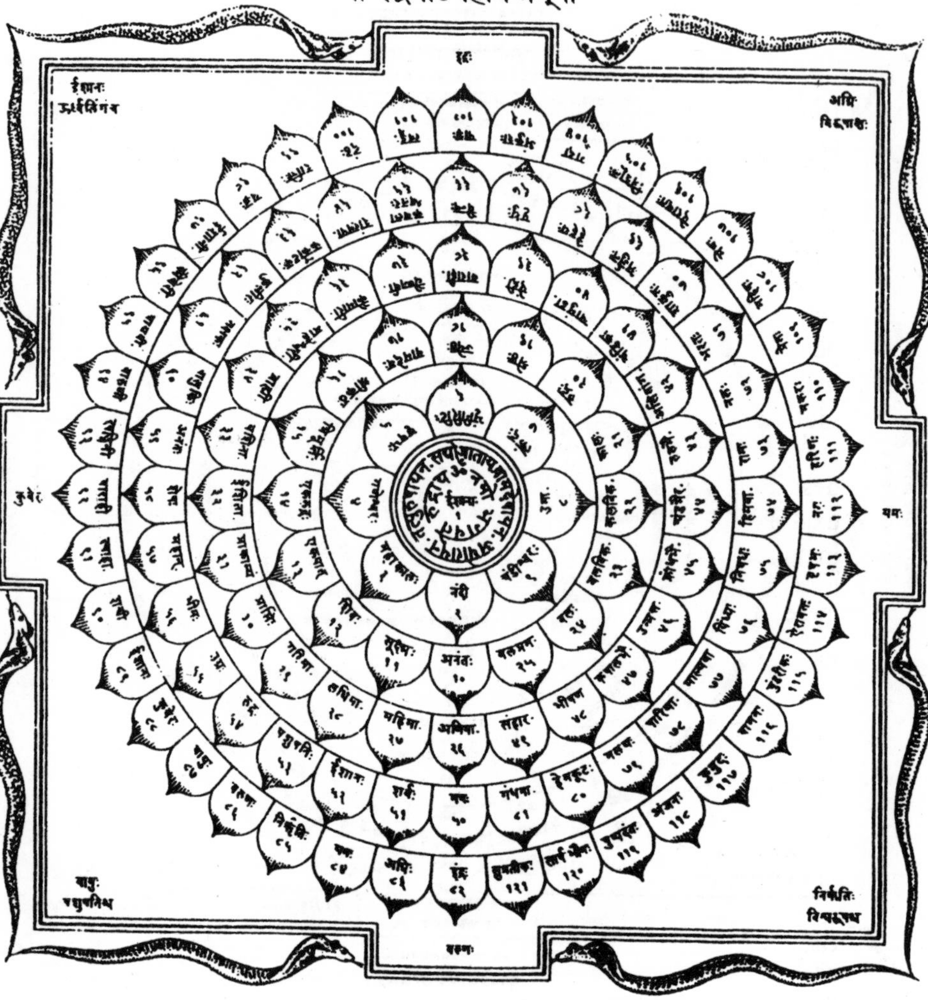

5. The *rudrapīṭhamahāyantra*

PART II. BHADRAMAṆḌALAS [1]

1 *Introduction*

Bhadramaṇḍalas are square-shaped maṇḍalas that are divided into a grid of squares.[2] Specific shapes are traced within the framework of these squares. In the course of the ritual, deities are invoked into different parts of these shapes. The maṇḍalas are used mainly as supports (*pīṭha*) for vessels (*kalaśa*). The vessels function as seats for icons of deities. The *bhadramaṇḍalas* are employed mainly in the concluding ceremonies of religious observances (*vratodyāpana*). It is believed that a ritual performed without the support of a *bhadra* is fruitless, whereas a ritual employing such a support is thought to yield excellent results (Bhadramārtaṇḍa, fol. 2a.5–6). The construction of the *bhadramaṇḍalas* is still alive in Mahārāṣṭra and described in ritual handbooks of priests. In the following I will explore the different types and structures of these maṇḍalas. My main textual source here is the 19th-century Bhadramārtaṇḍa written by Harikṛṣṇa, a text which has not been analyzed previously. Most[3] of the maṇḍalas found in the printed edition of the Bhadramārtaṇḍa have been reproduced in this book.

---

[1] In my paper entitled 'Bhadramaṇḍalas in the Ritual Practice,' published in the Wiener Zeitschrift für die Kunde Südasiens in 1987, I discuss *sarvatobhadras* and several types of *liṅgatobhadras*, the deities invoked into them and the ritual employment of the *bhadramaṇḍalas*. The paper includes diagrams of maṇḍalas and photographs of stages in their construction, together with translations of text passages and numerous references in the notes. This information has not been duplicated here. While the earlier paper refers only briefly to some modifications of these maṇḍalas, such as the *rāmatobhadras*, these modifications are described here in greater detail. Thus this essay complements my earlier paper.

[2] The square grid is described in section 1.3.2 of the previous essay.

[3] The printed edition does not illustrate all maṇḍalas described in the text. Illustrations of maṇḍalas 36, 38, 53–65 are missing. Moreover, some maṇḍala drawings are incomplete (24–25, 39–40 and 50–51) and have therefore not been reproduced in this book.

2 *The Bhadramārtaṇḍa and its Author*

The Bhadramārtaṇḍa (BM) is, to my knowledge, the most comprehensive compendium on *bhadramaṇḍalas*. The text describes as many as 76 *bhadras*, which are to be employed by the 'followers of the Veda' (*vaidika*).

The BM forms chapter (*adhyāya*) 17 of the sixth *skandha* of the Bṛhajjyotiṣārṇava, written by the astrologer (*jyotirvid*) Harikṛṣṇa in 1871 A.D. Harikṛṣṇa's father was Veṅkaṭarāma, an *audīcya* Brahmin of Gujarāt of the *audīcya-sahasra* branch who resided in Aurangabad. Veṅkaṭarāma belonged to the *vājasaneya-śākhā* of the White Yajur-Veda and the *gautama-gotra*.

To date, only parts of the comprehensive Bṛhajjyotiṣārṇava have been printed by the Veṅkaṭeśvar Press (also known as Khemrāj Śrīkṛṣṇadās). The printed parts of the text include the Baṭukabhairavopāsanā (Bombay 1909), the 124th *adhyāya* in the *dharmaskandha* of the work; the Cakrāvalīsaṃgraha (Bombay 1900), included in the sixth *skandha*; the Krīḍākauśalya (Bombay 1901), the 20th *adhyāya* in the sixth *skandha*; the Hanumadupāsanā (Bombay 1899), the 114th *adhyāya* of the *upāsanāstabaka* in the eighth *skandha*; and the Durgopāsanākalpadruma (Bombay 1907), the 128th *adhyāya* in the eighth *skandha*. Harikṛṣṇa is also the author of the Kārttikamāsamāhātmyaṭīkā and the Vaiśākhamāsamāhātmyaṭīkā.

Although Harikṛṣṇa's compilation is recent, descriptions of most of the maṇḍalas included in the BM can be traced back to older sources, such as the *vratakhaṇḍa* of Hemādri's Caturvargacintāmaṇi (ca. 1260–1270 A.D.), the *manoharakāṇḍa* of the Ānandarāmāyaṇa (ĀR) and to several other texts on *vratas* and *dharma*.[4] Among these texts, the ĀR[5] is the most important source for the BM. Bulcke 1962: 73 assigns this text to ca. 1500 A.D. According to Raghavan (†) 1998: 121, the ĀR was most likely produced during the Maratha rule

---

[4] Harikṛṣṇa names the following texts as his sources: the <Ānanda->Rāmāyaṇa; the Vratarāja; the Śāntisāra; the Tattvasāgara-Saṃhitā; 'the Pāñcarātra;' Hemādri<'s *vratakhaṇḍa* in his Caturvargacintāmaṇi>; 'the Purāṇas,' especially 'the Skānda' and 'the Laiṅga;' the Maṇḍalasaṃgraha; 'the Tantras,' especially the Rudrayāmala; the Rudrapaddhati, a text that may be identical with the Mahārudrapaddhati, or the Rudrānuṣṭhānapaddhati (Aufrecht 1: 530), which was authored by Nārāyaṇabhaṭṭa, son of Rāmeśvarabhaṭṭa; and the 'Kaumudī,' which may be identical with the Vratodyāpanakaumudī.

[5] For a summary of the narrative contents of the ĀR, see Raghavan (†) 1998: 72–124.

in South India, between the end of the 17th and beginning of the 18th centuries. This later date is more likely. Several of the maṇḍalas Harikṛṣṇa describes are detailed in contemporary ritual handbooks of priests in Mahārāṣṭra, and are currently employed in rituals.

3 *The Structure of the Bhadramārtaṇḍa and its Maṇḍalas*

The BM has been out of print for a long time and it is difficult to obtain copies. The work, comprising 36 printed folios, is written in verse with occasional brief prose explanations. Most verses consist of quotations from other texts. The work begins with a general section that provides definitions and explanations (*paribhāṣā*), and then proceeds with technical instructions for drawing the maṇḍalas. The 76 *bhadras* described in the text are divided into the following main categories:

1) *sarvatobhadras*
2) *liṅgatobhadras* for Śiva, including *bhadras* for Gaurī
3) *bhadras* for Rāma
4) the *pañcabhadra*
5) *bhadras* for Sūrya
6) the *bhadra* for Gaṇapati/Gaṇeśa
7) the *cakrāravindamaṇḍala*
8) the *svastikamaṇḍala*.

A complete list of maṇḍalas described in the BM is found in the appendix at the end of this paper.

Sarvatobhadra means 'auspicious from all sides'[6] and most likely refers to the symmetry of the maṇḍala design.[7] The name has been

[6] Dakshinaranjan Shastri 1940: 171 translates the name as 'beautiful in every aspect,' Brunner, p. 167 as 'thoroughly auspicious' and Rastelli, p. 124 as 'auspicious in every way.'

[7] Sarvatobhadra is also the name of a *bandha* composition in literature, in which verse quarters can be read in all four directions, forwards, backwards, horizontally and vertically. As Lienhard demonstrates, names of *bandhas* can be traced back to certain army formations (*vyūha*). A *sarvatobhadravyūha* can attack an enemy from all sides (Lienhard 1997: 346, 350, 351). For a drawing of a *sarvatobhadra* stanza, see Lienhard 1997: 353. The term *sarvatobhadra* is used in architecture to denote a house with a veranda all around (Bṛhat-Saṃhitā 53.31) and a type of temple (Bṛhat-Saṃhitā 56.18, 56. 27). In town-planning the term refers to an oblong or square-shaped town. For a *sarvatobhadra* town plan, see Lienhard 1997: 358.

used by different texts to designate distinct types of maṇḍalas. For example, the variations of this maṇḍala in the BM differ from descriptions in some other texts,[8] for example, the *sarvatobhadra* according to the third chapter of the Śāradātilaka, which Brunner reconstructs in her contribution. The *sarvatobhadra*, of which four types are explained in the BM (Illustrations 1–4), is the most versatile of all the *bhadras* in application. It can be employed in all the religious observances (*vrata*), regardless of whether the principal deity is Viṣṇu, Śiva or another deity. But it is believed to be particularly well suited for Vaiṣṇava rites. One type of *sarvatobhadra* described in the BM (Illustration 3) is an eight-petalled (*aṣṭadala*) lotus, which functions as a substitute for a *bhadramaṇḍala*.

The terms *liṅgatobhadra*, *rāmatobhadra* and so forth are derived analogically from the term *sarvatobhadra*. The term *liṅgato<bhadra>*, '<auspicious> because of a *liṅga*/*liṅgas*,' is used synonymously with *liṅgasamudbhava*, '<auspicious(ness)> arisen from a *liṅga*/*liṅgas*.'

The *liṅgatobhadras* described in the main section of the BM fall into many subcategories. The subcategories are named according to the number of phallic symbols of Śiva (*liṅga*) they depict, ranging from one to 1,008. In addition to their number, the arrangement of the *liṅgas* within the maṇḍalas is significant, as is the number of lines drawn while constructing the maṇḍalas. As one would expect, the *liṅgatobhadras* are employed in *vratas* connected with deities of the Śaiva tradition. Three *liṅgatobhadras* that are named *gaurītilaka*[9] (Illustrations 5–7) are prescribed for *vratas* connected with Śiva's

---

[8] For other types of *sarvatobhadra*, see the references in Bühnemann 1987: 43, note 2 and, in addition, the colour diagram in Banerji 1978: 176+ and the line drawing in V.V. Dwived/J. Pandey/S.S. Bahulkar (Bhāratīya Tantraśāstra, Sarnath, Varanasi: Central Institute of Higher Tibetan Studies, 1995): 682. A *sarvatobhadra* is included in the sketchbook of the painter Vishnu Bahadur Chitrakar of Bhaktapur, Nepal, which is reproduced in Vergati 1982: 56. Gaeffke 1987: 154 states that the *sarvatobhadra* is identical with the *navapadmamaṇḍala*; these maṇḍalas, however, usually differ considerably in structure. For a sketch of a *navapadmamaṇḍala* reconstructed according to the description in the Jayākhya-Saṃhitā of the Pāñcarātra, see Apte 1973: 514+, illustrated Figure 1. His sketch is based on a colour print prefixed to the foreword of only the first edition of the Jayākhya-Saṃhitā (1931); see also Colour Plate 15. The *navapadmamaṇḍala* is also described in the Lakṣmī-Tantra. A colour diagram is appended to Gupta's translation of the Lakṣmī-Tantra (= Diagram III), which is reproduced in black and white in Khanna 1979: 92. The Tantrasadbhāva (see Törzsök, p. 205, note 95) apparently refers to a type of *śrīmaṇḍala* as *sarvatobhadra(ka)*.

[9] For drawings of two different *gaurītilakamaṇḍalas* each with four *liṅgas* and five lotuses, see SP3, Plate XV and also p. 696; see also Sabarathinam 1995: 62.

consort Gaurī, also referred to as Śakti. Combinations of the *sarvatobhadra* and the *liṅgatobhadra* are frequently termed *harihara(ātmaka)liṅgatobhadras*, '*liṅgatobhadras* (consisting) of Hari and Hara' (for example, Illustrations 19–21). The *sarvatobhadra*, which usually appears in the centre of these maṇḍalas, represents Hari/Viṣṇu, while the *liṅgatobhadra* on the outside represents Hara/Śiva. The *harihara-liṅgatobhadras* can be employed in both Vaiṣṇava and in Śaiva rites. Liṅgatobhadras are also combined with the auspicious *svastika* symbol. Five additional *liṅgatobhadras*, which are used on special occasions, such as festivals, and in rites performed for the attainment of specific goals, are described separately in the final section of the BM. The total number of *liṅgatobhadras* described in the text is 41.

The 25 *bhadras* for Rāma, called *rāmatobhadras*, 'auspicious because of <the 'seal' of> Rāma,' are employed in rituals for Rāma and Viṣṇu. They are maṇḍalas inscribed with one or several 'seals' (*mudrā*). 'The seal' is defined as the words *rājā rāma* ('King Rāma') (see Table, Figure 9), or, in reverse order, *rāma rājā*. The *bhadras* for Rāma may also be inscribed with the name (*nāman*) *rāma rāma*. In such cases, they are classified as *rāmanāmatobhadras* (cf. ĀR, *manoharakāṇḍa* 4.49–45). Alternatively, they can be inscribed with the names *ramā rāma*, in which *ramā* refers to Rāma's wife. Some *bhadras* are inscribed with the seal *rājā rāma* together with *liṅgas*. These *bhadras* are termed *rāmaliṅgatobhadras* (see Colour Plates 6–7).[10] Various *bhadras* for Rāma, such as *rāmatobhadras* and *rāmaliṅgatobhadras*, many of which contain a *sarvatobhadra* in their centre, are elaborately described in *sargas* 4 and 5 of the *manoharakāṇḍa* of the ĀR. Combining a *rāmamudrā* and a *śivaliṅga* in the same maṇḍala poses no doctrinal problems. Rāma is said to have worshipped Śiva and established *liṅgas* (cf. ĀR, *sārakāṇḍa* 10.124), which are often called *rāmaliṅgas* in Mahārāṣṭra and Karṇāṭaka. Śiva, on the other hand, is said to utter a *rāmamantra* called *tārakamantra* for the benefit of those who pass away in Vārāṇasī. ĀR, *rājyakāṇḍa* 18.19 refers to a stone inscribed with the *rāmamudrā* in Rāmanāthapura, a site close to Rāmeśvara. According to legends, the stones used to build the bridge to Laṅkā were inscribed with the

---

[10] Of these two paintings, which come from private collections, the pattern of the first *bhadra* cannot be identified in the BM. The second *bhadra* bears the inscription *caturmudrārāmaliṅgatobhadra* and corresponds to Illustration 42 from the BM. It features four *rāmamudrās*, eight *liṅgas* and a *sarvatobhadra* in the centre.

rāmamantra or with Rāma's name. In the ĀR the power of the *rāmamudrā* is eulogized repeatedly. When a maṇḍala that combines *rāmamudrās* and *śivaliṅgas* is employed for the worship of Rāma, the *rāmamudrā* becomes the object of worship and the *liṅga*/Śiva acts as the worshipper.[11] But when the same maṇḍala is used in a ritual worshipping Śiva, the *liṅga* becomes the object of worship, and the *rāmamudrā*, the worshipper. A *rāmatobhadra* is employed in rites for Viṣṇu, while a *rāmaliṅgatobhadra* is suitable for either Viṣṇu or Śiva. A *bhadra* inscribed with the 'seal' *ramā rāma* is used for the goddess.[12]

Two types of *sūryabhadras* (Illustrations 67–68) are described for use in *vratas* connected with the sun. Each one contains 12 images of the sun, 12 being the number that symbolizes the sun, since it corresponds to the 12 months of the year and the 12 zodiac signs. The two *bhadras* differ in the number of lines drawn and in the way the icons are placed. The *bhadra* (Colour Plate 10) from Rājasthān can be identified as the *sūryabhadra* with 20 lines corresponding to Illustration 67 from the BM.

The BM describes only one *bhadra* for Gaṇapati/Gaṇeśa (see Illustration 69). It is a *bhadra* with a total of five icons of Gaṇapati, four in the cardinal directions and one in the centre (see Colour Plate 8).[13] But we know from other texts that several other types of *gaṇapatibhadras* exist.[14] One of these features 21 icons of Gaṇapati, 21 being an important number in the worship of the deity (see Colour Plate 9).

[11] Cf. ĀR, *manoharakāṇḍa*, 4.6 and 5.90cd–91ab.

[12] Cf. ĀR, *manoharakāṇḍa*, 5.375; BM, fol. 3a.8–9.

[13] The maṇḍala is reproduced from Gaṇeśkoś (edited by A. Gāḍgīḷ, Puṇe: Śrīrām Book Agency, 1981): 477. The *gaṇeśabhadra* reproduced in the BM features four icons of Gaṇeśa in the cardinal directions but no icon (only a lotus) in the centre. This *gaṇeśabhadra* is reproduced in colour in S.D. Deśikar (Gaṇapati, Tirvāvaḍuturai Adīṇam, 1984 [second edition] [in Tamil]): 141+.

[14] For *gaṇapatibhadras*, see also Bühnemann 1987: 48–49, 59, 63.

Other maṇḍalas in the BM include the *cakrāravinda*,[15] a lotus encircled by a wheel, and the *svastikamaṇḍala*,[16] which features the auspicious *svastika* symbol inside a square. The *svastika* also appears in other maṇḍalas, such as some *liṅgatobhadras* in combination with *liṅgas*, lotuses or other symbols. It is an ancient auspicious symbol which Auer/Gutschow 1974: 22, 38 consider an abstract form of a maṇḍala whose 'arms' establish the unity of the maṇḍala's four parts.

4 *Constituent Parts of the Bhadras*

Bhadras are constructed by drawing a certain number of vertical and horizontal base lines (*rekhā*) that form square grids. The squares are called *pada* or *koṣṭha* (see Table, Figure 1). The maṇḍala is made up of *padas* that are assembled to form different shapes. The *sarvatobhadra* usually has the following parts (see Table, Figures 2–9):

'enclosure' (*paridhi*) (Figure 2)
'well' (*vāpī*) (Figure 3)

[15] A more complex maṇḍala of this type is the *cakrābjamaṇḍala*. The Pauṣkara-Saṃhitā, which contains a description of the maṇḍala in chapter 8, states in verse 2ab that multiple variants of this maṇḍala exist. For a description of the *cakrābjamaṇḍala*, see Pādma-Saṃhitā, *caryāpāda*, chapter 2. The maṇḍala is discussed in volume 1, Appendix 10: 53–54 of the edited text (with references to parallel texts) and in volume 2: 569–571; see also Colour Plate 14 in this book (reproduced from a plate inserted in the back of volume 1) and the sketch in volume 2: 568. Another variant of the maṇḍala is reproduced in the appendix to Gupta's translation of the Lakṣmī-Tantra (= Diagram IV); in the maṇḍala reproduction the tips of the lotus petals are not oriented to the points of the compass. Gupta's diagram is reprinted in black and white in Khanna 1979: 93. For a sketch of a somewhat different *cakrābjamaṇḍala*, see Rao 1988–1992, volume 5: 27. The *cakrābjamaṇḍala* is also known as *bhadrakamaṇḍala* (see Rastelli, p. 124, note 28) because it is similar to a type of *sarvatobhadra*, namely the *sarvatobhadra* reconstructed by Brunner. One mark of distinction between the *cakrābjamaṇḍala* and the *sarvatobhadra* is that a conch shell is drawn in each of the four corners of the *cakrābjamaṇḍala*. For a *bhadrakamaṇḍala*, see the line drawing printed in Nāradīya-Saṃhitā, p. 576. The same line drawing also appears in an article by R.P. Chaudhary (in V.V. Dwived/J. Pandey/S.S. Bahulkar: Bhāratīya Tantraśāstra, Sarnath, Varanasi: Central Institute of Higher Tibetan Studies, 1995): 682. For a sketch of a simpler *bhadrakamaṇḍala*, see Rao 1988–1992, volume 5: 20.

[16] For a different *svastikamaṇḍala* reconstructed from the Siddhāntasārāvalī, see SP3, Plate XVI and p. 696; see further PauṣS2, appendix, p. XI and Rao 1988–1992, volume 5: 25 for different types of this maṇḍala.

'offset' (*bhadra*)[17] (Figure 4)
'creeper' (*vallī*) (Figure 5)
'chain' (*śṛṅkhalā*) (Figure 6)
'crescent moon' (*khaṇḍendu*) (Figure 7).

In the centre is usually a lotus with a pericarp (*karṇikā*).

In addition to these parts, the *liṅgatobhadras* contain one or several phallic symbols (*liṅga*) of Śiva (see Figure 8).[18] The *liṅgas* are also referred to as Rudra or Śiva in the BM. The number of *liṅgas* ranges from 1 to 1,008. Other constituent parts found in some *liṅgatobhadras* are a passage (*vīthī*) for circumambulation, which surrounds a throne (*pīṭha*), miniature creepers (*laghuvallī*) and miniature chains (*laghuśṛṅkhalā*).[19]

As noted before, a *rāmatobhadra* may contain *liṅgas* and/or a *sarvatobhadra*, but it mainly depicts the 'seal' of Rāma (Table, Figure 9), usually the words *rājā rāma*. The *gaṇeśa-* and *sūryabhadras* feature images of Gaṇeśa and the sun.

The parts of the maṇḍala are usually one of five colours:[20] the enclosure is yellow; the well, white; the *bhadra*, red; the creeper, dark green/blue; the chain, black; and the crescent moon, white. On the outside, the maṇḍala is enclosed by a square with three nested lines which are named after the three constituents (*guṇa*) of primary matter (*prakṛti*) in the Sāṃkhya system: *sattva*, *rajas* and *tamas*. These lines are coloured white, red and black in accordance with the symbolism of the *guṇas*. The lotus in the centre of the maṇḍalas often has a yellow pericarp and white petals, while the *liṅgas* are black and the *rāmamudrā* is white.

The BM recommends that one construct these maṇḍalas from powders or grains. The grains include unbroken rice grains (*akṣata*) (white), red lentils (red), chick-peas (yellow), black beans (dark) and moong gram (*mudga*) (Phaseolus mungo) (green) (BM, fol. 3a.1–2). The use of both coloured powders and grains in the construction of

[17] In architectural terminology, *bhadra* designates an offset projection common to North Indian temple plans.

[18] For additional constituent parts of the *liṅgatobhadras*, see Bühnemann 1987: 55.

[19] These parts are described and illustrated in Bühnemann 1987: 54–55.

[20] The significance of the five colours in ancient Indian culture is elaborately discussed in Goudriaan 1978: 190ff.

the *bhadras* can be observed in contemporary ritual practice in India (see Colour Plate 11).

5 *The Ritual Employment of the Maṇḍalas*

In Mahārāṣṭra, the *bhadras* are mainly employed in concluding rites (*udyāpana*) of religious observances (*vrata*), which frequently consist of a *pūjā* followed by the giving of a gift. This tradition has continued until the present. The size of the maṇḍalas can vary. In Mahārāṣṭra, the *bhadras* are frequently prepared on a low square table used in worship (*cauraṅga*) and are comparatively small in size. After the maṇḍala is constructed, the deities are invoked into areca nuts (*pūgīphala*) that have been placed in parts of the maṇḍala (see Colour Plate 12) and worshipped with such offerings as flowers. According to BM fol. 3b.1, the deities invoked into the *rāmatobhadras* and the *liṅgatobhadras* are said to be the same as those in the *sarvatobhadra*, but other texts appear to differ.[21] The group of deities invoked into the *sarvatobhadra* is a specific group led by Brahmā (*brahmādi-maṇḍaladevatā*).[22] After the offerings, a vessel (*kalaśa*) filled with water and auspicious objects is placed in the centre of the maṇḍala; additional vessels may be placed in the four corners. A flat dish filled with unbroken rice grains is placed on top of the vessel, which becomes the throne of the principal deity of the *vrata* (see Colour Plate 13).

In addition to being used in concluding rites of *vratas*, a *bhadra* can be employed as a seat for a deity in a *pūjā* ritual. The *sarvatobhadra* can be used in the rite of infusing life (*prāṇapratiṣṭhā*) into a statue, in rites for the heavenly bodies (such as the *graha-makha*) and in rites of pacification (*śānti*).[23] Vergati 1982: 57 reports that in Nepal the *sarvatobhadra* is covered with a piece of cloth on which a vessel (*kalaśa*) is placed. The maṇḍala is used in the seven-day ritual recitation of the Bhāgavata-Purāṇa (*bhāgavata-saptāha*) and in the nine-day ritual recitation (*navāha*) of the Rāmāyaṇa and other texts for Rāma. As noted above, the *sarvatobhadra* is employed for rites centring on Viṣṇu, but it can also be used for any other

---

[21] For the deities invoked into several *liṅgatobhadras*, see Bühnemann 1987: 58–59, 65–70.

[22] Their names are listed in Bühnemann 1987: 63–65.

[23] For detailed references, see Bühnemann 1987: 49–50 and 61.

deity. The *liṅgatobhadras* are employed in Śaiva rituals, and a subcategory of them, the *gaurītilakas*, in rituals for Śiva's consort, Gaurī.

The tradition of constructing *bhadramaṇḍalas* is still alive in Mahārāṣṭra and other parts of South Asia, including Nepal, although it is disappearing fast. The time-consuming construction, from the drawing of the lines with the help of threads to the filling of the squares with powders or grains of different colours, is now often obviated by the use of commercially produced charts, which can easily be called back into service.[24] Such coloured charts of one or more types of *sarvatobhadra, liṅgatobhadra, grahamaṇḍala, kṣetrapālamaṇḍala* and *mātṛkāmaṇḍala* are reportedly sold in shops in Vārāṇasī for use by priests. The printing and distribution of such charts promotes the standardization of certain variations of these maṇḍalas, just as the printing of a certain recension of a text does.

6 *Concluding Remarks*

It appears that the Smārtas included the *bhadramaṇḍalas* in their ritual practices under the influence of maṇḍala rituals performed by Tantric practitioners and maṇḍala patterns described in Tantric texts. The Pāñcarātra and the Tantras are referred to among the sources for the BM. One such source may have been the Īśānaśivagurudevapaddhati by Īśānaśivagurudevamiśra, an 11th- or 12th-century Śaiva manual of temple worship in four sections (*pāda*). This text describes maṇḍalas named *bhadraka, sarvatobhadra, pārvatīkānta (aṣṭaliṅgalatāpadmavīthīprākāra), latāliṅgodbhava, pañcabrahmamaṇḍala-gaurītilaka, svastikābjadvaya, svastikasarvatobhadra, cakrābja,*[25] *māyācakra* and *tripurāmaṇḍala.*[26] Some of these names are also included in the BM. One can observe structural similarities between some *bhadramaṇḍalas* and the maṇḍalas reconstructed by Apte in his

[24] Brunner makes a similar observation regarding the maṇḍala tradition in South India (Brunner, pp. 165–166, note 28).

[25] These maṇḍalas are described twice in the Īśānaśivagurudevapaddhati, in two very similar passages. The first description appears in *sāmānyapāda* 6.36–152 (= volume 1, pp. 51, 10 – 62, 2), and the second one in *kriyāpāda* 8.31–123 (= volume 3, pp. 77, 8 – 85, 6). The Ajita(-Āgama) and the Tattvasāgara(-Saṃhitā) are among Īśānaśivagurudevamiśra's sources.

[26] The last two maṇḍalas are only described in *sāmānyapāda* 6.132–152 (= volume 1, pp. 60, 8 – 62, 2).

edition of the Pauṣkara-Saṃhitā (Part 1). A detailed comparative study of maṇḍalas described in the Āgama texts has not been undertaken, but would be a prerequisite for tracing the development of the *bhadramaṇḍala*s.

7 *Appendix: List of Maṇḍalas Described in the BM*

Because the BM appears to be the most comprehensive text on *bhadras*, a complete list of maṇḍalas described in it is provided here.

0 General explanations (*paribhāṣā*) (fols. 1a.1–3b.3)
1 Sarvatobhadras (fols. 3b.3–10a.9)
1.1 Type 1 (fols. 3b.3–4b.6) (Illustration 1)
1.2 Type 2 and list of deities invoked into the maṇḍala with their respective mantras (fols. 4b.6–8b.12) (Illustration 2)
1.3 Type 3: The *aṣṭadalamaṇḍala* as a substitute for the *sarvatobhadra* and the deities invoked into it (fols. 8b.12–10a.2) (Illustration 3)
1.4 Type 4 (fol. 10a.2–9) (Illustration 4)
2 Liṅgatobhadras (fols. 10a.9–24b.11)
2.0 Deities invoked into the *liṅgatobhadra*s and their mantras (fol. 10a.10–10b.11)
2.1 Gaurītilakamaṇḍalas employed in *vrata*s connected to goddesses (fols. 10b.11–11b.4)
2.1.1 Ekaliṅgatobhadra *laghugaurītilaka* (fols. 10b.11–11a.3) (Illustration 5)
2.1.2 Caturliṅgatobhadra *bṛhadgaurītilaka* (fol. 11a.3–9) (Illustration 6)
2.1.3 Gaurītilaka (fol. 11a.9–11b.4) (Illustration 7)
2.2 Caturliṅgatobhadras (fols. 11b.4–12a.7)
2.2.1 Type 1 (fol. 11b.4–10) (Illustration 8)
2.2.2 Type 2 (fol. 11b.10–14) (Illustration 9)
2.2.3 Type 3 (fols. 11b.14–12a.4) (Illustration 10)
2.2.4 Type 4 (fol. 12a.5–7) (Illustration 11)
2.3 Aṣṭaliṅgatobhadras (fols. 12a.8–13a.5)
2.3.1 Type 1 (fol. 12a.8–12b.4) (Illustration 12)
2.3.2 Type 2 (fols. 12b.4–13a.2) (Illustration 13)
2.3.3 Two minor variations (fol. 13a.2–5)
2.4 Dvādaśaliṅgatobhadras (fols. 13a.5–18a.11)

2.4.1 Type 1 with a list of the names of deities invoked into the maṇḍala (fols. 13a.5–15a.3) (Illustration 14)
2.4.2 Type 2 (fol. 15a.3–13) (Illustration 15)
2.4.3 Type 3 (fol. 15a.13–15b.6) (Illustration 16)
2.4.4 Type 4 (*hariharātmakadvādaśaliṅgatobhadra*) (fols. 15b.6–16a.3) (Illustration 17)
2.4.5 Type 5 (fol. 16a.3–10) (Illustration 18)
2.4.6 Type 6 (*hariharātmakadvādaśaliṅgatobhadra*) (fol.16a.10–16b.2) (Illustration 19)[27]
2.4.7 Type 7 (*hariharātmakadvādaśaliṅgatobhadra*) (fol. 16b.2–10) (Illustration 20)
2.4.8 Type 8 (*hariharātmaka/[harihara]dvādaśaliṅgatobhadra*) (fols. 16b.10–17a.6) (Illustration 21)
2.4.9 Type 9 (*latāliṅgatobhadra*)[28] (fol. 17a.6–12) (Illustration 22)
2.4.10 Type 10 (*liṅgasvastikabhadra*) 1 (fol. 17a.12–17b.5) (Illustration 23)
2.4.11 Type 11 (*liṅgasvastikabhadra*) 2 (fols. 17b.5–18a.4)
2.4.12 Type 12 (*navanābhapadmasvastikamaṇḍala*) (fol. 18a.4–11)
2.5 Ṣoḍaśaliṅgatobhadras (fols. 18a.11–19a.3)[29]
2.5.1 Type 1 (fol. 18a.11–18b.10) (Illustration 26)
2.5.2 Type 2 (*ṣoḍaśaliṅgodbhavahariharamaṇḍala*) (fols. 18b.10–19a.3) (Illustration 27)
2.6 Saptadaśaliṅgatobhadras (fol. 19a.3–19b.12)
2.6.1 Type 1 (fol. 19a.3–13) (Illustration 28)
2.6.2 Type 2 (fol. 19a.13–19b.3) (Illustration 29)
2.6.3 Type 3 (fol. 19b.3–12) (Illustration 30)
2.7 Caturviṃśatiliṅgatobhadra (fols. 19b.12–20a.6) (Illustration 31)
2.8 Aṣṭāviṃśatiliṅgatobhadra (fol. 20a.7–8) (Illustration 32)
2.9 Pañcaviṃśatiliṅgatobhadras (fol. 20a.8–20b.13)
2.9.1 Type 1 (fol. 20a.8–20b.3) (Illustration 33)
2.9.2 Type 2 (fol. 20b.3–13) (Illustration 34)
2.10 Aṣṭottaraśataliṅgatobhadras (fols. 20b.13–22a.6)
2.10.1 Type 1 (fols. 20b.13–21b.10) (Illustration 35)
2.10.2 Type 2 (fols. 21b.10–22a.6)

---

[27] A variation of this maṇḍala is reproduced in Mookerjee 1971: 54 (plate 32).

[28] For a drawing of the *latāliṅgodbhavamaṇḍala*, see also Rao 1988–1992, volume 5: 23.

[29] Vergati 1982: 58 reproduces a *ṣoḍaśaliṅgatobhadra* from the sketchbook of the painter Vishnu Bahadur Chitrakar of Bhaktapur, Nepal. The *bhadra* differs from the two types explained in the BM and is erroneously labelled *sarvatobhadra* on p. 59.

2.11 Ekaviṃśottaraśataliṅgatobhadras (fols. 22a.6–23a.14)
2.11.1 Type 1 (fols. 22a.6–23a.4) (Illustration 37)
2.11.2 Type 2 (fol. 23a.5–14)
2.12 Aṣṭottarasahasraliṅgatobhadras (fols. 23a.14–24b.11)
2.12.1 Type 1 (fols. 23a.14–24a.8)
2.12.2 Type 2 (fol. 24a.8–24b.11)
3 Rāmabhadras (fols. 24b.11–32a.9)
3.0 List of deities to be invoked (fols. 24b.11–26a.8)
3.1 Ekamudrārāmatobhadra (fol. 26a.8–26b.7) (Illustration 41)
3.2 Caturmudrārāmaliṅgatobhadra (fol. 26b.7–10) (Illustration 42) (see also Colour Plate 7)
3.3 Aṣṭamudrārāmatobhadras (fols. 26b.10–27a.7)
3.3.1 Type 1 (fols. 26b.10–27a.4) (Illustration 43)
3.3.2 Type 2 (*aṣṭamudrārāmaliṅgatobhadra*) (fol. 27a.4–7) (Illustration 44)
3.4 Navamudrārāmatobhadra (fol. 27a.7–10) (Illustration 45)
3.5 Dvādaśamudrārāmaliṅgatobhadra (fol. 27a.10–27b.8) (Illustration 46)
3.6 Trayodaśamudrārāmatobhadra (fol. 27b.8–10) (Illustration 47)
3.7 Laghuṣoḍaśarāmamudrārāmaliṅgatobhadra (fols. 27b.10–28a.7) (Illustration 48)
3.8 Ṣoḍaśamudrārāmatobhadra and *ṣoḍaśamudrārāmaliṅgatobhadra* (fol. 28a.7–10) (Illustration 49)
3.9 Caturviṃśatimudrārāmatobhadra (fol. 28a.11–13)
3.10 Pañcaviṃśatimudrārāmaliṅgatobhadra (fol. 28a.14–28b.1)
3.11 Aṣṭottaraśatarāmaliṅgatobhadra (fol. 28b.2–9) (Illustration 52)
3.12 Śatarāmaliṅgatobhadra (fol. 28b.9–11) (Illustration 53)
3.13 Śatamudrārāmatobhadra (fol. 28b.11–13)
3.14 Aṣṭottaraśatarāmatobhadra (fols. 28b.13–29a.3)
3.15 Aṣṭottaraśatarāmaliṅgatobhadras (differing from 3.11) (fol. 29a.3–29b.10)
3.15.1 General description (fol. 29a.3–14)
3.15.2 Variation 1 (fol. 29a.14–29b.5)
3.15.3 Variation 2 (fol. 29b.5–10)
3.16 Aṣṭottarasahasrarāmanāmatobhadra (fols. 29b.10–30a.12)
3.17 Harihararāmaliṅgatobhadra (fol. 30a.12–30b.6)
3.18 Aṣṭottarasahasrarāmatobhadra (fol. 30b.6–14)
3.19 Aṣṭottarasahasrarāmaliṅgatobhadra (fols. 30b.14–31a.11)
3.20 (Aṣṭottara)sahasrarāmatobhadra (fol. 31a.11–12)

3.21 Aṣṭottaraśatarāmatobhadras (fols. 31a.12–32a.8)
3.21.1 Type 1 (fols. 31a.12–32a.2)
3.21.2 Type 2 (fol. 32a.2–8)
4 Pañcabhadra (fol. 32a.9–13) (Illustration 66)
5 Sūryabhadras (fol. 32a.13–32b.12)
5.1 Type 1 (fol. 32a.13–32b.6) (Illustration 67) (see also Colour Plate 10)
5.2 Type 2 (fol. 32b.6–12) (Illustration 68)
6 Gaṇapatibhadra *vighnamarda* (fols. 32b.12–33a.3) (Illustration 69)
7 Cakrāravindamaṇḍala (fols. 33a.3–34a.1) (Illustration 70)
8 Svastikamaṇḍala (fol. 34a.1–34a.5) (Illustration 71)
9 Liṅgatobhadras for special occasions and for the attainment of specific objectives (fols. 34a.5–35b.9)
9.1 Trayodaśaliṅgasamudbhavamaṇḍala (fol. 34a.5–10) (Illustration 72)
9.2 Caturdaśaliṅgatobhadra (fol. 34a.10–34b.6) (Illustration 73)
9.3 Viṃśatiliṅgatobhadra (fols. 34b.6–35a.1) (Illustration 74)
9.4 Catvāriṃśalliṅgatobhadra (fol. 35a.1–10) (Illustration 75)
9.5 Ṣaṣṭiliṅgatobhadra (fol. 35a.10–35b.9) (Illustration 76)
0 Colophon (fols. 35b.9–36a.3)

Figure 1. Basic square unit *(pada, koṣṭha)*

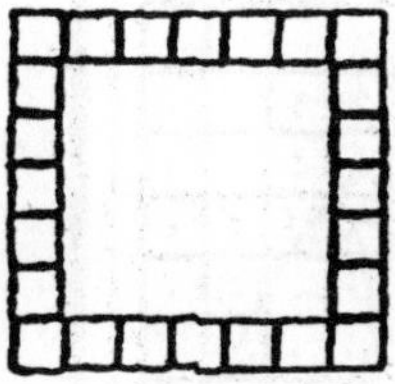

Figure 2. 'Enclosure' *(paridhi)*

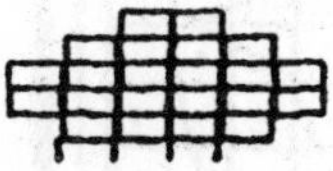

Figure 3. 'Well' *(vāpī)*

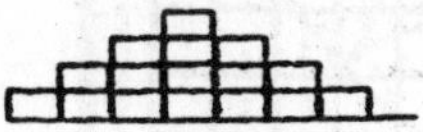

Figure 4. 'Offset' *(bhadra)*

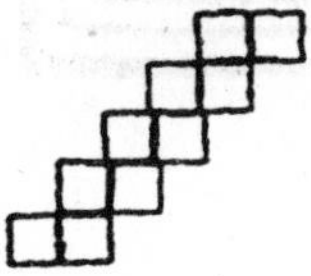

Figure 5. 'Creeper' *(vallī)*

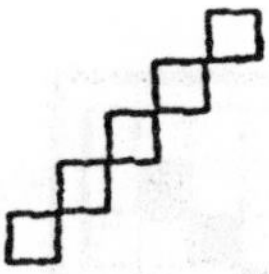

Figure 6. 'Chain' *(śṛṅkhalā)*

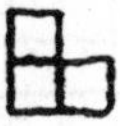

Figure 7. 'Crescent moon' *(khaṇḍendu)*

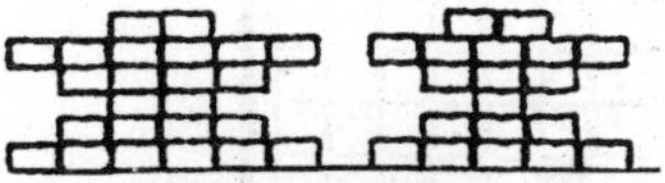

Figure 8. Phallic symbol *(liṅga)* of Śiva

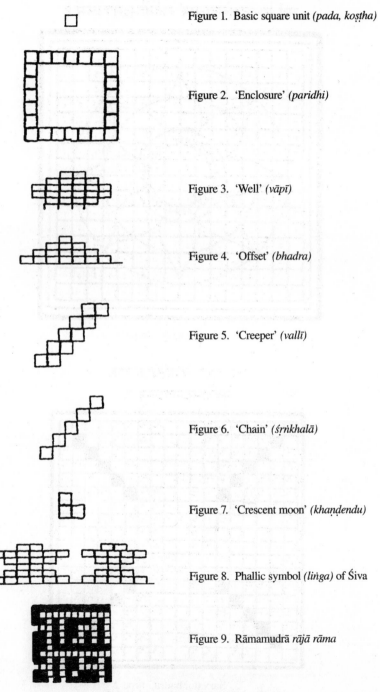

Figure 9. Rāmamudrā *rājā rāma*

Table: Constituent Parts of the Bhadras

अथ सप्तदशरेखात्मकं सर्वतोभद्रमण्डलम् १

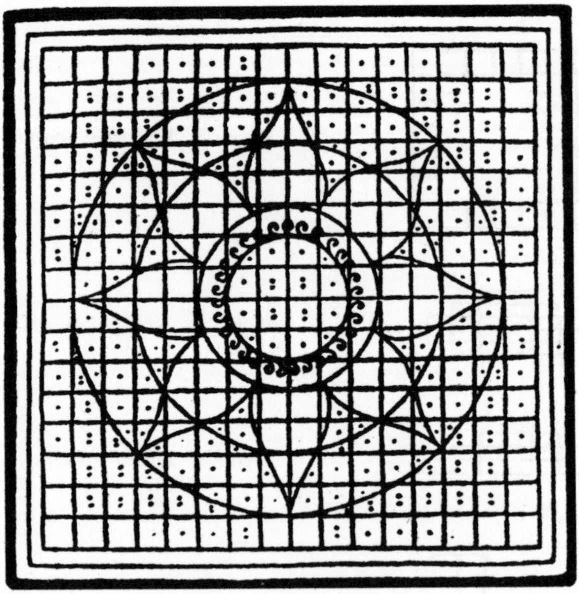

1. Sarvatobhadra, type 1

अथ एकोनविंशतिरेखात्मकं
सर्वतोभद्रमण्डलम् २

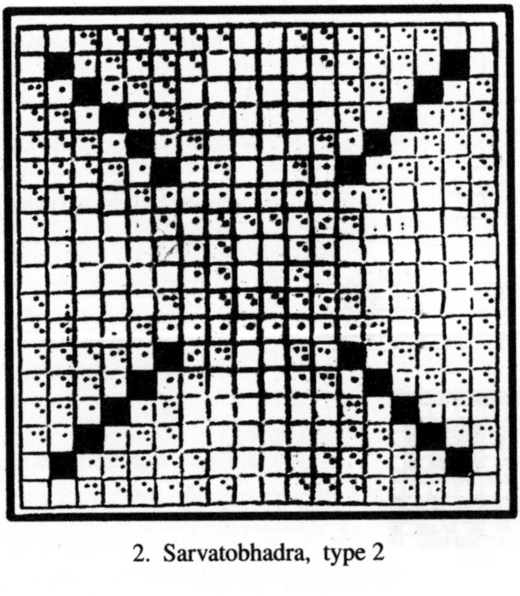

2. Sarvatobhadra, type 2

अथाष्टदलाख्यं मण्डलम् ३

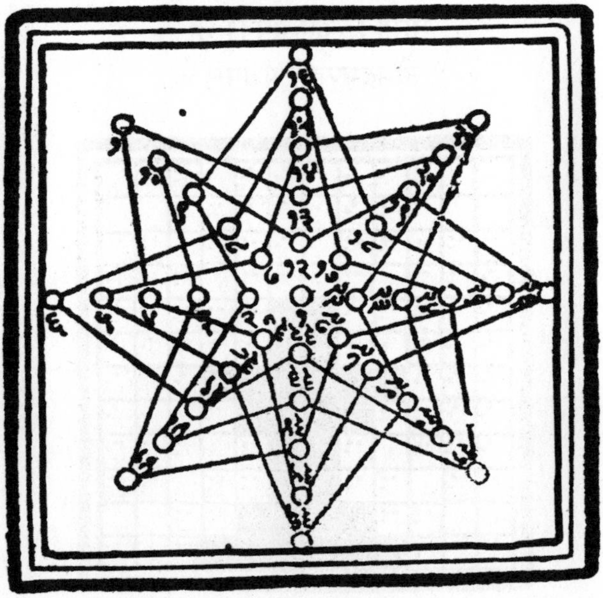

3. Sarvatobhadra, type 3

अथ त्रयोविंशतिरेखात्मकं सर्वतोभद्रमण्डलम् ४

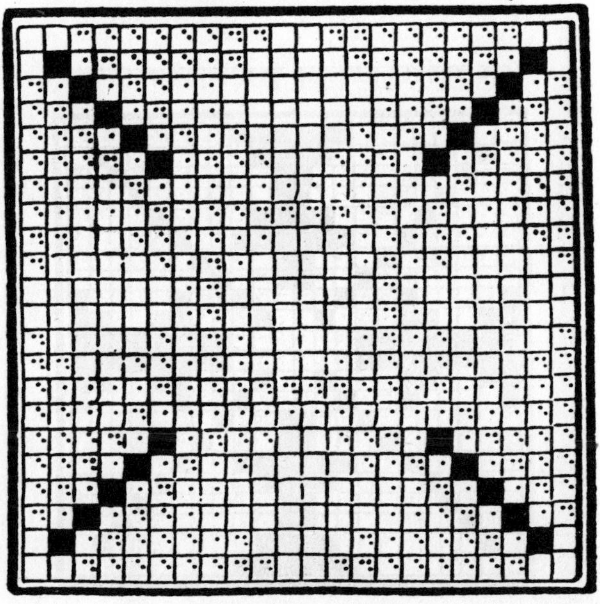

4. Sarvatobhadra, type 4

अथ त्रयोदशरेखात्मकं लघु-
गौरीतिलकाख्यमेकलिङ्ग-
तोभद्रमण्डलं पञ्चमम् ५

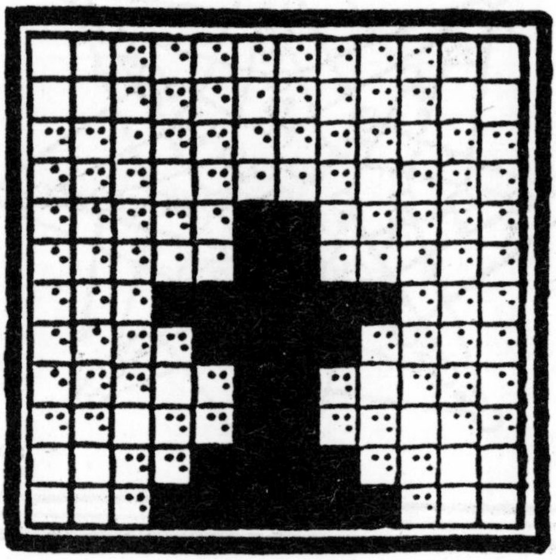

5. Ekaliṅgatobhadra *laghugaurītilaka*

अथ त्रयोविंशतिरेखात्मकं बृहद्गौरीतिलकमण्डलम् ६

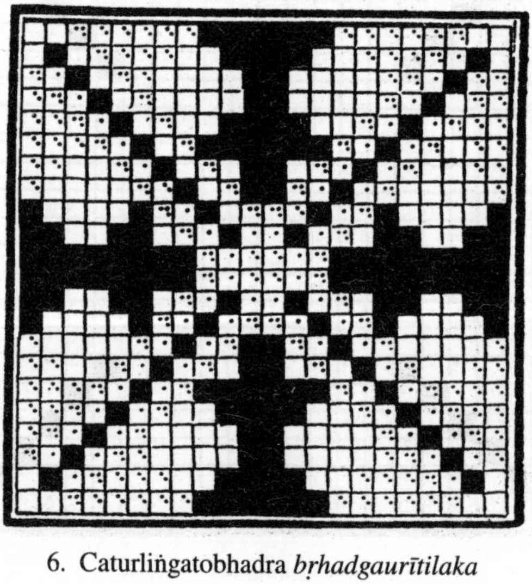

6. Caturliṅgatobhadra *bṛhadgaurītilaka*

अथ सप्तविंशतिरेखात्मकं गौरीतिलकमण्डलम् ७

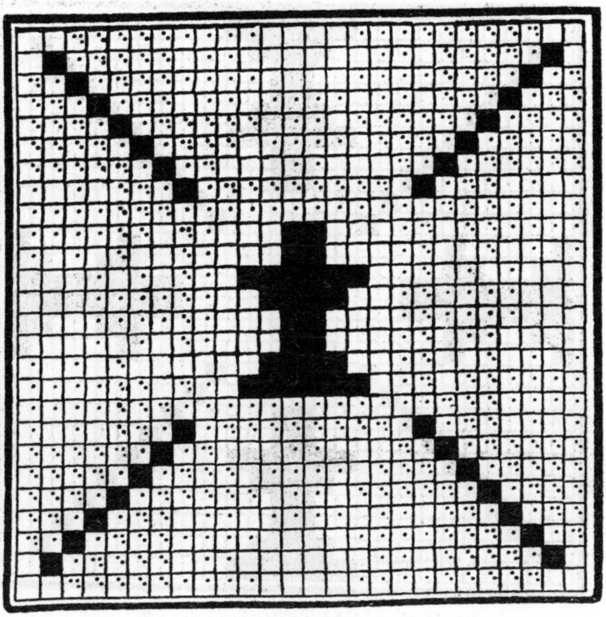

7. Gaurītilaka

अष्टादशरेखात्मकं चतुर्लिङ्गतोभद्रमण्डलम् ८

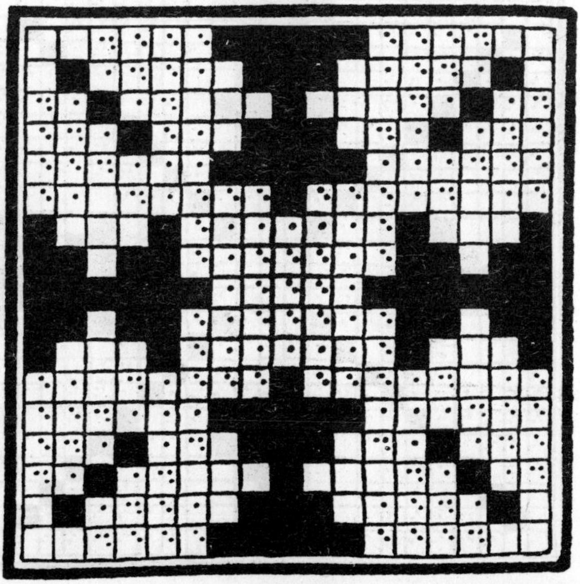

8. Caturliṅgatobhadra, type 1

सप्तविंशतिरेखात्मकं चतुर्लिङ्गतोभद्रमण्डलम् ९

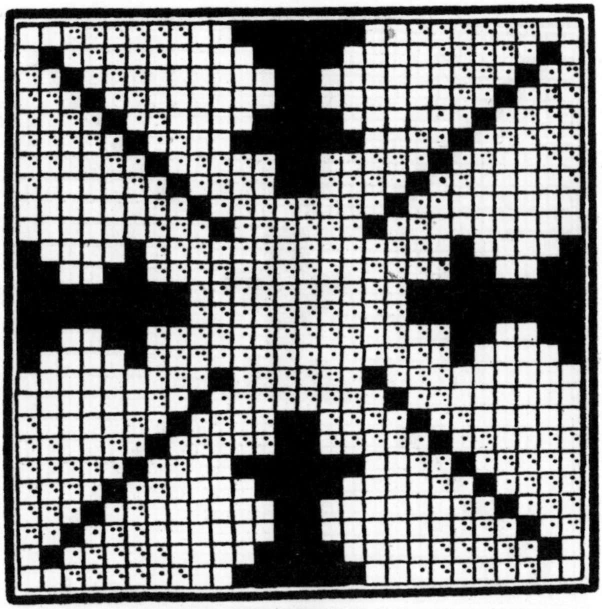

9. Caturliṅgatobhadra, type 2

अथ चतुर्विंशतिरेखात्मकं चतुर्लिङ्गतोभद्रमण्डलम् १०

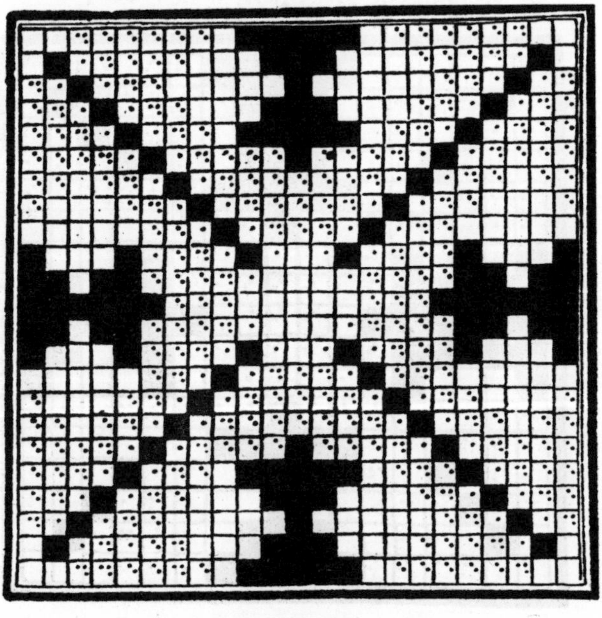

10. Caturliṅgatobhadra, type 3

द्वाविंशतिरेखात्मकं चतुर्लिङ्गतोभद्रमण्डलम् ११

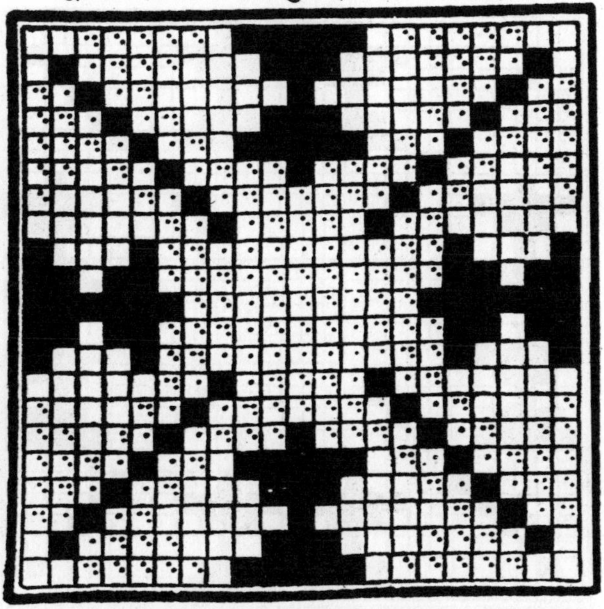

11. Caturliṅgatobhadra, type 4

चतुर्विंशतिरेखात्मकमष्टलिङ्गतोभद्रमण्डलम् १२

12. Aṣṭaliṅgatobhadra, type 1

अष्टाविंशतिरेखात्मकमष्टलिङ्गतोभद्रमण्डलम् १३

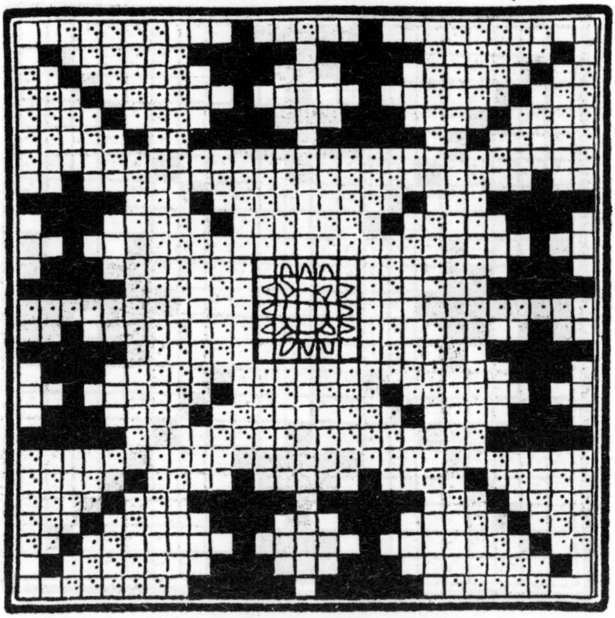

13. Aṣṭaliṅgatobhadra, type 2

अथ चतुस्त्रिंशद्रेखात्मकं द्वादशलिङ्गतोभद्रमण्डलम् १४

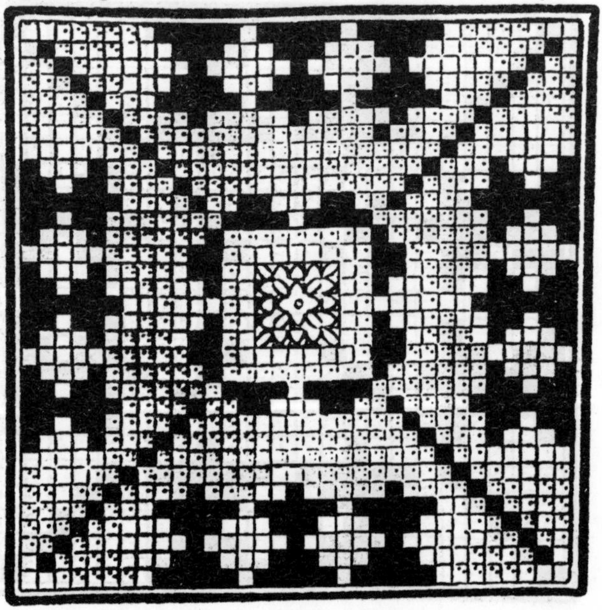

14. Dvādaśaliṅgatobhadra, type 1

अथ पञ्चत्रिंशद्रेखात्मकं द्वादशलिङ्गतोभद्रमण्डलम् १५

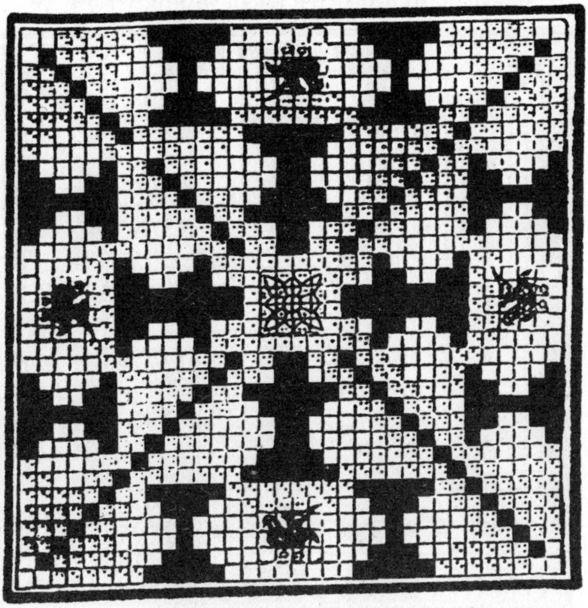

15. Dvādaśaliṅgatobhadra, type 2

पञ्चत्रिंशद्रेखात्मकं द्वादशलिङ्गतोभद्रमण्डलम् १६

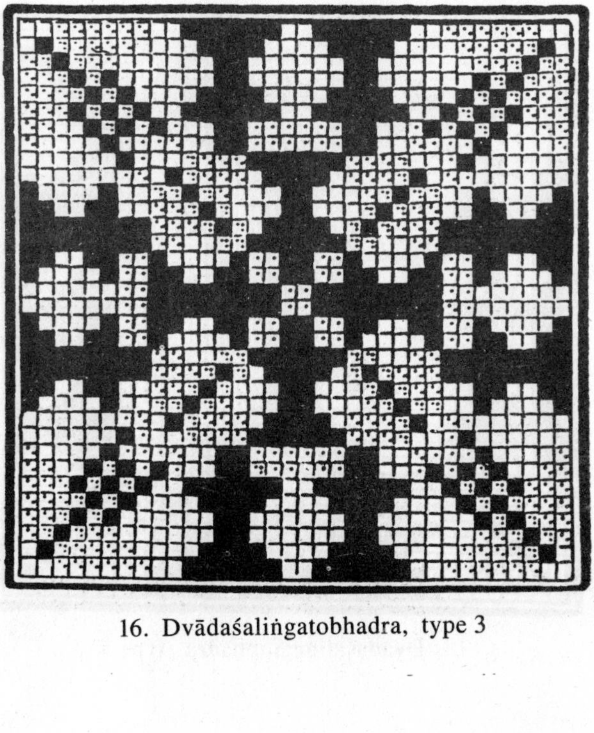

16. Dvādaśaliṅgatobhadra, type 3

षट्त्रिंशद्रेखायुतं हरिहरात्मकं द्वादशलिङ्गतोभद्रमण्डलम् १७

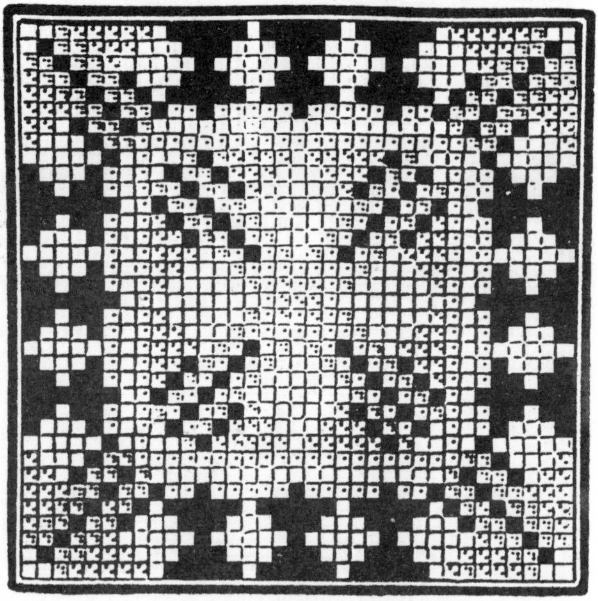

17. Dvādaśaliṅgatobhadra, type 4

अथ सप्तत्रिंशद्रेखात्मकं द्वादशलिङ्गतोभद्रमण्डलम् १८

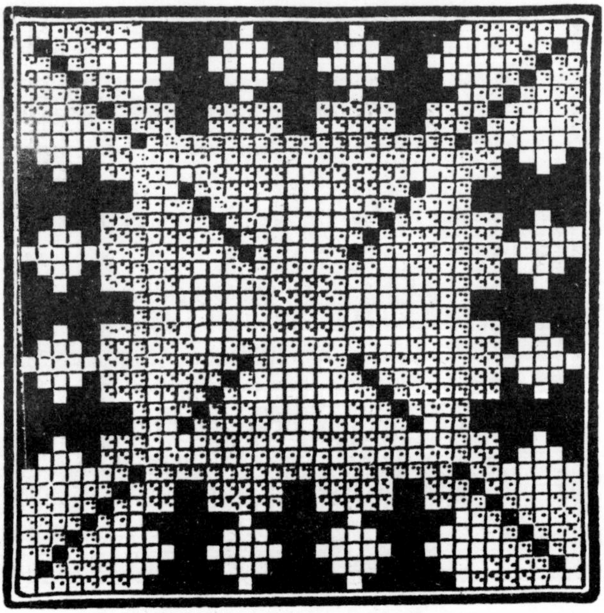

18. Dvādaśaliṅgatobhadra, type 5

अथ ४३ रेखात्मकं हरिहरात्मकं द्वादशलिङ्गतोभद्रमण्डलम् १९

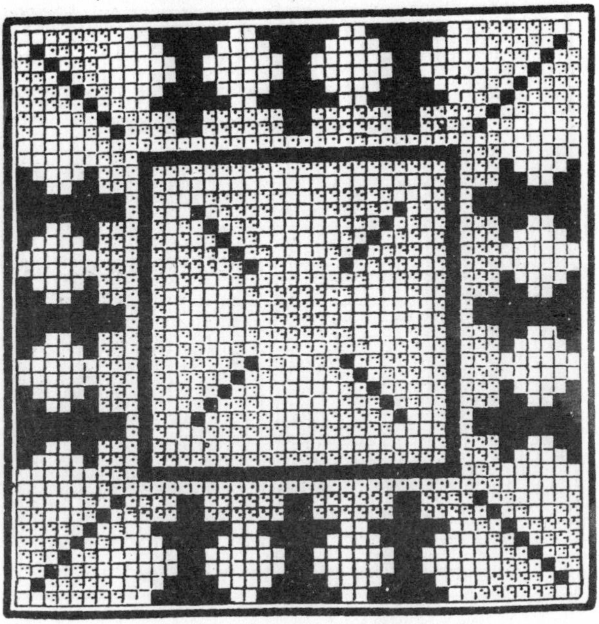

19. Dvādaśaliṅgatobhadra, type 6

३३ रेखात्मकं हरिहरात्मकं द्वादशलिङ्गतोभद्रमण्डलम् २०

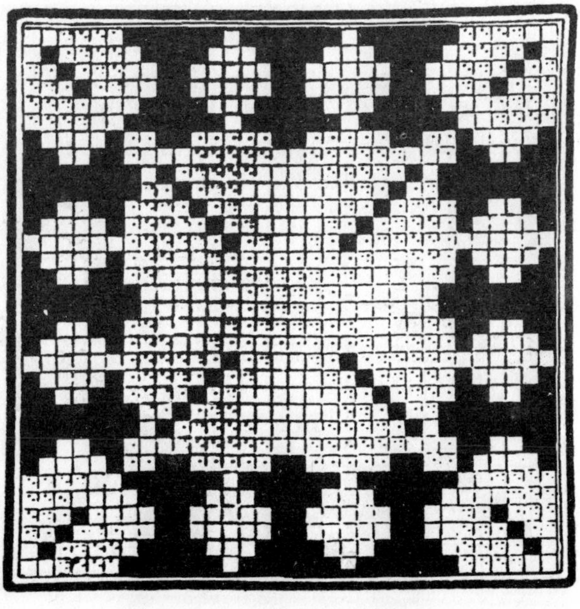

20. Dvādaśaliṅgatobhadra, type 7

अथ ३७ रेखात्मकं हरिहरात्मकं द्वादशलिङ्गतोभद्रमण्डलम् २१

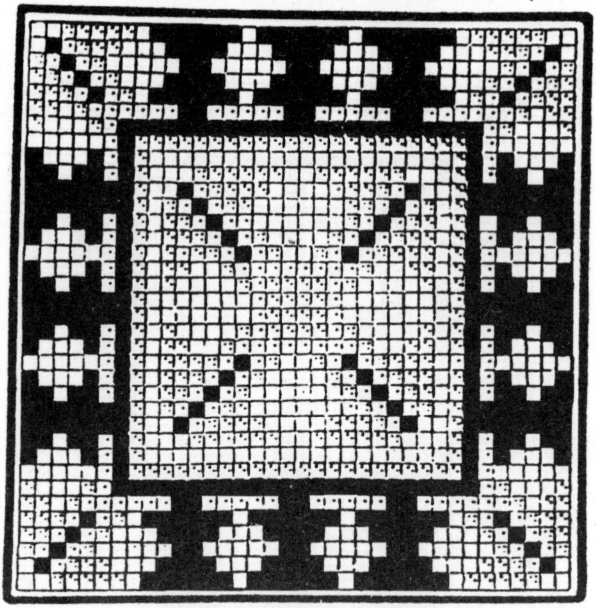

21. Dvādaśaliṅgatobhadra, type 8

अथ २२ रेखात्मकं लतालिङ्गतोभद्रमण्डलम् २२

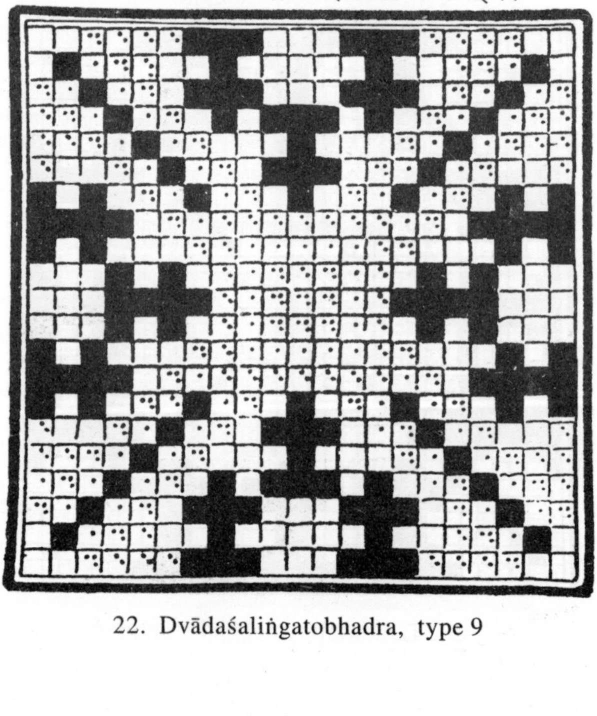

22. Dvādaśaliṅgatobhadra, type 9

अथ २४ रेखात्मकं लिङ्गस्वस्तिकं भद्रमण्डलम् २३

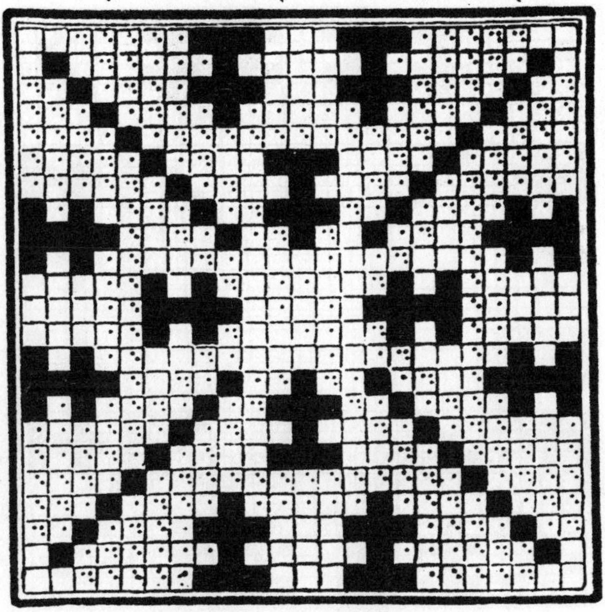

23. Dvādaśaliṅgatobhadra, type 10

अथ ३७ रेखात्मकं षोडशलिङ्गतोभद्रमण्डलम् २६

26. Ṣoḍaśaliṅgatobhadra, type 1

अथ २९ रेखात्मकं हरिहरात्मकं षोडशलिङ्गतोभद्रमण्डलम् २७

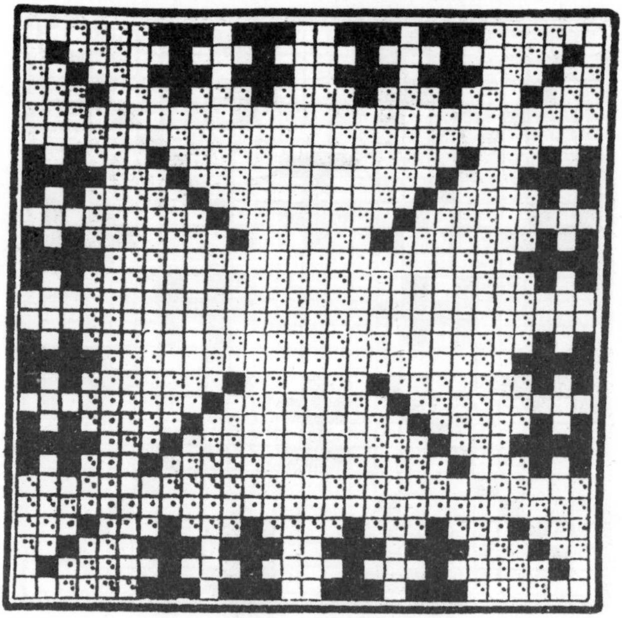

27. Ṣoḍaśaliṅgatobhadra, type 2

अथ ४० रेखात्मकं सप्तदशलिङ्गतोभद्रमण्डलम् २८

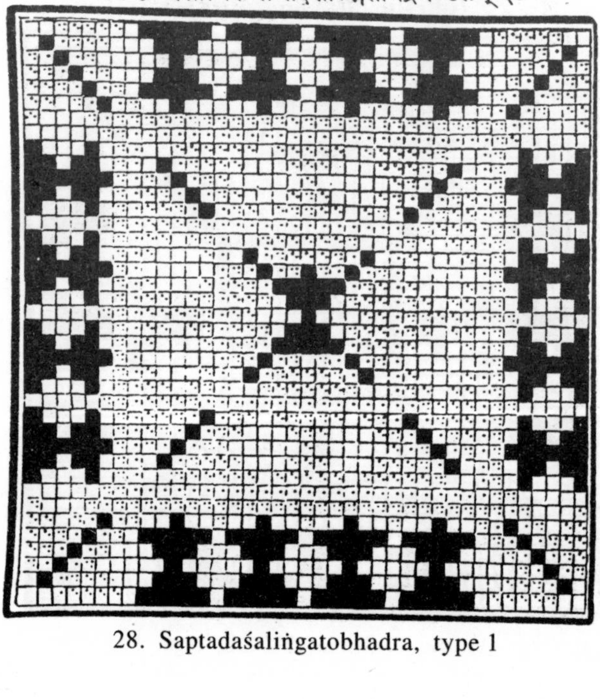

28. Saptadaśaliṅgatobhadra, type 1

अथ ४० रेखात्मकं सप्तदशलिङ्गतोभद्रमण्डलम् २९

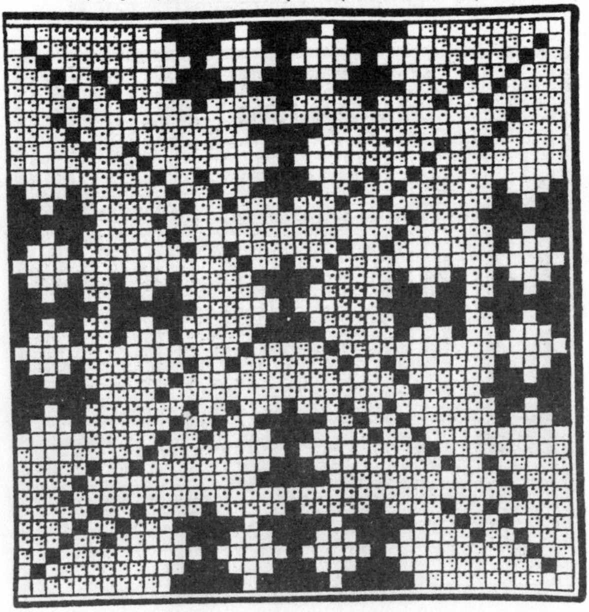

29. Saptadaśaliṅgatobhadra, type 2

अथ ४३ रेखात्मकं सप्तदशलिङ्गतोभद्रमण्डलम् ३०

30. Saptadaśaliṅgatobhadra, type 3

अथ ४२ रेखात्मकं चतुर्विंशतिलिङ्गतोभद्रमण्डलम् ३१

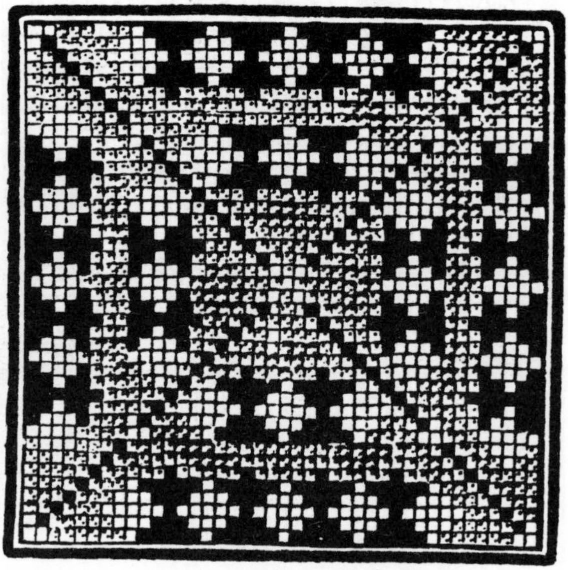

31. Caturviṃśatiliṅgatobhadra

अथ ४२ रेखात्मकम् अष्टाविंशतिलिङ्गतोभद्रमण्डलम् ३२

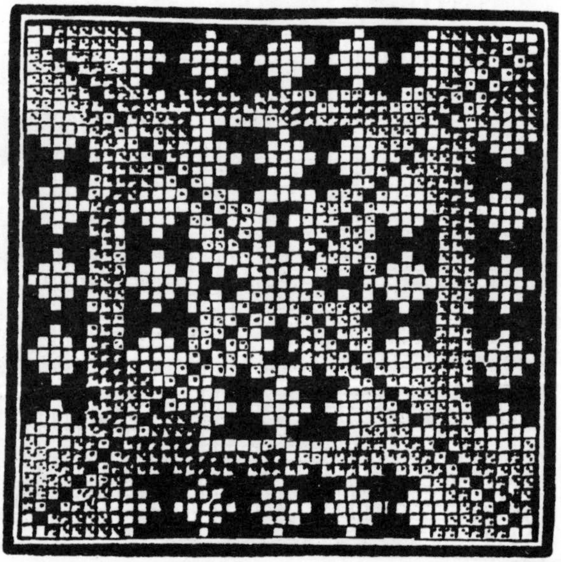

32. Aṣṭāviṃśatiliṅgatobhadra

अथ ५५ रेखात्मकं पञ्चविंशतिलिङ्गतोभद्रमण्डलम् ३३

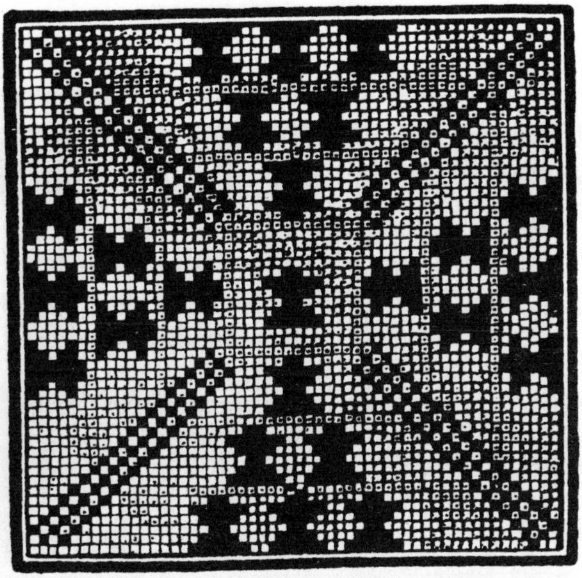

33. Pañcaviṃśatiliṅgatobhadra, type 1

अथ ४२ रेखात्मकं पञ्चविंशतिलिङ्गतोभद्रमण्डलम् ३४

34. Pañcaviṃśatiliṅgatobhadra, type 2

अथ ८६ रेखात्मकम् अष्टोत्तरशतलिङ्गतोभद्रमण्डलम् ३५ अग्रे प्रकारान्तरस्य स्वल्पान्तरत्वाद्ग्रन्थविस्तरभयाच्च न स्पष्टीकृतम् ३६

35. Aṣṭottaraśataliṅgatobhadra, type 2

अथ अष्टाशीतिरेखात्मकमेकविंशोत्तरशतलिङ्गतोभद्रमण्डलम् ३७ + अष्टत्रिंशत्तममण्डलस्य स्वल्पान्तरत्वान्न स्पष्टीकृतं ग्रन्थविस्तरभयाच्च ३८

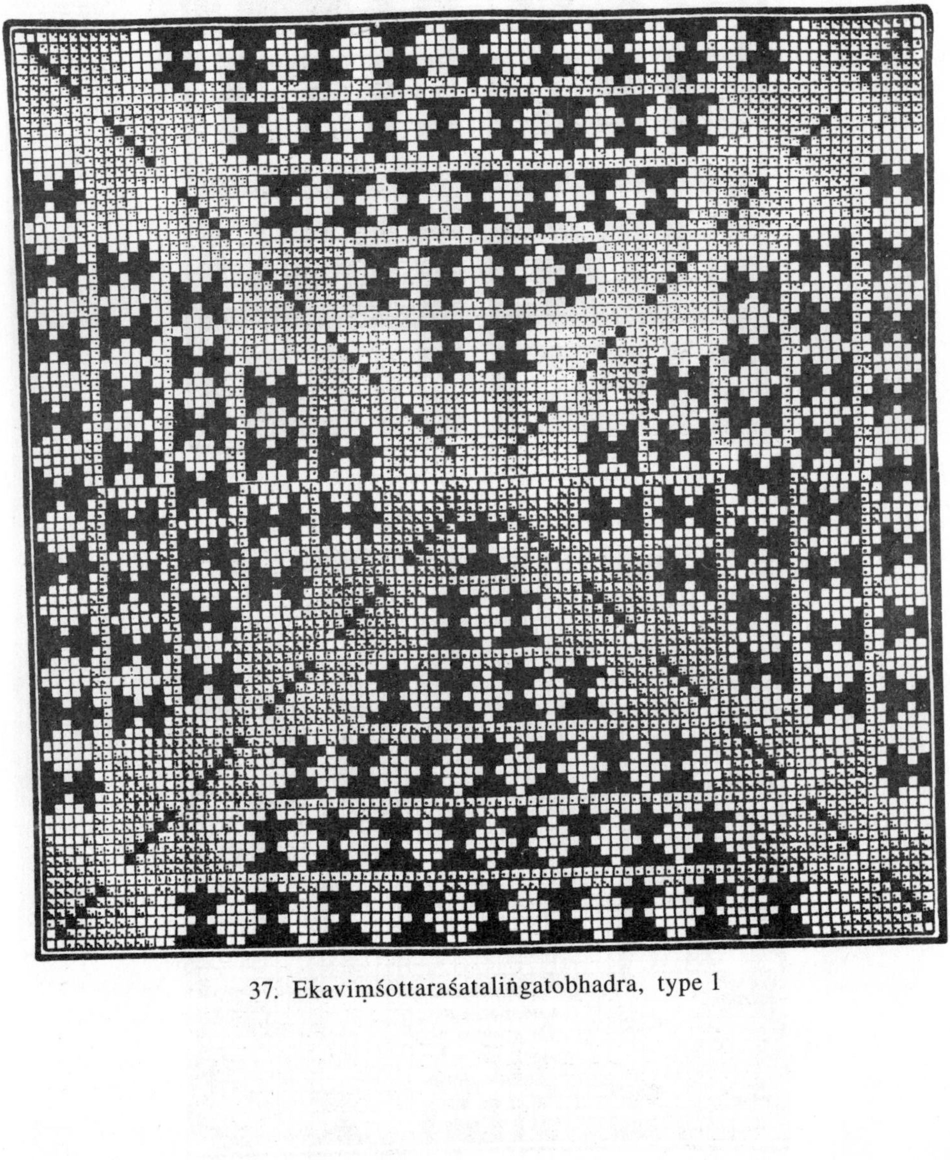

37. Ekaviṃśottaraśataliṅgatobhadra, type 1

अथ २६ रेखात्मकमेकमुद्रारामतोभद्रमण्डलम् ४१

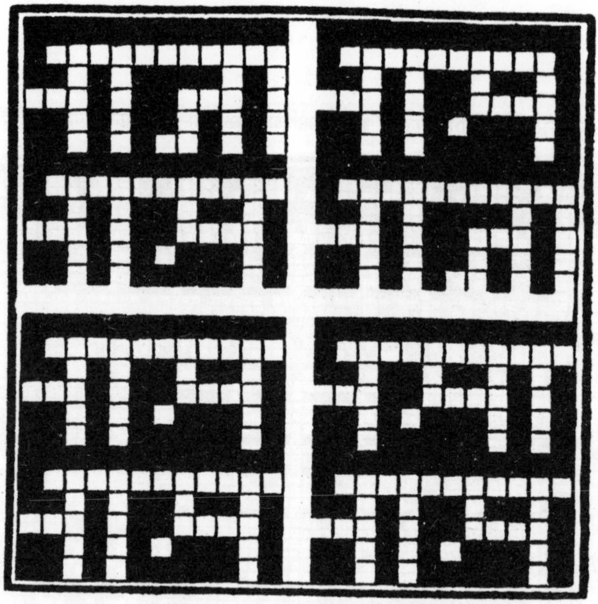

41. Ekamudrārāmatobhadra

अथ ५३ रेखात्मकं चतुर्मुद्रारामलिङ्गतोभद्रमण्डलम् ४२

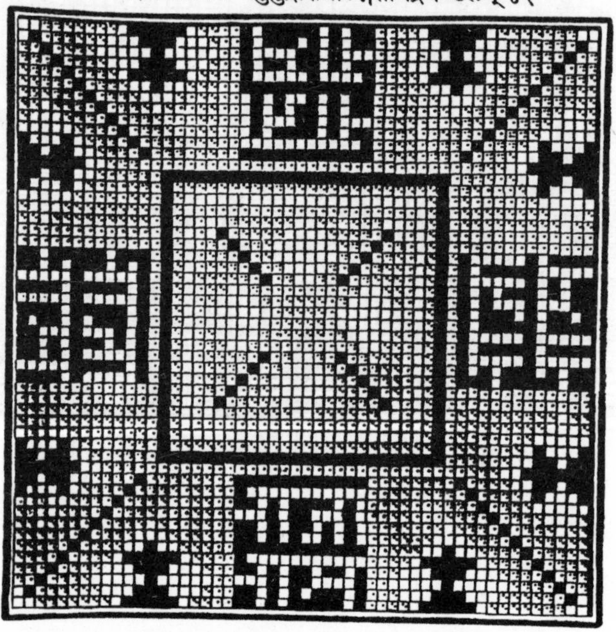

42. Caturmudrārāmaliṅgatobhadra

अथ ६१ रेखात्मकम् अष्टमुद्रारामतोभद्रमण्डलम् ४३

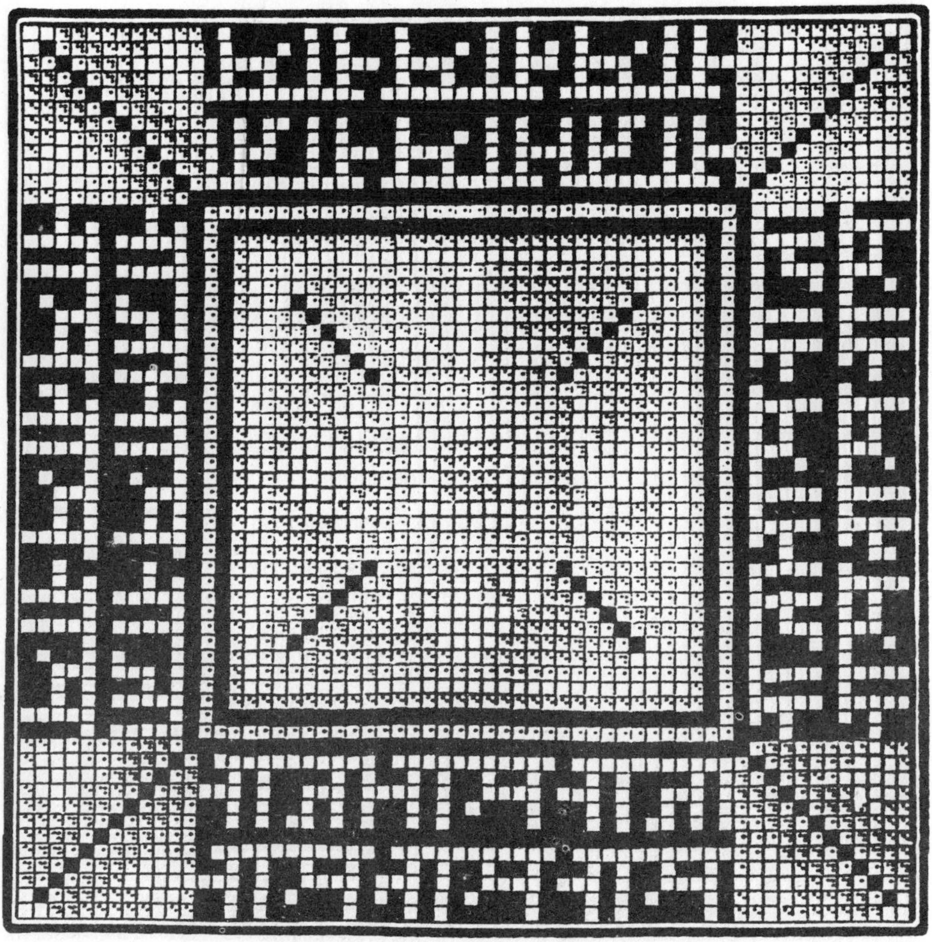

43. Aṣṭamudrārāmatobhadra, type 1

अथ ६१ रेखात्मकम् अष्टमुद्रारामलिङ्गतोभद्रमण्डलम् ४४

44. Aṣṭamudrārāmatobhadra, type 2

अथ ७९ रेखात्मकं नवमुद्रारामलिङ्गतोभद्रमण्डलम् ४५

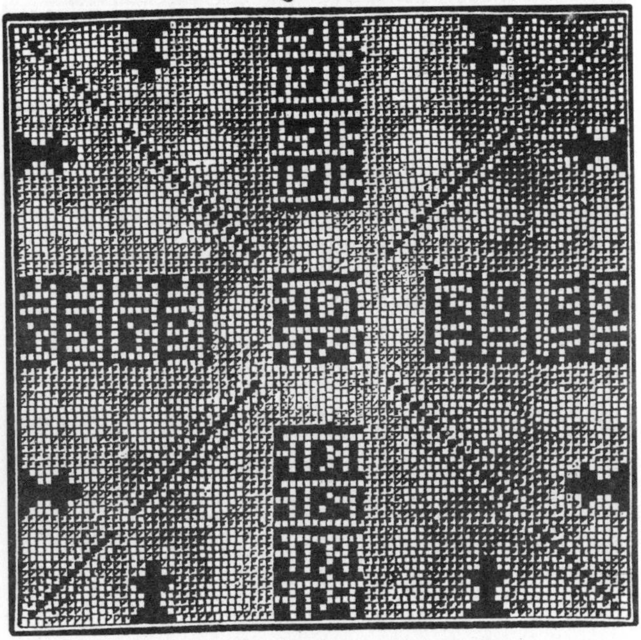

45. Navamudrārāmatobhadra

अथ ७३ रेखात्मकं द्वादशमुद्रारामलिङ्गतोभद्रमण्डलम् ४६

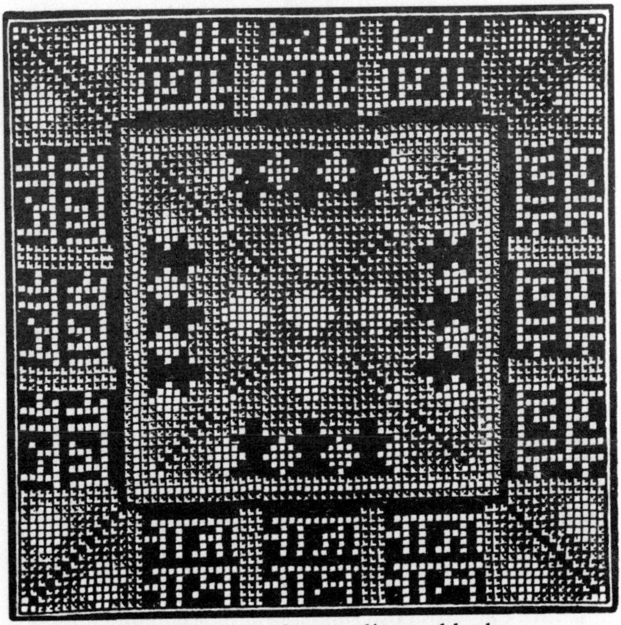

46. Dvādaśamudrārāmaliṅgatobhadra

अथ ७९ रेखात्मकं त्रयोदशमुद्रारामलिङ्गतोभद्रमण्डलम् ४७

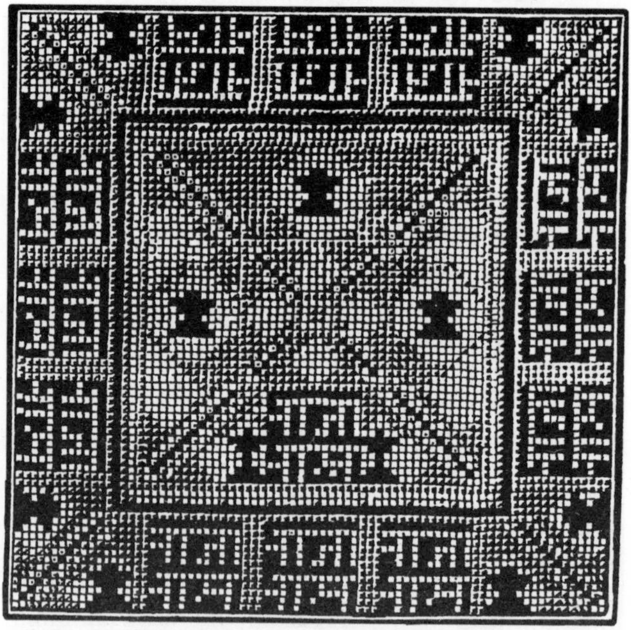

47. Trayodaśamudrārāmatobhadra

अथ ५१ रेखात्मकलघुषोडशमुद्रारामलिङ्गतोभद्रमण्डलम् ४८

48. Laghuṣoḍaśarāmamudrārāmaliṅgatobhadra

अथ ७९ रेखात्मकं षोडशमुद्रारामतोभद्रमण्डलम् ४९

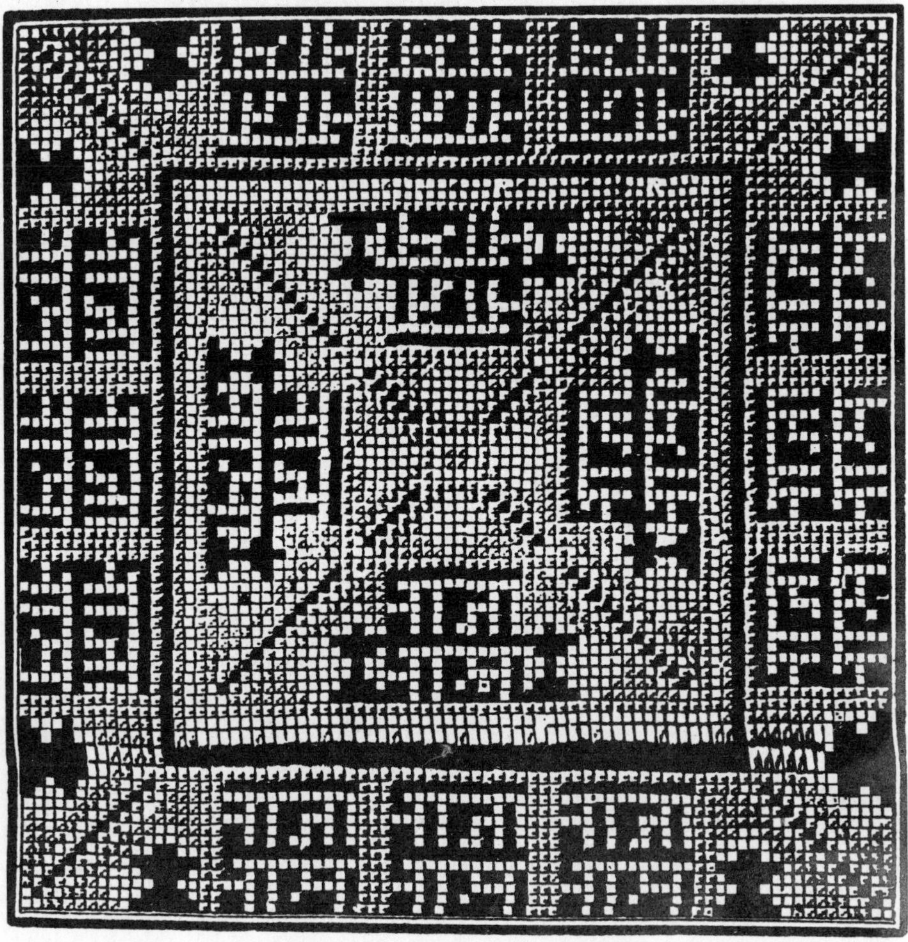

49. Ṣoḍaśamudrārāmatobhadra

अथ २०३ रेखात्मकम् अष्टोत्तरशतराममुद्रालिङ्गतोभद्रमण्डलम् ५२ एवमग्रे स्वबुद्ध्या अन्यान्यपि मण्डलानि कर्तव्यानि ग्रन्थविस्तरभयान्नात्रोच्यते.

52. Aṣṭottaraśatarāmaliṅgatobhadra

अथ ११ रेखात्मकं पञ्च-
भद्रमण्डलम् ६६

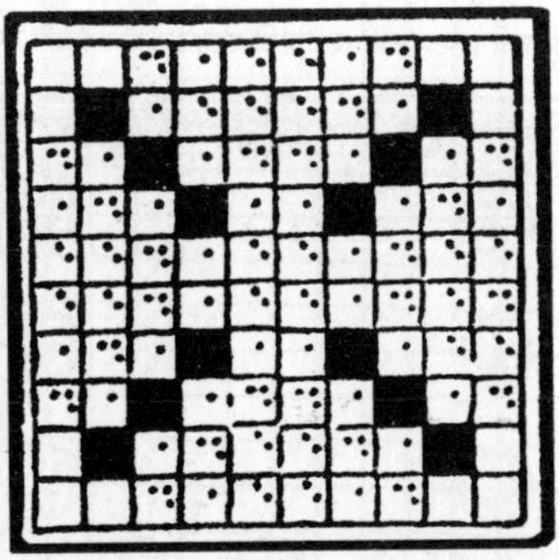

66. Pañcabhadra

अथ २० रेखात्मकं सूर्यभद्रमण्डलम् ६७

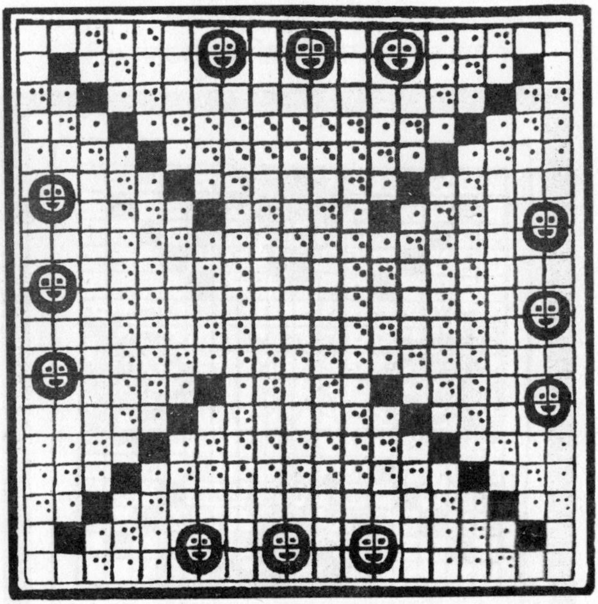

67. Sūryabhadra, type 1

अथ २१ रेखात्मकं सूर्यभद्रमण्डलम् ६८

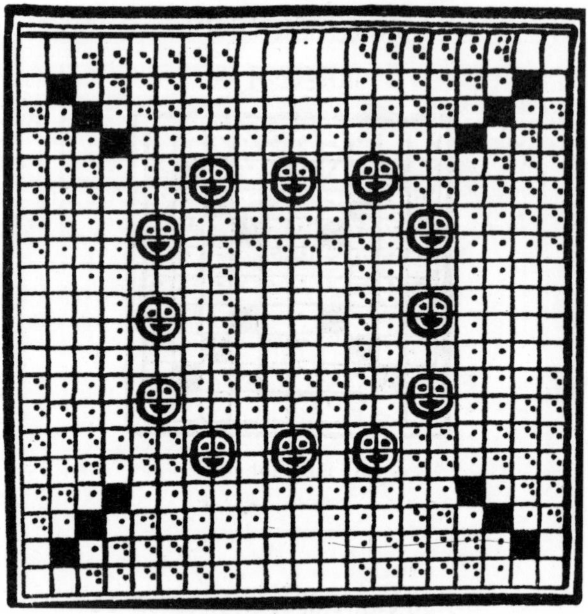

68. Sūryabhadra, type 2

अथ १७ रेखात्मकं गणपतिभद्रमण्डलम् ६९

69. Gaṇapatibhadra *vighnamarda*

अथ चक्रारविन्दमण्डलम् ७०

70. Cakrāravindamaṇḍala

अथ स्वस्तिकमण्डलम् ७१

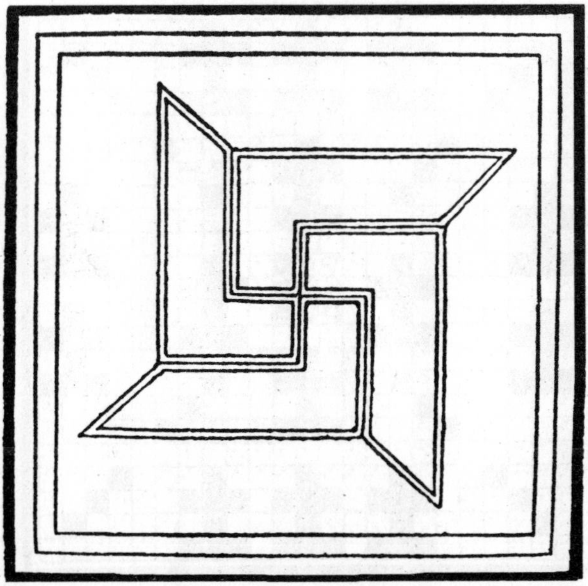

71. Svastikamaṇḍala

अथ २० रेखात्मकं त्रयोदशलिङ्गतोभद्रमण्डलम् ७२

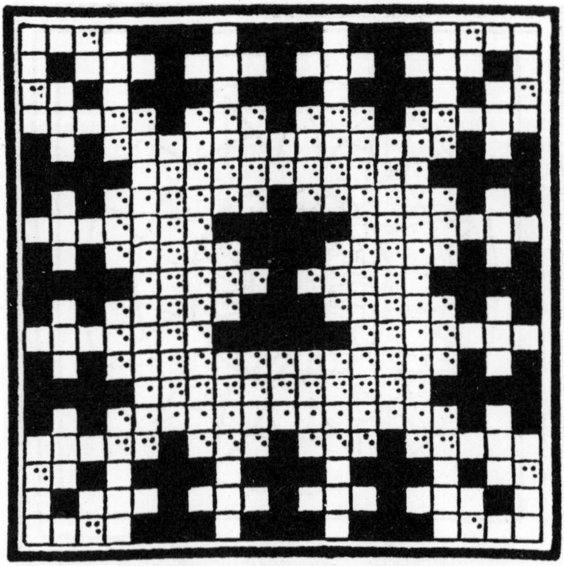

72. Trayodaśaliṅgasamudbhavamaṇḍala

अथ २४ रेखात्मकं चतुर्दशलिङ्गतोभद्रमण्डलम् ७३

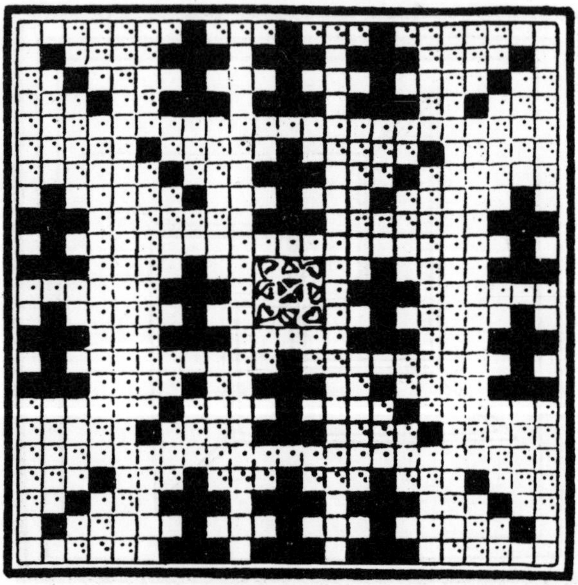

73. Caturdaśaliṅgatobhadra

अथ २८ विंशतिरेखात्मकं विंशतिलिङ्गतोभद्रमण्डलम् ७४

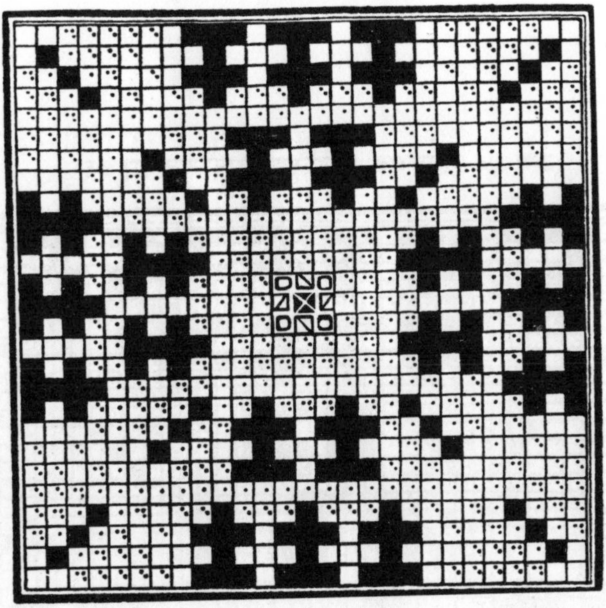

74. Viṃśatiliṅgatobhadra

अथ ३६ रेखात्मकं चत्वारिंशल्लिङ्गतोभद्रमण्डलम् ७५

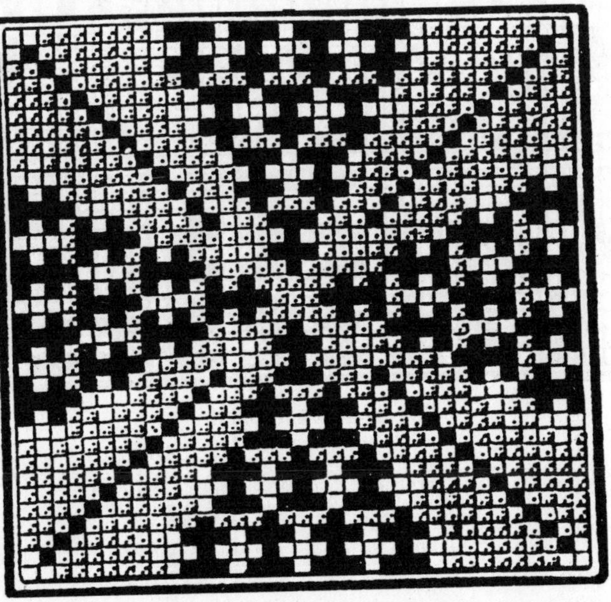

75. Catvāriṃśalliṅgatobhadra

अथ ४८ रेखात्मकं षष्टिलिङ्गतोभद्रमण्डलम् ७६.

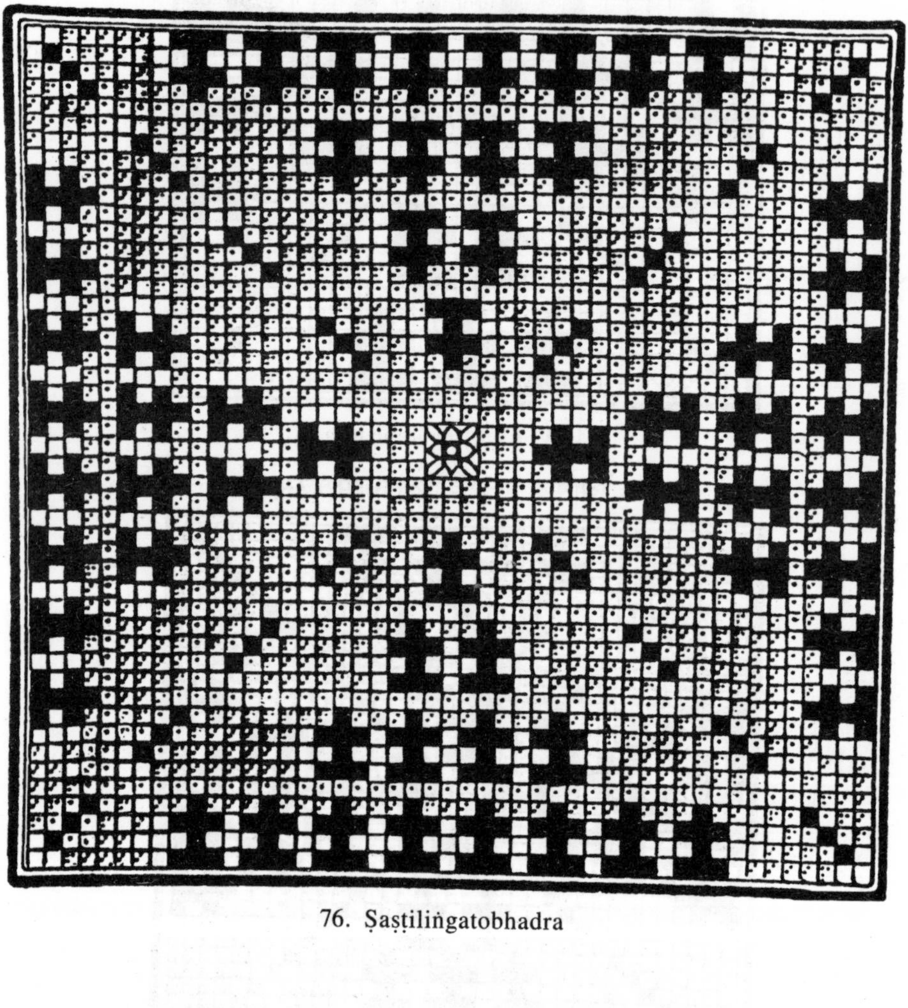

76. Ṣaṣṭiliṅgatobhadra

MAṆḌALAS AND YANTRAS IN THE PĀÑCARĀTRA TRADITION*

Marion Rastelli

This paper deals with the preparation and use of maṇḍalas and yantras in the Pāñcarātra tradition. The sources for this investigation are the Pāñcarātra Saṃhitās as far as they have been edited and were available to me.

Both maṇḍalas and yantras are diagram-like, often symmetric drawings that are invested with mantras. A maṇḍala, also called *pura*, *yāga*, and cakra,[1] is usually prepared by means of applying powder upon an immobile place. It serves as a place of worship. The deity is made present in the maṇḍala by imposing mantras that represent him and his aspects upon it, and he can then be ritually worshipped there.

A yantra is usually drawn upon a mobile material and can thus be carried around. Mantras are written on it, and the drawing and the mantras form an integrated whole that represents the deity or one of his aspects. Yantras are often used as amulets, which protect their wearers and help them to the fulfilment of their wishes.

The Construction of Maṇḍalas

Before drawing a maṇḍala, the practitioner must determine a suitable place and prepare it. The Pauṣkara-Saṃhitā, which is to a great part

---

* I am grateful to Cynthia Peck-Kubaczek for reading the English manuscript and suggesting various corrections.

[1] For the usage of the term *pura* for maṇḍalas, cf. Rastelli 2000b: 375, note 57. The term *yāga* is used mainly in the Pauṣkara-Saṃhitā, see, e.g., PauṣS1 2.8c, 4.13d, 14d, 96a, 5.5a. If not indicated otherwise, I use the Pauṣkara-Saṃhitā's edition from 1934, as the new edition from 1991 contains only the first 26 *adhyāyas*. The usage of cakra in the sense of maṇḍala is rare (examples are Parama-Saṃhitā 7.68b, 8.7c, 8c, Pārameśvara-Saṃhitā 17.499a, 501a). In the context of maṇḍalas, cakra more often designates a circle that forms a part of a maṇḍala (Jayākhya-Saṃhitā 30.51c, Parama-Saṃhitā 6.23b, Pādma-Saṃhitā, *caryāpāda* 25.134a).

devoted to maṇḍala construction,[2] provides very elaborate instructions on how this should be done. Places that are suitable for the construction of a maṇḍala are a mountaintop, a cave at the mountaintop, a pleasant forest abounding with trees and herbs, a lovely grove, a lotus-lake, a riverbank, a confluence of two rivers, a ford (*tīrtha*), a temple (*devatāyatana*), a meeting place (*goṣṭha*), and a hermitage of Brahmins that is free from evil beings, thieves, diseases, and dangers.[3] In general, these places are considered sacred, and similar lists are also given for places that are suitable for worship of the deity's descents (*avatāra*).[4]

It is important that the chosen place is without any faults as otherwise worship performed there would not bring the desired results.[5] Free from any faults means, according to the Pauṣkara-Saṃhitā, that the place should be provided with auspicious trees, fruits, flowers, soft young grass, tender herbs, and various species of lotuses. It should be pleasant to the touch and be supplied with cooling water, fragrances, and good flavours. It should not be saline, burnt by fire, a meteor or sunrays, or vile-smelling. The place should bestow ease, peace, and delight like the sight of one's beloved. It should be inhabited by beautiful birds, cows, deer, tigers, elephants, and human beings, and should be free of evil creatures. East of the place there should be a lake, west of it a forest of mango trees, north of it a large thicket and south of it a mountain. Moreover, in the north or north-east of it there should be a well or a water tank. The soil should be even and inclined to the north-east, of a single colour and free of serpents and similar creatures. In the summer it should be as cool as the moon, in the winter, hot, and in the rainy season, without moisture.[6]

---

[2] Maṇḍala construction has been given the same attention in the Pauṣkara-Saṃhitā as temple construction has been given in the later Pādma-Saṃhitā.

[3] PauṣS$_1$ 2.4–7b. For necessary emendations in this passage, see Rastelli 2000a: 120, note 75.

[4] Cf. PauṣS$_1$ 34.1–2 and 36.238–239c. For translations of the three passages of the Pauṣkara-Saṃhitā mentioned here and in note 3, see Rastelli 2000a: 120f.

[5] Cf. PauṣS$_1$ 2.10cd: "However, a faulty soil may produce many obstacles." (*sā tu doṣavatī bhūmir vighnān utpādayed bahūn //*) and 2.26: "Therefore, a different [soil with the] opposite [qualities] always bestows undesired results. [It] should be refused from afar since it inhibits success." (*ato 'nyā viparītā ca sāniṣṭaphaladā sadā / dūrataḥ parihartavyā siddhihānikarī yataḥ //*)

[6] PauṣS$_1$ 2.7c–20b and 24ab. PauṣS$_1$ 2.20b *rasānvā*: *'rasā yā*. Apte's emendation *rasānvitā* is not possible on account of the metre.

As described, this place is certainly an ideal and found only rarely if at all. Other Saṃhitās, being more realistic, make less heavy demands on the place for a maṇḍala and only prescribe that it should be pleasant, even, oriented toward the north-east, and free from thorns and other faults.[7] Even the Pauṣkara-Saṃhitā concedes that if one cannot find a place with all the described qualities, one can also make do with an ordinary one.[8]

Before the construction of the maṇḍala, the soil is tested and prepared just as before the construction of a building.[9] The Pauṣkara-Saṃhitā describes several methods for testing the suitability of the soil (*bhūparīkṣā*). One of these methods is digging a hole and filling it again with the earth taken out of it. The best result is if the earth overfills the hole. It is acceptable if the ground is even after filling the hole, but if the hole cannot be filled with the earth again, the place should be avoided.[10] Another method is to sow a seed. The soil is most suitable if it shoots forth within three days, a medium result is if it shoots forth within five days, the worst if it shoots forth within seven days.[11]

The place is to be worshipped with mantras and oblations and, on an auspicious day, ritually acquired. For this ritual acquisition, one must first distribute *bali* offerings for the cruel beings who are present there in all quarters, and ask them to go away.[12] Then one digs the ground to the water limit and fills it again. After that one grows grass, rice, and shoots of trees. Then one puts a herd of cattle out to pasture for three days. After the three days, the ground is ploughed and filled with burnt bricks. Upon them one scatters gold dust, silver dust, and jewel dust, fragrant flowers, grain, rice, fruits

---

[7] E.g., Jayākhya-Saṃhitā 23.69cd, Viṣṇu-Saṃhitā 9.2.

[8] PauṣS1 2.27.

[9] Cf. PauṣS1 2.7c–8: "At the beginning, he should test if the soil there, which [he has] examined well, is endowed with favourable signs for the sake of a house of gods, for the sake of a village for Brahmins, etc., for the sake of worshipping *yāgas* (i.e., maṇḍalas), for the sake of a house of a householder." (*tatra bhūmiṃ parīkṣyādau lakṣaṇāḍhyāṃ sulakṣitām // 7 devānām ālayārthaṃ tu grāmārthaṃ brāhmaṇādiṣu / yajanārthaṃ tu yāgānāṃ gṛhārthaṃ gṛhamedhinām //* 8)

[10] This procedure is meant to test whether the land is very loose or sandy; cf. Acharya 1946: 384.

[11] PauṣS1 2.21c–23. Pādma-Saṃhitā, *kriyāpāda* 1.32–36 gives the same methods for testing the soil before constructing a temple; cf. also Acharya 1946: 383–385.

[12] PauṣS1 2.30–34c. Cf. Pādma-Saṃhitā, *kriyāpāda* 1.40–49a for this rite before the construction of a temple.

and other substances.[13] The ground is made even, sprinkled with water, rammed by means of pestles, besmeared with clay, cow-dung, and water and swept with the hand or a cloth.[14]

The maṇḍala is to be constructed in a pavilion (*maṇḍapa*) that is adorned with canopies, banners, etc.[15] In the centre of the *maṇḍapa*, a platform (*vedi*) is made of wood and clay and besmeared with the five products of the cow (milk, sour milk, butter, and the liquid and solid excreta) or with cow-dung and water.[16] On the platform, one first draws the x-axis, then the y-axis, the diagonal lines, and the boundary lines in order to obtain a square. This square is divided into several other squares in which the various elements of the maṇḍala are drawn.[17] The preliminary grid is made by means of threads that are besmeared with a substance and thus leave lines on the floor when laid on it.[18] The maṇḍala is drawn by means of strewn powder (*rajas*). First the lines are drawn, and then the pattern is filled with powders in various colours.[19]

While strewing the powder, one must be very careful to apply it evenly. The Viṣṇu-Saṃhitā describes in detail how the maṇḍala should be drawn and which mistakes are to be avoided: "Many faults [arise] through protuberances, [lines that are] crooked, [too] thin, and [too] thick, cavities, elevations, irregularities, and holes. In no case [should] the lines [be] interrupted. If there are protuberances, etc., on

[13] PauṣS1 2.34d–39. The text is corrupt and thus not always intelligible.

[14] PauṣS1 2.42c–44. For similar rites before the construction of a temple, cf., e.g., Pādma-Saṃhitā, *kriyāpāda* 3.1–37.

[15] Cf. Jayākhya-Saṃhitā 13.14, PauṣS1 4.21ff., Lakṣmī-Tantra 37.3d, 55.10a, Viṣṇu-Saṃhitā 9.3–5b, Aniruddha-Saṃhitā 7.3ab.

[16] Jayākhya-Saṃhitā 13.15c–16, Pādma-Saṃhitā, *caryāpāda* 7.2–7b, Viṣṇu-Saṃhitā 9.5b, Viśvāmitra-Saṃhitā 15.2–6a. For the *vedi* as support of the maṇḍala, see also Jayākhya-Saṃhitā 18.36a, Īśvara-Saṃhitā 11.133c, 18.171c, Aniruddha-Saṃhitā 7.3c and 8a.

[17] Jayākhya-Saṃhitā 13.17–24, Lakṣmī-Tantra 37.4c–13b, Īśvara-Saṃhitā 11.135c–140. For an example of a preliminary grid, cf. the diagrams in Gupta's translation of the Lakṣmī-Tantra, pp. 228 and 230.

[18] Cf. Pādma-Saṃhitā, *caryāpāda* 7.9c: *candanārdrāṇi sūtrāṇi*, "threads moistened with sandalwood." Not all Saṃhitās mention the substance for besmearing the threads explicitly. Jayākhya-Saṃhitā 13.16c gives only: "having first besmeared the thread" (*upalipyāgratas sūtram*) and Lakṣmī-Tantra 37.5a mentions a "very white thread" (*susitaṃ sūtram*), which probably means a thread besmeared with a white substance. For the manner of drawing lines and circles by means of threads, cf. also Brunner 1986: 26 (cf. Brunner, p. 170) and Apte 1973: 503f. or Apte 1987: 130f.

[19] Jayākhya-Saṃhitā 13.25–40, Lakṣmī-Tantra 37.13c–19, Īśvara-Saṃhitā 11.141–161b. According to the Parama-Saṃhitā, the maṇḍala used in the *samaya-dīkṣā* can also be drawn with paint (*varṇaka*) (Parama-Saṃhitā 8.7c–8b).

account of carelessness when the maṇḍala is drawn by disciples, then the competent teacher[20] [should be] alert. He should have [the disciples] position the lovely pericarp, the filaments and the other [parts of the maṇḍala's lotus] by applying [the powder] only once and not by moving [it] to and fro."[21] In addition, the various constituent parts of the maṇḍala should be applied in varying thicknesses: "He should make the pericarp and the lines of the leaves around [it] elevated. The elevated lines are threefold, namely, equal to the little finger, to the middle finger, and to the thumb. The diminution of the [lines] with regard to the highest, the middle, and the lowest [elevation] should be modified in the order beginning with the lotus."[22]

The powders used for drawing the maṇḍala are made of various materials such as herbs, jewels, stones, leaves, fruits, seeds, fragrant substances, wood, metals, and minerals.[23] The Nāradīya-Saṃhitā and the Bhārgava-Tantra state in detail which materials should be used for which colours: ground rice or sandalwood powder for white, safflower for red, pure turmeric or turmeric mixed with a bit of white substance for yellow, burnt rice or sacrificial charcoal for black, and green leaves for green (*śyāma*).[24] Apart from powder, materials such as whole seeds (mustard seeds, sesame seeds, grain) or flowers can also be used.[25] Flowers are especially used for maṇḍalas employed during initiation (*dīkṣā*) or a festival (*utsava*).[26]

---

[20] Drawing maṇḍalas is primarily a task of the teacher (*guru*, *ācārya*), who belongs to the highest level of initiation (cf. Rastelli 1999: 153–158); cf. Jayākhya-Saṃhitā 17.56ab, Sātvata-Saṃhitā 21.49, and Ahirbudhnya-Saṃhitā 20.6c.

[21] Viṣṇu-Saṃhitā 9.39–41:
granthivaktrakṛśasthūlanimnonnatavimiśraṇaiḥ /
chidraiś ca bahavo doṣā rekhācchedo na sarvathā // 39
pramādād yatra śiṣyāṇāṃ maṇḍalasya tu lekhane /
granthyādi syād atandrī tu samaye kuśalo guruḥ // 40
karṇikākesarādīni lalitāni prayojayet /
sakṛdarpaṇamātreṇa na punaḥ parivartanaiḥ // 41

[22] Viṣṇu-Saṃhitā 9.42–43b:
karṇikām ucchritāṃ kuryāt patrarekhāś ca sarvataḥ /
kaniṣṭhāmadhyamāṅguṣṭhamitā rekhās tridhocchritāḥ // 42
mukhye madhye 'dhame 'bjādikramād ūhyaś ca tatkṣayaḥ /
This means that the maṇḍala's centre is the most elevated and its edge the lowest.

[23] Parama-Saṃhitā 7.61, Viṣṇu-Saṃhitā 9.37.

[24] Nāradīya-Saṃhitā 8.59c–61b, Bhārgava-Tantra 13.17–18.

[25] Sātvata-Saṃhitā 17.50c–51.

[26] For flowers used for maṇḍalas employed during the initiation, cf. Sanatkumāra-Saṃhitā, *indrarātra* 9.87c–88c, *ṛṣirātra* 5.1–17, Nāradīya-Saṃhitā 10.6b; for flowers

There are many different forms of maṇḍalas. The Pauṣkara-Saṃhitā, for example, gives a great choice of varying maṇḍalas.[27] The maṇḍala that is most often mentioned in the Pāñcarātra texts is the *cakrābjamaṇḍala*, also called *bhadrakamaṇḍala*.[28] The centre of this maṇḍala consists of a combination of a wheel (*cakra*) and a lotus (*abja*) that is then surrounded by three square enclosures with doors in the four quarters. The central combination of a wheel and a lotus is made up of five concentric circles. The innermost circle is the pericarp (*karṇikā*) of the lotus. In the second circle are the lotus' filaments (*kesara*), its petals (*dala*), and the hub (*nābhi*) of the wheel. In the third and the fourth circle are the spokes (*ara*) of the wheel, and the fifth circle is the felly of the wheel. In the two inner enclosures around the five circles, there are twelve lotuses each, one in each corner and on the left and right of the doors (*dvāra*). Conch shells (*śaṅkha*) are drawn in each of the corners of the outermost enclosure.[29]

The use of different maṇḍalas in worship effects different results. Thus, the kind of maṇḍala may be chosen according to the result one desires to achieve. The Pauṣkara-Saṃhitā, for example, distinguishes the maṇḍalas described in it as follows: "The first maṇḍala is known as 'auspicious in every way' as it causes prosperity. The second [maṇḍala] is called 'liberating from sins' as at the sight of it, the sin acquired in many births comes to an end. The third [maṇḍala] is the 'good path' and shows the way of the *dharma*. The fourth [maṇḍala] is called *dharma*. On account of [its] worship, it bestows the *dharma*. The fifth [maṇḍala] is the 'womb of wealth' [and] effects the increase of the *bhakta*s' wealth. (...)"[30]

---

used for maṇḍalas employed during a festival, cf. Īśvara-Saṃhitā 11.389–390, Viṣṇu-Saṃhitā 20.66c–75b, Viṣvaksena-Saṃhitā 26.167c–201.

[27] See PauṣS1 5–19.

[28] See the usage of the designation *bhadraka* for this maṇḍala in Pādma-Saṃhitā, *caryāpāda* 7.38c, Nāradīya-Saṃhitā 8.53a and Viśvāmitra-Saṃhitā 15.34d.

[29] Pādma-Saṃhitā, *caryāpāda* 7.12b–38b, Nāradīya-Saṃhitā 8.2–53b, Viśvāmitra-Saṃhitā 15.6c–34b, Bhārgava-Tantra 13.5–26b. PauṣS1 8 describes various kinds of *cakrābjamaṇḍala*s. For a drawing of the *cakrābjamaṇḍala* according to the younger Saṃhitās, see Colour Plate 14. Another example of a maṇḍala often used is the *navapadmamaṇḍala* (see Colour Plate 15).

[30] PauṣS1 5.2–4:

maṇḍalaṃ sarvatobhadraṃ bhadrakṛt prathamaṃ smṛtam /
aghanirmocanaṃ nāma dvitīyaṃ yasya darśanāt // 2
anekajanmopāttaṃ tu kalmaṣaṃ kṣayam eti ca /
sadadhvaṃ syāt tṛtīyaṃ ca dharmamārgapradarśanam // 3

Another reason to choose a particular maṇḍala may be the kind of ritual that is to be performed, as some maṇḍalas are considered particularly suitable to certain rituals: "When [the god] is sent to sleep (*prasvāpe*) one should prepare the best *yāga* (i.e., maṇḍala) called *svastika*, o twice-born, when [he] is awakened, [the maṇḍala] called 'distinction' or one of the design-complexes, at the festival, the *cakrapaṅkaja* (i.e., *cakrābja*) with one or more lotuses."[31]

Finally, the maṇḍala differs according to the deity that is worshipped on it. This is relevant especially with regard to the ritual of the *sādhaka* who worships a particular mantra or deity in order to gain *siddhis*. The maṇḍalas used here are specific to the mantras worshipped, and sometimes their shape even corresponds to the mantra that is worshipped in it. Thus, the maṇḍala of the *śaṅkha-mantra*, for example, has the shape of the conch shell or the maṇḍala of the *gadāmantra* is surrounded by eight maces.[32]

The Use of Maṇḍalas

A maṇḍala serves as a place where the deity can be invited and then worshipped.[33] In addition to a maṇḍala, there are several other places that can be employed for this purpose. Pots (*kumbha*, *kalaśa*), statues (*bimba*, *pratimā*), and fire (*vahni*, *agni*) are most often used, but also other places are possible such as the disk of the sun or a rosary (*akṣasūtra*).[34] Often the deity is worshipped in several places one after the other. In the daily ritual described in the Jayākhya-Saṃhitā,

---

dharmākhyaṃ syāc caturthaṃ tu dharmaṃ yacchati pūjanāt /
pañcamaṃ vasugarbhaṃ tu bhaktānāṃ vasuvṛddhikṛt // 4

For different results stemming from the worship of different maṇḍalas, see also Jayākhya-Saṃhitā 13.44–47b and Pādma-Saṃhitā, *caryāpāda* 7.85c–89.

[31] Pārameśvara-Saṃhitā 12.575–576b:
prasvāpe svastikaṃ nāma kuryād yāgavaraṃ dvija /
prabodhe tu vivekākhyaṃ vyūheṣv ekatamaṃ tu vā // 575
utsave hy ekapadmaṃ vā naikābjaṃ cakrapaṅkajam /

For the *svastikamaṇḍala*, see PauṣS1 5.151b–177c, for the *vivekamaṇḍala* 5.107b–117c, for the 'design-complexes' (*vyūha*), PauṣS1 7 (the translation of *vyūha* by 'design-complex' follows Apte; cf. his translation of PauṣS2 7).

[32] Jayākhya-Saṃhitā 30.63 and 42ab. For the shapes of the various mantras' maṇḍalas, cf. Rastelli 2000b: 325 and 360–371.

[33] E.g., Jayākhya-Saṃhitā 13.1, Parama-Saṃhitā 4.26.

[34] For the disk of the sun and a rosary as places for worship, see Parama-Saṃhitā 4.26c and Jayākhya-Saṃhitā 13.4a.

for example, the deity is worshipped in a maṇḍala, in a pot, and in the fire.[35]

In younger Saṃhitās, a hierarchy of suitable places for worship has been established, especially of the 'four places' (*catuḥsthāna*), as maṇḍala, pot, fire, and statue are called.[36] Worship of the deity in a maṇḍala is considered the best, then follow the pot, the fire, and finally the statue. On the other hand, maṇḍala worship is necessary only on special occasions; in other cases one could be content with the deity's worship in fire and a statue or only in a statue: "At an initiation, a festival, an ablution, the fruit festival,[37] the 'raising of the *damana* [flowers],'[38] the great flower festival, a special 'festival of the purifying thread,' the *jayantī* [festival],[39] at the time of the *kṛttikā* festival,[40] at a lunar or solar eclipse, an equinox, a solstice, particularly on the twelfth day of a half-month, in all expiations, and at the spring festival one should perform the worship in a maṇḍala. Otherwise, [the ritual] may cause faults. Worship [of the deity] in a maṇḍala is the best one, worship in a statue the lowest. Worship [of the deity] in a pot, a maṇḍala, a statue, and fire is the very best. Through the very best worship, all faults are destroyed, all sins of men are removed, [and] the king's country is promoted. A ritual without worship in [all] four places may be fruitless. Therefore, with all [one's] effort one should perform the worship in the four places. Four places are the best, three places medium, two places the lowest, the remaining single place mere appearance. A statue is taught as the single [place], a statue and fire are the two places, [these two] together with a pot are the three places, [all these and] a maṇḍala are the four places."[41]

---

[35] Cf. Rastelli 1999: 271–322.

[36] Cf. Pādma-Saṃhitā, *caryāpāda* 21.69.

[37] Cf. Aniruddha-Saṃhitā 22.9cd and 23.10c–26.

[38] Cf. Aniruddha-Saṃhitā 22.7cd and 23.1–10b.

[39] Cf. Aniruddha-Saṃhitā 22.14cd and 25.5c–27.

[40] Cf. Aniruddha-Saṃhitā 22.16cd and 25.28–49.

[41] Aniruddha-Saṃhitā 6.56c–64b:
dīkṣāyām utsave caiva snapane ca phalotsave // 56
damanāropaṇe caiva tathā puṣpamahotsave /
pavitrotsave viśeṣe jayantyāṃ ca tathaiva ca /
kṛttikotsavakāle tu grahaṇe somasūryayoḥ // 57
viṣuve cāyane caiva dvādaśyāṃ tu viśeṣataḥ /
prāyaścitteṣu sarveṣu vasantotsava eva ca // 58
maṇḍalārādhanaṃ kuryād anyathā doṣakṛd bhavet /
maṇḍalārādhanaṃ śreṣṭhaṃ jaghanyaṃ bimbapūjanam // 59

As in the other places that are suitable for the deity's worship, the deity must be made present on the maṇḍala. This is achieved by the imposition (*nyāsa*) of the mantras of the deity and of his various aspects such as his retinue, his weapons, and his ornaments. The deity's main mantra is usually placed in the maṇḍala's centre and the mantras of his retinue, etc., around him. An example is the *cakrābjamaṇḍala* (cf. p. 124) described in Nāradīya-Saṃhitā 8.61c–73. Viṣṇu is in the maṇḍala's centre, that is, the pericarp (*karṇikā*) of a lotus. His consorts Śrī and Puṣṭi are on his right and left side, that is, south and north of him. Viṣṇu's twelve limbs (*aṅga*), viz., heart (*hṛdaya*), head (*śiras*), tuft of hair (*śikhā*), armour (*kavaca*), weapon (*astra*), eye (*dṛś*), belly (*udara*), back (*pṛṣṭha*), arms (*bāhu*), thighs (*ūru*), knees (*jānu*), and feet (*pāda*), are on the petals of the lotus.[42] Viṣṇu's quiver (*iṣudhi*) and sword (*asi*) are south of the lotus, his bow (*dhanu*) and shield (*kheṭaka*) north of it. The garland of forest flowers (*vanamālā*) is east of the lotus, and *śrīvatsa* (a curl of hair on Viṣṇu's breast) and *kaustubha* (a jewel on Viṣṇu's breast) are north and south of the garland of forest flowers. The conch shell (*śaṅkha*) is at the directional points. Garuḍa is at the eastern and western door, Viṣṇu's discus (*cakra*) at the southern door, his mace (*gadā*) at the northern door. The eight guardians of the quarters (*dikpāla*) are outside the maṇḍala.[43] The 25 *tattvas* arising from the primary matter

---

kumbhamaṇḍalabimbāgnau pūjanaṃ cottamaṃ bhavet /
uttamārādhanenaiva sarvadoṣakṣayaṃ gatam // 60
sarvapāpaharaṃ puṃsāṃ rājarāṣṭravivardhanam /
catuḥsthānārcanāhīnaṃ karma niṣphalatāṃ nayet // 61
tasmāt sarvaprayatnena catuḥsthānārcanaṃ yajet /
catuḥsthānam uttamaṃ ca tristhānaṃ madhyamaṃ bhavet // 62
dvisthānam adhamaṃ caiva ekam ābhāsakaṃ param /
ekaṃ tu bimbakaṃ proktaṃ dvisthānaṃ bimbapāvakam // 63
tristhānaṃ kumbhasaṃyuktaṃ catuḥsthānaṃ tu maṇḍalam /

Cf. also Īśvara-Saṃhitā 13.88c–89: "With regard to the principal rule, one should worship the all-pervading one in a pot, a maṇḍala, a statue, and fire. With regard to the secondary alternative rule, one should worship [the deity] in a pot, etc., with the exception of the maṇḍala, or one should worship [him] in a statue and in fire." (*kumbhe ca maṇḍale bimbe vahnau ca yajanaṃ vibhoḥ // 88 mukhye kalpe prakurvīta hy anukalpe tu maṇḍalam / vinā kumbhādiṣu yajed bimbavahnyos tu vā yajet //* 89) Cf. also, with the same content, Pārameśvara-Saṃhitā 16.20c–22b.

[42] Cf. Nāradīya-Saṃhitā 3.8c–11b.

[43] For their names, see, e.g., Nāradīya-Saṃhitā 13.318–319.

(*prakṛti*) are in the *vīthi*.[44] Śiva, Brahmā, and Viṣṇu are in the hub of the maṇḍala's wheel, the twelve lords of the months (*māseśa*), Viṣṇu, Madhusūdana, Trivikrama, Vāmana, Śrīdhara, Hṛṣīkeśa, Padmanābha, Dāmodara, Keśava, Nārāyaṇa, Mādhava, and Govinda[45] on the spokes, the moon with its sixteen digits (*kalā*) and its light and dark half between the spokes (?), the sun (*sūrya*) on each spoke at the edge as well as the twelve Ādityas, viz., Dhātṛ, Aryaman, Vidhātṛ, Mitra, Varuṇa, Bhaga, Indra, Vivasvat, Savitṛ, Pūṣan, Tvaṣṭṛ, and Viṣṇu.[46]

Since the maṇḍala is a place for the deity's worship, it is used in many different rituals. According to the Jayākhya-Saṃhitā,[47] the daily ritual (*nityakarman*) consists of preliminary rites such as the bath (*snāna*), the purification of the elements (*bhūtaśuddhi*), and the imposition of mantras (*mantranyāsa*) upon one's body, of the mental (*mānasayāga*, *antaryāga*) and the external worship (*bāhyayāga*), and of the fire ritual (*agnikārya*).

Mental worship is composed of the same parts as the ensuing physical worship. Mental worship, however, consists only of visualization. During this process mantras are imposed upon the lotus visualized in the practitioner's heart in the same manner as they are upon a maṇḍala, and subsequently visualized and worshipped there.[48] Thus the lotus of the heart serves as a maṇḍala in mental worship.

In external worship, a maṇḍala is drawn as described above (pp. 122f.). Like the other materials used for worship, the maṇḍala is ritually purified before worship. According to the Jayākhya-Saṃhitā this ritual purification consists of sprinkling water upon the maṇḍala and burning and inundating it mentally by means of mantras.[49] After

[44] The *vīthi(kā)* or *vīthī* is the passage surrounding the *pīṭha*. The *pīṭha* surrounds the inner lotus wheel; cf. Nāradīya-Saṃhitā 8.10cd, Apte 1973: 504 and the drawing ibid. Figure 1.

[45] Cf. Parama-Saṃhitā 2.83–86.

[46] For other examples of mantra impositions, see the drawings in Apte 1973: 513ff. according to Jayākhya-Saṃhitā 13.107–125b or in Hikita 1990: 172 according to Sātvata-Saṃhitā 17.65c–72b.

[47] The following description of the use of the maṇḍala in the daily ritual relates to the Jayākhya-Saṃhitā. For a detailed description of the daily ritual as given in this text, see Rastelli 1999: 193–322.

[48] Jayākhya-Saṃhitā 12.81c–102b; cf. also Rastelli 1999: 264f.

[49] "Having anointed [his] hands with fragrance, having sprinkled [water] that is drawn up from the *arghya* vessel over the entire maṇḍala, pavilion [and] offering substances, he should cause [them] to burn by means of the *astramantra* [and] then

the purification, the mantras are imposed upon their places on the maṇḍala while imagining that they are arising from Viṣṇu[50] and thus made present there. Then the mantras are mentally visualized in anthropomorphic forms and worshipped by offering various things such as *arghya*,[51] water used for washing the feet (*pādya*), flowers, fragrances, various kinds of food, etc.[52] This kind of worship in which the mantras are imposed upon different places on a maṇḍala, visualized in a concrete shape, and worshipped is called *bhogayāga*, the 'offering of objects of enjoyment.'[53] Accordingly, the maṇḍala is called *bhogasthāna*, the 'place of the objects of enjoyment.'[54]

At the very end of the daily ritual, i.e., after the fire ritual, the mantras made present upon the maṇḍala are sent forth again: The practitioner offers *arghya* and fragrances again, takes the *arghya* and flowers offered during the external worship from the maṇḍala as his *prasāda*, puts them on his head, and draws a mark (*tilaka*) on his forehead with yellow and red powder from the maṇḍala. Then the practitioner visualizes that the mantras being present upon the maṇḍala enter the gross (*sthūla*) body of the main mantra, i.e., that of Viṣṇu himself. The main mantra's gross body enters its subtle (*sūkṣma*) body and the latter, its highest (*para*) body. This highest body enters the heart-lotus of the practitioner who then visualizes his body as shining and starts to tremble on account of the mantra's

---

inundate [them] by means of the *mūla*[*mantra*]. Then the substances are pure and fit for the offering." (Jayākhya-Saṃhitā 13.73c–75b: *gandhadigdhau karau kṛtvā arghyapātroddhṛtena ca // 73 maṇḍalaṃ maṇṭapaṃ prokṣya yāgadravyāṇy aśeṣataḥ / dāhayed astramantreṇa mūlena plāvayet tataḥ // 74 nirmalo dravyasaṅghaś ca yāgayogyo bhavet tadā /*) Cf. also Jayākhya-Saṃhitā 13.89 for a repeated ritual purification of the maṇḍala.

[50] Cf. Jayākhya-Saṃhitā 13.105c–106b: "Then he should visualize that Lakṣmī and the other [mantras] are coming forth as splendour from the venerable Viṣṇu's shining body like a mass of sparks." (*tato bhagavato viṣṇor bhāsā bhāsvaravigrahāt // lakṣmyādīr nissṛtā dhyāyet sphuliṅganicayā yathā /*)

[51] Arghya is a mixture of varying ingredients. According to Jayākhya-Saṃhitā 13.65c–66b, it consists of white mustard, sesame seeds, *dūrvā* grass, white rice, barley, water, milk, and fruits.

[52] Jayākhya-Saṃhitā 13.106c–178b.

[53] Jayākhya-Saṃhitā 12.83c–84b, 20.341ab (= Pārameśvara-Saṃhitā 15.839ab). For the use of the term *bhogayāga*, see also PauṣS$_{I}$ 19.59c and Lakṣmī-Tantra 38.84a.

[54] See, e.g., Jayākhya-Saṃhitā 13.106c and Lakṣmī-Tantra 38.28c. The *bhogayāga* is differentiated from the *layayāga*, 'the offering in dissolution,' in which the mantras are worshipped without visualizing their concrete form and without imposing them upon a particular place (see Jayākhya-Saṃhitā 12.75c–81b and Rastelli 1999: 261–263).

power. Next the food that was offered to the mantras (*naivedya*) is distributed among the persons who have participated in the ritual. Visvaksena is invited into the maṇḍala and the substances previously offered to the main mantra (*mūlamantra*), i.e., Viṣṇu, are offered to him.[55] After sending forth the mantras also from the fire pit, where they were worshipped during the fire ritual, and inviting and worshipping Viṣvaksena also there, the devotee worships him again in the maṇḍala, asks his forgiveness for any mistakes that have been made during the ritual, and sends him forth. The maṇḍala is left after having brought a vessel that is filled with milk, water, honey, and clarified butter and in that the *astramantra* has been imposed.[56] This vessel probably serves as the maṇḍala's safeguard, as protection is one of the functions of the *astramantra*.[57]

In other rituals, the maṇḍala is treated like any other place where the deity is invited and worshipped. So, maṇḍalas are used for the deity's worship in different rituals such as festivals (*utsava*), consecrations (*pratiṣṭhā*) of statues, temples, etc., or magic rites.[58] In the annual rite of *pavitrāropaṇa*, which is performed in order to make good all faults accumulated in the rituals during the past year,[59] the maṇḍala is invested with threads as the other places where the deity is present during worship are, such as the pot, the statue, and the fire pit.[60]

The maṇḍala is of particular importance in the initiation (*dīkṣā*). Although it is possible to perform the *dīkṣā* ceremony without a maṇḍala if one does not have the means for it,[61] using a maṇḍala

---

[55] Viṣvaksena always receives the residue of the offerings to Viṣṇu. For Viṣvaksena, cf. Gupta 1976.

[56] Jayākhya-Saṃhitā 15.230–231 and 233c–249.

[57] Cf. its employment in the *digbandha* rite in Jayākhya-Saṃhitā 9.21c–24, 11.6–7b, 16.91c–92b.

[58] Cf., e.g., Pārameśvara-Saṃhitā 17.89cd, Īśvara-Saṃhitā 10.275ab, Pādma-Saṃhitā, *caryāpāda* 11.232–233c (*utsava*); Jayākhya-Saṃhitā 20.137a, Nāradīya-Saṃhitā 15.23cd, Pādma-Saṃhitā, *kriyāpāda* 31.41 (*pratiṣṭhā*), Pādma-Saṃhitā, *caryāpāda* 32.218ab (for the purpose of expulsion [*uccāṭana*]), and Rastelli 2000b: 325f.

[59] Cf. Jayākhya-Saṃhitā 21.1–4b, Kane 1977, volume 5: 339f. and Gupta/Hoens/Goudriaan 1979: 158.

[60] Jayākhya-Saṃhitā 21.63–64b, PauṣS I 30.32c–35b, Īśvara-Saṃhitā 14.138c–140b, 14.215c–216, Nāradīya-Saṃhitā 23.23c–26, Pādma-Saṃhitā, *caryāpāda* 14.51c–53 and 19.93–94b.

[61] Cf. Jayākhya-Saṃhitā 16.4c–6: "For rich [people] he should cause to perform [the initiation] by means of an offering [to the god] in a great maṇḍala. For a person who is deprived of property and wealth [or] possesses very little property [but] is

during the initiation is often considered better[62] and sometimes even so essential that the term 'one who has seen a maṇḍala' (*maṇḍala-dṛṣṭa*) serves as a designation of one who has undergone the first initiation and thus has become a *samayin*.[63]

An examination of the different Pāñcarātra-Saṃhitās shows that the role of the maṇḍala in the initation was not always the same. It was used in diverse rites of the *dīkṣā* and so the meaning ascribed to it also varied.

The Pauṣkara-Saṃhitā distinguishes four kinds of maṇḍalas according to the rank of initiation. The *padmodaramaṇḍala* is used for the *samayin*, the *anekakajagarbhamaṇḍala* for the *putraka*, the *cakrābjamaṇḍala* for the *sādhaka*, and the *miśracakramaṇḍala* for the *ācārya*.[64] At the beginning of the initiation, the teacher draws the respective maṇḍala, worships it, and then shows it to his disciple.[65] His hand, upon which he has visualized and thus made the maṇḍala present,—maṇḍalas comprising all aspects of the deity in the form of the mantras imposed on them,—is subsequently laid on the disciple. Through this act, the teacher, who is identified with the deity himself,[66] liberates the disciple from transmigration: "Having recognized that the devotee is helpless and plunged into the ocean of sorrow, he should draw [him] out by means of the *yāga* hand

---

afraid of transmigration [and] is truly a devotee of Viṣṇu, the teacher should be gracious (i.e., perform the initiation for him/her) only with seeds, sesame, and clarified butter [that are oblated to the god who is present] in the fire, [and] for [a person] who is deprived of any substances, [he should be gracious] only by means of a word (i.e., a mantra)." (*mahāmaṇḍalayāgena vittāḍhyānāṃ tu kārayet // 4 vittayogavimuktasya svalpavittasya dehinaḥ / saṃsārabhayabhītasya viṣṇubhaktasya tattvataḥ // 5 agnau cājyānvitair bījaiḥ satilaiḥ kevalaiḥ tathā / dravyahīnasya vai kuryād vācaivānugrahaṃ guruḥ // 6*) Cf. also Lakṣmī-Tantra 41.9–10b for a variant of this passage. Possessing the necessary material means is an essential prerequisite for obtaining the initiation by means of a maṇḍala. Also according to the PauṣS, the first thing that the teacher asks from a disciple who has come for the initiation is to acquire the necessary means (PauṣS$_1$ 1.1–4).

[62] Cf. Bhārgava-Tantra 24.28: "The principal initation in the *cakrābjamaṇḍala* is praised for the [person who is devoted to the twelve syllable mantra]. The secondary alternative initiation is [performed] only near the fire." (*cakrābjamaṇḍale dīkṣā tasya mukhyā prakīrtitā / anukalpā bhaved dīkṣā kevalaṃ vahnisannidhau //*)

[63] See Sātvata-Saṃhitā 20.2a (= Īśvara-Saṃhitā 21.464c) and Alaśiṅga Bhaṭṭa's commentary on this passage (Sātvata-Saṃhitā-Bhāṣya, p. 410, 9–11).

[64] PauṣS$_1$ 1.8b–11. For different procedures with regard to the use of the maṇḍala in the *dīkṣā* for the different ranks, cf. also Parama-Saṃhitā 8.7c–11b, Viṣṇu-Saṃhitā 2.40–47 and 11.3–6.

[65] PauṣS$_1$ 1.6–8a.

[66] For the identification of the teacher with the deity, cf. Rastelli 1999: 168–170.

(*yāgahastena*). It is known that this teacher is similar to me (i.e., Viṣṇu)."[67] This procedure is called *yāgadīkṣā*, 'initiation into the *yāga* (i.e., maṇḍala).' After it, the teacher destroys the disciple's past, present, and future bonds[68] by sacrificing them into the fire, and causes the disciple to become identical to the deity.[69] The *dīkṣā* is completed.

After the *dīkṣā*, the devotees belonging to the various ranks of initiation vary in their worship of the maṇḍala. The *samayin* only looks at and worships the maṇḍala on the twelfth *tithi* of every half (*pakṣa*) of a lunar month. After one year he may become a *putraka*. A *putraka* should look at, worship and visualize the maṇḍala within his heart for another year. Then he may become a *sādhaka*. He should worship and visualize the maṇḍala for three months minus five days. If he is successful in this, he may undergo the initiation for an *ācārya*. After having worshipped and visualized the maṇḍala for four years, he may reach final emancipation.[70] According to the Pauṣkara-Saṃhitā, emancipation can be attained only by means of maṇḍala worship: "The ocean of worldly existence is not passable by any other [means] than the *yāga*."[71]

In the *dīkṣā* according to the Sanatkumāra-Saṃhitā, the maṇḍala plays an even more central role than in the Pauṣkara-Saṃhitā. In this text, 'one should undergo the initiation' is expressed by the phrase *praviśed dīkṣāṃ cakramaṇḍale*, 'one should attain the initiation in the *cakramaṇḍala*,'[72] which shows the centrality of the maṇḍala in the *dīkṣā*. The initiation ritual as described in the Sanatkumāra-Saṃhitā is very simple. After constructing a maṇḍala by means of flowers[73] and distributing various offering substances on it,[74] the teacher worships it, takes the disciple's right hand with his right hand, and, carrying a handful of flowers (*puṣpāñjali*), leads him

[67] PauṣS1 1.28:
jñātvā bhaktam anāthaṃ ca nimagnaṃ śokasāgare /
uddhared yāgahastena sa gurur matsamas smṛtaḥ // 28
For the visualization of the maṇḍala on the hand, see below, pp. 137f.

[68] These are often symbolized by a thread; cf., e.g., Jayākhya-Saṃhitā 16.131–134b and 260c–274.

[69] PauṣS1 1.37d–41. This passage is corrupt and not intelligible in all details.

[70] PauṣS1 1.13–23.

[71] PauṣS1 1.26ab: *bhavārṇavo hy alaṅghyas tu vinā syād yāgato 'nyakaiḥ /*

[72] Sanatkumāra-Saṃhitā, *indrarātra* 4.1cd, 3ab, 4ab, 5ab, 6ab, etc.

[73] Cf. above, p. 123.

[74] Sanatkumāra-Saṃhitā, *ṛṣirātra* 5.1–30b.

around the maṇḍala while turning their right sides towards it (*pradakṣiṇa*). Then the teacher has the disciple approach the maṇḍala and worship it with offerings of fragrances, flowers, etc. Following this he teaches him the rules that must be observed and makes him enter the maṇḍala. How far he may enter into the maṇḍala depends on his *varṇa* and his/her sex. A Brahmin may enter into the innermost enclosure (*prathamāvaraṇa*), a *kṣatriya* into the second enclosure, and a *vaiśya* into the third enclosure. Śūdras and women must stay outside the maṇḍala and are not allowed to enter it.[75] In the maṇḍala, the disciple is told three mantras, a Vedic one (*vaidika*), a Tantric one (*tāntrika*), and one that is both Vedic and Tantric (*vaidikatāntrika*). These mantras can be used in the various rituals henceforward.[76] With this the initiation is completed.

In other Saṃhitās the initiation ceremonies are much more elaborate. In the following description, only the rites concerning the maṇḍala will be discussed. A rite in the *dīkṣā* that is described very often in the texts is the tossing of one or more flowers, and sometimes also other substances such as fragrances and *arghya*, onto the maṇḍala. Usually, the disciple is led blindfolded around the maṇḍala and then given two handfuls (*añjali*) of flowers and other substances, or only one flower, which he must toss onto the maṇḍala. Then the blindfold is removed and the disciple may see the maṇḍala.

The older Saṃhitās do not clarify explicitly the meaning of this rite. The Jayākhya-Saṃhitā reads: "Having prepared an *añjali* of flowers (*puṣpāñjali*) [for each of the disciples] in sequence, he should have [the disciples], whose eyes are blindfolded as before, toss [the flowers] that are endowed with gold, jewels, and pearls. Then he should unveil [their] eyes and show [them] everything."[77] The Sātvata-Saṃhitā states: "Taking the [disciple] by the hand, he should go near the god's abode (i.e., the maṇḍala). Having placed [him] on his left side and again blindfolded [his] eyes, he should have [him], who is deprived of [his] eyesight [now], toss *arghya* [from] the *añjali*. [Then the disciple] may see the mantra's highest abode, which

---

[75] Also the kind of maṇḍala varies with regard to the disciple's *varṇa* or sex; cf. Sanatkumāra-Saṃhitā, *ṛṣirātra* 5.40c–43.

[76] Sanatkumāra-Saṃhitā, *ṛṣirātra* 5.30c–40b.

[77] Jayākhya-Saṃhitā 16.217c–218:
kramāt puṣpāñjaliṃ kṛtvā baddhanetrāṃś ca pūrvavat // 217
kṣepayec ca hiraṇyāḍhyaṃ maṇimuktāphalānvitam /
udghāṭya nayane paścād akhilaṃ saṃpradarśayet // 218

bestows the fruit of [the fulfilment of every] wish."[78] The reason for tossing flowers and other offerings onto the maṇḍala may be that the disciple, prior to seeing the maṇḍala, must worship the deity present in it in order to dispose him favourably, and that only then does he grant him his favour. This can be concluded from the Sātvata-Saṃhitā's statement that the maṇḍala that has been looked upon by the disciple, fulfills every wish.

A passage in the Īśvara-Saṃhitā also shows that the tossing of flowers, etc., brings the disciple into contact with the deity present in the maṇḍala. This contact causes or increases his devotion (*bhakti*) and purifies his internal organ (*antaḥkaraṇa*) as a result of the deity's grace: "He should have him, with a bowed head, toss the *añjali*['s contents] into the god's abode. If he sees that [the disciple], whose eyes have [then] been unveiled, who has not been seen by any other person [and] who has entered the auspicious path, [shows] the sign of devotion (*bhaktilakṣaṇa*), which involves bristling of the hair, eagerness, joy, tears of bliss, prostrations, exclamations of 'victory' (*jaya*), and circumambulations in [all] quarters (?*dikpradakṣiṇa*), [and] if he has understood that [the disciple's] internal organ is purified, he should recognize that he is suitable. When [all this has happened], then [the disciple] has received grace (*anugṛhīta*) through this (i.e., the teacher's) thought, which is named Acyuta (i.e., Viṣṇu)."[79] A passage from the Tantrāloka, although from the Kashmirian Trika tradition, may help further to understand the idea that is behind the described ritual. According to this text, when the blindfold is removed the mantras present in the maṇḍala enter the disciple

---

[78] Sātvata-Saṃhitā 19.39c–41b:
tam ādāya karād devadhāmasannikaṭaṃ vrajet // 39
kṛtvātmano vāmabhāge bhūyaḥ saṃcchādya locane /
prakṣepayet tathā sārghyam añjaliṃ muktalocanam // 40
saṃpaśyet paramaṃ dhāma māntram icchāphalapradam (v.l.) /

[79] Īśvara-Saṃhitā 21.131–134b:
prakṣepayed devadhāmni natamūrdhnāṃjaliñ ca tam /
tasyodghāṭitanetrasya tv adṛṣṭasyetarair janaiḥ // 131
kuśalādhvaniviṣṭasya dṛṣṭvā vai bhaktilakṣaṇam /
romāñcautsukyaharṣāḍhyam ānandāśrusamanvitam // 132
sapraṇāmajayālāpadikpradakṣiṇasaṃyutam /
pūtāntaḥkaraṇaṃ bu<d>dhvā yogyo 'yam iti bhāvayet // 133
yadā tadācyutākhyā yānugṛhīto dhiyā tayā /
Through the identification of the teacher's thought with the deity, the identity of the teacher with the deity is also emphasized here.

in an instantaneous possession (*āveśa*).[80] Perhaps the author of the Īśvara-Saṃhitā did not consider the 'signs of devotion' (*bhakti-lakṣaṇa*) as possession, but it is obvious that also according to the Īśvara-Saṃhitā, the disciple, when seeing the maṇḍala for the first time, comes into contact with the deity's power.

In many Saṃhitās, the tossing of a flower onto the maṇḍala is considered a means to determine the initiand's mantra or name. As described above (pp. 127f.), varying mantras are placed on the different constituent parts of the maṇḍala. The mantra that is present on the place where the flower tossed by the disciple falls is then his personal mantra or gives him his name. The Parama-Saṃhitā describes the first variant: "He should blindfold the disciple by means of a cloth, take [his] hand and enter the maṇḍala through its door. He should lead [the disciple around the maṇḍala,] turning their right sides towards [it] and have [the disciple] bow down before the guardians of the quarters. On which flower[81] this flower falls by chance, this [flower's] mantra is for his protection and prosperity. Having effected [his] faculty of seeing [again], he should show him the *cakramaṇḍala*."[82] Several younger Saṃhitās indicate that the purpose of tossing flowers onto the maṇḍala while blindfolded is to give the disciple a name (*nāmakaraṇa*). Among these texts is the Pādma-Saṃhitā, which states: "Directed by the teacher, [the disciple] should toss the flowers onto the maṇḍala. [The teacher] should assign to the disciple the names of the manifestations (*mūrti*) such as Keśava, etc., that are the sovereigns of that place upon which most of the flowers fall of their own accord. The word *bhāgavata* or *bhaṭṭāraka* is to be joined to the end of the name if [the disciple] is a

[80] TĀ 15.451c–452b. Cf. also Sanderson 1986: 169 and Takashima 1992: 51f.

[81] Obviously, the mantras are invoked in flowers being placed on the various parts of the maṇḍala. Bühnemann 1987: 47 describes a similar method using areca nuts for invoking mantras. This passage presumably does not mean that the maṇḍala is made of flowers (cf. p. 123), because the verses Parama-Saṃhitā 8.7c–9b prescribe that the maṇḍala is to be drawn with paint in the case of a *samayadīkṣā* and with powder during the *tantradīkṣā* (Parama-Saṃhitā 8.9b *tatra dīkṣitaḥ* em. *tantradīkṣitaḥ*).

[82] Parama-Saṃhitā 8.44–46:
vastram ekam upādāya śiṣyaṃ ba<d>dhvā mukhāntare /
haste gṛhītvā praviśet svena dvāreṇa maṇḍalam // 44
nītvā pradakṣiṇaṃ caiva dikpālān praṇipātayet /
tat puṣpaṃ nipatet puṣpe yasminn eva yadṛcchayā // 45
sa mantras tasya rakṣāyām udaye ca vidhīyate /
utpādya cakṣuṣī cainaṃ darśayec cakramaṇḍalam // 46

Brahmin. He should assign a name ending with *deva* to a *kṣatriya*, one ending with the word *pāla* to a *vaiśya*, [and a name] ending with *dāsa* to one who is born from [the Puruṣa's] feet.[83] Then he should remove the blindfold and show [him] the *cakramaṇḍala*."[84]

Although most of the Saṃhitās examined connect the ritual of tossing flowers upon the maṇḍala with the name-giving, this was not its original purpose. This can be seen in the Jayākhya-Saṃhitā that prescribes the name-giving ceremony as being at another moment of the initation than that of the first showing of the maṇḍala, and prescribes the ceremony being done with the help of a platform made of earth (*sthala*) upon which a maṇḍala is only imagined.[85] In the Sātvata-Saṃhitā, although the name-giving immediately follows the tossing of the *puṣpāñjali* upon the maṇḍala, the purpose of the tossing act is not to give a name. It is just done on the same occasion. The passage Sātvata-Saṃhitā 19.39d–41b quoted above (pp. 133f.) continues as follows: "On this occasion, he should give [him] a

---

[83] I.e., a *śūdra;* cf. Ṛg-Veda 10.90.12d: *padbhyā́ṃ śūdró ajāyata*. For the choice of the names for the members of the different *varṇas*, cf. also Manu-Smṛti 2.31-32. I am thankful to Professor Bühnemann for this reference.

[84] Pādma-Saṃhitā, *caryāpāda* 2.57–60:
puṣpāṇi vikiret tasmin maṇḍale gurucoditaḥ /
yasmin patati bhūbhāge puṣpāṇām utkaras svayam // 57
tadbhāgādhipamūrtīnāṃ nāmāny asya vinirdiśet /
śiṣyasya keśavādīni padaṃ bhāgavateti ca // 58
nāmnām ante prayoktavyaṃ yad vā bhaṭṭāraketi ca /
brāhmaṇaś cet kṣatriyasya devāntaṃ nāma nirdiśet // 59
vaiśyasya pālaśabdāntaṃ dāsāntaṃ pādajanmanaḥ /
tato vimucya dṛgbandhaṃ darśayec cakramaṇḍalam // 60
See also Viṣṇu-Saṃhitā 10.61–64b, Śrīpraśna-Saṃhitā 16.106 and 136–137, and Viśvāmitra-Saṃhitā 9.65–67.

[85] Cf. Jayākhya-Saṃhitā 16.124c–127b: "He should blindfold the disciple's eyes by means of a new, pure, white cloth upon which the *netramantra* has been used. Then he should have [him] cast for Viṣṇu a *puṣpāñjali* that is not invested with a mantra upon the platform. He should brand him with the name of the mentally imagined lotus upon which the [*puṣpāñjali*] falls—before [this] he should divide [the platform] into nine parts (here obviously the *navapadmamaṇḍala* consisting of nine lotuses is meant [cf. note 29])—, together with the words *viṣṇu* or *pati*, o Brahmin." (*vāsasā hy ahatenātha śuddhena susitena ca //* 124 *netramantrābhijaptena netre śiṣyasya bandhayet/ amantraṃ kṣepayec cāto viṣṇoḥ puṣpāñjaliṃ sthale //* 125 *yatra sā patati brahman buddhisaṅkalpite 'mbuje / navadhā vibhajet prāgvat tannāmānaṃ tam aṅkayet //* 126 *viṣṇuśabdānvitenaiva patisaṃjñāyutena* [em. of the edition] *ca /* The text is corrupt.) It is unknown if the branding of the name is to be taken literally. Usually in the *dīkṣā*, a *cakra* mark is branded on the right shoulder and a *śaṅkha* mark on the left one (cf. Sātvata-Saṃhitā 22.9d, Īśvara-Saṃhitā 21.284c–292b, and Rangachari 1930: 35).

suitable name of a [deity] who has a secret primary name and a secondary one accordant with circumstances."[86] According to the Īśvara-Saṃhitā, the disciple's name is determined with the help of tossing a *puṣpāñjali* upon the maṇḍala. This is described by means of the passage from the Sātvata-Saṃhitā quoted above, which the Īśvara-Saṃhitā has adopted from this text like many other passages.[87] However, the name-giving rite is performed one day after the first viewing of the maṇḍala,[88] which occurs during the preparations for the initiation (*dīkṣādhivāsana*). Thus, the rite of name-giving originally was not connected with the act of tossing flowers onto the maṇḍala.

At the end of this section on the *dīkṣā*, I would again like to consider the placing of the teacher's hand on the disciple that was mentioned above (pp. 131f.) as being part of the initiation. This placing of the teacher's hand can be done either before revealing the maṇḍala to the disciple or after.[89] The hand is mentally invested with the deity's power that is then transferred to the disciple. Investing with the deity's power is done either by imposing a mantra[90] or visualizing a maṇḍala on the hand: "On [his] right hand, he should visualize all principal deities as illuminating [it] by their rays of light [and] being in their respective supreme abodes in the centre of the *cakrābja*[*maṇḍala*]. He should [then] touch the [disciple] with this

[86] Sātvata-Saṃhitā 19.41c–42b:
tasminn avasare kuryān nāma yasya yathocitam //
rahasyasamjñaṃ mukhyaṃ ca gauṇaṃ vāsya yathāsthitam /

[87] Īśvara-Saṃhitā 21.319–325 ~ Sātvata-Saṃhitā 19.39c–46b. The Īśvara-Saṃhitā introduces this passages with the following words: "He should give a name to the disciple. The rule for this is given here." (Īśvara-Saṃhitā 21.318cd: *nāma kuryāc ca śiṣyasya tadvidhānam ihocyate //*)

[88] Cf. Īśvara-Saṃhitā 21.131–134b quoted on p. 134f.

[89] Before revealing the maṇḍala: Sātvata-Saṃhitā 19.38c–39b, Viṣṇu-Saṃhitā 10.46c–52b; after it: PauṣS1 1.28, Jayākhya-Saṃhitā 16.335, Pādma-Saṃhitā, *caryāpāda* 2.66–67b, Īśvara-Saṃhitā 21.134c–136b, Viśvāmitra-Saṃhitā 9.75c–76a.

[90] Cf. Jayākhya-Saṃhitā 18.82c–83: "Having thus spoken, the teacher himself should visualize the supreme Viṣṇu who is the supreme one [and] who consists of parts and is without parts (cf. Rastelli 1999: 101–105), in the form of the mantra on [his] right hand, worship him with fragrances, flowers, etc., and lay it on the [disciple's] head." (*ity uktvā dakṣiṇe haste svayaṃ sañcintya vai guruḥ // 82 mantrātmānaṃ paraṃ viṣṇuṃ paraṃ sakalaniṣkalam / saṃpūjya gandhapuṣpādyair dadyāt tasya ca mastake // 83*) and Sātvata-Saṃhitā 19.38c–39b: "He should touch [him] from the feet with the mantra hand and then he, who conquers the seed of suffering, should lay the mantra hand, which has a blazing form, on [his] head." (*ā pādān mantrahastena parāmṛśyātha mūrdhani // mantrahastaṃ jvaladrūpaṃ dadyād yo duḥkhabījajit /* = Īśvara-Saṃhitā 21.282c–283b)

Acyuta hand that was [previously] wetted with water."[91] If a mantra is imposed upon the hand, it is called mantra hand (*mantrahasta*). If a maṇḍala is visualized on the hand, it is called *yāga* hand (i.e., maṇḍala hand; *yāgahasta*).[92] In both cases it can also be called Viṣṇu hand (*viṣṇuhasta*) (or Acyuta hand as in the passage just quoted) as in both cases Viṣṇu is present on the hand: "The hand on which Viṣṇu is present is called Viṣṇu hand."[93] According to the Viṣṇu-Saṃhitā it destroys all sins that were ever accumulated: "All sins that were formerly accumulated in thousands of other births are dissolved without doubt by the mere touch."[94] According to the Pauṣkara-Saṃhitā it liberates one from the world of transmigration (cf. pp. 131f.).

All the examples of various Saṃhitās given show that the maṇḍala plays a central role during the initiation, although its meaning and function vary in the different texts. First of all, the first viewing and first worship of the maṇḍala is the initiation into maṇḍala worship, which is in the centre of the devotee's religious practice in the Pauṣkara-Saṃhitā especially but also in other Saṃhitās. But the maṇḍala as a place of the deity's presence is also a means for encountering the deity: by worshipping him there in order to dispose him favourably, but also by experiencing his favour by the mere sight of the maṇḍala, by obtaining a name and a mantra that were not chosen by a human being, but by the powers present in the maṇḍala, and last but not least, by the physical contact with him through the Viṣṇu hand.

---

[91] Īśvara-Saṃhitā 21.134c–136b:
smared dakṣiṇapāṇau tu cakrāmburuhamadhyagam // 134
pradhānadevatābṛndaṃ sve sve dhāmni pare sthitam /
svamarīcigaṇenaiṣa dyotayantaṃ tu cākhilam // 135
tenācyutakareṇaiva sodakenālabheta tam /
Cf. also PauṣS$_1$ 1.28 (quoted on pp. 131f.), Pādma-Saṃhitā, *caryāpāda* 2.66–67b, Viṣṇu-Saṃhitā 10.46c–52b, Viśvāmitra-Saṃhitā 9.75c–76a.

[92] Cf. Sātvata-Saṃhitā 19.38c–39b (quoted in note 90) and PauṣS$_1$ 1.28.

[93] Viṣṇu-Saṃhitā 10.50cd: *haste viṣṇuḥ sthito yasmin viṣṇuhastas tu sa smṛtaḥ* // For the use of the term *viṣṇuhasta*, cf. also Jayākhya-Saṃhitā 16.335a, Pādma-Saṃhitā, *caryāpāda* 2.67a, and Viśvāmitra-Saṃhitā 9.75d.

[94] Viṣṇu-Saṃhitā 10.51:
janmāntarasahasrais tu yat pāpaṃ sañcitaṃ purā /
sarvaṃ tat sparśamātreṇa vilayaṃ yāty asaṃśayam // 51

The Symbolic Meaning of the Maṇḍala

As mentioned several times above, the maṇḍala is a place where the deity and his various aspects are made present by imposing their mantras upon it. Invested with mantras, the maṇḍala is very powerful and merely looking at it has an effect.[95]

However, the Pāñcarātra Saṃhitās not only assign a meaning to the maṇḍala but also to its constituent parts. As a place of the deity's presence, the maṇḍala is considered to be his body and thus, the maṇḍala's constituent parts are considered to be the constituents of the body. Since the body's constituents, i.e., the principles (*tattva*) arising from the primary matter (*prakṛti*), also constitute the universe, the maṇḍala is also a representation of the universe.

Such a conception is found in the Sātvata-Saṃhitā, which is also adopted by the Īśvara-Saṃhitā: "Having thus constructed [the maṇḍala], he should consider [it] as having the nature of the universe like a body. Know that the white, yellow, etc., powders are the [five] elements (*bhūta*). The *upaśobhas*[96] are the subtle elements (*tanmātra*), the *śobhas*[97] the organs of action (*karaṇa*), and in the same way, all the corners and doors are the sense organs. The outer enclosures are the three [constituents of the primary matter] *sattva*, etc. The wide *vīthī*[98] is the mind (*manas*); the *pīṭha*[99] is called conceit (*garva* = *ahaṃkāra*). The intellect (*dhī* = *buddhi*) is the lotus. Its ruler is the *puruṣa* who consists of pure thought in the form of a seed syllable (*bījātman*), and the Lord (*īśvara*), who is characterized by bliss [and] whose mere sight pleases the mind forever, is present there without a concrete form."[100]

---

[95] Cf. PauṣS1 10.34d–35b: "I explain to you [now] the entire [great maṇḍala], through which, if it is merely looked at, the fetters of worldly existence are destroyed." (*taṃ ca kṛtsnaṃ vadāmi te // yena sandṛṣṭamātreṇa bhavabandhakṣayo bhavet /*) Cf. further Viṣṇu-Saṃhitā 10.64cd: "If a maṇḍala is merely looked at, the accumulated sins are destroyed." (*dṛṣṭamātre praṇaśyanti maṇḍale pāpasañcayāḥ //*)

[96] Apte 1973: 504 and 1987: 131 explains *upaśobhās* as 're-entrants or the inverted counterparts of the offsets occupying the space in between offsets and corners of the enclosures.' For a better understanding of this explanation, cf. the drawing in Hikita 1991: 319.

[97] The *śobha* is the space between the *upaśobhas*; cf. the drawing in Hikita 1991: 319 (here the feminine forms *śobhā* and *upaśobhā* are used).

[98] Cf. note 44.

[99] The *pīṭha* is the part of the maṇḍala which surrounds the lotus(es); cf. Figure 1 in Apte 1973 and also Nāradīya-Saṃhitā 8.10c.

[100] Sātvata-Saṃhitā 11.32c-36:

A similar conception can be found in the Viṣṇu-Saṃhitā. In this text, the maṇḍala's constituent parts are seen as parts of the body on one hand, and as cosmic and divine powers on the other. Possibly, two texts that were originally different are joined here as the two conceptions are combined without a real inner connection. In addition, some principles (*tattva*) and deities appear twice: "He should consider the maṇḍala as a human being (*puruṣa*). The lotus is its heart. [The maṇḍala's] centre is between the arms. The stalk of the lotus is at the base of the navel. The two back doors in the south and the north are to be known as the two feet. The stalk of the lotus, which has nine holes, is the seat of the *kalās* Vimalā, etc.[101] Its root is the subtle Janārdana in the form of a seed syllable (*bījarūpa*), since one should know that the root of the lotus, which supports everything, is based on his greatness. The phonems *a*, etc.,[102] became the winds [of the body]. On the stalk are the finger-nails.[103] The knot (?*granthi*) is the 'great one' (i.e., the intellect [*buddhi*]) consisting of the [three] constituents [of the primary matter]. The eight petals are then the various [modifications of] the intellect, *dharma*, *adharma*, etc. Within the stalk is the endless ego principle that carries the subtle elements, the sense organs, and the elements. The lotus [of the god's throne (*āsana*) visualized upon the maṇḍala] is the unevolved [primary matter]. Some [teach] that the circles of sun, moon, and fire[104] are the different phonems *a*, etc.,[105] and others consider them

---

kṛtvaivam anusandhāya sarvātmatvena dehavat // 32
rajāṃsi viddhi bhūtāni sitapītādikāni ca /
tanmātrāṇy upaśobhāni śobhāni karaṇāni tu // 33
evaṃ sarvāṇi koṇāni sadvārāṇīndriyāṇi ca /
bahirāvaraṇaṃ yad vai sattvādyaṃ tritayaṃ hi yat // 34
manaḥ suvitatā vīthī garvaḥ pīṭham udāhṛtam /
dhīḥ padmaṃ tadadhiṣṭhātā bījātmā cinmayaḥ pumān // 35
amūrta īśvaraś cātra tiṣṭhaty ānandalakṣaṇaḥ /
yasya sandarśanād eva śaśvad bhāvaḥ prasīdati // 36
(~ Īśvara-Saṃhitā 11.161c-165).

[101] These are Viṣṇu's nine *śaktis*, viz., Vimalā, Utkarṣiṇī, Jñānā, Kriyā, Yogā, Prahvī, Satyā, Īśā, and Anugrahā (Viṣṇu-Saṃhitā 6.44c–45).

[102] Here, phonems imposed upon the maṇḍala are probably meant.

[103] The finger-nails are identified with the thorns on the stalk, both of which are called *kaṇṭaka* in Sanskrit.

[104] These also belong to the throne (*āsana*) that is visualized upon the maṇḍala. For the mental visualization of an *āsana* upon the maṇḍala, cf. also Ahirbudhnya-Saṃhitā 28.17c–18. For the constituent parts of the *āsana*, cf. Rastelli 2002.

[105] The phonems are considered as parts of the worldly creation; cf. Viṣṇu-Saṃhitā 9.53: "[The universe] is to be known as being pervaded by the first sound in

as born of the eight *śakti*s Vimalā, etc. The lotus that is the great support of the universe is in the centre of the egg (?*aṇḍa*).[106] The Māyā is in the egg-shell below the egg, Vidyā is above it.[107] He should consider the border (*prativāraṇa*) as the pericardium of the heart-lotus. Out of the [border], god Vairāja (i.e., Brahmā) is taught as [being present] in the shape of the rampart. In the yellow, white, red, black, and dark powders are the [five elements of] the earth, etc. The Vasus are on the tips of the lotus' petals; the Rudras and Ādityas are the filaments, the Maruts are on the junctures of the petals; the planets and stars are the powders. On the lines of the petals' upper [edges] and between [them] are the rivers and oceans. [Mount] Meru is in the pericarp, the *muni*s are on the seed syllables. Viṣṇu is in sun, moon and fire. (...) The thorns are Yakṣa, etc., the hairs on the stalk are known as the Apsaras. The thread is Prajāpati; the roots of the leaves are the winds [of the body] such as *prāṇa*, etc. The *ātman*, who is the lord of the universe, who is Hari, who is known as having no parts (*niṣkala*), [and] who abides in the supreme abode, is [present] in the centre of the *cakramaṇḍala*. He who has thus recognized that the god is present in the maṇḍala leaves Viṣṇu's Māyā behind and attains the supreme abode. He who worships or visualizes (*paśyet*) the god as present in the maṇḍala, even if it is not prescribed directly, beholds the lord of the gods forever. In the maṇḍala, the one who has all forms is eternally near here [in this world]. Therefore, worship in the maṇḍala is better than [worship in] auspicious places such as *tīrtha*s, etc."[108] In both passages quoted

---

the shape of the *nāda*. Viṣṇu's supreme abode is beyond the creation of the phonems, etc." (*nādarūpeṇa vijñeyaṃ vyāptam ādyakṣareṇa tu / varṇādikalpanātītaṃ tad viṣṇoḥ paramaṃ padam //*) and Rastelli 1999: 125f.

[106] Here, the lotus arising from Viṣṇu's navel on which Brahmā sits and creates the world, is possibly meant.

[107] Māyā and Vidyā are constituents of the universe; cf. Viṣṇu-Saṃhitā 3.48cd and 6.42ab.

[108] Viṣṇu-Saṃhitā 9.58c–76b:

puruṣaṃ maṇḍalaṃ vidyāt padmaṃ hṛdayam asya tu // 58
bāhvantaragataṃ madhyaṃ nābhimūle 'bjanālakam /
pade dve paścimadvāre jñātavye dakṣiṇottare // 59
padmanālaṃ navacchidraṃ vimalādikalāśrayaṃ /
tasya mūlaṃ bhavet sūkṣmo bījarūpo janārdanaḥ // 60
ādhārabhūtaṃ sarvasya mahimni sve vyavasthitam /
padmamūlaṃ vijānīyād yato 'kārādayo 'bhavan / 61
marutaḥ kaṇṭakā nāle granthir guṇamayo mahān /
buddhibhedā dalāny aṣṭau dharmādharmādayas tataḥ // 62
nālānte 'haṃkṛto 'nantas tanmātrendriyabhūtabhṛt /

here, the maṇḍala is seen as the body of the deity. Like any other body, it consists of the *tattvas*, of limbs, and of organs. However, the maṇḍala also consists of principles, and of cosmic and divine powers that constitute the universe. Thus it is also a representation of the universe. Again, the universe is a manifestation of the deity.[109] Thus, the maṇḍala, even if it is not yet invested with mantras, is considered here as being a representation of the deity.[110]

Yantras

Like maṇḍalas, yantras consist usually of diagram-like drawings and mantras made present in them. There are, however, essential differences between maṇḍalas and yantras.

Yantras are generally drawn on mobile materials. For drawing and writing, powders are not used, but rather liquid substances; metal

---

padmo 'vyaktam akārādibhedo 'rkendvagnimaṇḍalam // 63
buddhigarvamanomātrā dakṣiṇādidalāṣṭakam /
ity anye vimalādyaṣṭaśaktijaṃ cāpare viduḥ // 64
aṇḍamadhyagataṃ padmaṃ viśvasyāyatanaṃ mahat /
māyāṇḍādhaḥ kapālasthā vidyā cordhvaṃ vyavasthitā // 65
purītataṃ hṛdabjasya kalpayet prativāraṇam /
tadbāhyataḥ purākāro vairājo deva ucyate // 66
pītācchāruṇakṛṣṇeṣu śyāme ca kṣmādayaḥ sthitāḥ /
vasavo 'bjadalāgrasthā rudrādityāś ca kesarāḥ // 67
maruto dalasandhisthā reṇavo grahatārakāḥ /
dalāntarāgrarekhāsu saritaḥ sāgarās tathā // 68
merus tu karṇikāntastho bījeṣu munayaḥ sthitāḥ /
sūryendvagnigato viṣṇus (...)
yakṣādyāḥ kaṇṭakā nāle romāṇy apsarasaḥ smṛtāḥ // 71
sūtraṃ prajāpatiḥ patramūle prāṇādivāyavaḥ /
cakramaṇḍalamadhyastha ātmā sarveśvaro hariḥ // 72
niṣkalas tu samākhyātaḥ parame vyomni saṃsthitaḥ /
evaṃ yo vetti devaṃ taṃ maṇḍalāntargataṃ tathā // 73
sa hitvā vaiṣṇavīṃ māyām āpnuyāt paramaṃ padam /
avidhāne 'pi yo devaṃ maṇḍalāntaḥsthitaṃ yajet // 74
paśyed vā tena deveśaḥ sākṣād dṛṣṭo bhaved dhruvam /
maṇḍale 'tra bhaven nityaṃ sānnidhyaṃ sarvarūpiṇaḥ // 75
tasmāt tīrthādipuṇyebhyo viśiṣṭaṃ maṇḍale 'rcanam /

Viṣṇu-Saṃhitā 9.69d–71b is an insertion that does not make sense with regard to the contents of the passage.

[109] All constituent parts of the universe are manifestations of the deity (cf. Rastelli 1999: 98f.); thus the universe is also his representation.

[110] The Saṃhitās teach similar notions with regard to the temple; cf. Rastelli 2003.

yantras can also be engraved. Thus yantras can be carried everywhere and also worn as amulets.

When maṇḍalas are prepared, a diagram is drawn and only then are the mantras made present upon it by imposition (*nyāsa*). When preparing a yantra, drawing and writing of the mantras are done in a single process, and, as just mentioned, the mantras are *written*. This is not the case with maṇḍalas.

This is probably connected with the fact that in most cases yantras are not considered to be just places where the deity can be made present and worshipped as maṇḍalas are, but are considered to be representations of the deity himself (see below pp. 144f.).

Yantras are used mainly for worldly purposes (see below pp. 146ff.).[111]

The writing materials most commonly used for the preparation of yantras are birch-bark (*bhūrja*) and cloth (*vastra*, *karpaṭa*).[112] Other materials mentioned in the texts are gold (sometimes embellished with jewels, corals, and pearls), silver, copper and other metals, wood, and stone.[113] The writing paint is prepared from *rocanā*,[114] saffron (*kuṅkuma*), sandalwood (*candana*), talc (*ghana*), camphor (*tuṣāra*), musk (*kastūrikā*), milk, *agaru*[115] and dew.[116] The writing utensil is a golden needle (*hemasūcī*).[117] The yantras described in Aniruddha-Saṃhitā 5 seem to be special cases. According to the prescription of this text, the yantras should be prepared and worshipped on a platform (*vedī*) in a pavilion (*maṇḍapa*).[118] These yantras are, of course, not mobile.

[111] These differences between maṇḍalas and yantras have emerged from my study of the Pāñcarātra-Saṃhitās. For a list of differences that varies slightly from mine, cf. Brunner 1986: 19 (cf. Brunner, pp. 162–163). The differences noted by Brunner may also apply to Pāñcarātra, but I have not yet found evidence for this in the texts.

[112] Jayākhya-Saṃhitā 26.97b, 29.96b, 164a, Pādma-Saṃhitā, *caryāpāda* 25.102c, 32.46b.

[113] Pādma-Saṃhitā, *caryāpāda* 32.92c, Ahirbudhnya-Saṃhitā 26.3ab, 74cd, 85cd.

[114] According to Apte 1957 (*s.v. gorocanā*), *rocanā* is "a bright yellow pigment prepared from the urine or bile of a cow, or found in the head of a cow."

[115] *Aquilaria agallocha*. Perfumes, ointments, and oil are obtained from its fragrant wood (Syed 1990: 31).

[116] Jayākhya-Saṃhitā 26.89c, 97a, 106ab, 29.95c–96a, 163cd, Ahirbudhnya-Saṃhitā 26.4ab, 75d, Pādma-Saṃhitā, *caryāpāda* 25.102d–103, 32.45–46a.

[117] Ahirbudhnya-Saṃhitā 26.4c, Pādma-Saṃhitā, *caryāpāda* 25.103c, 32.45a.

[118] See Aniruddha-Saṃhitā 5.1c–3 and 59.

According to the Ahirbudhnya-Saṃhitā, the yantra's material is determined by the qualification (*adhikāra*) of its user.[119] In addition, different materials lead to different results following the yantra's worship. For example, a yantra made of gold, jewels, corals, and pearls bestows sovereignty, or a yantra made of birch-bark and drawn with saffron and sandalwood, when worn on the head, effects the fulfilment of all wishes.[120]

As already mentioned, when a yantra is prepared, drawing the diagram and writing the mantras are done in a single process. The following is an exemplary prescription for the preparation of a yantra that is used for paralyzing (*stambhana*) divine beings: "Furnished with *rocanā* and saffron, he should write [the divine being's] name intertwined[121] with the [*mūla*]*mantra* in the centre of a [drawn] *kaustubha* that contains sixteen sixteenth parts (*kalā*). Previously each sixteenth part has been provided with nectar,[122] o sage. Above the sixteenth parts of nectar he should place [the *mūlamantra*], which resembles the moon's rays, resting on the *viśvāpyāya* (= *ṭa*). Outside of the [*mūlamantra*], he should draw an eight-petalled lotus with a pericarp. [Then] he should write the god's *aṅga*[*mantras*] on the petals just as in worship."[123]

The drawing and writing of the yantra are seen as a unit. The drawing is not just a place for making the deity present by means of mantras, but the yantra's drawing and writing as a unit is a representation of the deity. The deity assumes the form of the yantra.

---

[119] Ahirbudhnya-Saṃhitā 26.3.

[120] Ahirbudhnya-Saṃhitā 26.74c–77.

[121] There are several interpretations of what *vidarbha* or *vidarbhita* means. Generally, it means that parts of the name and of the mantra, i.e., one or two syllables of each, are alternated. Cf. Padoux 1977 and 1986–1992: 69f.

[122] That is, the letter *sa*. Each letter of the Sanskrit alphabet has several names that are used as codes in the description of mantras; cf. Jayākhya-Saṃhitā 6.32c–57.

[123] Jayākhya-Saṃhitā 26.89c–92:
rocanākuṅkumair yukto nāmamantravidarbhitam // 89
likhet kaustubhamadhye tu kalāṣoḍaśasaṃyute /
ekaikā tu kalā vipra purā yuktāmṛtena tu // 90
sāmṛtānāṃ kalānāṃ ca yojayec ca tathopari /
viśvāpyāyasthitaṃ vāpi candraraśmisamaprabham // 91
tadbāhye 'ṣṭadalaṃ padmaṃ vilikhec ca sakarṇikam /
devyo 'ṅgāni (em. *divyāṅgāni*) *yathārcāyāṃ daleṣv abhyantare likhet* // 92
For other examples, see Jayākhya-Saṃhitā 26.97–111b, 29.163c–172, 32.66–79b, Sātvata-Saṃhitā 17.333c–359b (translation in Hikita 1992: 193–190; for a drawing of the yantra described in this passage, see Hikita 1990: 170), Pādma-Saṃhitā, *caryāpāda* 25.104–107b, Aniruddha-Saṃhitā 5.

Thus, the installation (*pratiṣṭhā*) of the *saudarśanayantra* (which is established and worshipped like a statue; see below pp. 148ff.) is prescribed with the following words: "Having established the god, [who is] the Lord having the shape of a yantra, in the centre (...)."[124] Further, the deity is described as 'consisting of all yantras' (*sarva-yantramaya*).[125] Thus, a yantra is a representation of the deity on one hand, and the deity encompasses all yantras on the other.

Two other kinds of mantric safeguards (*rakṣā*) that are described in the Ahirbudhnya-Saṃhitā are closely related to yantras. One is called *jyotirmayī*, 'consisting of light,' and the other *vāṅmayī*, 'consisting of language.'

The first is a wheel (*cakra*) whose constituent parts are represented by divine beings and their activities. The *brahman* is considered as being the wheel's axle, the *śakti* as its hub, the *śakti*'s five activities, viz., disappearance (*tirobhāva*), creation, maintenance, destruction, and favour, as its spokes, the Vyūhas and Vyūhantaras as its felly, and the Vibhavas as flames outside the felly. It is obvious that this kind of *rakṣā* can only be visualized mentally.[126]

The safeguard that consists of language (*vāṅmayī rakṣā*) is a wheel (*cakra*) whose shape is formed by writing mantras instead of drawing lines. The Ahirbudhnya-Saṃhitā describes several forms of this kind of safeguard.[127]

Nowhere in the Ahirbudhnya-Saṃhitā's text are these two kinds of safeguards called yantra. The term yantra is mentioned in the title lines of chapters 23 and 24 of the Ahirbudhnya-Saṃhitā and in two subtitles on p. 218 of the first volume of the Ahirbudhnya-Saṃhitā's edition,[128] but not in the body of the text itself. Thus the two kinds of *rakṣā* probably cannot be interpreted as yantras in the actual sense.

However, these safeguards, which are very similar to yantras, can help to clarify the meaning of yantra as representation of the deity. Both the *rakṣā* 'consisting of light' and the one 'consisting of language' are direct representations of the divine power, the first having divine beings as its constituent parts, the latter consisting

---

[124] Ahirbudhnya-Saṃhitā 47.21cd:
madhye devaṃ pratiṣṭhāpya yantrarūpadharaṃ prabhum //

[125] Ahirbudhnya-Saṃhitā 47.56d and 65a.

[126] Ahirbudhnya-Saṃhitā 21.4–29b.

[127] Ahirbudhnya-Saṃhitā 22–24.

[128] Ahirbudhnya-Saṃhitā 23 is called *vāsudevādiyantranirūpaṇa*, Ahirbudhnya-Saṃhitā 24, *yantradevatādhyānanirūpaṇa*

merely of mantras that are manifestations of the deity and his aspects. These *rakṣās* are not places where the deity can be made present, but they are the deity's presence itself. The same is true of yantras, which, in this aspect, are much more similar to the two kinds of *rakṣās* just described than to maṇḍalas.

However, seeing yantras as representations of the deity is not the only notion found in Pāñcarātra Saṃhitās. According to the Pādma-Saṃhitā, after the preparation of a yantra, the deity should be invited into it in order to worship him there.[129] Here, similar to a maṇḍala, the yantra is treated as being a place for the deity's worship.

What purpose do yantras have and how are they used? It is often emphasized that mere visualization of a yantra or concentration upon it is enough to reach a certain goal; for example: "He who recollects it in danger, in a battle, or in a dispute has victory in his hands; here there should not be any doubt." Or: "This yantra, o excellent sage, destroys all calamities. There is nothing that cannot be obtained by wearing, recollecting, [and] visualizing [it]."[130] Also the yantra's mere drawing can have effect: "Everything accrues to the people through its mere drawing."[131] In general, however, worshipping it with offerings, oblations and ablutions is seen as the prerequisite for the effect of a yantra.[132]

Yantras are frequently worn on the body as amulets, often bound with thread and/or covered with metal. Using them in this way, yantras are considered to protect and to have positive effects: "He should wrap this yantra with a five-coloured thread [and] put it into a golden casket. [If] he puts [it] on [his] right arm or a woman between [her] breasts he/she is liked forever, even among enemies. The *sādhaka* can easily cross female and male rivers or the oceans for many purposes; and because of its power, he does not sink in the

---

[129] Pādma-Saṃhitā, *caryāpāda* 25.107cd.

[130] Ahirbudhnya-Saṃhitā 26.80:
bhayāgame ca saṃgrāme vāde vā yaḥ smared idam /
vijayas tasya hastastho nātra kāryā vicāraṇā //
and Jayākhya-Saṃhitā 26.104c–105b:
yantro 'yaṃ muniśārdūla sarvopadravanāśanaḥ //
dhāraṇāt smaraṇād dhyānān nāsti tad yan na sādhayet /
See also Jayākhya-Saṃhitā 26.93c, Ahirbudhnya-Saṃhitā 25.17c.

[131] Ahirbudhnya-Saṃhitā 25.21cd:
etallekhanamātreṇa sarvaṃ sampadyate nṛṇām //

[132] See Jayākhya-Saṃhitā 26.93c, 27.214c, 28.12a, 29.52d, Pādma-Saṃhitā, *caryāpāda* 32.115c–116c, Aniruddha-Saṃhitā 5.59. Cf. also Rastelli 2000b: 350f.

water. Fear of beings of the jungle or the forest does not exist [for him]. Inauspicious planets bestow favourable [things]. Manifold terrific and exceedingly frightening poisons do not trouble [him]. Weapons of thieves, etc., do not enter the joints of [his] body. (...) The demons who injure children, etc. (*bālagrahādayaḥ*), leave the child and go far away if this yantra is present on its body. A pregnant woman bears easily on account of wearing [this yantra]. A barren woman [and] a [woman] whose new-born children die will have children."[133]

Likewise, it is considered auspicious to have a yantra in one's house: "He who has placed a yantra in his house accomplishes everything."[134]

The yantras' protecting and auspicious effects are also used on other occasions. So, at a funeral, the dead body is put upon a yantra that is covered by a cloth.[135] A pill (*gulikā*) that has been prepared for the acquisition of supernatural powers must be purified with incense in a casket upon which a yantra has been drawn (*yantrasampuṭa*).[136]

Other than protection, a yantra may bestow anything one wishes as already indicated in the passage quoted above: elimination of sorrow, diseases and obstacles, attainment of children, friends,

---

[133] Jayākhya-Saṃhitā 29.172d–180b:
tad yantraṃ pariveṣṭayet // 172
pañcaraṅgeṇa sūtreṇa kṣipet kanakasaṃpuṭe /
dordaṇḍe dakṣiṇe kuryāt strī vā stanayugāntare // 173
priyatvaṃ satataṃ yāti vairiṣv api ca sādhakaḥ /
nadīnadān samudrān vā līlayā parilaṅghayet // 174
bahvarthaṃ tatprabhāvāc ca no majjati jalāntare /
nāraṇyavanajānāṃ tu sakāśād vidyate bhayam // 175
bhajanti sānukūlaṃ ca viparītasthitā grahāḥ /
na bādhate viṣaṃ ghoram anekaṃ cātibhīṣaṇam // 176
corādiśastrasaṃghāto gātrasandhiṣu no viśet / (...)
bālagrahādayo dūraṃ tyaktvā bālaṃ prayānti ca // 178
yatredaṃ tiṣṭhate yantraṃ kiṃ tu taddehagaṃ tu vai /
lagnagarbhā ca yā nārī sukhaṃ sūte ca dhāraṇāt // 179
bhavet putravatī vandhyā mṛtavatsātha putriṇī /
(Jayākhya-Saṃhitā 29.177c–178b is corrupt.) Cf. also Jayākhya-Saṃhitā 29.102c–103, 32.81–84, Sātvata-Saṃhitā 17.352–357b. Not only yantras can be worn as amulets. A mantra written on birch-bark or a piece of cloth can also be used as such; cf. Rastelli 2000b: 350.

[134] Ahirbudhnya-Saṃhitā 25.18cd:
yantraṃ yasya gṛhe nyastaṃ tasya sarvaṃ prasidhyati //

[135] Jayākhya-Saṃhitā 24.8cd.

[136] Jayākhya-Saṃhitā 26.69ab.

consorts, kingship and wealth.[137] Yantras are considered to be so powerful that even antidotes against them could be necessary in the case of an enemy using them against one. Such antidotes are presented in the Jayākhya-Saṃhitā: the *varāhamudrā* and the *jayāmantra* are successful in destroying the power of yantras.[138]

A particular yantra is the *saudarśanayantra*, which is described in the Ahirbudhnya-Saṃhitā and, based on the Ahirbudhnya-Saṃhitā, also in the Pārameśvara-Saṃhitā.[139] It not only contains linear diagrams and writings of mantras, but also pictorial representations of various deities.[140] Furthermore, the writing material, which should be solid such as metal or stone, is covered with a yantra diagram not only on the obverse side but also, with a different drawing, on the reverse.[141]

The *saudarśanayantra* is used especially by kings and those who want to attain kingship. They should install it in a temple and worship it daily in order to secure their kingship: "Hear the peculiarity of the protective prescription for kings, o Nārada. He who desires kingship, he who is deprived of kingship, or he who is overpowered by [other] kings, having realized that the most distinguished teacher who bestows the yantra of Sudarśana exceeds all, should worship this [teacher] with great wealth and then should worship the four-armed Nārāyaṇa, the god, whose eyes are as large

---

[137] E.g., Jayākhya-Saṃhitā 26.104c–105b, 110c–113b, Ahirbudhnya-Saṃhitā 26.73, 36.26c–30b.

[138] Jayākhya-Saṃhitā 8.30a, 27.131a.

[139] The description of the *saudarśanayantra* in Pārameśvara-Saṃhitā 23 is based on that in the Ahirbudhnya-Saṃhitā. The Pārameśvara-Saṃhitā even refers explicitly to the Ahirbudhnya-Saṃhitā as its source. Compare Pārameśvara-Saṃhitā 23.2c–3: "In former times in order to appease the great sin of cutting Brahmā's head Nārāyaṇa taught, at the auspicious Badarikāśrama, [the yantra] that removes all sins to Śaṅkara, who was asking for it." (*purā nārāyaṇenoktaṃ puṇye badarikāśrame // 2 brahmaṇaḥ śīrṣavicchedamahāpātakaśāntaye / pṛcchataḥ śaṅkarasyātha sarvapāpāpanodanam //* 3) with Ahirbudhnya-Saṃhitā 25.14c–15: "In order to appease the great sin of cutting Pitāmaha's head Nārāyaṇa taught me [the yantra] that pacifies all afflictions [and] keeps off all pain at the auspicious Badarikāśrama." (*mama nārāyaṇenoktaṃ puṇye badarikāśrame //* 14 *pitāmahaśiraśchedamahāpātakaśāntaye / sarvabādhāpraśamanaṃ sarvaduḥkhanivāraṇam //* 15) Cf. also Pārameśvara-Saṃhitā 26.43abc: "(...) according to the rule, as Ahirbudhnya has taught it at length to Nārada, who has asked [for it] (...)" (*pṛcchate nāradāyaitad ahirbudhnyena vistarāt / yathopadiṣṭaṃ vidhivat*).

[140] The most important deities on the *saudarśanayantra* are Sudarśana, Viṣṇu's discus to whom the Ahirbudhnya-Saṃhitā is especially devoted, and Nṛsiṃha.

[141] Ahirbudhnya-Saṃhitā 26.5–72, Pārameśvara-Saṃhitā 23.16–117b.

as a lotus, who is dark-coloured, who [wears] yellow garments, and who is adorned with all [kinds of] ornaments according to the prescriptions as taught by the teacher. He should have an excellent yantra made, which is made of gold, is decorated with jewels and corals, and furnished with all [kinds of] ornaments. By merely doing this does he attain sound kingship. Having installed [this yantra], which bestows the attainment of everything, he should worship it respectfully. Then he will obtain the earth with [its] seven divisions (*saptadvīpām*) [and its] towns."[142]

In the Ahirbudhnya-Saṃhitā, the temple (*vimāna*) for the *saudarśanayantra* and the prescriptions for worship to be performed there are not described in detail.[143] However, the author of the younger Pārameśvara-Saṃhitā, who strongly emphasizes temple worship in general, has elaborated the descriptions of the temple (*prāsāda*) or pavilion (*maṇḍapa*) that should be built for the *saudarśanayantra*'s worship, and also the prescriptions for its worship.[144] The yantra's worship is very similar to the common daily ritual in a temple. This means that this yantra takes the position of a place for the deity's worship, similar to, e.g., a statue or a maṇḍala.[145]

---

[142] Ahirbudhnya-Saṃhitā 26.82–87:
rājñāṃ rakṣāvidhāne tu viśeṣaṃ śṛṇu nārada /
rājyārthī hṛtarājyo vā paribhūto 'thavā nṛpaiḥ // 82
saudarśanasya yantrasya pradātāraṃ guruṃ param /
sarvebhyo hy adhikaṃ matvā tam abhyarcya mahādhanaiḥ // 83
tato nārāyaṇaṃ devaṃ puṇḍarīkāyatekṣaṇam /
śyāmalaṃ pītavasanaṃ sarvābharaṇabhūṣitam // 84
ārādhayec caturbāhum ācāryoktavidhānataḥ /
taptajāmbūnadamayaṃ maṇividrumacitritam // 85
sarvālaṃkārasaṃyuktaṃ kārayed yantram uttamam /
etatkaraṇamātreṇa rājyam āpnoty anāmayam // 86
pratiṣṭhāpyārcayed etat sādaraṃ sarvasiddhidam /
tato bhūmim avāpnoti saptadvīpāṃ sapattanām // 87
Cf. also Pārameśvara-Saṃhitā 23.8c–9b: "Kings who are disposed to protect [their] people are to perform continuously this worship. Otherwise a lack of firmness arises." (*prajāpālanaśīlānāṃ bhūpānām etad arcanam // nairantaryeṇa kartavyam anyathā jāyate 'dhṛtiḥ /*)

[143] The temple is mentioned only in Ahirbudhnya-Saṃhitā 36.35c, 36c, and 40c.

[144] See Pārameśvara-Saṃhitā 23.12–18b for the temple and Pārameśvara-Saṃhitā 25–26 for the ritual prescriptions.

[145] There is much inscriptional and literary evidence that images of Sudarśana were worshipped in Pāñcarātra temples, often in special shrines. Several such images have been preserved (cf. Begley 1973: 68ff.). Illustration 1 shows a bronze image of Sudarśana within a yantra. This image is dated by Begley 1973: 90 to about the 17th century. Although it does not look exactly like the *saudarśanayantra*

The *saudarśanayantra* is not the only yantra that is worshipped in a temple or pavilion. As already mentioned, yantras are worshipped in a *maṇḍapa* also according to the Aniruddha-Saṃhitā. Here, however, they are drawn directly on a platform (*vedi*) and not upon a mobile material.[146] According to the Parama-Saṃhitā, a yantra is used in place of a statue during the procession that is a part of the consecration (*pratiṣṭhā*). The yantra that represents Viṣṇu is carried around the temple. After this, it is installed in the temple, and only then is the statue of Viṣṇu established.[147]

Finally, a particular yantra that is related to the *saudarśanayantra* should be mentioned. This is the *dhārakayantra*, the 'yantra of the wearer,' i.e., the wearer of the *saudarśanayantra*. The power of the *saudarśanayantra* is considered to be so great that a human being cannot wear it without additionally having a *dhārakayantra*: "[Nārada:] 'Who wears this very wonderful divine ornament? I do not perceive anyone to have the power (*śakti*) to wear it. Please remove [my] doubt [that has arisen] on account of its excessive power.' Ahirbudhnya: 'Truly, no one can wear this [yantra] of great splendour without [also wearing] the following, other yantra that is full of power, o divine seer. Hear now its nature [and] energy, o best sage.' (...)"[148] The *dhārakayantra*'s most exterior part is the square earth maṇḍala with the seed syllable (*bīja*) of the earth on each corner and two Nāgas on each side. Within the earth maṇḍala is the fire maṇḍala having the shape of a hexagram with the fire seed

described in the Ahirbudhnya-Saṃhitā, it gives an idea of what it may have looked like.

[146] Cf. p. 143.

[147] Cf. Parama-Saṃhitā 19.62–63b: "He should then prepare a yantra of the great god and, after having asked for permission, have the initiated guardians of the statue lift the yantra that is Hari onto a comfortable palanquin that is endowed with an arch." (*tato devasya mahato yantram ekaṃ vidhāya ca / dīkṣitair mūrtipair juṣṭāṃ śibikāṃ toraṇānvitām / abhyanujñāṃ ca yācitvā yantram āropayed dharim /*) Cf. Parama-Saṃhitā 19.70cd for the yantra's and 19.72b for the statue's installation.

[148] Ahirbudhnya-Saṃhitā 27.2c–5b:

[*nāradaḥ* –]
etad atyadbhutaṃ divyaṃ dhriyate kena bhūṣaṇam // 2
na cāsya dhāraṇe śaktiṃ kasyacit kalayāmy aham /
atiśaktitayāsyemaṃ saṃśayaṃ chettum arhasi // 3
ahirbudhnyaḥ –
satyaṃ na kenacid dhartuṃ pāryate tan mahādyuti /
ṛte yantrāntarād asmād devarṣe śaktiśālinaḥ // 4
śṛṇu tasya muniśreṣṭha svarūpaṃ vīryam adya vai /

Cf. also Ahirbudhnya-Saṃhitā 27.24c–26.

syllable. The round wind maṇḍala with its seed syllable[149] is within it, and within the latter, a wheel with ten spokes. Two syllables each of the *saudarśanamantra* and the *nārasiṃhamantra* are written on nine spokes, and on the tenth spoke, the word *hana*, 'kill.' Obviously, this combination keeps the *saudarśanayantra*'s power in check. An eight-petalled lotus with the mantra *oṃ* and the names of the desired object and the person the yantra is directed to (*sādhya*) is in the centre of the wheel.[150] The penultimate item seems strange in the case of the *dhārakayantra* whose only purpose is the fitness for wearing the *saudarśanayantra*. The person it is directed to can only be its wearer. The example of the *dhārakayantra* shows how powerful yantras were considered to be, and that their power could get out of control if they were not treated properly.

---

[149] For the shapes of the elements' maṇḍalas, cf. also Jayākhya-Saṃhitā 10.26, 36c–38a, and 43c–44b and Gupta/Hoens/Goudriaan 1979: 172–174. The *bījas* of the elements vary in the different traditions. According to the Jayākhya-Saṃhitā, the earth's *bīja* is *ślāṃ*, the fire's *srāṃ*, and the wind's *hyāṃ* (Jayākhya-Saṃhitā 10.17c–20b), cf. also Gupta/Hoens/Goudriaan ibid.

[150] Ahirbudhnya-Saṃhitā 27.5c–16.

1. The 16-armed Sudarśanacakrapuruṣa in the Śrī-Kālamekaperumāl Temple

MAṆḌALA AND YANTRA IN THE SIDDHĀNTA SCHOOL OF ŚAIVISM: DEFINITIONS, DESCRIPTION AND RITUAL USE*

Hélène Brunner

(Translated from the French by Raynald Prévèreau)

Introduction

It is common to refer to the ritual use of more or less complex drawings among the defining characteristics of every denomination of Tantrism. Generally, such drawings are called maṇḍalas, but also yantras and cakras, with little consideration as to whether these terms are synonyms or not.

This paper essentially aims at clarifying this terminology, and this will be done in the first part. In the second part, I will discuss the maṇḍalas used in the cult of Śiva: analyzing a simple example, I will describe their general structure and indicate how exactly they are used in the rituals.

It is first out of personal interest that I began investigating the subject on which I here report my conclusions. Perplexed, undoub-

* This paper is, broadly, a remake of an article published in French some fifteen years ago (Brunner 1986). That article reproduced almost verbatim a lecture given in Paris in June 1984 on the occasion of a conference organized by A. Padoux in the context of the research team no. 249 of the Centre national de la recherche scientifique (CNRS) entitled 'L'Hindouisme—textes, doctrines, pratiques.' The present paper is a complete revision of the previous one. Not only did I eliminate the oral character of the presentation, but I also modified several expressions that seemed correct in 1984 but that progress in the study of Śaivism now shows to be inexact. I also reworked some long passages by introducing useful precisions, added many references and inserted some comments in part inspired by the discussion (not reproduced here) that followed the lecture in Paris. It was, however, not possible for me to extend my research. Therefore, works on the subject which appeared after 1986 are not taken into consideration.

Note by G. Bühnemann: In this article the author uses the term 'cult' in the sense of 'sectarian affiliation' and 'worship'/'ritual.' The word is not used in a derogatory sense.

tedly like many other scholars, by the coexistence of three terms that modern authors rarely distinguish and often translate, in English, as well as in French, by the same word 'diagram,' I had developed the habit over the years of taking note of the ritual contexts in which those terms appeared. Soon enough, I realized that mediaeval authors did not use the terms so freely as we do and thought that it would be good if we imitated their precision instead of creating confusion where it did not exist by using a single word in our translations (and I also accept this criticism). I was therefore pleased to seize the opportunity provided by a conference held on this theme in Paris in 1984 to expand my research and submit the result of my reflections to the participants. Their reactions inspired some of the additions that I have made to the original French paper.

I must insist at the outset on the fact that my research does not cover all Hindu schools, not even all Tantric sects. Rather, I limited myself to the following texts:

(1) the fundamental texts of the Siddhānta School,[1] those that have come to be called Śaivāgamas or even simply Āgamas (Mūlāgamas and Upāgamas), but could just as well be called Tantras since they often present themselves as such.[2] I looked at

[1] We must stop calling this school the 'Southern School,' for while it is true that it is the South of India that has kept its heritage alive, we now know that its most ancient texts come from the North (including the *paddhati* of Somaśambhu, see my introduction to SP4, pp. xliii–xlv). We could call it the Śaiva-Siddhānta School, but since this term was borrowed from the Sanskrit School of that denomination by the Tamil School that followed it and profoundly modified it, and since the name has remained attached to the latter, we should call it more precisely: 'Śaiva-Siddhānta School of Sanskrit expression' or simply 'Sanskrit Śaiva-Siddhānta School.' That is what I keep repeating (see, for example, Brunner 1977: 114–115 and 1992: 38, note 2). This appellation is here shortened into 'Siddhānta' for the sake of simplicity.

[2] See, for example, p. xix of the introduction to my translation of Mṛgendrāgama, *kriyāpāda* and *caryāpāda*, and more recently Goodall's introduction to his edition of the Kiraṇavṛtti, pp. xxxvi–xxxix. It is useful to note here that, among the Tantras of the Siddhānta that have reached us, rare are the texts that date from before the ninth century. Except for the Kiraṇa, the Mṛgendra and the Mataṅgapārameśvara, those that were published in India, including those excellently edited by N.R. Bhatt and published by the Institut Français d'Indologie, belong to a later period, even though some of them borrow the name of a work previously known and cited. For the Kāmika, see the introduction to my translation of the Mṛgendrāgama cited above, pp. xii–xv. I will, however, have to refer to such works, which in fact, with regard to the subject here under investigation, most probably repeat the traditional instructions.

all the ones that were at my disposal, namely about ten of them, plus some preserved fragments of lost treatises;

(2) some Śaiva Tantras of the Trika: Svacchanda (SvT), Netra (NT) and Mālinīvijaya;

(3) a fair number of handbooks (*paddhati*) of the Siddhānta, the most important of which being the Somaśambhupaddhati (SP), called Kriyākāṇḍakramāvalī, written in Kashmir in the 11th century, and of which I have published a complete translation. The following handbooks, written in the South, depend more or less directly on this work: the Aghoraśivācāryapaddhati, called Kriyākramadyotikā, of the 12th century; the yet unpublished Jñānaratnāvalī, the Siddhāntaśekhara and the Siddhāntasārāvali, all three probably dating from the 13th century; and finally the Īśānaśivagurudevapaddhati, a later work which is nonetheless better known since it was edited early in the 20th century and reprinted in 1988;

(4) some handbooks from the Trika School, such as the Tantrāloka (TĀ) of Abhinavagupta and the Śāradātilaka (ŚT) of Lakṣmaṇadeśika.

All these sources converge, so much so that the results of my research do not only concern the Śaivism of the Siddhānta School, as the title of this paper carefully suggests, but could probably apply to a wider range of traditions. It is not certain, however, that my conclusions could, without further precautions, be extrapolated to all Tantric schools, for example, to Śāktism or to Pāñcarātra, nor to all periods, for example, to the more recent Tantrism.

Nonetheless, I should note that the non-synonymy of the terms maṇḍala and yantra is accepted by the Śabdakalpadruma (s.v. yantra) which quotes the following passage from the Yoginītantra,[3] where the possible supports for the cult of the goddess are discussed:

liṅgasthāṃ pūjayed devīṃ pustakasthāṃ tathaiva ca /
maṇḍalasthāṃ mahāmāyāṃ yantrasthāṃ pratimāsu ca //
jalasthāṃ vā śilāsthāṃ vā pūjayet parameśvarīm /

[3] Text dating from the 16th century (see Goudriaan in Goudriaan/Gupta 1981: 85–86).

I. *Occurrence of the Three Terms in the Ritual Texts*

A. Maṇḍala

Let us now look at the first point, which concerns the occurrence of the terms maṇḍala, yantra and cakra in the ritual texts. I will begin with the one that is by far the most frequent in the standard rituals: 'maṇḍala'—a term that we spontaneously associate with those splendid drawings so characteristic of Tibetan Buddhism and of which we have seen a large diffusion over the last decades.

When and how do the Śaiva texts use this word? We must obviously set aside right from the start the rather banal meaning of 'circle' (construction circle or any other disk) as well as that of 'territory' or 'province,' with which we are not concerned here, at least not directly. I shall therefore consider only the specific ritual objects that the texts call 'maṇḍalas.' All appear as limited surfaces, of which I find three main types:

First type: a limited surface deprived of structure.
For example: the 'cow-dung maṇḍala' enjoined on numerous occasions to serve either as the seat for a god (for example, Naṭeśvara, when he is called to preside over the dances performed by the Devadāsīs in front of Śiva), for a man (the disciple, before his initiation), or for a revered object (the cooking pot for the deity's rice, when it is removed from the fire and placed on the ground).[4]

Such maṇḍalas are made by smearing a generally circular portion of the ground with a semi-liquid paste made of cow-dung or sandalwood. I will call them 'seat-maṇḍalas.'

Second type: a limited surface showing a drawing generally made of the accumulation of coloured powders.

This is the most interesting type of maṇḍala, one that we must most carefully distinguish from those other drawings called 'yantras,' because they bear some resemblance. Here are its characteristics:

- These maṇḍalas serve as supports for the worship of divinities. They have no other use.
- They are temporary, being destroyed once the ceremony for which they were built is completed.

[4] See SP3, Index, p. 737, s.v. "maṇḍala (quelconque)."

- They are constructed on a plane and purified area, and oriented. The drawing (made with strings and compass) is geometrical; it often shows a central symmetry (or, if one prefers, an axial symmetry, with reference to an axis perpendicular to the plane and going through the centre);[5] and it is entirely covered with coloured powders (three, four or five different colours)—hence the exact name of these objects: *rajomaṇḍalas.*[6]
- Their dimensions are sometimes considerable since they vary, depending on the type or the text, from one to eight (according to the Mṛgendra)[7] or even eighteen cubits (according to the Mataṅgapārameśvara), that is to say from half a metre to about four or even nine metres. The officiant is there described entering and leaving through 'doors,' moving around along 'streets'—instructions that must be taken literally for the bigger structures.

Let us go over the first of these characteristics; namely, that these maṇḍalas serve as supports for worship. The way to perform this cult will be described in the second part of this paper, but it will be good at this point to specify the nature of the worship in question. Here the texts from the Siddhānta diverge from those of the Trika. While the latter recommend doing all the cults, including the daily cults,[8] on a maṇḍala, the vast majority of the texts of the Siddhānta insist on using the maṇḍala only for the occasional *(naimittika)* rituals[9]—such

---

[5] The square maṇḍala, of central symmetry, with, at its centre, an eight-petalled lotus, is by far the most common maṇḍala, at least in the normal cult of Śiva. For the other gods, the maṇḍala may take other shapes. For example, according to the Mṛgendrāgama (*kriyāpāda* 8.36c–37b), the maṇḍala of Caṇḍa is semi-circular, and that of the goddesses invoked to seduce women takes the form of a vulva, an eye or an arc. The shape and colour also vary according to the purpose of the ritual (Mṛgendrāgama, *kriyāpāda* 8.37c–38).

[6] There are, as we will see, drawings that, by their aspect and their use, partake of the nature of the maṇḍala, but that are not constructed by the accumulation of powders.

[7] See Mṛgendrāgama, *kriyāpāda* 8.30 and Mataṅgapārameśvarāgama, *kriyāpāda* 1.26a.

[8] See, for example, SvT$_1$, chapter 2, introduction to verse 155. It is the same for the Mṛgendrāgama (see note 11).

[9] According to the Vedic classification, which in fact does not apply well at all to Tantric rituals. The *pratiṣṭhā* is generally taken as an example of occasional (*naimittika*) rites; but since it is performed on the initiative of a person who wishes to acquire merit, it is sometimes classified among the optional (*kāmya*) rituals. The *utsava*s may be spoken of as 'occasional' if one considers their periodicity, but they should be called 'optional' on account of their being performed with a definite aim

as the *dīkṣā*, the *pratiṣṭhā*, the *pavitrārohaṇa*, the *utsava*—and the optional (*kāmya*) cults, that is to say all the rites performed for a desire-oriented purpose.[10] For the daily (*nitya*) cult of Śiva, even for the private one, they prefer the *liṅga*.[11] It is therefore with regard to

---

in view. The *pavitrārohaṇa* (see SP2, section II) belongs to the '*prāyaścitta*' category, which is associated with the occasional rituals out of convention only. Finally, the *dīkṣās* are said to be 'occasional' only from the point of view of the *guru* performing the rite; those that are conferred upon the *sādhakas* to let them acquire *siddhis* should logically count among the *kāmya* rituals. One should note that these long rituals (which spread over several days, of which the first days are used for preparatory rites designated by the general term *adhivāsa*) can be performed only by the *ācārya*, if they are public rituals, or by the *sādhaka*, if they are private cults (on the *sādhaka*, see Brunner 1975), and that it is only these high ranked initiates who can trace and use the *rajomaṇḍalas*.

[10] The only maṇḍala described in the Sārdhatriśatikālottara (7.1ab) is presented in the context of the *kāmyakarman*, and this shows, according to its commentator, that it concerns only the *sādhaka*. The interpretation expressed in this work seems unusual, however. Indeed, it must be noted that some of the desire-oriented rituals that concern a group of people and not just one person, such as the purification or pacifying (*śānti*) rites, can be and usually are performed by the *ācārya*.

[11] With a few exceptions, for example, the Mṛgendra, which describes the daily cult of Śiva on a *sthaṇḍila* before considering the possibility of using a *liṅga* (Mṛgendrāgama, *kriyāpāda* 3.54c–56b). It is the opposite elsewhere, see, for example, SP1, pp. 226–229, verses 102–103, where Somaśambhu, after describing the cult on a *liṅga*, gives a list of equally acceptable supports (for the private cult), but concludes: *liṅge 'py atyantam uttamam*. The later works take in general a more radical position. Quoting the Pūrva-Kāraṇāgama, chapter 30, will suffice. In the first passage (30.2c–3b), that text lists the different supports for the private cult: the personal *liṅga* given by the *guru*; the *sthaṇḍila*; oneself; a temporary (*kṣaṇika*) *liṅga*; a maṇḍala; the water. Immediately afterwards (30.3c–4b), and in a somewhat different list, it assigns a value to the cults performed on these supports: the cult performed on a maṇḍala is rated at 100; at 1000 if performed on a *sthaṇḍila*; at 10,000 on a *kautuka* (probably a narrow stripe of cloth with drawings, later called *paṭa*), and at 10 billion on a *liṅga*.

datte ca guruṇā liṅge sthaṇḍile svayam ātmani //
kṣaṇike maṇḍale toye 'py ātmārthayajanaṃ smṛtam /
maṇḍale tu śataṃ puṇyaṃ sthaṇḍile tu sahasrakam //
ayutaṃ kautuke liṅge koṭikoṭiguṇaṃ bhavet / (30.2c–4b)

The same work takes up again the problem a little farther (30.7–8), and establishes the following series, listing the cults in an increasing order in terms of their value: the mental cult; the cult on a maṇḍala; on a temporary *liṅga*; on a stripe of cloth (with drawings? *paṭa*); on a painted image (? *ābhāsa*); on an image in the round (*bimba*); on a *liṅga* (with faces, to distinguish it from the next one); on a *liṅga* deprived of anthropomorphic traits (*niṣkala-liṅga*).

mānasān maṇḍalaṃ śreṣṭhaṃ maṇḍalāt kṣaṇikaṃ param /
kṣaṇikāt phalam utkṛṣṭaṃ paṭaṃ caiva tataḥ param //
paṭād ābhāsam utkṛṣṭam ābhāsāt bimbam ucyate /
bimbād vai liṅgam utkṛṣṭaṃ liṅgād vai niṣkalaṃ param // (30.7–8)

the occasional rituals, especially the *dīkṣā*, that the Siddhānta texts give a description of the maṇḍala: some will describe only one, like the Mṛgendra (*kriyāpāda* 8.25c–53) and the Sārdhatriśatikālottara (chapter 7), but in general several kinds of maṇḍalas are suggested for the officiant to choose from (see below). All these maṇḍalas have a complex structure, are rather long to elaborate, and remain present for the complete duration of the ritual for which they are used. When one considers using a maṇḍala for the daily cult of Śiva,[12] the maṇḍala, which will have to be drawn each day, is of course much simpler. It is limited to the eight-petalled lotus that occupies the centre of the larger maṇḍalas. According to the Suprabheda (*kriyā-pāda* 8.8), it is drawn on a portion of the ground previously smeared with cow-dung, while according to other texts it is drawn on a square platform made of sand and grains named *sthaṇḍila* (thus the frequent confusion between *sthaṇḍila* and maṇḍala). But there is never any mention of coloured powders. The same instructions apply to the maṇḍalas used in the daily cult of the secondary divinities, such as Sūrya (see SP1, p. 71, under [1d]).

In all cases, this second type of maṇḍala corresponds to the following definition: it is a temporary divine image traced, with some exceptions, by the accumulation of coloured powders and which must be beautiful to rejoice men and gods. I will call it the 'image-maṇḍala.'

Third type: a limited surface that is squared but has no drawing. We also find under the name maṇḍala some square surfaces suitably squared and in the boxes of which the officiant (rapidly) invokes

---

The idea, as we can see, is to exalt the *liṅga* as the ideal support for the private cult. As for the temple cult, the question does not crop up: it can only take a permanent image as its support, that is to say a fixed *liṅga* for Śiva, a sculpted image for the goddess.

[12] There are circumstances when one has to. That is what Īśānaśivagurudeva explains (see Īśānaśivagurudevapaddhati, *kriyāpāda* 20.23–27 [= volume 3, p. 200, 6–15]): if the adept is affected by a family impurity, he cannot touch the *liṅga*, nor the fire; he must therefore have someone else perform the public cult, while mentally reciting the mantras; then he must himself perform his daily cult (compulsory) on a maṇḍala, always mentally reciting the mantras. One could ask if that rule can be explained by the fact that, the maṇḍala being temporary, no impurity coming from the officiant can impinge on it definitively, while it would have a lasting effect on the permanent *liṅga*; or if it can be explained simply by some essential inferiority of the maṇḍala compared to the *liṅga*: the simple maṇḍala used here would be less precious than any *liṅga*, even the temporary *liṅga* that would be allowed in the first hypothesis. See also note 55.

some divine or evil powers in order to make them favourable to his cause with a food offering called *bali*.

These *balimaṇḍala*s are found in many rituals, including the daily ritual. The best known of these is certainly the one called *vāstumaṇḍala*, where 45 gods and 8 demons are worshipped (and fed) before any construction, as well as at some critical moments associated with a given site. The works of Stella Kramrisch[13] made it famous and loaded it with a symbolism that I for one have some difficulty seeing but on which I do not have to elaborate here. What I would like to emphasize, however, is that the term *vāstumaṇḍala*, which we use systematically, is rare in the texts with which I am most familiar.[14] In the vast majority of cases, these texts prefer the terms *pada* and *padavinyāsa* to refer to these squared surfaces and their construction; the same terms are used when they describe the division of any square area (the ground of a sacrificial pavilion, the site of an agglomeration, etc.) in four concentric zones destined to serve as guides for the ulterior arrangement of the site.[15] In all these cases, we must take the term *pada* in the sense of 'domain' and understand *padavinyāsa* as the attribution of their respective domain to different entities. However, it will happen that the term maṇḍala be used in this context, and that is why I refer to these squared surfaces as a third type of maṇḍala—the only one, in fact, for which the translation 'diagram' is appropriate.

I will include in the same category some simple geometrical figures allowing for the distribution of objects, for example, the square divided in nine boxes which, according to some texts, serve to fix (with the fall of a flower) the name of a Śaiva initiate;[16] or the

---

[13] See Kramrisch 1946, volume 1: 29–97.

[14] It is not found in this context in the following Āgamas: the Pūrva-Kāmika, the Suprabheda, the Ajita and the Kiraṇa nor is it found in the Mayamata or the Bṛhat-Saṃhitā. We find the word maṇḍala twice in the description of the Pūrva-Kāraṇa, once *balimaṇḍala* in the Śāradātilaka, once "*maṇḍalād bahye*" in a handbook dealing with *pratiṣṭhā*, and twice the term *vāstumaṇḍala* (once abbreviated to maṇḍala) in the Somaśambhupaddhati (see SP4, pp. 46 and 386).

[15] The name of these four zones are, starting from the central zone: *brāhmapada*, *daivikapada*, *mānuṣyapada* and *paiśācapada*. A fifth zone called *rākṣasapada* is sometimes added, see Mayamata, volume 1, p. 126, note 56 and Figure 9; and SP2, pp. 332–333 and Plates I and II. The term *pada*, while referring here to the entire zone, does not lose the meaning of 'unit box.'

[16] See Suprabhedāgama, *caryāpāda* 4.12–15b. The central box and the four boxes of the principal directions are those of the five Brahmans; the corners belong to four

squared surfaces on which the *pañcagavya* and other mixtures are prepared.[17] We can call these maṇḍalas 'distributive diagrams.'

Fourth use of the term: There is finally one last use of the term, but it is totally heterogeneous with the preceding ones and does not correspond to a category of objects that could be integrated into our classification. The maṇḍalas of which I am thinking are not, by the way, material objects used for concrete rituals. Even though we can draw them, they are mental objects that the imagination must create and which, under certain specific circumstances, serve as supports of meditation. This is the case with the maṇḍalas of the five elements mentioned in the descriptions of *bhūtaśuddhi* as well as the descriptions of the subtle body; this is also the case with the three maṇḍalas of the moon, the sun, and fire (to which a *śaktimaṇḍala* is sometimes added) that appear at the upper end of the throne of Śiva. The idea of cosmic domain is there inseparable from that of a geometric symbol, so that the inclusion of these maṇḍalas with the preceding ones becomes impossible and all attempts at a translation fail.

We therefore arrive at three well defined types of maṇḍalas: the seats, the divine images and the distributive diagrams.[18]

B. Yantra and Cakra

I now resume my terminological exploration by looking at the terms yantra and cakra, on which I will not elaborate so much. But first, here are two preliminary remarks.

The first one is negative: to my knowledge, the maṇḍalas that I have just discussed, no matter the type, are never called yantras or cakras in the Āgamas. I, however, found one exception: the Upā-

---

of the six 'members' (*aṅgas*). The point of fall of the flower determines the beginning of the name of the initiate, see SP3, p. 102.

[17] See SP2, p. 320.

[18] The distinctions between the three types of maṇḍalas are certainly not as clear as this paper leads to believe. In particular, a quick outline of a lotus or any other adequate drawing can transform a 'seat' into an 'image;' just as a drawing that is a little complex, made, for example, with hulled grains on a raw grains background, transforms a *sthaṇḍila* (see above) into something that could be called a maṇḍala. On the other hand, it also happens (ŚT 3.17c–18a) that the *vāstumaṇḍalas* are covered with coloured powders—a fact that brings them closer to the second category of maṇḍalas and could create confusion if we forget this essential difference: the *vāstumaṇḍalas* do not serve as supports for the cult of a main god—they are not even connected to any particular form of Hinduism.

gama named Vātulaśuddha describes in its third chapter, under the title *cakrabhedapaṭala*, what is, in fact, an image-maṇḍala; it calls it cakra throughout the description, even once yantra. The explanation for this infringement is doubtlessly contained in the final lines of that section, where it is said that the cakra can be drawn on a bark and kept as an amulet. The *śrīcakra* represents a better known exception.

My second remark will again contrast the texts of the Siddhānta with those of other schools: the terms yantra and cakra are rarely encountered in the Siddhānta (these terms do not appear in the lists of appropriate supports for the cult of Śiva), while they are frequent elsewhere. It is therefore from the Tantras of the Trika, in particular the SvT and the NT, that I draw the characteristics of these objects.[19]

1) Yantras are drawings that differ in several ways from maṇḍalas:

- They serve only for the *kāmya* rituals, the desire-oriented rites, and therefore concern essentially the *sādhaka*. The cult based on yantras in fact only marks the first stage of their use. Indeed, the yantras are generally kept after the cult and worn as amulets; or buried for subsequent magic rituals; or eaten, after crushing the support and mixing the resulting powder with milk or honey.
- They are traced on durable materials: birch-bark (*bhūrjatvac*, *bhūrjapattra*), copperplates, pieces of cloth, and now paper; they are therefore small and mobile.
- The representations they carry are linear.

[19] On the basis of these same two Tantras and their commentaries by Kṣemarāja, Professor Alexis Sanderson commented, at the conference mentioned above (see Padoux 1986: 33), that they confirmed the distinction that I made between maṇḍala and yantra: "...Your precise distinction between *yantra* and *maṇḍala* is confirmed by Kṣemarāja who defines the former (in its more complex form) as a collection of mantras written in a particular pattern (on NT_2 20.59c: *yantracakraṃ viśiṣṭa-saṃniveśalikhito mantrasamūhaḥ*), while in its most basic form it is simply a spell written on a piece of birch-bark (*bhūrjapatram*)...." And he continued with a very pertinent remark concerning the more subtle distinction between maṇḍala and cakra: "As for the subtler distinction between *maṇḍala* and *cakra*, if the *maṇḍala* is the *ādhāraḥ* (locus) and the *cakra* (of deities/mantras) the *ādheyam* (located), then it would follow that it is only the former that one can 'trace' and that when one speaks of the *maṇḍala* to include the circle of deities (*devatācakram*) or mantras (*mantra-cakram*) worshipped in it, then this is by extension of the primary sense."

We find a number of drawings of yantras in the handbooks of popular Tantrism, in Hindī, abundantly distributed by Indian bookstores. Of more refined art, the drawings of the Balinese sorcerers (see the posthumous book, Hooykaas 1980) also have something of the yantra.

- The drawing is engraved (rare) or (more often) traced with a liquid—some ink—made from a variety of often surprising substances, such as blood and the bile of a corpse in some cases of black magic.
- The drawing is always completed with the inscription of letters, of *bījas*, each of which makes a divinity present, and of mantras often containing imperative orders such as: "Kill such and such!", "Heal such and such!"
- Their layout and use are secret.

The dominant idea of the yantra is contained in its name, derived from the root *yam*: with a yantra, the *sādhaka* 'constrains' a divinity to carry out a certain action for him.[20] Just as those other machines bearing the same name, the ritual yantra is first an ingenious instrument.

The NT keeps mentioning these yantras among the sovereign remedies (for example, NT1 19.198b) and among the weapons of magicians or sorcerers (NT1 18.88c).

2) The use of the term cakra is much less precise. Apparently, it does not refer to a category of objects different from the maṇḍalas and the yantras.

Sometimes, the idea of 'wheel' is obvious, as in the case of the cakra of thirty-two Śaktis included in the maṇḍala of the Svacchandatantra (9.16ab and 9.24). But the term often simply expresses the idea of a 'collection' or a 'mass:' the mass of the divinities assembled on the same limited surface. Finally, cakra is frequently used as a synonym for yantra, though we cannot always tell if this practice is due to a lack of rigour in the vocabulary or to a change of perspective. In those cases, the author may be talking of cakra to refer to the mass of the divinities that are present, or to their configuration, while using the word yantra to refer to the use of the object. But more research than what I was able to do would be necessary to arrive at a convincing conclusion on this point.

Let us note, however, that the term maṇḍala is never used in the designation of these magic figures (will we call them 'coercive

---

[20] See another analysis of the term in Kulārṇava-Tantra 6.86 cited in the Śabda-kalpadruma (s.v. yantra) as coming from another source:
kāmakrodhādidoṣotthasarvaduḥkhaniyantraṇāt /
yantram ity āhur etasmin devaḥ prīṇāti pūjitaḥ //

diagrams'?)—except, of course, for the construction circles or round elements of the total yantra.

II. *Description and Ritual Use of the Image-maṇḍalas*

A. Importance

I mentioned earlier that the maṇḍalas were quasi indispensable elements in the occasional rituals. The chosen maṇḍala is constructed on the altar (*vedī*) that stands in the centre of the pavilion (*maṇḍapa*, more exactly *yāgamaṇḍapa*) where the ritual is taking place and it serves as the principal[21] support for the worship of Śiva during the few days of the ceremony. It is therefore present as a divine image, and only as a divine image; that explains why, though that would not be considered a good solution, the maṇḍala can be substituted with a mobile *liṅga* placed on a *sthaṇḍila*.

B. Varieties

There are tens of well differentiated forms of maṇḍalas, each being designated with a specific term that sometimes expresses a characteristic of the drawing, sometimes the virtue of the object. The list found in Īśānaśivagurudevapaddhati, *kriyāpāda* 8.31–123 (= volume 3, pp. 77, 8 – 85, 6) comes down to seven terms: *bhadra, sarvatobhadra, pārvatīkānta, latāliṅgodbhava, svastikābjadvaya, svastikasarvatobhadra* and *cakrābja*.[22] But some other texts are more prolix, such as the Aṃśumat, which gives twenty names or so.[23]

---

[21] 'Principal,' since there are other supports on which Śiva must be worshipped during the ceremony that uses the maṇḍala. In the *maṇḍapa* itself, aside from the *guru* and eventually the disciple, there are, firstly, a vase of water placed on the north-eastern corner where Śiva is installed as the guardian of the sacrifice and, secondly, the fire (see SP2, pp. 58–80; pp. 86–88 and Plates I–IV). If the ceremony is organized by a temple, the god of the sanctuary nonetheless continues to receive his cult, so that the priests often feel the need to remind through a special ritual the essential identity of all these apparently distinct Śiva(s).

[22] The list of the Rauravāgama (*kriyāpāda* 25.59–62) also counts seven terms, but is somewhat different. There, N.R. Bhatt gives in the notes the construction of each of these maṇḍalas, as found in the hitherto unpublished Śaivāgamapaddhati.

[23] See Aṃśumat 43.40–47, quoted in Rauravāgama, volume I, p. 158, note 11. The Siddhāntasārāvali, verses 78–91, describes ten maṇḍalas: *latāliṅgodbhava* (in two sizes), *navanābha, anantavijaya, bhadra, purākāra* (two sizes), *latākāraliṅga, subhadra, umākānta* and *svastika*—plus another one used for the cult of Caṇḍa; and

These numbers quickly multiply if we take into consideration all of the possible variations on a same theme, so that we finally arrive at hundreds of different maṇḍalas.

Some Āgamas maintain that the choice of the maṇḍala to be used in a given ritual is not arbitrary but depends on the type of ritual to be performed (for example, *dīkṣā* or *pratiṣṭhā*). The selection is even more limited if we distinguish the private (*ātmārtha) pratiṣṭhā* from the public (*parārtha) pratiṣṭhā* and, in the case of the public *pratiṣṭhā*, if we take into account the nature of the *liṅga*, which can be self-manifest (*svāyambhuva*), established by the gods or other supernatural beings (*daivikādi*), or established by men (*mānuṣa*).[24] Elsewhere, we are asked to take into account the season or other contingencies of that order[25] or, if it is a *dīkṣā*, the social class of the initiate.[26] But even if we accept all these restrictions (which not all texts do mention), the definitive choice theoretically remains quite vast, and in the end it is probably some traditions of the schools that were decisive, each master most probably mastering the construction of only a small number of these structures.[27]

C. *Description of a Particular Maṇḍala Destined for a Dīkṣā*

If I just spoke in the past tense, it is because the maṇḍala tradition is not so alive in South India anymore.[28] We are left with the texts,

we find a list of eleven in Īśānaśivagurudevapaddhati, *sāmānyapāda* 6.36–152 (= volume 1, pp. 51, 10 – 62, 2). At the opposite end, the Mataṅgapārameśvarāgama (*kriyāpāda* 1.26–57) describes only two maṇḍalas for Śiva and the Kiraṇa (*paṭala* 20) only one, as is the case for the Mṛgendrāgama as mentioned earlier.

[24] See Aṃśumat, loc. cit.

[25] See, for example, Pūrva-Kāraṇāgama 110.15c–17:
maṇḍalaṃ vedikordhve tu vasantādi ca ṣaḍ ṛtu //
vasante svastikābjaṃ ca grīṣme tu sarvabhadrakam /
prāvṛṭ ca bhadram ākhyātaṃ liṅgābjaṃ svastikaṃ tathā //
śarady eva tu hemānte pārvatīkāntamaṇḍalam /
padmasvastikam ākhyātaṃ śiśire tu viśeṣataḥ //

[26] See the Śāradātilaka, quoted in a South-Indian handbook called Dīkṣādarśa (p. 96, transcript no. 76 of the Institut Français d'Indologie, Pondicherry); the stanza is not found in the printed editions of the Śāradātilaka:
viprāṇāṃ sarvatobhadraṃ gaurītilā nṛpasya tu /
vaiśyānāṃ tu latāliṅgaṃ śūdrāṇāṃ svastikaṃ bhavet //

[27] Financial considerations were also present, see note 47.

[28] Most of the officiants now use some drawings prepared in advance on cardboard or cloth, which will seem aberrant if we think of all those passages in the

which are rich in long and apparently very detailed descriptions, and should in principle suffice. But alas! Whoever takes with enthusiasm his ruler and pencil to translate these instructions into drawings will soon be disappointed: the descriptions, as long as they may be, are everything but clear. Therefore, all of the attempts that I have seen of constructing a maṇḍala strictly on the basis of textual indications have been disappointing: when they were not purely whimsical, the drawings that were proposed were often hypothetical and always incomplete, because a number of constituting elements could not be identified.[29] I know the problem quite well for having wrestled with it when translating the *kriyāpāda* of the Mṛgendra.[30] I still have to situate correctly the thirty-two doors of the big maṇḍala that is described there, and until recently, more exactly until the conference in Paris that I mentioned earlier, a series of technical terms found in that description remained mysterious to me. To most of the problems left unanswered up to that point I found the key in a very clear text that I had ignored until then. It is the Śāradātilaka of Lakṣmaṇadeśika (chapter 3) and its commentary by Rāghavabhaṭṭa.[31] The maṇḍala that I could draw (see Illustration 1)[32] and on which I will

---

scriptures that explain the virtues of the maṇḍalas through those of the powders of which they are composed.

[29] For example, the *śūlābjamaṇḍala* of which Gnoli gives the 'essential structure' in his translation of the Tantrāloka (1972, beginning of p. 520) [note by G. Bühnemann: In the version published in 1999 the diagram appears on p. 614. For a diagram of the maṇḍala, cf. also Sanderson 1986: 171 and Illustration 2 in Padoux's first paper in this book]; and the *mahāmaṇḍala* given by N.R. Bhatt in Mataṅgapārameśvarāgama, volume II, Figure 6.

[30] See Mṛgendrāgama, *kriyāpāda* 8.47c–51.

[31] This commentator, who wrote at the very end of the 15th century, quotes many sources, in particular several handbooks from the Siddhānta School.

[32] Note by G. Bühnemann: Brunner's reconstruction of the maṇḍala is almost identical with the *sarvatobhadramaṇḍala* reproduced in colour (but not analyzed) in Dakshinaranjan Shastri 1940: 170 and 1963, opposite p. 1 and Banerji 1978: 176+. Both of these books reproduce the same maṇḍala drawing. This must be a popular drawing since it also appears on the book cover of an Indian edition and translation of the Devīmāhātmya (Devi Mahatmyam [Glory of the Divine Mother]. 700 Mantras on Sri Durga, <Sanskrit Text and> English Translation by Swami Jagadiswarananda, Madras: Sri Ramakrishna Math, fifth impression, no date). Brunner's drawing can further be compared to the coloured print of the *sarvatobhadra* in Ghoshal Sastri 1983: 56+ and to a drawing in manuscript A 246/25 (labelled *tāntrikakarmakāṇḍa*) preserved in the National Archives, Kāṭhmāṇḍu. The same manuscript also contains a simpler variant called *laghusarvatobhadra*. For a simpler *sarvatobhadra/bhadraka*, see the sketch in the appendix, p. i in Apte's edition of the Pauṣkara-Saṃhitā (Part 1) and the description of the maṇḍala in chapter 5.21–28 of the text. For a colour print

comment is one of the maṇḍalas enjoined there for the *dīkṣā*, the 'thoroughly auspicious' one (*sarvatobhadra*). I chose it not only because I had succeeded in tracing it using only the textual instructions and the commentary (to tell the truth, this was not so difficult at all), but because its simple structure allowed me to show an immediate symbolism equally applicable to the other maṇḍalas.

The drawing starts with a squaring of the initial square in 256 (16 x 16) boxes, indifferently called *pada* or *koṣṭha*. These boxes are grouped in four zones, the exact dimensions of which are given in *padas* in the text and reproduced in the legend that accompanies my drawing.

1) The central zone (A) is called 'lotus' (*padma*) because its space is fully occupied by an eight-petalled lotus, the full geometrical description of which is found in the text. Like all of the lotuses appearing in the maṇḍalas,[33] this one counts four parts; namely, starting from the centre: the pericarp (*karṇikā*); the stamen (*kesara*), covering the base of the petals; the petals (*patra*, *dala*), or rather the region where they are visible and knitted together; and the tips of the petals (*dalāgra*), not knitted together and whose form varies in accordance with the goal in view.

2) The next zone (B), the width of a *pada*, is called *pīṭha*, a term that must be translated, as we will see, by 'throne.' This *pīṭha* is made of four *pādas* and four *gātras*, and it is the interpretation of these terms that will give its meaning to the whole structure.

Indeed, while *pāda* evidently means 'foot,' the meaning of *gātra* is far from obvious. I understood it only when I found a text (Siddhāntasārāvali, verse 76) that gives the colours of these parts as follows, starting from the east: black and white; white and red; red and yellow; yellow and black. That reminded me of the description of the second section of the throne of Śiva, the *siṃhāsana* which rests upon the *anantāsana*. That *āsana* is similar to a low square table

---

of the same maṇḍala, see: Prakṛti: The Integral Vision. Volume 3: The Āgamic Tradition and the Arts (edited by B. Bäumer, New Delhi: D.K. Printworld (P) Ltd., 1995): 193+, 'Illustration's P.P. Apte 1.1.'

[33] The big maṇḍalas, such as the one found in the Mṛgendra (see note 30) or the *mahāmaṇḍala* of the Mataṅga, usually contain many lotuses: a central lotus for Śiva, eight peripheral lotuses for the divinities of the first 'circle' (most of the time the Vidyeśvaras), and sometimes still others.

whose four legs (*pādas*), situated at the corners, each take a different colour. It has on its sides four edgewise boards, named *gātras* (because they are imagined as the bodies of men or animals), that are often referred to as bicolour because each half borrows its colour from the leg to which it is attached.[34] We should therefore understand the *pīṭha* of the maṇḍala to correspond to the *siṃhāsana* of the throne constructed for the cult of Śiva.[35] A full confirmation of this parallelism is given in the Śāradātilaka, since upon following its instructions to draw the maṇḍala, we find the *pādas* and *gātras* appearing where we would expect them to appear if we accepted the preceding hypothesis.

It is worth noting that, if the *pīṭha* is equivalent to the *siṃhāsana*, it is the entire square that should be called this way, and not only the zone that projects beyond the lotus. And this is indeed what we find in many works.

Now to come back to the lotus itself, one will understand that it is nothing other than the lotus in full bloom, with eight petals, that forms the upper part of the throne of Śiva, the one generally called *padmāsana* (see SP1, p. 154, note 1) on which the god is seated in order to be worshipped. We therefore arrive at a first conclusion: the central part of the maṇḍala (the lotus and its *pīṭha*) represents the throne of Śiva reduced to its two essential parts; not as it could materially be constructed, but as the practitioner mentally creates it during the cult to project it on the material pedestal of the image that he uses.[36] Except for that—a better faithfulness to the ritual model—this central part is equivalent to the pedestal (*pīṭha*) of the *liṅga*, in particular the *liṅga* of a sanctuary. And since the plane projection of the *liṅga* itself would superpose on the *karṇikā*, we can

---

[34] See SP1, p. 162, note 1, quoting Aghoraśivācāryapaddhati, *nityakarmavidhi* 35 (p. 88 of the *grantha* edition).

[35] In fact, to justify the colours of the *gātra* of the maṇḍala, the commentator of the Siddhāntasārāvali (a certain Anantaśambhu) quotes two lines appearing in the *paddhati* of Aghoraśiva in the context of the *āsanapūjā* and which we will find quoted, with the half-*śloka* that follows them, in SP1, p. 163, under [50b]. Also, Nārāyaṇakaṇṭha, while commenting on Mṛgendrāgama, *kriyāpāda* 8.34–35, which discusses the central lotus of the maṇḍala, refers, for another technical term, to a line of the SvT taken from the description of the throne of Śiva. It is therefore certain that the Śaiva masters of old were fully aware of the identification at which I painfully arrived—that the *pīṭha* of the lotus in a maṇḍala represents the *siṃhāsana*.

[36] See the *āsanapūjā* in SP1, pp. 154–176 or SvT $_1$ 2.55c–82. The imaginary throne, made of mantras, must overshadow the concrete pedestal, just as the form of Sadāśiva that will be visualized will overshadow the material *liṅga*.

even say that the lotus and the *pīṭha* of our maṇḍala are equivalent, from the point of view of the ritual, to the *liṅga* of a temple, provided with its *pīṭha*.

3) Zone (C) is the 'street' or 'lane' (*vīthī*) where the officiant moves around during his cult. It is therefore equivalent to the inside space within the *garbhagṛha* of a temple, where movement is possible.

4) Finally, zone (D) represents the enclosure, constituted here of four kinds of elements:

a) the doors (*dvāras*), that is to say the passages for entrance and exit;
b) the *śobhās*, which are not just any 'embellishments' (like I used to believe, and like some later commentators also suggested), but the monumental doors themselves (*dvāraśobhās* in architecture);[37]
c) the *upaśobhās*, of which I do not know if there exists an architectural model;[38]
d) the 'corners' (*koṇas*), first called 'weapons,'[39] and which in fact vaguely have the form of a *vajra*.

All in all, the maṇḍala of the Śāradātilaka represents, very schematically of course, a minimal temple, with its unique enclosure. And, just as the architecture of a temple can become complicated with the addition of successive enclosures, so the maṇḍala can become complicated, the bigger ones presenting up to four enclosures (with two doors on each side, for a total of 32).[40] In the end we get a kind of citadel.

---

[37] The *dvāraśobhā* is the entrance pavilion of the first enclosure of a palace or temple, see Acharya 1946: 158, 243 and Mayamata 24.2–22 (the word is sometimes abbreviated to *śobhā*).

[38] Since *śobhā* is sometimes used for *dvāraśobhā*, the word *upaśobhā* probably refers to the pavilions that top the secondary doors (for the *upadvāras*, see Mayamata 9.58–59b), which should be called *upadvāraśobhās*.

[39] In ŚT 3.112a, which announces that the two most external zones of *padas* are reserved for *dvāras*, *śobhās*, *upaśobhās* and *astras*. Can we invoke here the tridents often seen on the walls of temples, at the corners?

[40] We must be careful not to push the parallelism too far. In particular, the successive enclosures of a maṇḍala host the circles' divinities (*āvaraṇadevadatās*) that the ritual places around Śiva, not those that, according to our Āgamas, reside in the enclosures of temples. Anyway, it is clear that the maṇḍala is not made in the image of the temple (the opposite would be more likely): there are simply between the two a certain number of essential correspondences that have to be kept in mind.

Such an assimilation is warranted by the usual appellations of the maṇḍalas that are presented as 'houses' (*bhavanas*) of Śiva; and, for the bigger ones, as towns or citadels (*puras*). It is confirmed also by the fact that many names given to particular maṇḍalas are also the names of some types of towns. It is not likely, however, that we would have arrived at any result in trying to interpret our maṇḍala and explain the technical terms that come up in its description if we had started from that observation, since we would not have thought of trying to understand the central part of the maṇḍala via the ritual.

As far as I am concerned, the work of interpretation is not complete. However, a clarification of the technical terms which have not yet been explained would essentially not modify the general vision of the maṇḍala that I was keen to present.

D. Construction of the Maṇḍala

I now leave the narrow context of the Śāradātilaka to present in a more general manner the ritual activity associated with maṇḍalas.

First, their construction. This must be done on the same day of the ceremony that requires them[41] and includes the following steps:

1. The *ācārya* must first purify the ground[42] (leveled and prepared beforehand) and locate appropriately the north-south and east-west directions.
2. He or his assistant carefully then traces the axes of the future square, then its sides, and finally the chosen drawing, all of this with the help of simple instruments: a cord, white powder and a piece of chalk. For the straight lines, one stretches between two fixed points the cord covered with powder and, pulling it up by its middle, immediately lets it go so that it hits the ground, leaving a trace; for the circles, one improvises a compass with a cord of the desired length and a piece of chalk attached to one extremity, the other being held fixed. The drawing must be precise and respect scrupulously the given measurements.

---

[41] So, for the big rituals, after the *adhivāsa*, see SvT I 3.90c–91b with commentary and 4.34–35; or SP3, p. 228, note 155.

[42] This instruction is not incompatible with the fact that the maṇḍala is generally traced on a *vedī*: the *vedī* is made of beaten earth and must undergo the same purification process as any portion of the ground destined to a ritual use.

3. The *ācārya* then pours some coloured powders on the drawing, in sufficient quantity to form a notably thick layer. Each part of the lotus and each of the other elements of the whole receives a particular colour, duly specified in the text that is followed. Finally, everything must be covered, even the lanes, according to some of our texts.

The fingers used to pour the powders and the way in which to proceed depend on the goal in view.[43] The same principle applies to the materials used to get the three, four or five necessary colours. While some Āgamas, such as the Kiraṇa, have modest demands in this regard (cereal flour for white, minium or crushed cooked bricks for red, coal or burnt chaff for black, curcuma or ochre for yellow, crushed leaves for green),[44] others, like the Mṛgendra, accept these substances only in the case of ordinary *dīkṣās*, adding that if one wishes for special powers or good fortune (and this must be applicable to other rituals than the *dīkṣā* for which this is said), precious materials must be used; namely, pearls, coral, gold and cat's eye for white, red, yellow and black respectively; whereas some impure or harmful substances are well indicated for black magic.[45] Finally, some works offer different solutions (a good one, a middle one and an inferior one) according to the financial possibilities of people;[46] but we are then brought back to the opinion of the Mṛgendra since it is agreed that in all these cases the one who wishes to get a precise favour from a divinity must not mind the expenses.[47]

---

[43] See, for example, Īśānaśivagurudevapaddhati, *kriyāpāda* 8.45c–47b (= volume 3, p. 78, 16–21) (emend the first word *bhukty-* to *mukty-*).

[44] See Kiraṇāgama 20.15–17b:
yavagodhūmajaiś cūrṇaiś śālitaṇḍulajais sitam /
dhātusindūrajaṃ raktaṃ mṛdbhiḥ pakveṣṭakair bhavet //
kṛṣṇaṃ rajas tuṣair dagdhair aṅgārair vā sucūrṇitam /
haridrāsambhavaṃ pītaṃ gairikodbhavam eva vā //
haritaṃ cūrṇitaiḥ patrair haritais tat prakalpayet /

[45] See Mṛgendrāgama, *kriyāpāda* 8.39–40.

[46] For example, Suprabhedāgama, *caryāpāda* 3.61c–65 successively proposes for white, red, black and yellow:
a) pearls, rubies, sapphires, gold;
b) shells, *jātiliṅga* (?), collyrium (*kṛṣṇāñjana*), realgar (*manaśśilā*);
c) rice flour, cooked bricks, burnt cereals, curcuma.
All of this must of course be crushed.

[47] That is why the passages that enjoin the use of precious stones and gold must not be considered merely as theoretical. To be sure, most of the adepts, in order to meet with these textual injunctions, must have been satisfied with mixing, for each

These precisions provide us with a double teaching. The first is that the use of maṇḍalas was a standard practice for the desire-oriented rituals. This is amply confirmed by a number of other instructions concerning the form of the tips of the petals, the thickness of the lines, the number of 'circles' of divinities to be worshipped around Śiva, etc. The insistence on these details could lead one to believe that despite the Āgamic passages systematically associating the maṇḍalas with occasional rituals, it is for the *kāmya* rites that these multicoloured drawings were first conceived. But that does not assimilate the maṇḍalas to the yantras. Contrary to the yantra, the maṇḍala used in a *kāmya* ritual certainly is not the direct instrument in the action to be performed: it is not a magician's tool, but simply a means, for the *sādhaka*, to obtain the favour of a chosen deity. By worshipping it on a splendid and costly support, he improves his chances of pleasing the deity and, as a consequence, of obtaining the boons that he craves.

The second teaching to get from these same passages is essential: our authors believed in the intrinsic virtue of the materials used in the fabrication of the powders. In general, they seem to consider as obvious the fact that precious substances bring good fortune,[48] and harmful substances misfortune. In addition to that, some texts give a more precise teaching concerning the correspondence between the

---

colour, a pinch of a precious material with a cheaper one; but there must have been others rich enough to cover at least a small, or even a big, maṇḍala with these costly powders. We must recall, when reading our texts, that there was no lack of money in Middle Age India, especially among the kings or princes who, more often than not, were those who sponsored the important rituals. That is why I tend to believe that maṇḍalas made of precious stones were actually constructed; not frequently of course, and they were probably not very big, but I do not believe that their descriptions are purely theoretical. We should also note that these materials were not lost for everybody; they became the property of the main officiant, like all the rest of the material used in the *yāgamaṇḍapa* (see SP4, p. 251, verse 72bc). To think that some *ācārya* could have pushed their rich disciples to engage in such sumptuous expenses is a step that we may or may not want to take.

Note also that financial considerations already play a role in the choice of the maṇḍala, the bigger and more complex ones requiring bigger quantities of coloured powders. See Rauravāgama, *kriyāpāda* 25.60d which, after describing seven maṇḍalas, adds that one will choose a maṇḍala according to his own means (*yathāvibhavam*).

[48] It must be noted here that each of the precious stones possesses a given virtue, but that does not seem to be the first reason for their use in the maṇḍala.

colours, some deities and some fortunate effects;[49] but these indications vary too much between the sources to speak of a solid tradition and a real conviction. The only point on which everybody agrees is that these powders make the maṇḍala powerful—an idea repeated over and over.

E. Worship of Śiva on the Maṇḍala

No mantra is enjoined during the construction of the maṇḍala. Once completed, the maṇḍala therefore is not yet a divine image—no more than a carved *liṅga*, before the *pratiṣṭhā* ceremony. It will become one when the cult will have brought Śiva and the powers that accompany him down on the maṇḍala.

That cult, again, is a cult of Śiva on the maṇḍala, not a cult of the maṇḍala as such, despite the term *maṇḍalapūjā* sometimes used. It is performed like the *liṅgapūjā*, a cult of Śiva on a *liṅga*:[50]

- The stages of the *pūjā* are the same, with the difference that, the support being temporary, the invitation (*āvāhana*) and the dismissal (*visarjana*) of the god must be understood in the strictest sense. It goes without saying that the ablutions are made mentally.
- The mantras recited are also the same, most especially the phonic seeds (*bīja*s) that are their essential part since, properly pronounced, they make present the divinities of which they are

[49] See, for example, the passage of the Mahākapilapañcarātra quoted by Rāghavabhaṭṭa (p. 123, 17–22) in his commentary on ŚT 3.124. Each colour—five, in that text—is connected with an element, placed under the influence of a divinity and supposed to bring a specific effect. These effects, in reality, are all of the same order, that is to say the destruction of demonic powers; the result is simply that "the gods are happy."

The position of the Suprabhedāgama (*caryāpāda* 3.56c–59) is different but not much more convincing. That text, even though it suggests five colours for the maṇḍala, only speaks of the symbolism of the colours white, red and black, which it naturally connects to the three *guṇa*s and the three goddesses (Vāmā, Jyeṣṭhā and Raudrī). In a last passage it says that the yellow is added "in order to obtain the fruit from the *yāga*."

On the symbolism of colours and their magic use, see Goudriaan 1978, chapter 4.

[50] That cult is described in all the Tantras and handbooks. See the numerous references given by N.R. Bhatt in his edition of the Ajita, chapter 20, note 1. Among the texts quoted there, only the Kiraṇa, the Mataṅgapārameśvara and the Mṛgendra are earlier than the Somaśambhupaddhati whose description (SP1, section III), though concise, is complete, logical and one of the most reliable ones we have.

the sound body. The officiant imposes them (by means of flowers) unto the maṇḍala as he would do on a *liṅga* and its pedestal. The result is that the group of divinities that inhabit the maṇḍala when all the invocations are completed is identical to the group of divinities who inhabit the sanctuary of a temple (or what stands for it in a private cult) during the cult of Śiva. That these divinities be represented or not on the maṇḍala by a particular symbol (lotus, *svastika*, etc.) is of no importance whatsoever.

- The meditations and visualizations are those involved in any cult; they have no special features that would link them to the particular structure of the maṇḍala. Moreover, the texts do not mention any mental 'course,' leading, for example, from the periphery to the centre, as is enjoined in other traditions. There is indeed a motion, but it is on the whole a centrifugal one imposed by the normal enacting of the *pūjā*. Starting from the central lotus, where the throne of the god, then the god, are successively worshipped, the cult progressively includes the peripheral deities by enlarging each time the concerned circle (*āvaraṇa*). These remarks remain true in the case of a *dīkṣā*: though said to be indispensable, the maṇḍala is treated like any other cult support, without any particular role; and it is used as it would be in the context of another ritual, a *pavitrārohaṇa*, for example. In other words, the Śaiva *dīkṣā* does not take advantage of the particular form of the maṇḍala of which it requires the construction.[51]

F. Virtues and Symbolism of the Maṇḍala

If the Śaiva maṇḍalas are neither privileged means of reintegration, nor direct instruments of initiation, then what proper quality do they possess that makes them more appropriate for some rituals than other cult supports?

I already mentioned the particular virtue attributed to the powders of which they are made, and the incessantly repeated affirmation that, because of them, the maṇḍala is a powerful image. Another characteristic often advanced is its beauty, due to the brightness and

[51] Some texts, such as the Mṛgendra and the SvT, suggest the use of the big maṇḍala to fix the name of the initiated disciple. But this ritual can be done on a very simple 'distributive' maṇḍala, and it is certainly not for this purpose that the *rajomaṇḍala* is constructed.

the richness of the colours used. The initiate who constructs the maṇḍala is asked to make it "as beautiful as possible." Through the fineness and exactitude of the drawing, the precision of the colouring and the good taste evinced in the confection of the ornaments that are left to his initiative, the officiant must strive to create a perfect image. Is it to rejoice men, as it is sometimes suggested—or to charm the gods, as other texts would have it?[52] Probably both. Faced with a splendid maṇḍala, men are happy and feel their love of the gods growing,[53] and the gods are better disposed toward men. We must admit that for cults that are performed in an open pavilion, exposed to the view, beauty and brightness of the support are no negligible qualities. However, it seems that a statue or a richly draped *liṅga*[54] would be just as impressive to the spectators (and probably also to the gods ...); and I tend to believe that, despite the importance given to aesthetics in the Āgamas, the choice of a maṇḍala as the support of a cult is more dictated by faith in its intrinsic power than by the desire to create beauty.[55]

Or could there be more pertinent reasons? One would hope to find further justification for the eulogy of the maṇḍala through other considerations than the nature of the pulverized materials and the brightness of their colours, to dig out of the arid texts the profound signification of these objects that other traditions have loaded with so many virtues.

We naturally think of the cosmic symbolism[56] on which all the authors who discussed the question have insisted. And, certainly, we cannot deny that even the very simple maṇḍala that I tried to analyze possesses one. But that same symbolism exists in the pair formed by

---

[52] See TĀ 31.41cd.

[53] The Suprabhedāgama goes further: the mere vision of the maṇḍala cleanses from all sins (*caryāpāda* 3.2); the soul is delivered from all the fetters that turned it into a *paśu* (*caryāpāda* 3.41ab). Such passages, which of course must not be taken literally, at least show the importance of the *vision* of the maṇḍala—never equated, to my knowledge, to the *darśana* of the god who inhabits it: the idea is to see the exterior form itself.

[54] Just as the maṇḍala, but contrary to the fixed *liṅga* of the sanctuary of a temple, these mobile images can be seen by all.

[55] Why then is the maṇḍala disqualified for the daily ritual, at least in the Siddhānta? I can only see one logical reason for this: the fact that the maṇḍalas used for daily rituals are, as we have seen, necessarily simple, probably deprived of coloured powders, and therefore share none of the virtues attributed to the *rajomaṇḍalas*. The question, however, merits further investigations.

[56] On the symbolism of colours, see note 49.

a *liṅga* and its *pīṭha*, in the temple, in the city; and it is not expressed here with any more precision or enthusiasm than there. We must be careful not to give in to our imagination or our desires and add to the texts that we have at our disposal; and these texts do not encourage us to do so. To my knowledge, they do not even make explicit the immediate symbolism that makes the maṇḍala a miniature temple or even a city, though it is suggested by their vocabulary. They dwell even less on that cosmic symbolism with which we Westerners are so obsessed. It is not that they ignore it, but they leave it to the description of the ritual as such to bring out the correspondences between the different parts of the maṇḍala and the cosmic realities, and it seems vain or even dangerous to want to add more. It is by orienting the research in that direction, that is, by analyzing closely the rituals that have maṇḍalas as their support or pretext, that we must attempt to bring some precision to those symbolisms, instead of desperately trying to make them come out of the static structure of these same objects.

Conclusion

I am afraid that many readers will be disappointed, or even shocked, by my stripping the ancient Śaiva maṇḍalas of everything that the imagination, drawing from other sources, had superimposed on them. However, by bringing them back to what I consider their real status, that of divine images, no more and no less charged with symbolism than the others, but characterized by the special power provided by the powders of which they are made and by the power of seduction that results from their beauty, I have not deprived the maṇḍalas of all signification. Rather to the contrary. However, I did separate them, much to my regret, from our mental model of the maṇḍala, the one found in Tibetan Buddhism.

I will not try to explain this troubling disparity between the two schools, but hope that future research will bring some light on this point. My purpose here was simply to bring out the testimony of the Śaiva texts on the nature and ritual function of the maṇḍala.

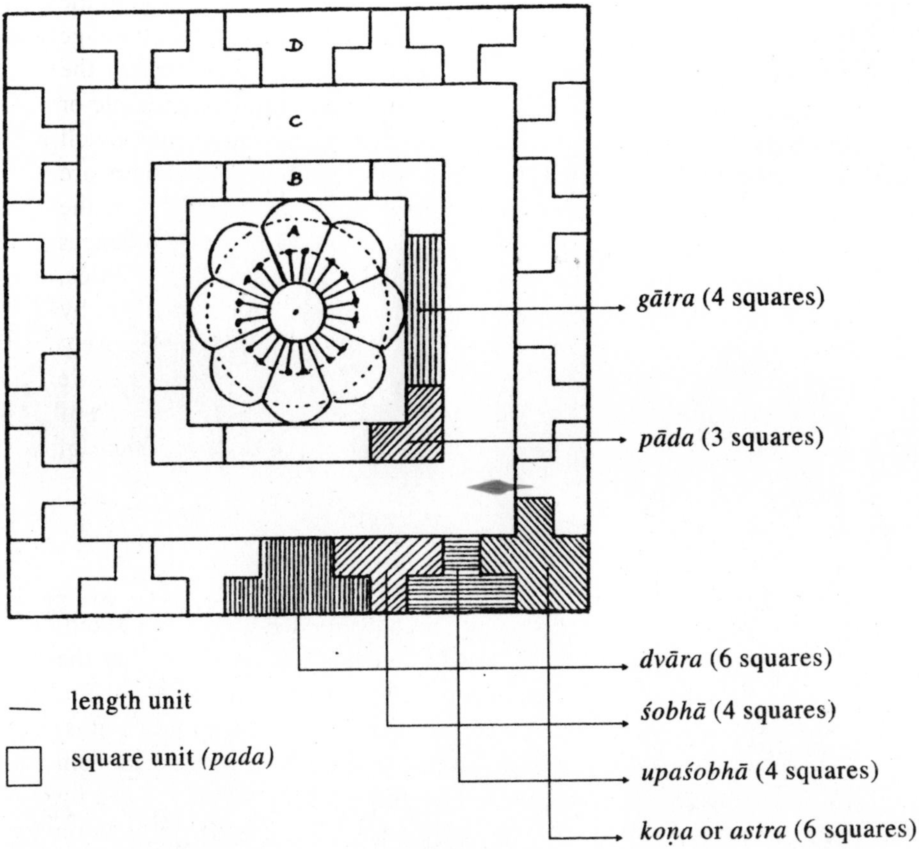

4 zones: A = main lotus (6 x 6 = 36 squares)
B = *pīṭha* (1 unit wide: 28 squares)
C = *vīthī* (2 units wide: 80 squares)
D = *dvāra*s + *śobhā*s + *upaśobhā*s + *koṇa*s (112 squares)
(The entire maṇḍala consists of 256 squares.)

1. The *sarvatobhadramaṇḍala* reconstructed according to the Śāradātilaka and Rāghavabhaṭṭa's commentary

ICONS OF INCLUSIVISM: MAṆḌALAS IN SOME EARLY ŚAIVA TANTRAS*

Judit Törzsök

Introduction

This study is very much inspired by and indebted to A. Sanderson's excellent article (Sanderson 1986) on the way in which various texts of the Trika school of Śaivism encoded their superiority to other schools in their maṇḍalas. It aims at examining some Śaiva maṇḍalas not examined by Sanderson, most of which are not based on the trident image used in the Trika. I shall try to explore how these images represent the relationship of certain branches of Śaivism with other Śaivas as well as with non-Śaivas and how these relationships are visually translated in the image of the maṇḍala. The discussion on maṇḍalas as icons of inclusivism is preceded by a short terminological investigation and a summary of some problems concerning initiation maṇḍalas.

Most of the texts considered here and consequently the maṇḍalas they describe date from before the Kashmirian exegetes, i.e., before the 10th-11th century A.D. Occasional reference is made to later texts such as the Īśānaśivagurudevapaddhati. Although evidence has been brought together from various branches of Śaivism, there are a number of demonstrably early Tantras that have been omitted from the discussion.[1] Thus, this study does not present a synthesis of all

---

* I would like to thank Paul and Guillaume Coatalen for having prepared the maṇḍala illustrations, and I dedicate this essay to them. I thank Professor Alexis Sanderson for a printout of a draft article on maṇḍalas he gave me some years ago, which I have lost unfortunately and thus cannot cite. I have tried to avoid topics I remember he discusses there in detail and hope not to have plagiarized anything unconsciously. I thank Professor Gudrun Bühnemann for drawing my attention to and correcting awkward points in my argument and style; I am fully responsible for whatever remains uncorrected, of course.

[1] From the demonstrably early Siddhāntas, two important texts have not been included in the discussion, although they contain relevant information: the Sarva-

the material one could have access to, but is to be considered the summary of a work in progress. This, to some extent arbitrary, choice of sources means that whatever conclusion is drawn here is limited and needs to be tested on further evidence. Moreover, the discussion on maṇḍalas as icons of inclusivism focuses only on two texts teaching the worship of Bhairava: the Svacchandatantra (SvT) and the Netratantra (NT).

1 *Maṇḍalas and Cakras*

The Sanskrit term maṇḍala and its several meanings have been analyzed in detail in the Śaiva context by Brunner 1986: 13–18 (cf. Brunner, pp. 156–161), and the word has been subjected to some analysis in almost everything that has been written on maṇḍalas. Without reiterating the arguments and all the meanings here, there is one point which is perhaps not unnecessary to reconsider: the question of the difference between the terms maṇḍala and cakra. Both words have the general meaning of circle, and thus by extension they can both denote a circle of deities or mantras (which are the same, since Tantric deities are mantras and spoken of as such): *devatācakra*. That in this meaning the two words are interchangeable can be shown by a number of passages, for instance, in the Siddhayogeśvarīmata,[2] in which both terms are used when the visualization of a circle of Yoginīs or mothers *(mātṛ)* is prescribed.[3] But the interchangeability of these terms is reflected in more than their use in the same context. Looking at the description of the circles of Yoginīs in the same text, it is somewhat confusing for the reader that in the same passage, the central deity—usually a Bhairava—is described as placed on the pericarp of a lotus or on the hub of a wheel, and the surrounding deities are said to be on the petals of a lotus or on the

---

jñānottara, whose full text is available only in manuscripts to which I have no access; and the Kiraṇa, whose only edition (Devakōṭṭai 1932) is also unavailable to me at present. For the dating of early Siddhāntas, see Goodall's introduction to his edition of the Kiraṇavṛtti, pp. xxxviff. I have also omitted maṇḍalas of two texts teaching more esoteric Yāmala and goddess worship: the Brahmayāmala and the Jayadrathayāmala. They teach several maṇḍalas, some of which have been discussed in Sanderson 1986. Moreover, no Kaula sources are included.

[2] The Siddhayogeśvarīmata is one of the root-texts of the Kashmirian Trika, which I have very tentatively dated to around the seventh century A.D. in Törzsök 1999a: vii.

[3] See, for instance, verses 22.23 and 28.40 for maṇḍala and 21.1 for cakra.

spokes of a wheel. The words describing the circle of deities as a wheel or as a lotus are mixed up, showing that what matters here is simply a circular arrangement: the lotus terminology recalling a typical maṇḍala with the lotus in its centre and the wheel terminology confirming that the same arrangement can be called a cakra.[4]

However, in spite of this confusion of lotuses and wheels only the word maṇḍala is commonly used when an actual drawing is described or referred to in a text, i.e., one following a rather precise outline and coloured with powders. This confirms what was stated by Sanderson in a discussion recorded in Padoux 1986: 33: the fact that maṇḍala normally denotes the *locus* of worship (*ādhāra*) and the cakra [of deities or mantras] is what is located on it (*ādheya*). Therefore, instructions to trace or draw (*likh-*) a diagram and to fill it with coloured powders are given for maṇḍalas, but not for cakras.[5] This is not contradicted by the fact that the circle of deities is sometimes called maṇḍala as an alternative, for that can be considered a metaphoric usage as noted above. But the consistent use of maṇḍala and the lack of the word cakra in contexts of elaborate drawings show that the former does indeed denote the *locus* of worship, at least in an early stratum of texts.[6]

There are nevertheless a few examples in which it seems that instruction is given to draw a cakra. However, in these cases the cakra is not the full circle of deities, for what is enjoined is that one is to draw an actual wheel with a hub, spokes and a circumference. Such instruction is given, e.g., in SvT2 9.16ff., prescribing that a wheel is to be drawn outside the central lotus of the maṇḍala.[7] Thus, this cakra is an equivalent image of the *lotus* rather than that of the

---

[4] See, for example, a description starting with verse 22.25 mentioning a lotus (*padma*) and finishing with the wheel terminology in verses 28–31.

[5] As noted in the same discussion by Sanderson, the terminology of the Śrīvidyā is a special case, and probably reflects a later and looser use of the terms cakra and yantra.

[6] This was questioned by Brunner in the same discussion, referring to the SvT and the NT, which allegedly use the word cakra for the drawing itself. Since no references are given there, and since I myself have not found any appropriate examples—only actual wheels which are to be drawn inside a maṇḍala or yantra and which are discussed below—it seems doubtful whether such confusion of cakra and maṇḍala is present in these texts. Nevertheless, no firm conclusion can be drawn until all these texts are available in electronic form to facilitate such terminological searches.

[7] This passage is mentioned as an example for the meaning 'wheel' in Brunner 1986: 20 (cf. Brunner, p. 163).

maṇḍala, and when its drawing is enjoined, it forms *part* of a maṇḍala, but does not replace it.

A similar idea may underlie the combined lotus-wheel image described in the Īśānaśivagurudevapaddhati, *kriyāpāda* 8.106–123, which calls it a maṇḍala of the wheel and the lotus (*cakrāmbuja-maṇḍala*). The text is rather corrupt and appears to give several alternatives at the same time. However, it is clear from verse 109 that at least in one of the versions, there is a lotus in the centre, and the lines drawn from the centre to the tips of the petals and to where the petals are joined are to be lengthened further, outside the lotus, to form the spokes of a wheel.[8] Here again, one has to draw a wheel just as one is to draw a lotus, but the result, the whole of the image, which includes the passageway outside it (*vīthī*), the doors, etc., is called a maṇḍala.

That the maṇḍala is the whole of the drawing itself is also confirmed by the synonyms used for it: *bhavana*,[9] *veśman*,[10] and *pura*[11]—words denoting house or abode, i.e., the place where the deities reside.[12] It appears that the maṇḍala is also identified as the seat (*pīṭha*) of the deity or deities, probably in the sense that it is the *locus* of the deities,[13] although this very word also denotes a central part of the maṇḍala.[14]

---

[8] Note that it is pointed out in verse 106 that in this case there is no *pīṭha* in the sense given in Appendix 1, i.e., the central circular image is not surrounded by a square-shaped seat. This is probably because the lotus is surrounded by the wheel itself, which may be considered to replace the seat.

[9] Mentioned in Brunner 1986: 25 (cf. Brunner, p. 170) without examples; see, e.g., SvT$_2$ 5.34d. A similar word, *bhuvana* is used in the Niśvāsa, fol. 25v5ff., which I understand to be a *varia lectio* for *bhavana*.

[10] E.g., SvT$_2$ 5.19.

[11] See, for example, SvT$_2$ 5.19.

[12] While the first two words mean abode or residence in their first sense, *pura* denotes a town or city as its first meaning. This may be the reason why Brunner 1986: 25 (cf. Brunner, p. 170) interprets the term to denote larger maṇḍalas (without giving examples). However, as Brunner remarks, larger maṇḍalas do not show any special relation to city plans or anything related to towns. Therefore, it seems quite possible that *pura* is used in the sense 'abode' rather than 'town' in the context of maṇḍalas, especially if we consider that as the above examples show, the SvT uses *pura* as a synonym of other designations without any apparent distinction. Moreover, Siddhayogeśvarīmata 25.8 and Mṛgendra, *kriyāpāda* 8.29c use the term *pura* to denote square maṇḍalas of 2, 3 or 4 *hastas* on each side, which are definitely not of extraordinary size.

[13] This is how I understand the use of the word in apposition to maṇḍala in a citation of the Siddhayogeśvarīmata given by Jayaratha *ad* TĀ 31.8b. The Siddhayogeśvarīmata seems to identify *pīṭha* with maṇḍala in a metonymic way. Note that

In short, the term cakra does not seem to be particularly vague and its use does not appear particularly inconsistent; it has primary and secondary as well as metaphoric meanings just as the term maṇḍala. But as far as the terminology of maṇḍalas as more complex images is concerned, I think it can be safely affirmed that maṇḍala usually denotes the whole of a particular image onto which deities are placed. Cakra either denotes an actual wheel as part of such drawings or refers to the deities themselves. Moreover, cakras are not necessarily associated with yantras—small drawings on durable material including mantra syllables, used as charms—in particular.[15] They are only associated with yantras inasmuch as mantra-deities or rather their seed syllables (*bīja*) can be incised in a circular design (*cakra*) on these charms.

This short terminological investigation leads us to the question of how these circles of mantra-deities are present on a maṇḍala. This subject, the visualization and placement of mantra deities on the maṇḍala, is usually treated as a topic distinct from the drawing of the maṇḍala, for indeed the maṇḍala is only one of the supports onto which deities can be projected and visualized. Moreover, the way in which deities are to be seen or meditated upon does not depend on the support, but on the purpose of the ritual. The same deity or deities can be visualized as more frightful for rites to acquire lower supernatural powers and as milder for appeasement and the like.[16] Even if the visualization of deities can vary considerably for *siddhi*s, there appears to be a standard visualization for initiation. And in the context of initiation, it should be remembered that what the practitioner of a ritual is supposed to see in a maṇḍala is not only the geometric drawing, but the deities placed on it. Consequently, when texts emphasize how the initiate is impressed by seeing the maṇḍala for the first time, especially at the time of his preliminary initiation (*samayadīkṣā*), it is not the precision of the drawing or the beauty of the colours that produce this effect, but the fact that the initiate sees

this passage is not found in the short recension edited in Törzsök 1999a and Törzsök *forthcoming*.

[14] See Appendix 1, Illustration 1 and Colour Plates 16–17.

[15] As suggested by a summary in Brunner 1986: 18–20 (cf. Brunner, pp. 161–164).

[16] See, e.g., Siddhayogeśvarīmata 28.29–30 and 22.27–29 and 38 for the *sāttvika/ rājasa/ tāmasa* visualizations of Yoginīs. See also various forms of Bhairava, alongside Svacchandabhairava, such as Koṭarākṣa, etc., in SvT2 9.3ff. and forms of Sadāśiva in Mṛgendra, *kriyāpāda* 3.41ff. and commentary. See also Sanderson 1990: 68.

the deity or deities.[17] This is clear from passages which do not prescribe an elaborate and colourful maṇḍala at the time of this initiation, but one drawn up quickly with sandalwood paste (*maṇḍalaka*).[18] Such a simple maṇḍala surely cannot impress the initiate by its exceptional beauty. Furthermore, Kṣemarāja also explains *ad* SvT2 3.128 that when the blindfold of a new initiate is removed and he sees the maṇḍala, he is enlightened, and is thus able to see the deity.[19] The text of the Tantra itself suggests the interpretation that the removal of the blindfold is symbolic, as if it was the removal of the darkness of ignorance. The Tantra also states that what the initiate sees are the deities.[20] Kṣemarāja goes on to say that since this is the first time the initiate sees the Lord after thousands of births, he is very much surprised, looks at him again and again and falls on the ground. This shows that he can be possessed by Śiva, for he has discarded the [false] perception of identifying his self with the body and so forth [instead of Śiva].[21]

What is important in the above lines of the SvT and its commentary is not simply the fact that the deities are present in the maṇḍala (which is quite obvious), but that for initiates they are *visible* there. Therefore the deities should be considered to form part of the visual appearance of the maṇḍala once they are installed on it.[22] Moreover, it must also be remembered that these deities are normally not represented by icons because they are too powerful and consequently too dangerous to be depicted.[23] Thus, it is when they are installed on a maṇḍala that their visual aspect seems to be the

---

[17] This aspect is worth emphasizing, for Brunner 1986: 30 (cf. Brunner, p. 175) tries to argue that it could be the external appearance of the maṇḍala that makes it special.

[18] See, e.g., SvT2 3.90.

[19] *prāgavastho yaḥ paśuḥ sa idānīm eva prabuddhaḥ ... punaḥ punar bhagavantam īkṣate.*

[20] *... mukham udghāṭya darśayet /*
vidyāmantragaṇaiḥ sārdhaṃ kāraṇaṃ sasadāśivam /
ajñānapaṭanirmuktaḥ prabuddhaḥ paśur īkṣate /
daṇḍavad dharaṇīṃ gatvā praṇipatya punaḥ punaḥ /

[21] *... ata eva janmasahasrāpūrvabhagavatsvarūpāvalokanād vismayāviṣṭaḥ punaḥ punar bhagavantam īkṣate / daṇḍavadgamanena dehādipramātṛtāpahastanāt śrīśiva-samāveśānusaraṇe yogyatāsya darśitā.*

[22] Such an image, including the deities, is reconstructed in Sanderson 1986: 187 (the drawing is reproduced as Illustration 3 in Padoux's first contribution to this book).

[23] This point is discussed briefly below, in subsection ii of section 2.

most prominent. It is there that each of them is represented in drawing by his or her distinct place such as a petal of a lotus, which serves not only as a *locus* or support of worship, but perhaps also as a crutch for those who perform the elaborate visualization.

The moment of seeing the maṇḍala with the deities is considered so important that its mention can metaphorically refer to the whole ritual of initiation.[24] However, maṇḍalas are not used exclusively at the time of initiation, although for some—or possibly even for most—initiates the ritual of initiation may actually be the only time they see a maṇḍala.[25] As pointed out in a number of studies,[26] maṇḍalas are mentioned as optional supports for daily worship and they figure quite prominently in rites to acquire supernatural powers (*siddhi*). No special maṇḍalas are prescribed for regular worship: the maṇḍalas used in regular worship are just small-size reproductions of initiation maṇḍalas. In what follows, focus will be laid on initiation maṇḍalas and maṇḍalas used for the acquisition of supernatural powers.

2 *Initiation Maṇḍalas and their Role*

i. *The Two Initiation Maṇḍalas*

It has been pointed out in various discussions[27] that just as there are two major parts of Śaiva initiation,[28] there are two different maṇḍalas

[24] See, e.g., Parātriṃśikā 19 and -laghuvṛtti *ad loc.* The text says that even without seeing the maṇḍala, one who knows the doctrine of this text becomes initiated. The seeing of the maṇḍala is thus considered the principal element of initiation, as the commentary confirms, saying that it includes rites from the night spent at the place of worship (*adhivāsana*) up to the fire ritual, i.e., initiation proper. The Siddhayogeśvarīmata has the colophon *samayamaṇḍala* at the end of the chapter describing the whole *samaya* rite, which also suggests that the principal element of the rite is considered to be the maṇḍala itself.

[25] This may be the case of someone who aspires only for liberation and who does not take the trouble to draw up a maṇḍala for daily worship, which was probably a rather laborious procedure (on this, see Sanderson 1986: 170, note 3). At some point this was perhaps the most common category of initiates.

[26] E.g., Brunner 1986: 20–21 (cf. Brunner, pp. 164–165) and Sanderson 1986: 169–170.

[27] See, for instance, Padoux 1986: 34, Sanderson 1986: 196, note 128 and Brunner in SP3, pp. xxx–xliii.

[28] In some traditions, there is also a third part between what I call here the preliminary initiation (*samayadīkṣā*) and initiation proper (*dīkṣā*). It is termed special preliminary initiation (*viśeṣasamayadīkṣā*), and is found in the Somaśambhu-

drawn for these occasions. It seems that according to most ritual manuals, the first maṇḍala, which is drawn for the preliminary initiation or *samayadīkṣā*, is not at all elaborate. It is made without coloured powders, including only a basic outline, for which sandalwood paste is used. The details of this basic drawing usually dubbed as *gandhamaṇḍala* ('scent maṇḍala')[29] or *maṇḍalaka* ('small maṇḍala')[30] are not given. However, one can often read detailed descriptions of what is called the powder maṇḍala (*rajomaṇḍala*). This is a larger drawing filled with coloured powders, to be used for what is initiation proper, sometimes also called *nirvāṇadīkṣā*, for it bestows final liberation.

While manuals seem to share their opinion on these two maṇḍalas as given above, canonical texts differ on several points. These differences concern not only the maṇḍalas, but to some extent also the way in which the two initiation rituals are performed.[31]

The first or preliminary initiation—which is not always named initiation[32]—consists mainly of a symbolic rite of entry into the Śaiva community. It involves the seeing of the maṇḍala and ends with the announcement of the rules (*samaya*) the neophyte is to observe as a new member of this community. This initiation can be termed preliminary initiation because it is a prerequisite to initiation proper, which follows after a night spent on the grounds of worship together with the *guru* (*adhivāsa*).[33]

Initiation proper is performed next day for those who can and want to receive it. It involves the rites of purification, deification of the body, etc., as well as a rite of prognostication, which is based on

---

paddhati as well as in South Indian manuals. As Brunner points out in SP3, p. xxxv, it seems to be a 'rite bâtard' containing elements of the *dīkṣā* itself.

[29] See, e.g., TĀ 15.387.

[30] See, e.g., SvT2 3.90c.

[31] It would require a separate study to discuss all the details and problems concerning the *samayadīkṣā*. Therefore I shall only point out problems pertaining to the use of maṇḍalas. For a more detailed discussion, see Brunner in SP3, pp. xxxff. and Törzsök 1999b.

[32] I have shown elsewhere that this rite is not called initiation (*dīkṣā*) in a considerable number of early texts including the Svāyambhuvasūtrasaṃgraha, the Brahmayāmala, the Siddhayogeśvarīmata and the Mālinīvijaya. For details of alternative terminology, see Törzsök 1999b.

[33] An important exception is the Vīṇāśikhatantra, which knows only of one initiation, preceded by the *adhivāsa* In this text, the rite of entry using the maṇḍala is performed on the same day as initiation proper, and the rules (*samaya*) are announced only at the end of the latter (verse 49).

the neophytes' dreams and on the way in which their tooth twigs[34] fall on the ground. Then another maṇḍala is prepared and another variant of the same kind of rite of entry is performed as the day before, but this time without being followed by the announcement of the rules. It is then that the main part of initiation is done. This is basically a rather complex ritual of purification of the 'bound soul' and its detachment from lower levels of existence. The rite involves fire offerings at the completion of which the soul of the initiand is joined to Śiva.

As even this brief summary shows, there is a repetition with variants of what appears to be essentially the same rite, whose culmination is the seeing of the maṇḍala. Most texts agree that there are two maṇḍalas and two rites, the first of which usually gives people the right to perform Śaiva worship using the mantras of the cult they are initiated into. However, the texts diverge on very significant details.[35]

Some texts[36] prescribe that the first maṇḍala should be the simple one drawn with sandalwood paste as mentioned above. When the initiand is led to it blindfolded, he is to throw a flower or flowers there. He then sees the maṇḍala, which has a profound effect on him. The maṇḍala drawn up the following day is larger, more elaborate and decorated with coloured powders, etc. The same person or persons are led to it blindfolded, but this time they toss one flower on the drawing each. The name of the deity on whose part of the maṇḍala the flower falls will form part of the person's initiatory name, thus suggesting that the initiate was chosen as it were by the deity who attracted his flower on the empowered diagram.

Some other texts, which may prescribe a smaller maṇḍala for the first rite, clearly envisage a colour maṇḍala even for the first rite of entry. This maṇḍala is probably identical to the second maṇḍala except perhaps for its size. Moreover, the *guru* is instructed to perform the name-giving as part of the first rite, while nothing particular is said about the second maṇḍala.[37]

---

[34] These are twigs used for cleaning one's teeth.

[35] The Vīṇāśikha differs as pointed out above, knowing only one maṇḍala rite.

[36] Such as SvT, chapter 3.

[37] The Siddhayogeśvarīmata, for instance, prescribes a colour maṇḍala for the *samaya* rite as 6.13 shows. But the second maṇḍala—although seemingly elaborate, for it can be double the size of the former—is not described in detail; the reader is referred to a manual instead (8.11).

There are yet other versions of these twin-rites. They involve a sandalwood paste maṇḍala in the first rite, which is nevertheless used for performing the name-giving.[38] It is tempting to argue[39] that the second version given above, which prescribes the use of the colour maṇḍala and the name-giving in the *samaya* rite, appears more functional[40] and is perhaps the primary version. However, it may be more important to consider the fact that the first version of the rites appears in the SvT, a text which is relatively old among the demonstrably early Tantras.

Without trying to establish which order and method of performance of the twin-rites is primary, it can be stated that the two rites resemble each other very much and thus may reflect the doubling of a ritual which was originally one.[41] Moreover, since there is an early Tantra, the Vīṇāśikha, which knows only of one combined initiation ending with the announcement of *samayas*, it may represent a very early stage of development, when even the *samaya* rite was not yet independent or separable.[42] Judging from the stage represented by this text, it seems a possible development that first the maṇḍala rite and initiation proper became separated, which was followed by the doubling of the maṇḍala rite. An additional argument for the theory of doubling could be that as some later developments show, a further extension of the preliminary initiation occurs[43] under the name of *viśeṣasamayadīkṣā*. To this a new repetition of the maṇḍala rite is added by Aghoraśiva's commentator, Nirmalamaṇi, who prescribes it if too much time has ellapsed since

[38] As in SP3, pp. 37 and 103.

[39] In Törzsök 1999b I tried to establish a possible chronology and development of this rite in various texts, but I am no longer sure if there is enough justification for all my hypotheses. An attempt at reconstruction has been made by Brunner in SP3, pp. xxxi–xxxiii in a more general way, omitting details of the maṇḍala.

[40] I.e., it seems to be more appropriate to draw up an elaborate maṇḍala for a rite which focuses on this instrument. Furthermore, it could be argued that the seeing of the uncoloured maṇḍala in the SvT, without the name-giving ritual, appears to be odd. Why should one be impressed by the sandalwood paste maṇḍala rather than by the coloured maṇḍala? What is the point here in casting flowers on the diagram if the name-giving is omitted? For a discussion of these problems, see Arraj 1988: 144ff. and Törzsök 1999b.

[41] For this hypothesis and arguments in the case of the Siddhānta, see Brunner in SP3, pp. xxxi–xxxiii.

[42] This confirms Brunner's hypothesis in SP3, pp. xxxi.

[43] This is the case, for example, in the Somaśambhupaddhati and the Aghoraśivapaddhati.

the performance of the *samaya* ritual.[44] Thus, the *samaya* rite seems to be particularly liable to doubling and expansion.

In spite of these possibilities, it must be reiterated that no early Tantra apart from the very brief Vīṇāśikha seems to refer only to one maṇḍala.[45] If a redoubling took place at some point, we have no way of knowing how exactly it happened and through what stages.

This means that the role of initiation maṇḍalas cannot be determined in general by covering the descriptions and versions of all early texts. However, a number of significant points can be summarized concerning their nature and importance in this ritual.[46]

1. It is the maṇḍala—either in its simpler or its more colourful and elaborate version—and the ritual connected to it that usually determine the initiation names of initiates and thus not only qualify them to use the mantras of the cult, but also give them a new identity in their Śaiva community. The initiate comes to be chosen as it were by one particular deity of that tradition, who attracts the flower he casts on the maṇḍala.[47]
2. After the disciple's blindfold is removed, the seeing of the maṇḍala—no matter which kind is used—with the deities on it is usually considered to have a profound effect on him, for this is

---

[44] See Aghoraśivapaddhati 254.

[45] It must also be added that the Vīṇāśikha does not mention the name-giving itself, but the editor of the text, T. Goudriaan, supposes that it was understood (cf. p. 139 and p. 16).

[46] In what follows, I assume that the more elaborate maṇḍala is a larger and expanded version of the colourless or smaller one. This is suggested in all texts which describe only one of them. To my knowledge, the only text according to which the two maṇḍalas are explicitly very different is the TĀ. But that exceptional choice is probably motivated by Abhinavagupta's intent to integrate various levels of the Trika in a hierarchy of initiations. For more information on this topic, see Sanderson 1986: 196.

[47] While texts contradict each other on whether the elaborate colour maṇḍala or the simpler *gandhamaṇḍala* is used for this rite, one could perhaps find more evidence by examining initiation names. From initiation names found in inscriptions in Darasuram, it seems that names of the Vidyeśvaras, *aṅgamantras* and mantras of the throne were used as well as the *brahmamantras* (see Srinivasan 1987, and the evidence summarized in Goodall 2000: 207). The name of Somaśambhu may show that even *lokapālas* were perhaps included in the initiation maṇḍala, which was then probably a more elaborate one. But since the above inscriptional evidence comes from the tradition of the Siddhānta in the Cōḷa country of the 12th century, its testimony cannot be taken for what happened in other regions and periods.

his first contact with the deities of his chosen school.[48] In the daily rites which he is obliged to perform ever after the initiation, the disciple is in fact supposed to recreate this first sight of the deities in visualizations.[49]

3. The seeing of the deities in the course of initiation is not the privilege of some, but is experienced by all categories of initiates. In a number of texts, the name-giving is also performed for all candidates as part of the initiation.
4. While there are Vedic parallels to initiation proper (*dīkṣā*) as a whole, the central part of the *samaya* rite performed at the maṇḍala has no such obvious Vedic predecessor.[50]

ii. *The Initiation Maṇḍala as the Largest Detailed Representation of Esoteric Deities*

The paragraphs above do little more than summarize what has already been analyzed in detail in Sanderson 1986 concerning the Trika, namely the fact that the maṇḍala plays a particularly important role in creating and maintaining a new, Śaiva and sectarian, identity of the initiate. This identity is then repeatedly confirmed in the course of the performance of daily worship. This must be one of the reasons why the moment of seeing the maṇḍala is considered so important. But in addition to this, there may be yet another reason. It is not mentioned or expressed explicitly, but is perhaps still an important factor here, at least as far as early texts and practices of Bhairavatantras[51] are concerned. The initiation maṇḍala, in addition

[48] Even if only the name-giving version is described for the *samaya* rite, as in the Tantrasadbhāva, for example, it is made clear that the initiate is duly impressed and falls on his knees. See 9.124d, where the subject must be the initiate or the initiate with the *guru*.

[49] For this process in the Trika, see Sanderson 1986: 169–170.

[50] Brunner in SP3, pp. xxxvi draws a parallel between the *samayadīkṣā* and the *upanayana* rather than between *dīkṣā* proper and Vedic rites. However, what is similar in the *upanayana* and in the *samayadīkṣā* is not the nature but the function of the two rites, for both bestow the qualification to study the scriptures. Moreover, it is only the *viśeṣasamayadīkṣā* that creates a twice-born in the same way as the *upanayana* does, and this is not common to all versions of the *samayadīkṣā*. My point in drawing a parallel between *dīkṣā* proper and Vedic rites is that fire ritual has obvious Vedic predecessors, while the rite involving the maṇḍala is rather unique to the Tantric context.

[51] The term is used here for Tantras teaching the worship of Bhairava as well as for Yāmalatantras and Tantras teaching goddess worship. For details of these

to being the paradigmatic image, is probably also the largest or one of the largest images representing esoteric deities in detail which is used in communal worship (in the sense that several people use it, but not at the same time). This point requires a brief investigation into the question of what objects were used for the worship of esoteric deities and how: the nature of worship and what substrates it may require, the role and scope of *liṅga* worship, the question of anthropomorphic images and what size various substrates were prescribed to have.[52]

Most Bhairavatantric ritual prescriptions envisage that ritual is performed in an abandoned place specially prepared for this purpose, and not in a permanent building with permanently installed images in it. This suggests that at least in the case of some esoteric cults (in the Bhairavatantras and 'above') and at a relatively early period, near the composition of the earliest Tantras, no permanent building or image was used to perform ritual.[53] It must also be noted that the list of supports for daily worship given by Abhinavagupta[54] mostly includes various small objects as supports for visualization which do not actually depict the deities of the cult. He mentions, for instance, a rosary, a mirror or a sword-blade as well as a private *liṅga*. When images are mentioned, they are small ones made of painted clay (perhaps what is meant is terra-cotta), deodar wood or gold or images painted on a piece of cloth or drawn on a skull. They are images of small size for private worship, never larger ones made of stone. Moreover, early Bhairavatantras do not normally include references to rituals which empower icons made for common worship (*pratiṣṭhā*).[55]

---

categories, see Sanderson 1988. For the fact that Tantras teaching goddess worship also categorize themselves as Bhairavatantras in a broader sense, see, e.g., Siddhayogeśvarīmata 1.19d and 8.4cd, the latter passage reading *mahābhairavatantre 'smin siddhayogeśvarīmate.*

[52] An appropriate treatment of the subject would require a monograph. Therefore, what is presented below is only a brief summary of a few points relevant to the present discussion on maṇḍalas in some early Śaiva Tantras, without a full presentation of all the evidence. It is hoped that the study 'Idols and Other Substrates of Worship in the Trika' announced in Sanderson 1990 shall be soon available.

[53] This hypothesis would of course need further investigation and a full presentation of the early sources on the subject.

[54] See TĀ 26.32ff. and Tantrasāra 179–189 and the summary of these passages in Sanderson 1986: 170.

[55] The only such text I know of is the unedited Piṅgalāmata referred to in Sanderson 1990: 40 and cited on the visualization of the deities of the Trika. Its

It must be mentioned that in the demonstrably early sources of the Siddhānta, even if the installation of deities in permanent, durable images is commonly discussed, these images were not used for public rites. They were used only by members of the particular community (*maṭha*) for individual worship. As Brunner observes in her study and translation of the *pratiṣṭhā* section of the Somaśambhupaddhati (SP4, p. v), at the time of the writing of this manual, no public temple rites were performed.[56] What is envisaged by Somaśambhu is that when a *liṅga* is established in a *maṭha*, for example, it is worshipped by several people one after the other.[57]

Private, portable (*cala*) *liṅgas* were also used in more esoteric cults, as mentioned above, even if the worship of larger, shared *liṅgas* does not seem to be mentioned in Bhairavatantras.[58] Moreover, as Abhinavagupta writes in Tantrāloka (TĀ) 27.2–3, these shared *liṅgas*—even if envisaged for Bhairavatantric worship—are not to be installed with secret, i.e., esoteric, mantras; for those mantra-deities possess their power in their esoteric nature and once

Nepalese manuscript is reported to be dated A.D. 1169–1170. The same title occurs in the list of the Bhairava canon as cited by Jayaratha from the Śrīkaṇṭhīya *ad* TĀ 1.17, but it is not cited by Abhinavagupta or Jayaratha himself. Although the text claims to be part of the Bhairava canon as Goudriaan 1981: 46 points out, it mainly deals with temple construction and installation of *liṅgas*. Goudriaan 1981: 46 also observes that "Śākta tendencies are almost completely absent" in this work, which would explain why a Saiddhāntika author, Vidyākaṇṭha II (pupil of Rāmakaṇṭha II), refers to it many times in his Bhāvacūḍāmaṇi (for details, see Goodall's introduction to his edition of the Kiraṇavṛtti, pp. xxvi–xxvii). From the above cited accounts of the contents of this text, it seems that only its chapter 5 on painting (and possibly some passages in its chapter 4 on icons) could be relevant in a Bhairavatantric context. These passages seem to give the iconography of paintings made on cloth, a substrate for private worship mentioned by Abhinavagupta in the above citations. The NT also gives some details in a few verses, which are discussed below.

[56] One of the few, relatively detailed, surviving passages about the installation of *liṅgas* and small size statues is found in the Mataṅga, *kriyāpāda* 13–14, the only longer passage pointed out in the above edition as a parallel. For some additional texts in manuscript form which also deal with the subject, see, e.g., Niśvāsatantra, Guhyasūtra, chapter 2 and Sarvajñānottara summarized in Goudriaan 1981: 36, 39. See also two Pratiṣṭhātantras, the Mohaśūrottara and the Mayasaṃgraha described in Goodall's introduction to his edition of the Kiraṇavṛtti, pp. x–xi and referred to as sources of Somaśambhu's account in Goodall 2000: 216.

[57] This is also what Abhinavagupta refers to in TĀ 27.53–54.

[58] This lack of interest in commonly worshipped large *liṅgas* may also be related to the fact that Bhairavatantras seem to focus on the acquisition of supernatural powers, which requires private rituals in secluded places in most cases, i.e., rites performed 'without one's companions.' The solitary performance of these rituals is enjoined, e.g., in Siddhayogeśvarīmata 12.14, 13.11, 18.18 and 19.17.

installed, they would lose their real nature as well as their power. Therefore, stable or larger *liṅga*s are to be installed with the mantras of the Siddhānta, even if other deities can be invoked in them temporarily. Furthermore, following the Sarvajñānottara, Abhinavagupta adds that secret mantras should be avoided especially in case one installs a so-called manifest (*vyaktarūpin*) image—a warning which shows that what is to be avoided here is first of all an anthropomorphic or figurative image.[59]

Nevertheless, there was one, undoubtedly 'anthropomorphic image' which was not excluded from communal esoteric worship and even recommended for certain days: the body of the *guru*, that of other Śaivas and certain women. In the list of 11 possible substrates of external worship given in TĀ 6.3,[60] the last one, *mūrti*, a word that could possibly refer to an icon in similar contexts, is glossed by the commentator as "the body belonging to the *guru* or others" (*mūrtir gurvādisambandhinī*). The long description of what is called 'The Worship of Embodiments' (*mūrtiyāga*) or 'The Worship of the Circle' (*cakrayāga*), which makes this somewhat enigmatic gloss clearer, is then given in chapter 28.60ff. by Abhinavagupta: it is a rite in which the preceptor, various other practitioners, their wives

---

[59] The exceptional installation of a Bhairavāgamic mantra in NT_2 18.119–121 is discussed by Sanderson 1990: 78, who understands the passage of the Tantra to prescribe the installation of an ectype of the esoteric mantra of Svacchandabhairava in the icon. He then argues that Abhinavagupta in TĀ 27.8 in fact contorts the intended meaning of the Tantra by interpreting the passage to refer to the installation of a non-Bhairavāgamic mantra such as that of Netranātha, so that the prescription should conform to the fundamental rules of *pratiṣṭhā*. Although Abhinavagupta's interpretation does seem forced, it must be noted that the passage of the Tantra itself refers back (by saying *prāgvidhānataḥ*) to some previous verses on general rules about *pratiṣṭhā*. These verses, 18.104c–109, prescribe the installation of the non-esoteric Amṛteśa/Netranātha alone or with the also non-esoteric goddess Mahālakṣmī. Even if this is not enough to support Abhinavagupta's interpretation, it is significant that installation is generally envisaged here using non-esoteric mantras, in spite of the general tendency of the NT to mix up various Āgamic prescriptions (for which see NT_2 13.45–46).

[60] These substrates are a maṇḍala, leveled ground, a vessel, a rosary, a manuscript [of Śaiva scripture], a *liṅga*, a skull, a piece of cloth (no details given), a clay/terracotta image (not discussed in any detail, but mentioned in 27.19 as coloured [*citra*]), a mirror (or any mirror-like surface, such as a sword mentioned in 27.44) and a *mūrti*:

maṇḍalaṃ sthaṇḍilaṃ pātram akṣasūtraṃ sapustakam /
liṅgaṃ tūraṃ paṭaḥ pustaṃ pratimā mūrtir eva ca //

and women of lower castes or prostitutes are propitiated by alcohol and offerings which include meat and fish.[61]

Even when an apparently figurative image or anthropomorphic icon seems to be mentioned in a Bhairavatantra, such as a 'Dakṣiṇāmūrti' in the SvT, commentators understand such references as denoting something which is different from an icon as an embodiment.[62]

As for the size of images used, icons of deities in the Siddhānta are described, e.g., in the Mataṅga, *kriyāpāda*, chapter 14 as being between ten *aṅgulas* and one *hasta* (0.2–0.45 metre).[63] The size of a *liṅga* is said to be three *hastas* (1.35 metre) in the same text (13.9),[64] which would be the size of the smallest maṇḍalas.

The initiation maṇḍala used by all the initiands is thus the largest image (as envisaged in a number of Bhairavatantras) or one of the largest images (if we consider shared *liṅgas*) a Tāntrika may see and use, for its side usually measures at least three or four *hastas* (eight or nine is also recommended), that is at least 1.35–1.8 metres. But unlike the other communal or shared support of a relatively large size, the *liṅga*, it contains a clear visual mapping of the esoteric deities of one's tradition.

Among objects used as supports for the worship of esoteric deities, portable images used for private worship are small. Therefore, even if kept over a longer period of time, they can be hidden from the uninitiated. Other supports such as a mirror or a sword are not easily recognizable as religious objects. But an image as large as an initiation maṇḍala is not so easy to hide, and this is perhaps one of the reasons why it has to be temporary: a maṇḍala drawn up for the occasion and effaced ritually after it has served its purpose.

---

[61] Note that according to Abhinavagupta his summary of this *yāga* is based on the Siddhayogeśvarīmata. However, the short recension of that text does not contain anything on this particular subject. For more information, see Törzsök 1999a: 229–230.

[62] See Kṣemarāja *ad* SvT_2 3.129, who remarks on *dakṣiṇāṃ mūrtim*: *na tu pāśavīṃ dehamayīm*. However, it is not clear to me what image Kṣemarāja had in mind.

[63] One *hasta* is the distance between the tip of one's middle finger and the elbow. I have taken one *hasta* to be equal to at least 0.45 metre and rounded up the figures.

[64] Somaśambhu envisages *liṅgas* of up to nine *hastas*, but it is questionable if such large *liṅgas* were common or if they were in use at an earlier date as well.

3 *The Inclusion of Lower Revelation in the Maṇḍala from the Vedas to the Siddhānta: The Case of the Svacchandatantra*

The way in which the trident image of the maṇḍalas of the Trika encodes the supremacy of that school has been analyzed in detail by Sanderson 1986.[65] He points out firstly, how scriptural sources represent the superiority of their system by raising the throne of their deities higher, and secondly, how Abhinavagupta's exegesis adds further hierarchies by stretching what is implied in the scriptural sources of the Trika and related schools. Thus, when the trident image, which includes the full cosmic hierarchy from earth up to the three goddesses on the tips of the trident, is installed in the line of inner sensation in regular worship, it reveals "the Trika's supremacy by taking [the practitioner] through and beyond the maṇḍala-thrones of all other Śaiva claimants to the worship and assimilation of absolute power."

In the same article, reference is made to the ranking of the doctrines of outsiders, i.e., non-Śaivas, in scriptural sources as well as in the Kashmirian exegetical literature.[66] In what follows, I shall take up this line of inquiry with special reference to the SvT, which gives a particularly detailed account of its relation to other doctrines, in order to illustrate the following two features of its initiation maṇḍala.

1. While the trident image of the Trika creates its hierarchy and encodes its supremacy to others in a vertical ascent, the SvT as well as a number of other texts and their maṇḍalas use a concentric image and arrangement of deities to express their domination:[67] they place the supreme deity of their system in the middle of the maṇḍala, surrounded by other deities often representing other schools of thought. This method of concentric encoding seems to be more common than that of the trident image of the Trika, whose maṇḍala is in fact quite exceptional in that it is to be seen as three-dimensional, building its central trident upon the usual concentric image of other Tantras. For in the trident maṇḍala, the central lotus is not the seat of the

[65] For an illustration of one of the several versions of the trident maṇḍala of the Trika, see Colour Plate 19.

[66] See Sanderson 1986: 172, especially note 8.

[67] This idea is also referred to briefly in Sanderson 1986: 172.

principal deity but is the lotus of gnosis, from which the trident of the three goddesses arises and is seen as coming out of the surface of the maṇḍala.

2. The example of the SvT also shows that the maṇḍala can visually represent and include not just other branches of Śaivism, but also non-Śaiva doctrines or traditions in the form of lower revelation. In this respect, the SvT is a special case, because it seems to be the only Bhairavatantra to include a relatively detailed discussion of other, non-Śaiva and early Śaiva (Pāśupata, etc.), doctrines and to include them in its cosmic hierarchy.

The SvT ranks the doctrines of outsiders in its 11th chapter (11.68ff.), which seems to have become something of a *locus classicus* on the subject later on, judging from the series of citations given by Jayaratha *ad* TĀ 1.33.[68] In this passage of the Tantra, schools of thought are assigned various levels of the universe or principles (*tattva*), from intellect (*buddhi*) to Sadāśiva. The equivalences with the *tattvas* are not explained in a fully systematic way, for while some *tattvas* are not assigned to any school,[69] others are said to represent the level of liberation or consciousness of several schools at the same time.[70] In addition, there are also principles which are not *tattvas* but are nevertheless said to be the place of certain schools.[71] It should be noted that these inconsistencies may be due to the fact that it is not uncommon in early Tantras that the number of *tattvas* fluctuates. Such fluctuations can be explained on the one hand as a result of redactional cutting-and-pasting, on the other by the fact that it was perhaps not felt to be necessary to fix the number of *tattvas* at an earlier stage of doctrinal development.[72]

---

[68] The citations are not identified in the edition. Jayaratha quotes SvT_2 11.68c–71d.

[69] None of the five coverings (*kañcuka*) is mentioned explicitly in the list, nor is the level of pure knowledge (*śuddhavidyā*) above *māyā*.

[70] Two sects, the Mausulas and the Kārukas are both given the 30th level, that of *māyā*; and the level of Īśvara also represents several sects.

[71] Thus, the Jainas are said to be established in the three strands of material existence (*guṇa*), which do not form a *tattva*. However, *guṇa* is sometimes listed as a *tattva*, such as in the Parākhya recorded in Goodall's introduction to his edition of the Kiraṇavṛtti, pp. liii.

[72] For a detailed discussion on the number of *tattvas* in the Siddhānta and what they may imply, see Goodall's introduction to his edition of the Kiraṇavṛtti, pp. li–lv.

In spite of these inconsistencies, a number of elements of the hierarchy are very clearly defined and some of them correspond to other ranking systems. Thus, while Kṣemarāja adopts a different hierarchy in his Pratyabhijñāhṛdaya (*ad sūtra* 8), he also assigns the level of intellect (*buddhi*) to the Buddhists.

In the ranking of the SvT, non-Brahminical schools are placed the lowest, below the 24th level, that of material cause (*prakṛti*): the Buddhists are made to reside in *buddhi* and the Jainas are at the level of the three *guṇas* of *sattva*, *rajas* and *tamas*. Now it could be said that the *guṇas* and material cause are at the same level, for the *guṇas* are the three strands of *prakṛti*. However, in this passage, they seem to be treated as separate from and inferior to *prakṛti*.[73] It should also be noted that in verse 68ab, *buddhi* itself is said to be produced from the three *guṇas*, suggesting a direct relationship between these two principles and possibly between the schools placed at these levels.[74]

The 24th principle, *prakṛti*, is assigned to 'Promulgators of the Veda,' which is interpreted to allude to the Vedānta by Kṣemarāja *ad loc.*,[75] but could just refer to anyone for whom the Veda is the highest revelation. The 25th principle, *puruṣa*, is the highest reality for the Sāṃkhya, which seems quite natural.[76] Above them, the 26th principle is the highest level for the Yoga. This is normally the level of *niyati*,[77] causal determination, but in this passage, the SvT does not speak explicitly about any of the five coverings, of which *niyati* is normally the first.

This exposition is followed by the placement of various schools of the Śaiva Atimārga, schools of Pāśupatas and Lākulas, in the cosmic hierarchy. First, the *pāśupata-vrata* is equated with the 33rd level of Īśvara. Following Kṣemarāja, this expression refers to the doctrine expounded by Lakulīśa. Then the text returns to a lower level, the 30th. It is the level of *māyā*, which is the highest level for Mausulas

---

[73] In the same way, the Kiraṇatantra also lists the *guṇas* below *prakṛti*, as reported in Goodall's introduction to his edition of the Kiraṇavṛtti, pp. lv.

[74] Note that Buddhist schools are distinguished, but in fact all are placed at the level of *māyā* in TĀ 4.29–30. Kṣemarāja puts the Saugatas together with the Mīmāṃsakas, Naiyāyikas and Cārvākas at the level of *buddhi*, while the Vedāntins and Mādhyamikas are above them.

[75] This can be inferred from the fact that he cites the Śvetāśvatara-Upaniṣad.

[76] However, Kṣemarāja upgrades them to the level of *mahāmāyā* in the Pratyabhijñāhṛdaya.

[77] That Yoga must be then at the level of *niyati* is also confirmed by Jayaratha *ad* TĀ 1.33: *teṣāṃ* [i.e., *pātañjalānāṃ*] *puṃstattvordhvavartiniyatitattvaprāptir uktā*.

and Kārukas, who are followers of disciples of Lakulīśa, according to Kṣemarāja. They are said to identify this level with the deities Kṣemeśa and Brahmasvāmin respectively. It is then stated that Vaimala and Pramāṇa (or Pañcārtha) Pāśupatas can reach up to the level of Īśvara, identified with their highest deities, Tejeśa and Dhruveśa. After this, Śaivas—probably in the general sense meaning Saiddhāntikas as well as those of other currents—are mentioned and declared to be above the rest.

Further in the same chapter, another passage discusses doctrines of other schools, this time without ranking them in an unambiguous way. The categorization of other doctrines is based on their relation to *dharma*/*adharma*, detachment/lack of detachment (*vairāgya*/*avairāgya*), knowledge/ignorance (*jñāna*/*ajñāna*) and powerfulness/lack of power (*aiśvarya*/*anaiśvarya*). According to verse 186, these eight concepts make the wheel of the *saṃsāra* turn round incessantly as eight spokes. In this passage, non-Śaiva and other Śaiva schools are hierarchized in the following way. Verses 174–179b describe treatises of logic (*hetuśāstra*) and declare them to be characterized by *adharma*, lack of detachment, ignorance and lack of power. It seems they receive the lowest grade here; for, as the SvT says: they are devoid of knowledge, Yoga and deities, and are useless for the attainment of any of the four goals of men in life.[78] After this, all the other schools are described mentioning at least one good point about their teachings. Mundane or common knowledge—covering agriculture, politics, etc., as Kṣemarāja points out—is characterized by *dharma*, while the doctrines of both the Pāñcarātrikas and the Vaidikas involve *dharma* as well as knowledge. Buddhist as well as Jaina doctrine is endowed with detachment, while the school of Sāṃkhya possesses both detachment and knowledge. The best-placed of the non-Śaivas is again the doctrine of Yoga, which is associated with knowledge, detachment and power at the same time. The only doctrine exhibiting all the good characteristics, and which thus goes beyond (*ati-*) the others, is the Śaiva doctrine of the Atimārga. For

[78] This particularly low ranking of the science of logic is not followed by the exegetes. Kṣemarāja places the Nyāya in the same group as the Mīmāṃsā and the Buddhists both in the Pratyabhijñāhṛdaya and in Spandanirṇaya *ad* 4 and 12–13. In the latter work, he places even the Sāṃkhya and the Vedānta at the same level. It could be argued that Hetuśāstra is not the same as the school of Nyāya. Nevertheless, in general statements of the above kind, they may not be differentiated in a very precise manner.

adherents of the Atimārga, i.e., those who practice the Skull observance, and the Pāśupatas (verse 184), there is no further creation, they are established in Īśvara/Dhruveśa. The ranking stops here, and no other Śaivas are mentioned.

This way of ranking of other doctrines reveals two important distinguishing features of the SvT. One is that it includes all Brahminical schools of thoughts from the level of *prakṛti* upwards. Now, it may be argued that the Pāñcarātrikas are omitted from the hierarchy of levels. However, it is arguable that they are understood next to the Vaidikas, which is demonstrated in two other passages. One is the verse referred to above, which states that the doctrine of both Vaidikas and Pāñcarātrikas is characterized by *dharma* and knowledge. Another passage (5.44–46) prescribes that one should not condemn Bhairava, his and other Śāstras, the latter including the Sāṃkhya, Yoga, Pāñcarātra and the Vedas, for they have all come forth from Śiva himself and bestow liberation.[79] These passages show that the Vaidikas, Pāñcarātrikas and the adherents of the Sāṃkhya and Yoga are all consciously felt to be very closely related to Śaiva doctrine, and consequently they are placed at the level of *prakṛti* and above.[80]

Secondly, the SvT also gives a particularly detailed account of how it sees itself in relation to the Atimārga. Judging from the number of Pāśupata branches, they must have been flourishing or recognized at the time of the redaction of this Tantra. It is also noteworthy that the SvT particularly insists on the superiority of the Atimārga, leaving the doctrine about the superiority of Bhairavatantras vis-à-vis other Śaivas implicit. It sees itself as the continuation of the Atimārga rather than of the Siddhānta.[81]

The whole issue of ranking other doctrines according to the *tattvas* gains particular significance in connection with the worship of the deities on the maṇḍala. The drawing of the maṇḍala of nine lotuses

---

[79] Kṣemarāja reports a reading from 'old manuscripts,' which states in the last line that everything comes forth from Śiva and bestows the fruit of [reaching] Śiva's abode.

[80] Although doctrinal affinities remain important, other texts do not state this relationship so explicitly.

[81] Kṣemarāja (commenting on 11.184c) seems somewhat uncomfortable with the fact that the ranking stops at the level of the Atimārga. He supplies an additional statement to the effect that if followers of the Atimārga are liberated, then how much more the Śaivas. He also understands the word *ca* in the sense of *api* in order to read this meaning into the text.

(*navanābha*) for initiation is described in chapter 5 (from verse 19), followed by an explanation concerning the deities to be worshipped on it (from 5.37c). The nine lotuses are arranged in a concentric design in such a way that the lotus in the centre is surrounded by eight others, and each lotus has eight petals.[82] On the pericarp of the central lotus, one is to place and worship the supreme deity of this system, Svacchandabhairava, surrounded by eight Bhairavas on the eight petals. The eight Bhairavas are placed on the petals as eight mantra-syllables extracted from the *navātmabīja*.[83] In what follows (verse 40), the text points out that one should recognize these deities as standing for [the principles] from Sadāśiva down to *prakṛti*, and they are also worshipped on the pericarps of the surrounding lotuses.[84] By including the principles from *prakṛti* up to Sadāśiva in the maṇḍala as secondary deities, the Brahminical schools from the Vedavādins upwards are also implicitly included and their levels represented by Vidyārāja and the other Bhairavas.[85]

Thus, doctrinal inclusivism also appears implicitly in a cult image in a fairly consistent way, since non-Brahminical schools, the Buddhists and the Jainas represented by *tattvas* below *prakṛti*, are left out of the maṇḍala and its deities. The SvT's example also illustrates the common way to express the superiority of a tradition in a concentric icon, in which the supreme deity of the school is worshipped in the centre, surrounded by its retinue of deities (*parivāra*) standing for lower levels of the universe and lower revelation.[86]

---

[82] For a reconstruction and illustration of this maṇḍala, see Appendix 2 and Colour Plate 18.

[83] See Kṣemarāja's commentary on *hakāreṇa*: HA for Kapālīśa, RA for Śikhivāhana, KṢA for Krodharāja, MA for Vikarāla, LA for Manmatha, VA for Meghanāda, YA for Somarāja and Ū for Vidyārāja.

[84] They swap places with Svacchanda as the text and the commentary clarify further on.

[85] We do not necessarily need to follow Kṣemarāja here, who assigns the *tattvas* of Sadāśiva, Īśvara, *vidyā*, *māyā*, *kalā*, *niyati*, *puruṣa* and *prakṛti* to the eight deities, for the text itself simply specifies that they represent levels from Sadāśiva down to *prakṛti*. The author(s) of the Tantra may not have had an exact distribution in mind, just as the distribution of *tattvas* to schools is uneven. It is also to be remarked that Kṣemarāja (*ad* 5.19) understands that the size of the maṇḍala, which measures 224 inches on each side, symbolizes the 224 *bhuvanas* or worlds of the universe. This is an interesting idea, but again one that the Tantra itself does not teach.

[86] The disadvantage or imprecision of this arrangement compared to the hierarchy expressed in the vertical arrangement of the trident icon is that the surrounding deities are not arranged in a hierarchy in relation to each other: Vidyārāja standing

4 *Maṇḍalas bestowing Supernatural Powers*

Although initiation maṇḍalas—whether they are used for the *samaya* rite or for the *dīkṣā*—appear to be the basis and model of maṇḍalas used for acquiring supernatural powers (*siddhi*) as well as for daily worship, *siddhimaṇḍalas*[87] seem to differ sometimes from their model in several ways. The ways in which maṇḍalas are transformed or visualized differently for *siddhi* can be divided into three groups:

i. Specialization
   Some maṇḍalas become reduced in that an element and a deity is taken out of the more elaborate version and the deity is then worshipped separately for specific supernatural powers.

ii. Expansion
   By contrast, some other maṇḍalas are expanded with a set or sets of other deities not necessarily present on the basic version, who seem to increase the power of the deity-circle without disturbing the hierarchy of the central deities of the cult.

iii. Substitution
   Lastly, some maṇḍalas are retained in their form as described for initiation except that the deities installed and worshipped on them are changed; thus the maṇḍala as a drawing is considered some kind of framework.

i. *Specialization*

A good example of how a maṇḍala is reduced, or rather, how one of its deities is focused on for specific purposes can be found in the ninth chapter of the SvT. The chapter starts with the description of the worship of Svacchandabhairava and how his maṇḍala of one lotus and four doors is to be constructed (9.12ff.). The drawing of the

---

for *prakṛti* and Vedic revelation has the same position as Śikhivāhana embodying the level of Īśvara and the Pāśupatas.

[87] The term *siddhimaṇḍala* is used in the colophon of the Siddhayogeśvarīmata, chapter 25, which thus distinguishes between this maṇḍala and the trident-based one used for the name-giving *samaya* rite. However, the Siddhayogeśvarīmata seems to envisage this very *siddhimaṇḍala* for *dīkṣā*, judging from an aside in 25.16cd: *dīkṣāyāṃ sādhane hy asminn evaṃ mānavikalpanā*. This usage may reflect the view of the Siddhayogeśvarīmata on the subject, namely that liberation is just one of the *siddhis* (see 29.8–11). It should also be noted that the Niśvāsa, on the other hand, uses the term 'maṇḍala bestowing liberation' (*muktimaṇḍala*) on fol. 20r4.

maṇḍala begins with a single lotus, on whose pericarp Svacchanda is later to be installed with mantra-syllables and worshipped. This lotus is then surrounded by a wheel of 32 spokes (9.16), on which the practitioner worships a set of 32 goddesses, starting with Aruṇā.[88] The size of this square maṇḍala can vary. Verse 14 envisages maṇḍalas of one, two, four or eight *hasta*s on each side; while the one with nine lotuses for initiation is prescribed as measuring nine *hasta*s on each side.

This maṇḍala of Svacchanda is said to bestow all kinds of supernatural powers, especially power over all the worlds. Some of these worlds are well-known from Purāṇic cosmography; they include the various hells, underworlds (*pātāla*) and the seven *loka*s. Others are identical with principles (*tattva*) of the universe in the Śaiva sense from *prakṛti* and *puruṣa* up to Sadāśiva and Śakti. The diagram translates into an image of what is elsewhere insisted upon in doctrinal passages: the idea that the supreme deity ultimately controls the whole universe, even if lower levels are assigned to other Bhairavas as their regents, and thus it is this supreme deity that is able to bestow full power upon the practitioner.

However, the other eight Bhairavas of the initiation maṇḍala are not forgotten in the context of *siddhi*, either. But while the worship of Svacchanda is prescribed on a maṇḍala as a support, the other Bhairavas are placed and worshipped on small charms written on pieces of birch-bark (yantras or *rakṣās*[89]). They are worshipped for the attainment of much more specific goals than the control of the whole universe.

The first yantras described are those of the first and last Bhairava, Vidyārāja and Kapālīśa, who can protect the practitioner from death. Their mantras are to be incised in the centre of a wheel, and the spokes are occupied by the 32 goddesses starting with Aruṇā, just as in the maṇḍala of Svacchanda above. The other yantras are based on the same model, with one Bhairava in the middle and the goddesses around him, except that in each case, some additional details are

[88] Following verse 16, which states that the wheel is outside the lotus, Kṣemarāja remarks at verse 24 that there are four goddesses in each of the eight directions, and that they are outside the lotus. However, the text of verse 24—contrarily to 16—suggests that the lotus and the wheel somehow overlap, because it says that the goddesses are on the petals and the spokes at the same time.

[89] As the examples below show, *rakṣā* is not always a protective amulet, despite its name.

given. These include instructions to incise the name of the person who is to be protected, controlled or killed in the middle; or the addition of other mantras to the whole yantra which envelope or inflame it, or the use of substances collected in the cremation ground (9.64–65). Among the other Bhairavas, Śikhivāhana is employed to cause one's enemy to suffer; Krodharāja can kill someone or make him mad; Vikarāla can frighten one's enemy; Manmatha is invoked for subjugation; Meghanāda to exile someone and Somarāja to acquire wealth.

The resemblance between the maṇḍala of Svacchanda and the yantras of the other Bhairavas shows that in spite of the differences between maṇḍalas and yantras, they are closely related, especially in the context of *siddhis*. Just as Svacchanda represents the truest doctrine of all Brahminical doctrines which are included in the initiation maṇḍala, so here, too, he stands for all-encompassing power. Other Bhairavas are seen as specializing in more specific tasks. The initiation maṇḍala of the nine lotuses includes all these Bhairavas as different levels of reality, for its purpose is to bestow qualification upon the initiate who can subsequently employ any of these Bhairavas for whatever goal he may want to. But for specific aims, he is to use only the Bhairava most appropriate for his purpose. Judging from the construction of these maṇḍalas and yantras in the SvT, *siddhi* is viewed here as the specific application of the power acquired in an all-inclusive way at the time of initiation.

ii. *Expansion*

This view of the SvT is not shared unanimously by all Tantras. In a number of texts, the maṇḍalas prescribed for *siddhis* contain several circles of deities who are not necessarily present in the initiation maṇḍala. The Mṛgendratantra, for instance, allows an initiation maṇḍala of just the central group of five deities or *brahmamantras*,[90]

[90] This is referred to in *kriyāpāda* 8.44 as an option, although it is emphasized in the preceding verse that one should try and make a maṇḍala with several circles of deities. Verses 8.52–53 also suggest that all the deities may not be present inside the maṇḍala, which should ideally include three circles of deities (*āvaraṇa*) around the central group. In case of these smaller maṇḍalas, one can worship the outer circles on ornamental elements, such as *svastikas*, lotuses or dots, or one can just worship Śiva on the four-petalled lotus. This last solution is interpreted by Nārāyaṇakaṇṭha to be used in case of lack of time, place or material means.

but prescribes additional outer circles of deities to be worshipped for certain supernatural powers. For the acquisition of knowledge, it is sufficient to worship the Vidyeśvaras around the central group of five *brahmamantras*. For 'divine' supernatural powers one should add the circle of the Gaṇeśas. For 'middle' *siddhis*—probably meaning attracting women and the like—the guardians of directions should be further added outside the Gaṇeśa circle. For 'lower' powers—such as killing—all the gods should be there, extending outward to the guardians' weapons on the periphery of the maṇḍala.[91] Moreover, according to *kriyāpāda* 8.46, in case the practitioner has various aims of different kinds, he is to worship the central deity surrounded by three or four outer circles of deities on a *śaktimaṇḍala*, which is endowed with an additional circle of the mothers.[92] These mothers are not present on any version of the initiation maṇḍala, yet they are employed for *siddhis* of all kinds, in an extension of what is or could be the same as the initiation maṇḍala.[93]

These prescriptions of the Mṛgendra show that the outer circles of deities in its maṇḍala are responsible for *siddhis* of increasingly low kinds. However, they are not worshipped on their own for these specific functions, but always remain in the outer circles of the maṇḍala whose centre is occupied by Śiva in the form of the five *brahmamantras*. This visual arrangement implies that various *siddhis* are not specific functions of the central deities (as was the case in the SvT), but rather that the bestowing of supernatural powers is seen as an extended function of these deities, who do not bestow *siddhis* themselves, but delegate lower gods, *lokapālas* and the like, for these tasks.[94]

---

[91] Cf. *kriyāpāda* 8.45. Note that according to Nārāyaṇakaṇṭha, in each case only one circle is to be worshipped around the centre and not several circles extending outward to the circle including those deities. The centre with the five mantra-deities and the guardians, for instance, should be worshipped for 'middle' *siddhis*, omitting the Vidyeśvaras and Gaṇeśvaras in between. However, the text of the Tantra does not support this interpretation, for it uses compounds such as *patiprāntaḥ* and *gaṇāntaḥ* (qualifying *yāgaḥ*).

[92] See also commentary *ad loc.*: *śaktīnāṃ mātṝṇāṃ sambandhi yan maṇḍalaṃ tatra....*

[93] The addition of female deities for *siddhis* is also a feature of the SvT as shown above, which positions the goddesses around the central Bhairavas.

[94] It may be tempting to speculate on the basis of this that the Mṛgendra's above arrangement reflects its dualistic position, while the SvT's way of attributing powers corresponds to a non-dualistic view. However, it is unlikely that cults, especially

iii. *Substitution*

The third way of changing the initiation maṇḍala for *siddhi* can be illustrated by two examples taken from the Siddhayogeśvarīmata. Chapter 25 first describes the initiation maṇḍala in a rather cursory way. Its side measures three or four *hasta*s and it has a 32-inch lotus with eight petals in the middle—thus resembling the basic type reconstructed in Illustration 1 and Colour Plates 16–17 (following the more detailed prescriptions of the *śrīmaṇḍala* in the NT).[95] After a brief statement of how the placement of mantras is to be performed on the body, the text appears to shift subject to give details of rites to acquire supernatural powers which are to be performed in the cremation ground. The placement of the mantras is followed by the filling of the maṇḍala outline with powders. Verse 34 specifies that white powder is to be produced from powderized human bones and red from blood. Then, the practitioner is to place a human skull on the pericarp of the lotus and on the eight petals and should write the mantra of Bhairava with his consort on the central skull with blood taken from his left arm. This Bhairava holds a trident in his right hand, on which the three principal goddesses of the Trika, Parā, Parāparā and Aparā, should be projected. On the remaining eight skulls the eight mantra-goddesses who form the retinue of Parāparā should be written, starting with Aghorā.

So far, this *siddhimaṇḍala* basically follows the arrangement of deities prescribed in chapter 6 for the *samaya* rite: the three goddesses occupy the prongs of the trident and the group of eight is

early ones, were based on such principles. For the problem of dualism and non-dualism in scriptural sources, see Sanderson 1992: 282ff.

[95] The same type of maṇḍala is given in another Trika text, the Tantrasadbhāva (9.104ff.), which calls it the *sarvatobhadra(ka)*. Although the Siddhayogeśvarīmata seems to agree with the Tantrasadbhāva on this matter rather than with a third surviving Trika text, the Mālinīvijaya (which gives a maṇḍala of a trident and the lotuses), the subsequent verses on *siddhi* show that there is a trident present on the maṇḍala of the Siddhayogeśvarīmata, too: but instead of being drawn on the ground inside the maṇḍala, it is drawn in blood on a skull placed in the middle. Nevertheless, it must be mentioned that the text does not give an unambiguous account of the maṇḍalas. This chapter as well as chapters 7 and 8 suggest that the initiation maṇḍala (*dīkṣāmaṇḍala*) may well resemble the Tantrasadbhāva's *sarvatobhadra*, without the trident, even though chapter 6 clearly prescribes the maṇḍala with the trident for the *samaya* rite. Moreover, Abhinavagupta's summary of the principal maṇḍala of this text—on the basis of which I have attempted to reconstruct the maṇḍala in Colour Plate 19, but which is not included in the surviving short recension—unambiguously gives one with the trident.

placed on the petals of the lotus. However, after giving the *bījamantras* for the goddesses and promising the successful invocation of Yoginīs, verses 53–55 give a new set of eight goddesses one can equally worship with the same or other *bījas* on the diagram. Their names indicate that they are probably recommended for lower *siddhis* such as killing.[96] The diagram itself becomes a framework which can accommodate various groups of deities depending on the *siddhi* envisaged.

A procedure similar to this seems to be at work in chapters 21 and 22 of the same text. Chapter 21 describes, again very briefly, a wheel-diagram with 12 spokes, which appears to be recommended for worship in various months of the year. Twelve Rudras of different names are placed on the spokes, and a Bhairava, identified with one's self, performs the churning of the nectar of immortality in the middle. Subsequently, the text gives a summary in a few verses of a *samaya* type ritual, in which this very wheel-diagram is employed to determine the *gotra* name of the initiates (verses 20–21), implying that the wheel is used as the central image of a maṇḍala. The wheel is to be drawn red, with a mixture including blood. Now a passage in the next chapter prescribes the visualization of the same kind of wheel as the one mentioned for the *gotra* attribution. However, this time the wheel, whose basic colour is red and which is to be visualized in the middle of an Ocean of Blood, is mentally projected in the air. Instead of 12 Rudras, 12 frightening Yoginīs—or optionally six Yoginīs accompanied by six Rudras as consorts[97]—are to be placed on the spokes. They churn *amṛta* from the Ocean of Blood and bestow success upon the practitioner.

The wheel-diagram used for a *gotra* name-giving initiatory rite and recommended for monthly worship is thus employed as a framework on which more fierceful deities are installed to gain supernatural powers, just as the lotus maṇḍala of the main goddesses can also accommodate goddesses associated with black magic (*abhicāra*).

Although the above examples are fairly representative of the major ways in which the initiation maṇḍala can be transformed to bestow *siddhis*, they are not exhaustive. Two additional common

---

[96] The first of them is called Jambhanī and the last, Pramathanī.

[97] This is how the conjunction *vā* may be interpreted in verse 34, followed by the mention of the two sets of six in verse 35.

types of procedure should be mentioned in this context: certain graphical differences which are associated with particular *siddhi*s and the change of materials with which the maṇḍala is prepared.

As for graphical changes, after describing the principal maṇḍala, whose base is square-shaped, the Niśvāsatantra mentions briefly how to draw the outline of circular (*vartula*) maṇḍalas, maṇḍalas of a semi-circular (*ardhacandra*) type and triangular (*trikoṇa*) ones. This is followed by the statement that for rites of propitiation or appeasement as well as for prosperity, one should use the square or circular type; the semi-circle should be used for the maṇḍala of Caṇḍeśa and the triangular type, for black magic.[98]

A different sort of graphical change is prescribed for the worship of various deities and for the acquisition of *siddhi*s in the Mṛgendra, which draws the shape of the petals of the lotus in the maṇḍala differently for different purposes.[99] For supernatural powers in general (*bhūti*), the petals should have curled-up tips; they should be even for liberation (*mukti*).[100] For the worship of Kāmeśvara and other deities bestowing good fortune, the petals are to have pointed tips, while if one worships the *lokapāla*s, the *graha*s, the *gaṇa*s, Caṇḍeśa or Gaṇeśa, the petals must be broad and curved at the edges.[101] The *gaṇa*s are also given round-shaped petals in another verse. The worship of the Vidyeśvaras requires petals shaped like cow's ears, and Gaurī, the goddess of speech (*vāk*) and the Rudras are to be worshipped on lotuses whose petals look like the leaves of the Aśvattha tree.

In the subsequent verses, the Mṛgendra gives yet more alternatives, which concern the shape of the mandala and its colour according to the deities or the purpose of the worship. Thus, agreeing with the Niśvāsa, it prescribes a semi-circular maṇḍala for worshipping Caṇḍeśa, but it adds the worship of the Amṛtavidyās[102] to this category and specifies that the colour of the diagram should

---

[98] *vartulaṃ caturasraṃ vā śāntike pauṣṭike tathā /*
ardhacandraṃ tu caṇḍeśe abhicāre trikoṇakam // fol. 26r3.
(The reading of the manuscript *caṇḍīśe* has been emended to *caṇḍeśe*.)

[99] See Mṛgendra, *kriyāpāda* 8.31–33.

[100] I follow Nārāyaṇakaṇṭha's interpretation of the verse, who understands the somewhat enigmatic *sphuṭam* to mean *animnonnatāgraṃ samam*.

[101] Following Nārāyaṇakaṇṭha's interpretation of the word *mantharāgrakam*.

[102] These are female mantra-deities bestowing immortality and the like.

be white. The maṇḍala of the Saubhāgyavidyās[103] is said to be red and vulva-shaped or bow-shaped. The description continues with further options for purposes of well-being, for rain and for the worship of the Vidyeśvaras.

The materials used for the preparation of the maṇḍala should also be different when used for liberation and when employed for lower supernatural powers (*abhicāra*) according to the same passage of the Mṛgendra (*kriyāpāda* 8.40):[104] the coloured powders are to be made from pearls, corals, gold and the like for liberation, but they are to be produced using substances from the cremation ground for the lower powers.

However, if the same maṇḍala is used for liberation as well as for the acquisition of supernatural powers,[105] the Mṛgendra instructs practitioners to make white powder from rice flour, red from red mineral from mountains—vermillion or red chalk according to the commentator—, yellow from yellow orpiment or turmeric[106] and black from burnt barley and the like. Since initiation maṇḍalas used for several people should not be made for a specific *siddhi*, this general type is probably what the text envisages for *dīkṣā*.

It must also be noted that a more esoteric text teaching goddess worship, the Siddhayogeśvarīmata, does not prescribe impure substances for specific *siddhis* as obligatory. At the same time it allows these substances as alternatives for initiation as well. Thus, in 6.12, the text gives the choice to the *guru* if he wants to use ashes (probably meant to be collected in a cremation ground) or flour for the *samayamaṇḍala*, and in 8.8 it also gives alternatives without restriction for the making of the thread to be used to prepare the outline of the maṇḍala: it can be made of human hair (*narakeśa-samutthena*, again probably obtained from corpses) or of cotton and the like. On the other hand, even for rites to acquire supernatural powers, the instructions state that flour or rice-powder may be used,

---

[103] According to Nārāyaṇakaṇṭha these are mantra-goddesses bestowing the powers of subjugation and attraction.

[104] It may be noted that as the above passages show, the Mṛgendra appears to mention a number of details about maṇḍalas which do not concern only initiation maṇḍalas, although the main subject of the passage is indeed initiation maṇḍalas. Therefore the distinction between *mukti* and *abhicāra* may not refer to initiation maṇḍalas of initiates with different purposes, but rather to *siddhimaṇḍalas*.

[105] This is what the commentary suggests at the beginning of the passage, saying *bhuktimuktiviṣayāṇāṃ yāgānām*.

[106] I again follow the commentator on *haridrakādinā*: *haridrāharitālādinā*.

although preference is given to impure substances, such as powderized human bones for white and blood for red.[107]

5 *Substitution and Change:*[108] *The Worship of Viṣṇu and the Inclusion of the Buddha in the Netratantra*

The *siddhimaṇḍala*s examined so far show that the pantheon worshipped on them can vary significantly and in several ways from the pantheon of the initiation maṇḍalas. However, in all these cases the deities worshipped remain those taught in the Śaiva systems: forms of Śiva or Bhairava, various Yoginīs or groups of deities forming their retinue such as the *lokapāla*s. It could be argued that for *siddhi*s, the SvT employs Bhairavas who embody lower levels of the universe in the initiation maṇḍala, and who consequently represent lower, non-Śaiva revelation: Vidyārāja who is employed to conquer death, for instance, stands for the level of *prakṛti* and by implication embodies the level attributed to Vedavādins. However, the deity remains a Śaiva mantra-deity with a visual appearance and name of a Bhairava. In this respect, the NT stands apart from other early texts in that for *siddhi*s it prescribes the alternative worship of deities who clearly belong to other systems, by substituting the central god of the cult, Mṛtyuṃjaya/Netranātha (as well as his consort), with non-Śaiva deities.

After describing the drawing and decoration of the maṇḍala, the NT lists the deities to be worshipped in its centre, on the pericarp of the lotus. First, the principal deity of the cult, Mṛtyuṃjaya is mentioned (18.62), who is to be worshipped with the goddess of prosperity, Śrī, as his consort. Secondly, an alternative is given

---

[107] Siddhayogeśvarīmata 25.34cd: *sitaṃ nṛśaṅkhajaṃ cūrṇaṃ raktaṃ kṣatajabhāvitam.* I have conjectured *nṛśaṅkhajaṃ* for the reading of the manuscripts *triśaṅkhajaṃ.*

[108] By this subtitle I intend to evoke the principal argument in Eivind G. Kahrs's unpublished dissertation entitled "Substitution and change: foundations of traditional Indian hermeneutics" (Oslo, 1996). I have not got direct access to this work, whose main thesis was summarized by the author in personal communications and in lectures at the University of Cambridge. The idea is also referred to briefly in Kahrs 1998: 278, who states that "change is achieved through substitution in that new meaning may be encoded into old terms by means of a substitutional model." In what follows, I hope to show that substitution is applied in the NT in a ritual context, not as a hermeneutic device, but as a method to include deities of other cults in its pantheon.

whereby Śrīdhara, that is Viṣṇu, can be substituted for the principal deity. Visualizations of Viṣṇu are described at the beginning of chapter 13, in which a number of Vaiṣṇava forms are listed which include various incarnations such as the Man-lion (Narasiṃha), the Boar (Varāha) and the Dwarf (Vāmana). But the list of alternatives does not stop here, for the text continues by giving the visualization of Sūrya, forms of Rudra, Harihara, Ardhanārīśvara, Brahmā, and finally the Buddha, who is said to specialize in granting liberation to women. The commentator, Kṣemarāja, introduces this passage[109] by saying that the text enumerates various alternative forms of Mṛtyuṃjaya. They can all be worshipped on a maṇḍala, too, which is first shown in the prescription according to which Sūrya is to be placed in the middle of a lotus (verse 23), and later by the mention of various *loci* of worship in 28. These deities or—following Kṣemarāja—forms of Mṛtyuṃjaya can be visualized on the ground, in fire or water, on the top of a mountain, or in any other place which is pleasing to the mind and shall all bestow the desired success. This is further confirmed in another passage of verses 37–43, which states that all kinds of deities lead to success if they are worshipped as prescribed. The text explicitly says that deities of other Tantric traditions can be invoked as well as those of the Nyāya, the Buddhists,[110] the Yoga, Vedic deities, etc.[111] The list shows that the Buddha is not visualized and regarded as a manifestation of Viṣṇu—which could also be the case—but is considered to be the Buddha of the Buddhists and is invoked as such.

What is most striking in the inclusivism of the NT is that it does not stop at the level of Vedic revelation and Brahminical *darśanas*, but includes the Buddhists, and that it allows the worship of forms of Viṣṇu and the Buddha as principal deities.

Now the SvT also includes the visualization of Brahminical deities who are not Śaiva strictly speaking, and who represent lower levels of the Śaiva universe situated below forms of Śiva. An example for such inclusion can be seen in the description of internal worship, in the course of building up the Śaiva universe internally. When visualizing the lotus of gnosis (*vidyāpadma*) on top of the

[109] Cf. the commentary before SvT_2 13.17.

[110] The NT_2 uses the irregular or *aiśa* form *ārahata* as does the SvT.

[111] The 'etc.' in the text is interpreted by Kṣemarāja to mean Purāṇic deities. This may include the worship of deities such as Durgā-Vindhyavāsinī mentioned subsequently.

throne, which is nailed together by the four Vedas and the four aeons (2.64c–65b), first a circle of Śaktis is described, which is to be placed on the petals with the goddess Manonmanī on the pericarp. This is followed by the placement of three circles (*maṇḍalas*/*maṇḍalakas*) on this lotus of gnosis: the circle of the sun on the petals, that of the moon on the filaments and the circle of fire on the pericarp.[112] Then the visualizations of three deities (of Purāṇic appearance) as regents of these three circles or spheres are prescribed: Brahmā, Viṣṇu and Rudra placed on the outer, middle and inner circles of the petals, filaments and the pericarp respectively. It is on top of Rudra, still on the pericarp, that the laughing Sadāśiva/Mahāpreta is then to be projected before the visualization and worship of Svacchanda's throne and of Svacchanda himself.

The difference between the place and role of Viṣṇu in the NT compared to the SvT is that on the one hand, the NT prescribes the worship of forms of Viṣṇu as the central deity, and on the other that it gives several alternative forms of Viṣṇu, which indicates its somewhat unusual interest for this deity in a Śaiva context.[113] Moreover, the appearance of the Buddha as central deity is undoubtedly unique here. By prescribing the worship of these deities, the NT goes much further than the SvT in including other cults. This may be considered not only another element showing the NT's relative lateness,[114] but also a feature that may reflect a different religious scene of its time.[115]

---

[112] According to Kṣemarāja (*avataraṇikā* of 2.72cd–73ab), these three circles represent the instrument, the object and the subject of gnosis (*māna*, *meya*, *mātṛ*) respectively as well as the three powers of knowledge, action and will (*icchā*, *jñāna*, *kriyā*).

[113] Although Vaiṣṇava inflections of Śaiva deities may be often encountered, the NT's interest in several such forms may be considered unusual. For a Vaiṣṇava version of Kālī worship, see the example from the Jayadrathayāmala teaching the worship of Kālī Mādhaveśvarī with Narasiṃha, given in Sanderson 1988: 154.

[114] That the NT belongs to a relatively later layer of the early, pre-10th century, scriptural sources has been argued on the basis of ample evidence in Brunner 1974: 126ff., who also cites Madhusūdan Kaul's introduction to the first edition.

[115] Ritual eclecticism and changing attitudes towards such phenomena were analyzed in a series of papers by Professor Phyllis Granoff at the École des Hautes Études en Sciences Sociales (Paris) in April-May 2000, especially in her first paper entitled "Other people's rituals: ritual eclecticism in early medieval religions." I am grateful to Professor Granoff for giving me a version of the final draft of her study and for drawing my attention to the ritual eclecticism of the NT. In the meantime part of this material has been published (Granoff 2000 and 2001).

What is perhaps less striking, but almost equally surprising, is the inclusion of the 'deity of the Nyāya'—whoever it is supposed to be.[116] The inclusion of the Nyāya is surprising because the SvT, which can probably be regarded as something of a reference work for the NT,[117] categorically rejects treatises of logic (*hetuśāstra*) and condemns them in a relatively long passage.[118]

At the same time, the NT can be said to follow a kind of logic already established in other Tantras. For the substitution of principal deities of the cult with less central ones in maṇḍalas employed for *siddhi* is a practice also seen in the example of the non-syncretic Siddhayogeśvarīmata. The NT applies the same procedure of substitution, except that it goes a step further and includes Vaiṣṇava and non-Brahminical deities or cult figures, who do not form part of its basic pantheon. The substitution can be justified in the same way as the SvT justifies its recognition of other scriptures: all scriptures as well as all deities and doctrines are created by and identical with the supreme deity of this Tantra.[119]

Conclusion

Instead of summarizing the major points of the above analysis of inclusivism or eclecticism—points which may well change in the light of further evidence—I would like to mention two particular features of the maṇḍala as *locus* of worship that may have contributed to inclusivism or ritual eclecticism in Bhairavatantras: the

---

[116] Kṣemarāja *ad loc.* interprets this reference to mean that the supreme deity of the Nyāya is one endowed with qualities of omniscience and the like, but who is ontologically different from men.

[117] For the NT's relying on the SvT, see Brunner 1974: 126ff.

[118] As mentioned above, even if Nyāya and Hetuśāstra (the latter possibly meaning any work questioning the authority of revelation) may not exactly cover the same branch of Śāstra, it is unlikely that they are strictly differentiated in these scriptural passages. The above mentioned passage about treatises of logic is long in that no other school of thought is treated or criticized in such detail in the text. See SvT 11.167–179b on what it calls Hetuśāstra, while all other traditions are dealt with in verses 179c–185.

[119] Something to this effect is stated in 13.44–46. This passage confirms that the principal deity of this cult is the soul of all mantras, and therefore there is no infringement of the rules prescribing that rites of different schools should not be mixed up. Kṣemarāja's commentary *ad loc.* adds a more strongly non-dualistic interpretation of this statement.

cosmic symbolism of the maṇḍala, and the fact that the drawing itself is an empty framework.

Although the initiation maṇḍala may not depict the Śaiva cosmos in a more explicit way than other supports of worship,[120] its concentric or vertical image of a hierarchy of deities and other elements is often seen as representing a cosmic hierarchy, too. Thus, the image of the maṇḍala is identified with the cosmic hierarchy in scriptural sources: the trident of the Trika is understood to represent the universe from earth to Śiva, the deities of the SvT represent levels from *prakṛti* up to Śiva-Bhairava and the five outer lines drawn around the maṇḍala of the NT stand for the five *kalās* which constitute the Śaiva universe (see Appendix 1). This identification is continued by Kṣemarāja in his commentary on the SvT, in which he states that the 224 inches of the side of the maṇḍala represent the worlds of the Śaiva universe. Since the maṇḍala is seen as representing the cosmic hierarchy, it includes lower revelation. Thus, at least for purposes of *siddhi*, deities of these lower revelations may be used effectively. They of course do not fully deprive the central deities of their importance and place in the hierarchy: for example, employing the Buddha's power is recommended mainly for women.

A second feature of maṇḍalas which may have contributed to the substitution and inclusion of non-Śaiva deities is that they do not actually depict the deities themselves.[121] Although Tantric deities can be visualized for worship, their identity lies first and foremost in their mantric form, as pointed out in Sanderson 1990: 78. In a number of texts, this means that they can be visualized in somewhat

---

[120] As Brunner 1986: 30 (cf. Brunner, p. 175) points out. However, as I have tried to argue above, the maṇḍala is a special case compared to the *liṅga* or a temple in that it gives a mapping of the deities of one's tradition.

[121] I think there is a practical reason for this, apart from the doctrinal reasons already mentioned. Since these maṇḍalas are mostly made of coloured powders, it would require an extremely large-size maṇḍala to be able to depict deities in detail on it. Such figurative images in coloured powders are made even today in Kerala. An example is the Kaḷam Eḻuttu, which depicts Bhadrakālī before the performance of a Muṭiyeṭṭu. This shows that even a single deity requires a rather large diagram. The construction of such a diagram would be quite unpractical for rites such as the name-giving *samaya* ritual. However, what is missing on the Śaiva Tantric image can be amply provided by detailed visualization, the result of which may not be as different from some Tibetan Buddhist maṇḍalas as Brunner 1986: 31 (cf. Brunner, p. 176) claims. Without trying to draw too many parallels between these two traditions, I would just like to emphasize again that the Śaiva maṇḍala is not simply the drawing itself, but the drawing and the visualization.

differing forms according to one's purpose, and thus the goddess Parā, for instance, is given a rosary and a manuscript as attributes—similarly to the goddess of speech, Sarasvatī[122]—when visualized to obtain eloquence, but she is pictured as pouring out the nectar of immortality to conquer death.[123] Taken to the extreme, this principle implies that any visualization can suit a mantra-deity, who may well take up the appearance of the Buddha if needed. The maṇḍala is quite well-adapted for such radical changes in visualization, for it does not depict the deities in their concrete forms. If one uses the geometrical framework of the maṇḍala, changing the deity's appearance in visualizations does not necessitate any change in the traditional maṇḍala, drawn according to Śaiva scriptural prescriptions.

In a final remark, it could be concluded that what renders the identity of Bhairavic mantra-deities weak is in fact their powerfulness. It is because they are too powerful and dangerous to be depicted with their iconographic features (TĀ 27.23) on objects such as the maṇḍala that their visualized images can be changed or replaced by the images of other deities; and it is this iconographic interchangeability that allows ritual inclusivism or eclecticism.[124]

---

[122] For this identification, see Sanderson 1990: 43.

[123] See Siddhayogeśvarīmata, chapters 11 and 12.

[124] It would require an altogether separate paper or monograph to explore why such eclecticism takes place in the NT in particular, which exhibits a somewhat lax attitude towards mixing prescriptions of different traditions (*tantrasaṃkara* in 13.46). In addition to an investigation into the changing religious scene of different periods, a rather precise chronology of the scriptural sources would also be needed.

Appendices

Appendix 1: The Construction of the Śrīmaṇḍala

Below is a brief description of how a simple maṇḍala is constructed, following the prescription of the NT with Kṣemarāja's commentary. Note that without the commentary it would be impossible to reconstruct the maṇḍala. Technical terms are given with illustrations so that this summary can serve as a basis for the reconstruction of other maṇḍalas. Their descriptions seem to follow mostly the same general terminology with a few minor differences. Some of these differences will be pointed out below. Ways in which the cardinal directions are determined on the ground, details concerning measurements, some problems pertaining to the actual drawing with the help of threads and the colouring with powders are not discussed here. However, it must be born in mind that these factors, too, form part of the process of maṇḍala construction, and are sometimes detailed in the middle of the description of the drawing. A good example is the discussion of how to establish the directions in SvT_2 5.29ff. What follows concerns only the actual drawing and the colours applied according to NT_2 18.31ff. A similar maṇḍala was reconstructed in Brunner 1986 (cf. Brunner, p. 177) on the basis of a later text, the Śāradātilaka and Rāghavabhaṭṭa's commentary, but without explanations of all the technical terms. For the construction of the *śrīmaṇḍala*, see Illustration 1, while the final result of the construction can be seen in Colour Plates 16 and 17 according to two versions.

The drawing of the maṇḍala starts with the construction of a grid, in which the size and number of the cells vary. The shape of the grid is square (*caturaśra*) and its lines are always drawn along the north-south and east-west axes. A cell is called a *koṣṭha* or *koṣṭhaka*, and the length of one of its sides is a *bhāga*. In the NT, the grid of 324 cells has 18 *bhāgas* on each side. There is an eight-petalled lotus in the middle occupying eight times eight cells.

In most maṇḍalas, the construction of a lotus follows the way in which this central lotus is produced in the NT. First, four concentric circles are drawn in the middle of the central square of the lotus. The first one has a radius of one *bhāga* and is the circle of the pericarp of the lotus (*karṇikā*). The second circle has a radius of two *bhāgas* and marks out where the fibres will end (*kesarāgra*). The third circle has a radius of three *bhāgas* to show where the petals will be joined to one another (*dalasaṃdhi*). The last circle has a radius of four *bhāgas*, to mark where the tips of the petals should end (*dalāgra*).

This is followed by the drawing of the lines where the petals of the lotus will meet. This means that first, one should draw eight lines from the centre in the cardinal and intermediate directions. These lines will intersect the outermost circle at the points where the tips of the petals are to be. Then one draws eight additional lines which must be in the middle of those eight radii. This halving is done in the same way as at the establishing of the square of the maṇḍala. In this case it is done by halving the line which one could draw between two petal tips, starting with the tips of the north-eastern and the northern petals. It is obvious from the description that since these latter lines represent the sides of the petals, they will be visible from outside the circle of the pericarp up to the third (*dalasaṃdhi*) circle. It is also mentioned that the petals have three fibres each (drawn from the pericarp up to the second circle).

The next step is the drawing of the outlines of the petals outside the *dalasaṃdhi* (i.e., the third) circle. Kṣemarāja says that one should draw two arcs with the help of a thread, fixing the thread with the left hand in between the line in the middle of the petal (*madhyasūtra*) and the line on the side of the petal (*pārśvasūtra*). Then one should draw two arcs on both sides [of the petal] with the right hand, starting from the point where the petals should intersect (already established by the intersection of the third circle and the *pārśvasūtras*).

After the description of the lotus, the text gives the colours for its various parts. It continues by stating that a white circle is to be drawn, its thickness measuring one inch, around the lotus. This is the so-called 'air-line' (*vyomarekhā*). Outside this circle, a square should be made, with a yellow line which is one inch (*aṅgula*) thick. This is the inner part of what is called the 'seat' (*pīṭha*), which is a square band occupying one *bhāga* outside the inner square. (The width is mentioned by Kṣemarāja in his commentary on 43cd.) Then this surrounding band is to be divided into the corners (*koṇa*) and the so-called 'limbs' (*gātraka*). These limbs are formed here by leaving two *bhāgas* on each side for the corners. Thus the 'limbs' occupy four cells each, as Kṣemarāja makes it clear. He also gives a brief definition of the 'limbs:' they are particular segments which should fall in between corners, outside the 'air-line' (*gātrakāṇi koṇāntarālagā avayavaviśeṣā vyomarekhāyā bāhye kāryāṇi*).

Next, one should leave a band which is two *bhāgas* wide around the 'seat.' This is the terrace or passage (*vīthī*). In Kṣemarāja's explanation the passage is the place to conduct the *pūjā*. Outside of this is the area where the doors are to be drawn, on a surrounding two *bhāga* wide band.

The door has two parts, here called *kaṇṭha* and *upakaṇṭha*. The former is the upper part, i.e., the part closer to the centre of the maṇḍala. In this maṇḍala it occupies four cells, as Kṣemarāja explains. He understands the prescription of two cells in the text to apply on both sides. Colour Plate 16 reproduces the maṇḍala according to Kṣemarāja's interpretation, while Colour Plate 17 gives the basic structure without the ornaments and without considering Kṣemarāja's remark about the size of the doors.

The base or lower part of the door is one cell wider on each side here. Kṣemarāja gives a definition of both *kaṇṭha* and *upakaṇṭha*: *kaṇṭhaṃ dvārordhvagam avayavaviśeṣam...*; *upakaṇṭhaṃ kaṇṭhādhogam avayavaviśeṣam*. Note that in a number of texts, this base is not called *upakaṇṭha*, but *kapola*.[125]

Next to the door, there is an ornamental part which has the shape of the door turned upside down.[126] The smaller and outer part of this element is called the *śobhā* and the wider upper part is the *upaśobhā*. Again, their measurements are based on Kṣemarāja's commentary, who himself mentions that some details are left out and understood to be supplied by the reader. Note that the *śobhā* and *upaśobhā* are called *kapola* and *upakapola* in the Īśānaśivagurudevapaddhati (*kriyāpāda* 8.58), in which they are also defined as having the shape of doors turned upside down and being placed next to them (*tatpārśvatas tadviparītavaktrās tadvat kapolopakapolakāḥ syuḥ*).

When the doors are ready, the text mentions that one is to draw three circles (inside the doors?), leaving out the western door, which faces the deity. This is not commented upon by Kṣemarāja, but there is a brief mention of a circle in the context of the door in TĀ 31.83, in which the door is said to be circular optionally. In the context of the NT, however, it seems that the function of these circles is to

---

[125] See, e.g., SvT2 5.34ff., Mālinīvijaya 9.31ab and TĀ 31.39, 31.84cd.

[126] See Kṣemarāja on 44d: *dvārapārśvayoḥ parāvṛttadvārasaṃniveśākāreṇa "tathā śobhopaśobhake" kārayet.*

close, cover or seal the doors, and this is probably the reason why the western door facing the deity has no circle. For this idea, see, e.g., the Lakṣmīkaulārṇava quoted by Kṣemarāja *ad* SvT2 5.35ab: *dvāra-trayaṃ pidhātavyaṃ paścimaṃ na pidhāpayet.* Nothing is said about the exact position or size of these circles in the NT.

This maṇḍala, being that of Śrī, is decorated with conch shells and lotuses in the *vīthī,* in the outer corners and outside. All colours are given in detail except those for the outer corners; and it is also not clear if the decorations in the *vīthī* should be black or the *vīthī* itself. Since all parts of a maṇḍala have to be covered with coloured powder so that the ground should not be seen,[127] it can be assumed that the corners also had some colouring. I have applied white for the *vīthī* as well as for the corners. The former is said to be always white in Īśānaśivagurudevapaddhati, *kriyāpāda* 8.73,[128] and as both the *vīthī* and the corners have the decorations of conch shells and lotuses, I assume they are also of the same colour. Consequently, the outlines of the conch shells and lotuses are mainly black, understanding that the NT refers to the outlines of ornaments when prescribing the black colour and not to the *vīthī.*[129] Verse 47cd–48ab prescribes the drawing of five lines around the maṇḍala, which represent the five *kalās*, the lowest (*nirṛti*) being the outermost one. According to Kṣemarāja *ad loc.*, they are white, red, black, yellow and transparent, starting from the outermost line.

[127] See, e.g., a brief aside in Īśānaśivagurudevapaddhati, *kriyāpāda* 8.61b: *yathā bhūmir na dṛśyate.*

[128] This passage states that the doors and the petals should also be white, which agrees with the NT.

[129] It is also unlikely that it should refer to the ornaments themselves, for it would be very odd to require conch shells and lotuses to be black.

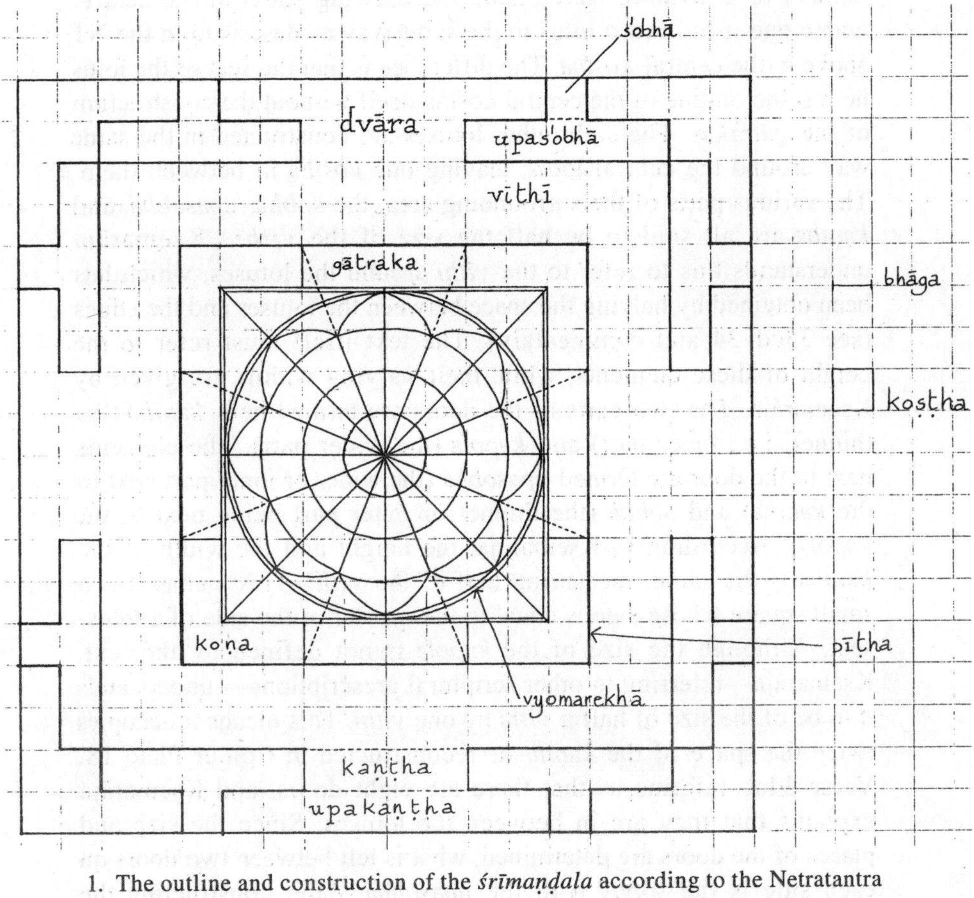

1. The outline and construction of the *śrīmaṇḍala* according to the Netratantra

Appendix 2: The Navanābhamaṇḍala

The maṇḍala of the nine lotuses (Colour Plate 18) has been reconstructed according to SvT_2 5.19–34 and Kṣemarāja's commentary thereon. The grid measures 224 x 224 *aṅgulas* and is divided into 7 x 7 large *bhāgas*. Kṣemarāja remarks that the number 224 reflects the number of *bhuvanas*. Here again, the drawing starts at the centre, where one is to draw a lotus in the same way as described in the NT above in the central *koṣṭha*. The difference is that the seat of the lotus here is the outline of the central *koṣṭha* itself without the construction of the *gātrakas*. The eight other lotuses are constructed in the same way around the central lotus, leaving one *koṣṭha* in between them. The various parts of the surrounding area, the *śobhā*, *upaśobhā*, and *kaṇṭha* are all said to be half the size of the *vīthī*. Kṣemarāja understands this to refer to the *vīthī* around the lotuses, which has been obtained by halving the space between the lotuses and the edges (see 33cd–34 and commentary). The text itself must refer to the height of these elements, while their varying widths are given by Kṣemarāja. The two parts of the doors are termed here *kaṇṭha* (the thinner, i.e., inner part) and *kapola* (the wider part). The elements next to the door are termed *upaśobhā* (the wider or inner part next to the *kaṇṭha*) and *śobhā* (the thinner or outer part being next to the *kapola*). According to Kṣemarāja, the height and the width of the *kaṇṭha* is the same, measuring half of the *vīthī*. This means it is a small square whose side is equal to the quarter of the side of a lotus-seat. Although the size of the *kapola* is not defined by the text, Kṣemarāja—referring to other scriptural prescriptions— understands it to be of the size of half a *vīthī* by one *vīthī*. This means it occupies twice the space of the *kaṇṭha* as reconstructed in Colour Plate 18. Verse 34ab informs us that there are eight doors, and Kṣemarāja explains that they are in between the lotuses. Since the size and places of the doors are determined, what is left between two doors on each side is the *śobhā* with the *upaśobhā*. After constructing the *śobhās* and the *upaśobhās* of the same size on each side of each door, the remaining parts form the four corners.

However, it is possible that in the text, *kapola* means what is added to the size of the *kaṇṭha* outside the *kaṇṭha*. This is suggested by the name *kapola*, 'cheek.' In that case, what is outside the *kaṇṭha* measures three times the square of the *kaṇṭha*. This would result in slightly different door-shapes, and the forms of the *śobhā*s, *upaśobhā*s and corners would also change.

As for the colours, Kṣemarāja points out that since they are not specified, one has to resort to other Āgamas. On the colours, he cites the Saiddhāntika Parākhya, which has the same prescription for the lotuses as the NT, but adds that the space between lotus petals is green and the corners are red. The fibres are slightly different, having the colours white, yellow and red starting from inside. I have made the doors and the *vīthī* white, as in the case of the NT's maṇḍala, and the *śobhā*s and *upaśobhā*s red and yellow. Kṣemarāja mentions that the western door, facing the deity, should be left open or uncovered, but since the covering is not explicitly prescribed in any graphic form, I have not tried to supply it.

Appendix 3: The Trident Maṇḍala

For the construction of the trident maṇḍala in the Siddhayogeśvarīmata, I have followed TĀ 31.155 with commentary as far as I have been able to. The outline is to be made on a square of three *hasta*s on each side, to which a surrounding band of 12 *aṅgula*s is added for the doors. The square of three *hasta*s on each side is divided into nine large cells, one square *hasta* each, and these are further divided into 6 x 6, i.e., 36 small cells each, so that each small cell measures four *aṅgula*s on each side. The lotus in the middle, similar to the one described in Appendix 1, measures one *hasta* on each side.

The trident is drawn in the large cell in the middle, i.e., leaving three small *bhāga*s untouched below.[130] On both sides, two half circles are to be drawn downwards, in the neighbouring two *bhāga*s. This implies that the radius of the smaller half-circles is half a *bhāga*, and the radius of the larger half-circles is one *bhāga*. The smaller half-circles continue in small arcs of quarter-circles above. The tip of the middle prong should end half a *hasta* inside the large *koṣṭha* above the *koṣṭha* of the central lotus, i.e., half a *hasta* below the door. The tips of the two other prongs should fall on the side-lines of the large *koṣṭha*s, i.e., on the lengthened side-lines of the square of the central lotus. I have made these tips by lengthening the lines that could be drawn between the centre point of the maṇḍala and the points where the two small arcs end. The two points where these lines intersect the side-lines of the large *koṣṭha* are the tips of the side-prongs. However, the exact drawing of the tips of the prongs are left to the reader's decision to some extent.

In addition to problems concerning the formation of the prongs of the trident, I have also had problems in interpreting the way in which the staff is to be drawn. As for its length, it reaches down as far as the edge of the outer square.[131] It is said to be three *hasta*s long counting from the tip of the middle prong, if I understand the text correctly. This means that the distance between the top of the trident and the bottom end of the staff is three *hasta*s, which is indeed the case if the staff reaches down to the edge of the outer square. Its thickness is two *aṅgula*s, which is probably to be applied on each

[130] Jayaratha states: *tatra madhyād adhastanaṃ bhāgatrayaṃ tyaktvā.*

[131] See Jayaratha's statement: *parivarjitabāhyadvādaśāṅgulāntam.*

side, i.e., its full thickness is four *aṅgulas*.[132] The staff should not cover the lotus, of course. It is not mentioned that the bottom end of the staff has got the thick ring called *āmalasāraka* as in the Mālinīvijaya's version of the maṇḍala, nor that the staff is pointed below. However, it is unlikely that the staff ended abruptly at the bottom, and one is probably to draw the pointed tip as well as the *āmalasāraka*. I have done so, assigning one *bhāga* to the pointed tip as well as to the *āmalasāraka*.

The lotuses on the tips of the trident measure half a *hasta*, i.e., their radius is half of the radius of the central lotus. Jayaratha mentions that the doors and the rest are to be fashioned as before. The last uncertainty concerns the central seat or *pīṭha*, which is not mentioned, but which I have supplied, for to my knowledge there are no occurrences of a central lotus without a *pīṭha* around it. I have chosen the seat to be one *bhāga* thick, which would be a standard measurement, similar to the measurement of the *pīṭha* in the NT, which is described in Appendix 1. I have not drawn the small stick-like element under the central prong called *gaṇḍikā*, which is prescribed for the Mālinīvijaya's trident in 31.67cd–68ab.

The colours are set out in verses 147ff. The colours for the central lotus are the same as in the NT. I have also followed the NT when colouring the doors and their surroundings. The *pīṭha* is coloured again as in the NT, for its prescription is the same as that of the Mālinīvijayottara in TĀ 31.80–81. I have followed verse 31.82 for the colouring of the trident, which is to be red, while its staff is black and the *āmalasāraka* is yellow. However, the *vīthī* is prescribed red in verse 149 following the lost Triśirobhairava. For the lotuses on the tips of the prongs, there may be two possibilities. One is that they are the same colours as the central lotus. The other is that their colours agree with the colours prescribed in the Triśirobhairava: red, red-black/brown and white for Parāparā, Aparā and Parā respectively, i.e., on the right, left and in the centre.[133] I have followed the Triśirobhairava concerning the colours of the small lotuses, but I

---

[132] I interpret the text to prescribe that the two vertical lines which form the staff are to be marked out on three points: in the lower, middle and upper part. Then these points are probably to be connected in one single line on each side, but I am not sure if this interpretation is correct.

[133] See TĀ 31.118. The three colours basically agree with the colours of the three goddesses in the Siddhayogeśvarīmata; see also Sanderson 1990: 51–53. Left and right are to be swapped in the drawing, see Siddhayogeśvarīmata 6.24.

have not followed its prescriptions concerning the forms of these lotuses. For the Triśirobhairava envisages the three small lotuses with different numbers of petals.

There is an alternative interpretation of the description of the trident, which is equally possible. This interpretation would change the shape of the upper part of the trident, which would somewhat resemble the reconstruction in Sanderson 1986: 171, except that it would be much broader than the central lotus and that the side-prongs would be curved. If this interpretation is followed, the thickness of the upper part of the trident is not determined at all in the text, therefore I have followed the first alternative.

MAṆḌALAS IN ABHINAVAGUPTA'S TANTRĀLOKA*

André Padoux

In the Tantrāloka (TĀ), 'Light on the Tantras,' the vast treatise Abhinavagupta composed during the first years of the 11th century, where he expounds his own interpretation of the notions and practices of the non-dualist Śaiva system of the Trika, maṇḍalas are mentioned a number of times. However, while the whole of chapter 31 in this work is devoted to these ritual diagrams, no general view is given there of the theory and practice of the maṇḍalas. It is only through his descriptions of how maṇḍalas are made use of in different rituals, and especially in the initiation (*dīkṣā*) ritual, that Abhinavagupta's conception of the nature of these devices appears.

Chapter 31 (163 *śloka*s), on the nature of maṇḍalas (*maṇḍala-svarūpam*), does not describe their nature, merely how to draw them. It consists almost entirely of quotations from earlier Tantras. It describes five different types of maṇḍalas, four of which are made of tridents and lotuses (*śūlābjamaṇḍala*), while one includes a *svastika*. The descriptions are those of four different Tantras, three of which have not come down to us: the Trikasadbhāva (also called Tantra-sadbhāva), the Devyāyāmalatantra, and the Triśirobhairavatantra. The fourth description is taken from chapter 9 (6–30) of the Mālinīvijaya, the Tantra on which according to Abhinavagupta the teaching of the TĀ is based; this text is still extant.[1] While the descriptions of the Trikasadbhāva and the Mālinīvijaya are clear enough, those drawn from the two other Tantras are difficult to understand (even with the help of Jayaratha's commentary). Only two forms of the *śūlābjamaṇḍala* can therefore be drawn with any

* The English of this paper has been checked by Mrs Barbara Bray whose kind help I wish (once more) to acknowledge very gratefully.

[1] See Bibliography. "There is nothing here," says Abhinavagupta in the first chapter of the TĀ (1.17) "that is not clearly said, or implied by the gods in the venerable Mālinī[vijayottaratantra]."

certainty.[2] The method for drawing the maṇḍalas given in these Tantras is the usual one, that is, to draw their lines with a powdered string on a pure, consecrated and oriented square surface, divided usually into small square sections. Coloured powders may be added once the pattern is drawn, so as to make it more beautiful, which is something the deities like (9.41–42): "one who knows how to do this is a real master of the Trika," says *śloka* 51. There are also maṇḍalas made of perfumed substances, called *gandhamaṇḍala*, and less frequently used.

What strikes one when looking at these diagrams is that they do not conform to the pattern generally considered as normal for maṇḍalas, which are usually centred geometrical structures which the user is to contemplate—and/or to use for his worship—by going mentally from their outward portion to their middle point; that is, ontologically, from an outer lower plane to the higher central plane of the deity: it is a centripetal move. Here the maṇḍalas are of a different type. On a square ground the main element is Śiva's trident (*śūla* or *triśūla*), whose staff goes vertically from the lower part of the maṇḍala to its centre, where it expands in the form of a lotus, above which its three prongs rise. On the tips of each of these is a full blown lotus—this is the *triśūlābjamaṇḍala*, the maṇḍala of the trident and lotuses described in the Mālinīvijaya. Or else it may consist of a vertical trident blossoming, in the centre of the diagram, into a lotus from which emerge on top and on the sides three lotus-topped tridents, thus forming the *tritriśūlābjamaṇḍala*, the maṇḍala of the three tridents and [seven] lotuses (see Illustration 1).[3] The mental movement of the user thus appears as an ascending one, or as centrifugal: the maṇḍala does not draw the user who meditates it to its centre, but appears to invite (and induce) a fusion through ascent to a higher level, or absorption into the shimmering luminousness of a radiating divine surface (a maṇḍala being always the receptacle—the *ādhāra*—of mantras/deities who are by nature luminous). While these maṇḍalas are different in their pattern, their ritual (and

[2] This was done by Stephanie Sanderson for Professor Alexis Sanderson's 1986 article 'Maṇḍala and Āgamic Identity in the Trika of Kashmir.' This very erudite paper is to date the only thorough study of the subject: the present brief survey is very largely indebted to it. Mrs Sanderson's drawings are reproduced here with her permission (see Illustrations 1–3).

[3] There seems also to be a four tridents and [eight] lotuses maṇḍala (*catustriśūlābjamaṇḍala*).

meditational) role is not different from that of other diagrams: they are structures on which to focus one's attention, in which to perceive the presence of the deity or deities, in which to worship them and finally unite with them: the aim is the same even if the mental and ritual course is different. This role of maṇḍala as a means of fusion with the godhead is underscored by Abhinavagupta who—for the maṇḍalas described in the TĀ—goes as far as to identify the maṇḍala and the supreme deity in TĀ 37.21 where he says: "because the term *maṇḍa* [forms the word] maṇḍala this word expresses the essence, it means Śiva" (*maṇḍalaṃ sāram uktaṃ hi maṇḍaśrutyā śivāhvayam*). As Jayaratha explains, the maṇḍala grasps (*lāti*—because of *la*) the essence which designates Śiva: *maṇḍalam iti maṇḍaṃ śivāhvayaṃ lātīty arthaḥ*.

The TĀ prescribes the use of maṇḍalas in various rituals. The maṇḍala is mentioned in TĀ 6.2–4 as one of the *sthānas*, the 'places' on or with which rites are performed or mental concentration is practiced (the case in this chapter being the transcending of time). For the TĀ as for all other Tantras, the maṇḍala is the ritually delimited and consecrated surface where deities and supernatural entities are installed by their mantras and on which rites are to be performed. If, however, a maṇḍala is to be used in various rituals and in ritual worship (*pūjā*), its more important use, in this treatise, is in initiation (*dīkṣā*) rites. Its role is so essential to initiation that seeing the maṇḍala may mean being initiated. TĀ 4.49 and 13.152 quote thus from *śloka* 18 of the Parātriṃśikā: *adṛṣṭamaṇḍalo 'pi*, "even if he has not seen the maṇḍala," which can be understood as meaning 'even if he is not initiated.' In this case, however, as Abhinavagupta explains in his commentary of the Parātriṃśikā, the word may be given several interpretations: it can be taken as referring to the system of bodily cakras or wheels of power where deities reside; or to the secret ritual meeting of Tantric initiates and Yoginīs (*melaka*), where the participants usually form a circle; or to the *triśūlābja-maṇḍala* seen during worship or initiation, or perceived in one's body (as we shall see below). These interpretations all refer to cases where the adept experiences mental cum bodily identification with the deity or its radiating power.

Since only an initiated (male) person can perform rites, we shall look at the role of the maṇḍala first in initiation (*dīkṣā*), then the occasional obligatory (*naimittika*) and the regular obligatory (*nitya*) ritual worship.

Chapter 15 of the TĀ describes in its latter part (436ff.) the *samayadīkṣā*, the first degree of initiation, by which one becomes a *samayin*, an initiate who abides by the rules (*samaya*) of the sect but cannot perform rites. The procedure is a comparatively simple one. For this, the sacrificial surface, the *sthaṇḍila*, is prepared by placing mantras on it and worshipping them, installing powers and offerings in vases, and then tracing a *triśūlābjamaṇḍala*, a maṇḍala of one trident and lotuses (described in TĀ 31.62–85, see Illustration 2), which in this case is a *gandhamaṇḍala* (15.387),[4] not traced with coloured powders but with perfumed substances. The initiating *guru* is to worship on it the three goddesses of the Trika "alone or with their consorts, or a *mantradevatā*" (388), which he has installed there by their mantras. He must then blindfold the initiand with a cloth on which mantras have been placed and lead him to the maṇḍala, make him fall on his knees and cast flowers on the maṇḍala, after which the cloth is swiftly removed: "The initiand, suddenly seeing the sacrificial area illuminated by the supernatural power of the mantras (*mantraprabhāvollasite sthale*), is possessed by them and identifies with them" (*tadāveśavaśāc chiṣyas tanmayatvaṃ prapadyate*) (15.451b–452a). "As a lover perceives directly the virtues of his beloved, in the same way [the initiand], made perfect by the descent of divine grace (*śaktipātasaṃskṛtaḥ*), experiences the presence of the mantras (*mantrasannidhi*)" (452). This direct luminous and purifying vision of a mantra pantheon[5] enclosed in the maṇḍala is only the first step in the initiation ritual, but it can be seen as the basic one since this initial empowerment of the initiate will not only make him a member of the sect, but will also induce a permanent state of identification with the deities of the maṇḍala, a state that will henceforth form the basis of his initiatic spiritual life. Though one of the terms used here to denote the condition of the initiand is *āveśa*, possession, he does not appear to be expected to fall in trance—as is the case in the Kaula initiation described in chapter 29, where the

[4] A *gandhamaṇḍala* is also used in the worship of the *guru* which takes place before the *samayadīkṣā* (TĀ 15.387).

[5] Tantric pantheons are as much (or perhaps more) structured groups of mantras as groups of deities.

mantras are so powerful that the initiate, merely by seeing them, is possessed and falls unconscious on the ground.

The next step in the Śaiva initiation is that of the *putrakadīkṣā*, (also named *viśeṣadīkṣā*, special initiation, or *nirvāṇadīkṣā*, liberating initiation) which transforms the *samayin* into a '[spiritual] son' of his *guru*. It is examined in chapter 16 of the TĀ, whose description (based on the teaching of the Mālinīvijaya and other Tantras) is more detailed than the preceding one. The ritual begins with the drawing of a *tritriśūlābjamaṇḍala*: "When the master wishes to promote a *samayin* to the state of *putraka*, of *sādhaka*, or of master (*deśika*), he must first perform the preliminary purification, then, the next day, draw the maṇḍala in the same way as for the composed sacrifice (*sāmudāyikayāge*)[6] and elsewhere" (1–2a). The use here of this more complex maṇḍalic structure, where more deities are installed, may be taken as showing that this initiation is of a higher order than the first one. Once the maṇḍala is drawn, the triad of the Trika supreme goddesses, Parā, Parāparā and Aparā, are to be placed (by their mantras) on the prongs of the three tridents and be fully worshipped (*pūrṇaṃ saṃpūjitam*). Then, the maṇḍala (which is apparently not made with powders) must be cleaned with a perfumed cloth (7b). After which the master, having bathed, worships, in front of the maṇḍala, the deities of the external retinue, then, on its 'doors,' the deities of the doors (*dvāradevatā*), then, going from the north-east to the south-east, he worships Gaṇeśa and other gods "down to the *kṣetrapāla*s" (8–9). We may note here that such prescriptions as these show that the maṇḍala is a rather large structure. The *guru* is now to worship with flowers, incense and other offerings the deities installed in the maṇḍala, starting with the *ādhāraśakti*, at the base of the trident, and up to Śiva at the tip of the tridents, the ritual being performed on each of the three tridents. Parā, Parāparā and Aparā with their accompanying Bhairavas are thus worshipped on the lotuses which are on the tips of the three tridents, then the transcendent goddess Mātṛsadbhāva—who is also Parā—in the central lotus where she abides accompanied by Bhairavasadbhāva. Parā, the supreme divine power, being thus centrally placed on all the tridents, is conceived as pervading the

[6] This refers to the maṇḍala used in the so-called inner sacrifice described in chapter 15 (295b–365) of the TĀ. This ritual is called composed, or complex, since it brings together several different elements.

maṇḍala, which "is entirely full of her presence" (*susaṃpūrṇas tadadhiṣṭhānamātrataḥ*—16). Several deities present in the maṇḍala are now to be worshipped. Several other rites follow, meant to infuse in the initiand the power of the goddesses of the maṇḍala[7] and bring him to enter the path of non-duality. A practice is also described (23–26) by which the initiating master, penetrating then leaving mentally (through a *prāṇāyāma* practice) the deity present in the maṇḍala, experiences an identification of his self with it (*maṇḍalātmaikyānusandhāna*), to use Jayaratha's expression (volume 10, p. 10). Thus pervaded with the power of the maṇḍala,[8] that is, the power of the mantras placed in this diagram, he will be all the more able to transmit this transforming power to the initiand, leading him from the lower condition of a *samayin* (or *samayadīkṣita*) to the higher one of *putraka* (or to the state of *sādhaka*, if he is a *bubhukṣu*, one who seeks power or supernatural rewards through the mastery of a mantra).

Maṇḍalas are also used in other forms of initiation described in the TĀ. A maṇḍala is used, for instance, in the funeral rite (*antyeṣṭi*), a kind of initiation rite, where it is to be drawn in the house of the dead person (24.10–12) before the funeral rites are performed. It is used, too, in the initiation of somebody who is absent (whether away or dead), briefly described in chapter 21. In this case, after preliminary purifications of the ritual place, of the rice used in the ritual, of the disciple and of the maṇḍala, the latter is used to bring about the presence of the mantras and to satisfy them (*mantrasaṃnidhisaṃtṛpti*), since these are the powers that are to be propitiated to initiate the disciple who is absent: as Jayaratha comments, the maṇḍala protects the disciple even if it is not seen by him. It is useful in spite of the fact that it is only one among eleven elements used to perform that initiation (21.13–15), the ritual having to be performed as richly as possible so as to satisfy fully the powers invoked in the maṇḍala. This maṇḍala is the *tritriśūlābjamaṇḍala*, which, Abhinavagupta says (21.19–20), is so powerful that simply by seeing it, without even propitiating the mantras placed on it, [the disciple] becomes a *samayin* (*mantramaṇḍale anāhute 'pi dṛṣṭaṃ sat*

[7] Sanderson 1986: 197 shows how Abhinavagupta superimposes on the Trika deities of the maṇḍala the fourfold sequence of the Krama tradition and even the system of the twelve Kālīs.

[8] TĀ 17.1–3 underlines the identification of the initiating *guru* and the maṇḍala.

samayitvaprasādhanam)—this sentence, however, is probably not to be taken literally. The likeness of the missing person used in the rite, as well as the mantras, must be luminous (*ākṛtir dīptarūpā yā mantras tadvat sudīptikaḥ*). After the maṇḍala has been drawn and the deity worshipped, adds the TĀ (22b–24), the *guru* must make with *kuśa* grass and cow-dung an image of the disciple he is to initiate, in which he will instil that disciple's mind (*citta*) so as to liberate him from his fetters before the rest of the ritual is performed.

The same maṇḍala is used for the initiation described in chapter 29, which is that of the Kaula Trika. This initiation is different from the one given to ordinary disciples. It is given by the Kaula *guru* to a few chosen disciples only—one in a hundred thousand, according to TĀ 29.187—that is, those who are able to perform rites (the Kaula sacrifice, *kulayāga*)[9] where a feminine partner (*dūtī*) plays a role and where the offerings include meat, and liquor, and also sexual secretions.[10] Such rites are in contradiction to the generally admitted rules of purity the Trika adept is supposed to respect in his outer social behavior. It is therefore to be kept secret. This is repeated several times in this chapter by Abhinavagupta, who states before describing the part of the ritual where the maṇḍala is used (29.169): "this cannot be described clearly by me because it is secret" (*na paṭhyate rahasyatvāt spaṣṭaiḥ śabdair mayā*). The passage which follows (170–174) is indeed quite obscure. I have not been able to render it very clearly in spite of the help extended to me by Professor Alexis Sanderson whom I consulted on the subject. As Jayaratha explains in his commentary on a preceding *śloka* (p. 114), Abhinavagupta refers here implicitly to the doctrine that the teachings of Bhairava have four foundations, namely mantra, *vidyā*, *mudrā* and maṇḍala,[11] the case here being that of the maṇḍala, which is identified with the body of the performer of the rite. In the section of chapter 29 (*ślokas* 166–177), concerning the secret practice with a *dūtī*, the divinized body of the Yogin is the substrate on and with

[9] Kulayāga, according to a common use of the term *yāga* in such texts, means also the pantheon of the Kula.

[10] It is the offering (*arghya*, *argha*) called *kuṇḍagola* or *kuṇḍagolaka* which includes the sexual secretions produced during the ritual by the adept and his feminine partner.

[11] Mantras (or *vidyās*, which are feminine mantras) are phonic forms of the deity. Mudrās, in Abhinavagupta's view (see TĀ, chapter 32) bring about the identification of the performer with the deity which is made present by arising from the image (*pratibimba*) thus produced. On this see Padoux 1990: 66–75.

which the ritual is performed. The passage we are concerned with runs as follows: "As all have [a body], so have the god and the goddess [that is, the Yogin and his *dūtī*]. This [body of theirs] is the supreme wheel (*tac cakraṃ paramam*) by which the goddess and the pantheon (*yāga*) are made present (170). The body is indeed the supreme icon (*deha eva paraṃ liṅgam*), made of all the *tattvas*. Auspicious, it is the highest place of worship for it is occupied by the wheel of all the deities (171). It is this [body] which is the supreme maṇḍala, made of the three tridents, the [seven] lotuses, wheels or voids (*kha*).[12] There and nowhere else must the wheel of deities be constantly worshipped, externally and internally (172).[13] [The performer] should first concentrate mentally on the mantra of each [deity] (*svasvamantraparāmarśapūrvam*), then touch [himself] with the richly blissful fluids that are produced from [the body,[14] this being done] following the order of emission and that of resorption (*sṛṣṭisaṃhāravidhinā*) (173).[15] By these contacts, the field of one's consciousness is awakened and, becoming the master of that [field], one reaches the highest domain (*paramaṃ dhāman*), having satisfied all the deities [which animate his senses and body] (174). [Then the Yogin] should gratify these [deities] in [his body] with all the heart-ravishing substances and by concentrating on each of their [mantras], following for this the procedure laid down for the auxiliary worship (*anuyāgoktavidhinā*)" (175). Abhinavagupta then sings the praises of the maṇḍala-body: "In the divine abode of the body (*dehadeva-sadane*), I worship you together, o my god and goddess, night and day, with the blissful nectar that fills the vase of offering of the heart, with the unmediated flowers of the spirit which spread their native natural fragrance, and by sprinkling over the world, bearer of all, with the pure essence of my wondering ecstasy (*camatkṛtirasa*)."

The use of maṇḍalas is prescribed not only for initiations but also for the performance of other rituals. For instance, for the worship of the newly consecrated master, the *gurupūjā*, which is to be per-

---

[12] Jayaratha glosses *kha* by *vyoman* which means space, void. Which void is this? I do not know.

[13] That is, by making offerings (meat, liquor, sexual fluids) to the deities on the maṇḍala, and by consuming them.

[14] This refers to the *kuṇḍagolaka*, see note 10.

[15] That is to say, beginning with the highest deity at the crown of the head and progressing downward, or beginning with the outermost deities of the maṇḍala, at the feet, and progressing upwards.

formed at the end of the initiation or consecration (*abhiṣeka*) ritual, the *guru* is to be seated on a seat 'of gold, etc.' (*haimādikāsanam*), placed on a maṇḍala on which a *svastika* is drawn (TĀ 28.425–426). What is the pattern of this *svastikamaṇḍala* is not specified there, but it is probably the pattern described in chapter 31, 132–154. Ślokas 147–154 of that chapter give precise details of the aspects and colours of the lotus petals and *svastikas* of the maṇḍala, which must not only be brightly coloured but also adorned with precious stones. The passage ends: "the sanctuary of the god of gods who satisfies all desires must be outwardly all red and shining (*jvalāruṇa*)." That the maṇḍala should be bright, shining, is often said, but it is difficult to gauge how 'bright' these diagrams really were. To be sure, they were brightly coloured, adorned with flowers, perhaps also gold and precious stones, but often the 'brightness' or even the fulguration mentioned in the texts is that of the mantras placed in the maṇḍala, not that of the diagram itself: a brightness, therefore, which was probably mentally perceived (shall we say imagined?) rather than actually seen.

Another, more interesting use of the maṇḍala, perceived as present in the body of the adept, is described in the 15th chapter of the TĀ. There, the maṇḍala is not identified with the body. It is felt to rise within it and then to overgrow it, thus bringing about a total surpassing of bodily existence and consciousness. This takes place during the first part of the daily ritual worship of the Śaiva adept, who, before performing the external phase (*bāhya*) of the worship, the *pūjā*, is to place mentally in his body the pantheon of the maṇḍala and to identify himself mentally with it: as the saying goes, *nādevo devam arcayet*: the officiant cannot worship a deity if he is not first formally deified. Here, however, the deification is of a very particular and especially intense sort since the adept is expected to transcend mentally his identity and limited consciousness by realizing it to be identical with the non-individual divine consciousness, a process that will fuse him with the unlimited power of the supreme godhead. Through this practice, to quote Alexis Sanderson, the performer "ritually internalizes a metaphysical ontology."[16] The diagram which is used to this end is the *triśūlābjamaṇḍala* (Illustration 2), to be visualized by the adept as present in his body,

[16] Sanderson 1986: 172; pp. 172–182 of this study describe and explain thoroughly the process and meaning of this ritual mental worship.

with all the cosmic entities and deities present in it. The procedure is as follows: first, controlling his vital breaths, the adept fuses his *prāṇa* and *apāna* breaths in the *samāna* breath, which is then burnt by the ascending *udāna* breath blazing up from below his navel along the *suṣumnā* up to the *dvādaśānta* (or *ūrdhvakuṇḍalinī*), the subtle centre deemed to be placed twelve finger-spaces above the *brahmarandhra*, therefore above his body. This awakening and rising of the *kuṇḍalinī* is the preliminary condition for the internal installation of the maṇḍala and for the worship of its deities. In this Yogic state of trance, which cuts him off entirely from the surrounding world, the adept is to visualize the *triśūlābjamaṇḍala* as present in his body (see Illustration 3). Four fingers below his navel, he places mentally the swelling at the base of the trident and worships it as being the *ādhāraśakti*, the power which supports the cosmos which he feels as present within him. Then he imagines (and worships as an ascending movement toward the deity) the staff of the trident which he sees mentally as rising in his body above the navel along the vertical axis of the *suṣumnā* up to the subtle centre of the palate (*tālū*) through the 25 *tattva*s constituting the world, from the earth-*tattva* to those of *puruṣa* and the *kañcuka*s, which are tiered along it. Thus all the constituents of the manifest, impure (*aśuddha*) world are present in the adept, constituting the throne of the Trika deities. Above the palate, he visualizes the 'knot' (*granthi*) of the trident, identified with the *māyā-tattva*, then he visualizes its 'plinth' (*catuṣkika*) together with the *śuddha-vidyā-tattva*, the first level of the pure universe (*śuddhādhvan*) which begins there and extends above *māyā* up to Śiva. On this plinth he imagines an eight-petalled 'lotus of gnosis' (*vidyāpadma*) as the *īśvara-tattva*. In the centre of that lotus the adept now mentally installs Sadāśiva (the 34th *tattva*), visualizing him as a blazing corpse (the so-called Mahāpreta), emaciated because he is void of the cosmos, gazing upward toward the light of the absolute and laughing boisterously (*aṭṭahāsa*).[17] Sadāśiva must be worshipped as made up of two and a half syllables[18] and as dominating everything. The adept is now to visualize the three prongs of the trident rising up through his cranial aperture (on the phonic level of *nādānta*) from Sadāśiva's navel and

[17] This mad laughter is a characteristic trait of fearsome Tantric deities. It is also to be used by adepts during certain rituals. The practice goes back to the Pāśupatas.

[18] As noted before, deities are mantras—or mantras deities.

going up to the *dvādaśānta*. These prongs are deemed to go through the subtle levels of resonance and consciousness named *śakti*, *vyāpinī* and *samanā*.[19] On the tips of the three prongs of the trident (on the level of the *dvādaśānta* and on that of *unmanā*, the trans-mental plane), he visualizes three white lotuses. On these he first enthrones the mantras of three Bhairavas, conceived of as lying on the lotuses, and then, seated on the Bhairavas, the three supreme goddesses of the Trika: first, on the central prong, Parā, the supreme, white, luminous, benevolent, pouring *amṛta*; then, on her left, Parāparā, the intermediate, red and wrathful; and on her other side, Aparā, the lower, dark-red, furious, terrifying. The three goddesses are garlanded with skulls, hold the skull-staff, etc. Now, the adept, seeing these goddesses mentally, must worship them together with their retinues, offering them (since this is a purely mental process) the transcendental consciousness he has of the fact that the universe is an expansion of the divine power and that his own consciousness is totally fused into this divine, omnipresent reality. To perform this Yogic practice of the maṇḍala is thus to experience the identity of the self and of the absolute. All the fantasmagory visualized in this way leads the Yogin to feel dissolved into the transcendental void of the absolute whilst being also inhabited in his body by the cosmos and its presiding deities. It is an interesting, but strange, process. If we consider that this Yogic, visionary trance-like state of bodily consciousness is to be experienced every day by the Śaiva adept, we may well wonder what psychological condition is thus induced in him, what kind of perception of the world he lives with. Can one feel fused with the absolute after having filled one's mind with such a fantastic scenery and still behave 'normally'? Of course, these ritual practices may have been performed merely in imagination without any real inner participation of the Yogin. They may even have been limited to the mere recitation of the mantras evoking the *tattvas* and the deities (*mantraprayoga*). But what if they were really experienced? What if the Kaula adept, practising the ritual at least once every day, carried always in him this scenery? This is an interesting question—but not one to be answered here.

---

[19] On the subtle levels of enunciation (*uccāra*) of a *bījamantra*, from *bindu* to *unmanā*, see Padoux 1990a: 404–411. Here as in other cases the planes (*kalā*) of phonic utterance (*uccāra*) are taken as a subtle prolongation of the levels of the cosmos (*tattvas*).

1. Outline of the maṇḍala of the three tridents and (seven) lotuses *(tritriśūlābjamaṇḍala)* prescribed by the Trikasadbhāvatantra

2. Outline of the maṇḍala of the trident and lotuses *(triśūlābjamaṇḍala)* prescribed by the Mālinīvijayottaratantra

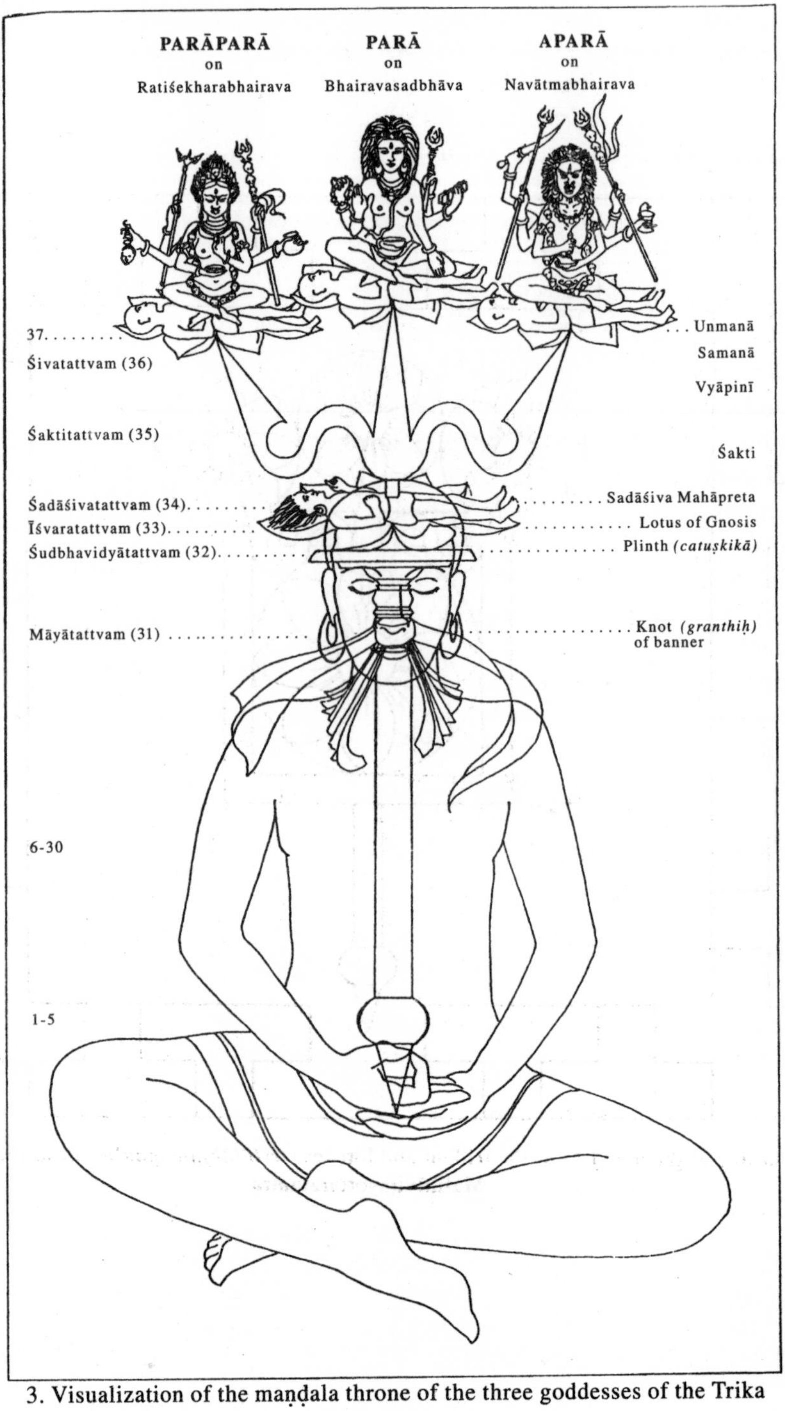

3. Visualization of the maṇḍala throne of the three goddesses of the Trika

THE ŚRĪCAKRA ACCORDING TO THE FIRST CHAPTER OF THE YOGINĪHṚDAYA*

André Padoux

The *śrīcakra*—the maṇḍalic form of the goddess Tripurasundarī, symbolic of her cosmic activity—is too well known to need describing here. It is indeed so well known that ritual diagrams are often believed to be all of the same type—i.e., centred maṇḍalic cosmic symbols—though, as Hélène Brunner explained in her article, this is not at all the case. The maṇḍalas of the Tantrāloka, also described in this book, are likewise of a different type. Cosmic diagrams of the same sort as the *śrīcakra* are to be found in the Kubjikāmatatantra, chapters 14–16, where they are to be visualized in the body, but not, apparently, to be materially drawn and used for worship.[1] This resemblance may be due to the links existing between the ancient Kubjikā tradition and the somewhat more recent Śrīvidyā,[2] to which the Yoginīhṛdaya (YH) belongs—it being, together with the Vāmakeśvarīmata/Nityāṣoḍaśikārṇava, one of its two basic texts. The description of the *śrīcakra* in the first *paṭala* of the YH is worth mentioning because, rather surprisingly, it does not say how the diagram looks and how to draw it,[3] but describes its apparition, its 'descent' (*cakrāvatāra*), as a divine cosmic process, an outward cosmic manifestation of the power of the godhead which is to be meditated, visualized, and even bodily experienced by the adept. The *śrīcakra* is shown here as a diagrammatic cosmic vision rather than

---

* The English of this paper has been—as usual—kindly checked by Mrs Barbara Bray to whom I am as always very grateful.

[1] See Heilijgers-Seelen 1994.

[2] This tradition is also called Tripurādarśana or Saubhāgyasampradāya. The name Śrīvidyā (which is also the name of its *mūlamantra*) is especially used for the modern, vedantized, form of the tradition. On the links between the Kubjikā and the Tripurā traditions, see Dyczkowski 1988.

[3] This is only briefly mentioned in the third chapter (3.95–97), where the cult of the goddess and of her retinue of deities—the *śrīcakrapūjā*, which is also to be performed—is described in some detail.

as a ritual diagram. The theological, metaphysical bias of the YH's description is emphasized by the earliest of the three known commentaries of the YH: the Dīpikā of Amṛtānanda (13th or 14th century), whose thought was very much influenced by the Kashmirian non-dualist Pratyabhijñā system, though he was probably from South India. The YH itself is in all likelihood a work from Kashmir, and may date from the 11th century.[4]

The *śrīcakra*, as is well known, is made up of a central triangle with a dot (*bindu*) in the middle, surrounded by four concentric series of triangles, themselves encircled by two concentric rows of lotus petals which in turn are encompassed by a threefold circle enclosed in a square ground forming the outer portion (see Illustration 1): nine parts altogether, each of which is called a cakra. These nine constitutive parts of the *śrīcakra* are regarded as an expansion of the divine power of the goddess, wherein abide all her different energies and all the deities emanating from her and forming her retinue. (These supernatural entities embody and relay her power, infusing the *śrīcakra* with it and therefore somehow constituting it.[5]) The *śrīcakra* as shown here is thus not a mere outline, nor a mere consecrated area, but a cosmic event and reality, to be meditated, realized, interiorized by the adept through the practice of *bhāvanā*; that is, by creative identifying meditation, a practice the fundamental importance of which in this context must be emphasized: the cosmic event, the expansion and unfolding of power of the *cakrāvatāra* is to be so intensely visualized, imagined, and felt to unfold in the cosmos as well as in the adept's mind *and* body, that he identifies with it.

An interesting aspect of the YH's approach to the *śrīcakra* is that its three chapters are called *saṃketa*, the first one being the *cakrasaṃketa*. The use of this term, which means agreement, appointment, meeting, underlines the fact that what is being described there is not a mere diagram, but the diagrammatic aspect and result of the meeting, the union of the goddess Tripurasundarī

[4] See Padoux 1994: 42ff. The YH may have been influenced by the Pratyabhijñā.

[5] Kashmirian Śaiva authors, such, for instance, as Kṣemarāja, tend to distinguish between yantra, conceived of as a pattern of mantras/deities, and maṇḍala as the actual, visible structure. This, as suggested by Sanderson in his comments on Brunner's contribution to Padoux 1986: 33, would have as a consequence that it is only the structure that one can 'trace,' that is the maṇḍala, and that (I quote) "when one speaks of the *maṇḍala* to include the circle of deities (*devatācakram*) or mantras (*mantracakram*) worshipped in it, then this is by extension of the primary sense."

and of her consort, Śiva/Bhairava, the common united presence of these two aspects of the supreme godhead in the *śrīcakra* bringing about its apparition and endowing it with their unlimited glory and power.

After eight introductory stanzas, the first chapter begins: "When she, the supreme power, [becoming] by her own free will embodied as all that exists (*viśvarūpiṇī*), perceives her own throbbing radiance (*sphurattā*), the cakra is then being produced."[6] It is a cosmic event: the goddess is taking on her cosmic form.[7] The YH then describes the development and play of the divine energies of the goddess, from the *bindu* in the centre to the outer square delimiting the *śrīcakra*. The *bindu* is said to issue from the initial, void (*śūnya*) phoneme *a*, which is the absolute. It is described (*ślokas* 11–12), not as a mere dot, nor as the place in which to visualize the goddess, but as "throbbing consciousness whose supreme nature is light and which is united with the flashing flow [of divine power]," being "the seat (*baindavāsana*) which is the [birth]place of the flow made up of the three *mātṛkās*." It thus assumes the form of the 'threefold *mātṛkā*,' which is to say the three planes of the word, *paśyantī*, *madhyamā* and *vaikharī* which appear together with the inner triangle of the *śrīcakra*. Then appears the cakra of eight triangles known as *navayoni* because it is considered as being made up of the central triangle plus the eight that surround it, nine in all, and because it is the origin, the *yoni* from which the following cakras are born. It is described as a huge compact mass of consciousness and bliss (*cidānandaghanaṃ mahat*), absolutely pure, transcending time and space: a cosmic vision, not a mere outline. Then, by an inner process of transformation and interaction, the other constituting cakras of the *śrīcakra* appear, each described as luminous, in each of which goddesses or mantras and phonemes are deemed to abide (and are to be imagined as present), each also associated with *tattvas* down to the level of the earth *tattva*, on the outer square. The cakras correspond, too, to the divisions of the cosmos called *kalā*, from the *śāntyatītakalā*, the highest, in the centre, to the *nivṛttikalā*, that of the earth, in the square part. This is to be expected since the *śrīcakra* as it appears or unfolds is an image

[6] *yadā sā paramā śaktiḥ svecchayā viśvarūpiṇī /*
sphurattām ātmanaḥ paśyet tadā cakrasya sambhavaḥ //

[7] In the non-dualistic vision of Śaivism, the cosmic manifestation (*sṛṣṭi*), though 'emitted,' results from an act of consciousness of the godhead and remains ontologically within it.

of the cosmos *in statu nascendi*, extending from the godhead to this world. The 'descending' cosmic structure of the *śrīcakra* appears also in the fact that its nine cakras are regarded as forms or creations of the powers (*śakti*) of Śiva and from this point of view are considered as divided into three groups, deemed respectively to correspond to the powers of will (*icchā*), knowledge (*jñāna*) and activity (*kriyā*) of the deity.[8] "The cakra," concludes *śloka* 24, "is thus threefold. It is an aspect of *kāmakalā*[9] and is in reality and essence expansion (*prasāraparamārthataḥ*)."

After this first cosmogonic phase, this cosmic vision, the adept must now (*śloka*s 25–36) turn to a different sort of mental exercise. He is to 'meditate' (*bhāvayet*), that is, visualize the nine portions of the *śrīcakra*, from the outer square to the central *bindu*, as present in nine centres (here called *padma*) of his Yogic 'subtle' body.[10] These nine centres are to be visualized with their shapes, colours and residing deities as tiered along the *suṣumnā*, from the *akulapadma*,[11] situated at its base, where he mentally places the outer square (called the *trailokyamohanacakra*), to the *ājñā*, between the eyebrows, where he imagines the central *bindu*. The movement is therefore now centripetal: the adept not only feels identified with the *śrīcakra* and imagines or perceives it in himself; he also follows mentally, linked with his Yogic imaginary inner structure or 'body,' an ascending movement towards the centre of the *śrīcakra* and thus to the supreme goddess. The movement does not, however, stop in this centre but takes on a different and more subtle (*niṣkalā*) form, for the adept is now to meditate the *kalā*s, the subtle phonic 'parts'—the subtle

---

[8] These are—in this order of decreasing status—the three powers or energies of Śiva through which he manifests the universe.

[9] To say that the *śrīcakra* is *kāmakalā* is to say that it is made up of the combined presence of Śiva (*kāma*) and Śakti (*kalā*).

[10] The pattern of centres (*cakra* or *granthi*) and canals (*nāḍī*) which the Yogin is to visualize as present in his body and where the *prāṇa* or the mantras flow, is often called the 'subtle body,' because it is a visionary, not an anatomically existing structure. But this is wrong because 'subtle body' is a translation of *sūkṣmadeha* (or *sūkṣmaśarīra*), the transmigrating portion, made of *tattva*s, of the human being: something quite different.

[11] This centre is specific to the YH (or to the Tripurā tradition). Since there are nine constituting cakras in the *śrīcakra*, to be visualized in the bodily centres, these must of necessity be nine in number. Above the *akulapadma* there is thus a *kulapadma*, a *lambikapadma* (on the *uvula*) being added between the *viśuddha* and the *ājñā* (see Illustration 2).

forms of phonic energy, that is,—of the *bījamantra hrīṃ*,[12] starting with the *bindu* (the *anusvāra* following the *m* of the mantra). He must visualize and meditate all the other *kalās*: *ardhacandra, nirodhinī, nāda, nādānta, śakti, vyāpinī, samanā* and *unmanā*[13] of the *uccāra* of *hrīṃ*, to which is added in fine the so-called *mahābindu*, which "transcends space, time and form:" an utterly transcendent aspect of the phonic vibration. In this mental practice the adept, having meditated and visualized each of the nine parts of the *śrīcakra* as present in each of his bodily centres, is now to perceive the central *bindu* not as the centre of the *śrīcakra* but as the first phonic *kalā* of *hrīṃ*, thus shifting from a spatial type of meditation to a more subtle, phonic one. This meditation is in fact not purely phonic since all the *kalās* have a visual aspect or symbol which is also to be evoked: these aspects are described in *ślokas* 27–34, which also mention the length of time during which they are to be mentally 'uttered' (*uccāraṇakāla*). These fractions of time are so minute (ranging from 1/4th to 1/256th of a *mātra*[14]) that they cannot possibly correspond to any actual utterance. They rather suggest the *uccāra*'s growing degree of subtleness. They express or correspond to a progression of the Yogin towards a total transcending of all empirical reality either of form or of sound/word. The adept is indeed finally to reach the transcendent plane of what is called *mahābindu*, where he is to meditate and fuse with (to quote Amṛtānanda) "the supreme Śiva, supreme light, the power of supreme awareness that is the supreme goddess Mahātripurasundarī." It is therefore a totally non-material (*niṣkalā*), mystical experience of the supreme godhead. This transition from a diagrammatic, spatial or visual dimension of meditative practice to a phonic, mantric one, with the attainment of the supreme plane of the deity, is expressed in *śloka* 36, which is as follows: "When this supreme energy (*paramā kalā*) sees the effulgence of the self (*ātmanaḥ sphuraṇam*), she assumes the aspect of Ambikā: the supreme word (*parā vāk*) is being uttered."[15]

The notion that the meditation of a maṇḍala should lead the adept to see or participate in the power of a deity is not uncommon. The

---

[12] The Tripurā/Śrīvidyā tradition has both a particular cakra and a particular mantra, the 15 phonemes *śrīvidyā*, the three parts of which all end with the *bīja hrīṃ*.

[13] On the *kalās* of *hrīṃ, oṃ*, etc., see Padoux 1990a: 402–411.

[14] A *mātra* or 'mora' is, in Sanskrit, the duration of a short vowel.

[15] *ātmanaḥ sphuraṇaṃ paśyed yadā sā paramā kalā /*
ambikārūpam āpannā parā vāk samudīritā //

notion that it should bring about an identification (*sāmarasya*, says the commentary) with the supreme plane of *vāc* is less frequent; this is perhaps a further proof of the Śaiva Kashmirian origin of the YH.

Ambikā, being the supreme mother and supreme level of the word, is the source of the cosmos. The *sādhaka* having mentally attained this level is now (*śloka*s 37–49) to imagine again the supreme goddess's intent on manifesting the universe with all it contains, a cosmic process conceived, however, as developing along the pattern of the *śrīcakra*. To quote *śloka*s 37–40, "When she is about to manifest the universe which [she holds within herself] as a germ, assuming an oblique aspect, [she becomes] Vāmā because she vomits the universe (*viśvaśya vamanāt*). Then, as the energy of will (*icchāśakti*), she has the visionary [word] (*paśyantī*) as her body. When she is the power of cognition (*jñānaśakti*), she is Jyeṣṭhā, and the intermediate word (*madhyamā vāk*) is then uttered. When the maintaining of the universe prevails, her figure spreads out into a straight line. Then, in the state of resorption she takes on the shape of the *bindu*. When the reverse process takes place, her body becomes [shaped like] a *śṛṅgāṭaka*.[16] She is then the power of activity (*kriyāśakti*): she is Raudrī, the corporeal [word] (*vaikharī*), appearing as the universe."

What the adept is to realize here is the first creative movement of the supreme goddess manifesting the inner triangle, together with four forms of energy and four divine forms of herself, while retaining all this within herself—hence the fourth goddess, Raudrī, and the return to the inner *bindu*.

In or around this central triangle other entities are now to appear, who like the preceding ones are to be conceived of both as existing in the cosmos and as abiding in the *śrīcakra*. First (*śloka*s 41–43) are produced the four *pīṭha*s, the sacred seats of the goddess, Kāmarūpa, Pūrṇagiri, Jālandhara and Oḍyāna, described here not as abiding in the central triangle (called the *sarvasiddhimayacakra*) but as being in the Yogic imaginary body (in the *mūlādhāra*, the heart, the *bhrū-madhya* and the *brahmarandhra*) of the adept: the process, as we have already noted, is inseparably cosmic, diagrammatic and Yogic, these three aspects being both imagined, visualized (the colours and shapes of the *pīṭha*s are described) and bodily experienced.

---

[16] The *śṛṅgāṭaka* is the *trapa bispinosa*, the water-chestnut, whose fruit is triangular in shape. The word *śṛṅgāṭaka* is therefore used to mean a triangle.

Then four different *liṅgas* (*svayambhū*, *bāṇa*, *itara* and *para*) are imagined as being each in one of the four *pīṭhas*, each being of a different colour and aspect,[17] and each associated with different sets of Sanskrit phonemes, so that the whole power of *vāc* in the form of the Sanskrit alphabet abides in them (41–44). All these elements, the *mātṛkā*, the *pīṭhas* and the *liṅgas*, are described as being 'expressed' (*vācya*) by (that is, as produced by) the mantra of the goddess, the *śrīvidyā*, which is taken as being fourfold (that is, the mantra as a whole plus its three parts), and are considered as corresponding to the five conditions or states of consciousness (*avasthā*), *jāgrat*, *svapna*, *suṣupti*, *turya* and *turyātīta*. The adept thus has a vision of the *śrīcakra* in its cosmic diversity and power. This is expressed by *śloka* 50: "[This] universe which has come forth as the cosmic outline born from her own will is consciousness, the [visible] form of the self, uncreated bliss and beauty."[18] Then the goddess herself, supreme consciousness, is to be visualized in the centre of the *śrīcakra* embracing her consort Kāmeśvara,[19] both holding the goad and the noose "made up of the energy of will" (*icchāśaktimaya*), the bow and the arrow "which are energy of action" (*kriyāśaktimaya*), so that the two, male and female, aspects of the supreme deity are seen as present in the diagram which they pervade and animate, as they do the cosmos, by their united power and will. To quote *śloka* 55: "Such is the supreme splendour, the *śrīcakra* as her cosmic body (*vapuḥ*), surrounded by the dazzling waves of her multitudinous power,"[20] a vision which fills the adept with wonder and awe.

Having thus visualized the *śrīcakra* in its cosmic aspect overflowing with the glory of the goddess, the adept is now to visualize and understand the role of another group of powers or deities residing in this diagram, the Mudrās, which are ten in number (*ślokas*

---

[17] A Śaiva *liṅga* is not necessarily of a more or less phallic shape. Here, for instance, the *itaraliṅga* is said to be round like a *kadamba* flower. The best *liṅga* is often said to be a *tūra*, an incised skull. As for the four *liṅgas* listed here, they are the usual four types of *śivaliṅgas*.

[18] *svecchāviśvamayollekhakhacitaṃ viśvarūpakam /*
caitanyam ātmano rūpaṃ nisargānandasundaram //

[19] Tripurasundarī with Bhairava as her consort is also conceived as Kāmeśvarī with Kāmeśvara, these latter being in fact the basic deities of the Dakṣiṇāmnāya (Padoux 1994: 38). On Kāmeśvarī, see, for instance, Bühnemann 2000–2001, volume I: 131.

[20] *evaṃrūpaṃ paraṃ tejaḥ śrīcakravapuṣā sthitam /*
tadīyaśaktinikarasphuradūrmisamāvṛtam //

56–71). Though this is another phase in the vision and practice of the *śrīcakra* by the adept, it is not described by the YH as something he is to do, but as a development taking place in the supreme consciousness, in the goddess, who now takes on the aspects of these ten goddesses, the Mudrās, who incarnate and express ten different phases of her cosmic activity and power. To quote *śloka*s 56–57: "When [the goddess] becomes luminously aware of the universe [appearing] on the screen of her own consciousness (*cidātmabhiṭṭau prakāśāmarśane*), being fully possessed by the will to act, she acts by her own free will. [Such is] the power of activity which, because it gladdens the universe and causes it to flow, is called *mudrā*." The last sentence of this stanza explains the name *mudrā*: these deities are so called because they gladden (*modanāt* [√ *mud*]) and cause to flow (*rodanāt* [√ *ru*]), hence *mud-rā*.

The first Mudrā is said to pervade (*vyāpaka*) the whole *śrīcakra*. The nine others abide each in one of the constituting cakras of the diagram, going from the outer square to the centre: the movement is centripetal because these deities, born from the play of the powers of the goddess, incarnate or symbolize nine stages of the return of the cosmos to its unmanifest source. The adept, therefore, visualizing them and identifying somehow with each of them, realizes that "this is how the play of the godhead's energy of activity (*kriyā*), whose nature is pure consciousness, is identical with the *śrīcakra*" (*kriyā caitanyarūpatvād evaṃ cakramayaṃ sthitam*—*śloka* 71). But what the adept must first and foremost always intensely meditate (*sarvadā bhāvayet*) is the supreme luminous power (*paraṃ tejas*) which is the willpower (*icchā*) of the godhead—his attention is to be focused on the supreme, on the source of all that exists. The YH merely describes these Mudrās as luminous deities to be visualized as they are described, and quotes their cosmic functions. What is prescribed here is therefore only one more perception and realization of the presence and play (here tending toward the resorption of the cosmos [*saṃhāra*]) of the goddess in and as her cakra: the practice by the adept remains a purely mental, meditative one. It is, however, worth noting that in his commentary on these stanzas Amṛtānanda describes the *mudrās* as hand gestures the adept is to display so as to identify with the role of each of the Mudrās, so that these *mudrās*, in practice, are at the same time deities to be visualized and worshipped *and* hand-gestures—an act of mental and bodily participation and identification of the adept with the deities: this aspect of the practice of the *śrīcakra* should not be overlooked.

The chapter ends by prescribing two other ways of perceiving the *śrīcakra* in meditation, first by considering it as divided into three portions each comprised of three cakras, going from the centre to the outer part, and then as consisting of its nine cakras, going from the outer part to the centre. The adept thus follows the process first of emanation then of resorption.

The chapter concludes (*śloka*s 85–86): "This is where the great goddess Mahātripurasundarī is to be worshipped. [Such is] in its absolute fullness the great cakra, giver of eternal youth and immortality. Thus has been said, o supreme goddess, the practice (*saṃketa*) of the great cakra of the goddess Tripurā, bestower of liberation while still in life."

To conclude, we may note that this chapter, which at first sight looks rather disorderly, is in fact rationally constructed, emanation and resorption succeeding each other and every successive moment increasing the awareness of and identification with the cosmic dynamism of the *śrīcakra*. First is expounded the succession of the different parts of the *śrīcakra* (8–21), then the play of energies that manifest the cosmos (22–24): this is an outward tending movement manifesting the world. After which, the *bhāvanā* of the *kalā*s of *hrīṃ* (25–36) and eventually the Mudrās (56ff.) turn the attention of the adept towards resorption, towards the centre of the diagram that is, towards liberation. The description of all the deities and entities present in the *śrīcakra* also manifests its power of creation and of resorption. The adept, by visualizing and meditatively identifying with this cosmic play, progresses towards liberation. As an active cosmic symbol (or as a display of the goddess's creative and salvific action and power), the *śrīcakra* appears very efficacious.

We may finally note that the origin of the *śrīcakra* remains shrouded in mystery. This ritual diagram is to be found in the older texts of the Traipuradarśana (which is the less ancient of the Kaula traditions), but where does it come from and when did it appear? We do not know. The source is probably to be looked for in the older Kubjikā tradition, though this is not certain.[21] A South Indian origin,

---

[21] Mark Dyczkowski (personal communication) believes that some aspects at least of this cakra come from the Śrītantrasadbhāva, a long (about 5000 stanzas) and yet unedited text which he is currently studying.

too, has been suggested by some, but this theory has so far not been conclusively proved. Whatever its origin, the *śrīcakra*, which we have just seen as it is shown in a chapter of an ancient text, is still very much in use (in ritual and meditation) in India today: not only in the South Indian 'de-tantricized' Śrīvidyā but also in the centre and the north of the sub-continent.[22] It therefore deserves some attention.

[22] The most complete study of the *śrīcakrapūjā* is that of Madhu Khanna (1986) in an unfortunately as yet unpublished Oxford thesis. Available, precise and complete is Sanjukta Gupta's description of the cult in Gupta/Hoens/Goudriaan 1979: 139–157.

1. The *śrīcakra*

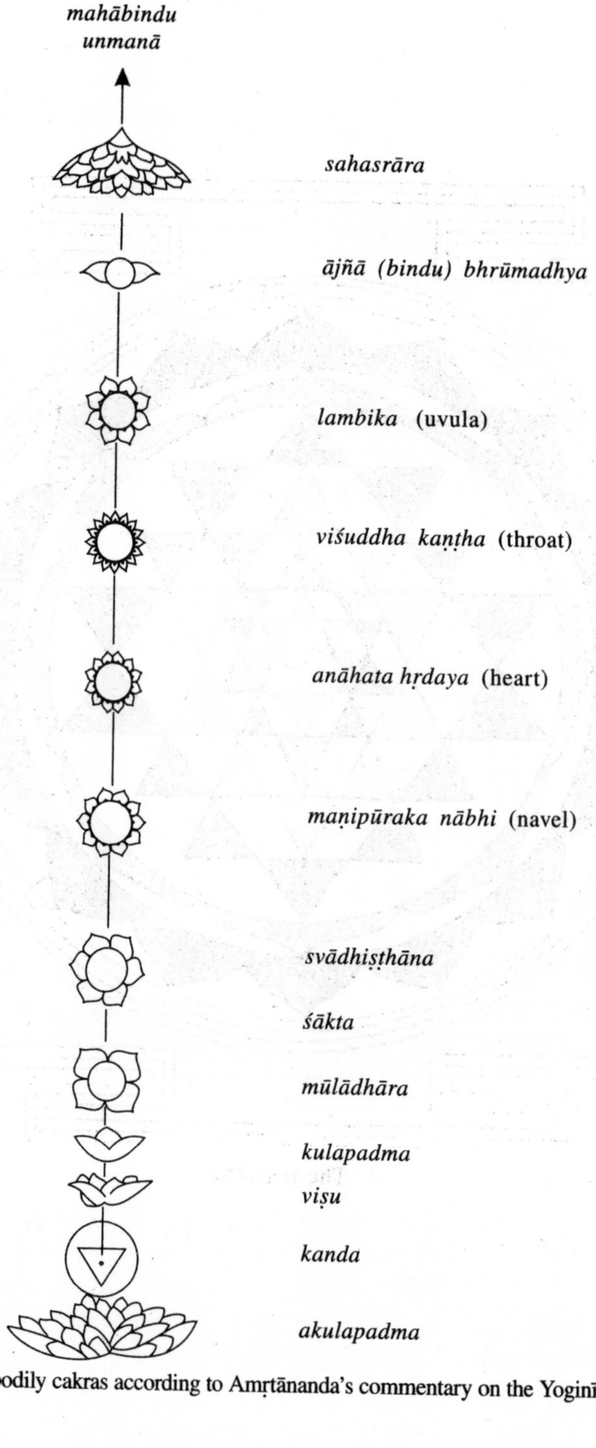

2. The bodily cakras according to Amṛtānanda's commentary on the Yoginīhṛdaya

VĀSTUPURUṢAMAṆḌALAS: PLANNING IN THE IMAGE OF MAN

Michael W. Meister

Diagrams for planning and meditation permeate South Asia, as tools for praxis, practical and religious. Psychedelic or pragmatic, they remain utilitarian at their core. They do not constitute a single reality, but have a history that makes of each a palimpsest. By the sixth century A.D., these layers had been combined to provide a tool, both religious and practical, for the constitution of a shelter for deities and worshippers—the temple—as a new form of Hindu worship began. This paper explores evidence found by recent scholarship in built monuments for the application of such diagrams to the construction, validation, proportioning, and designing of such shelters for the first early centuries of their use.

Indus Valley cities, with their gridded street plans dating from the third to second millennium B.C., have been cited as early examples of the city as 'pivot of the four quarters' (Wheatley 1971) even though their rhomboidal layouts and orientation only approximate a cardinal grid. They should perhaps remain in the pre-history of South Asian urban planning (Kenoyer 1998).

The mystic cosmogony of the Atharva-Veda, on the other hand, from early in the first millennium B.C., does provide us with a paradigm for cosmic planning in South Asia. In book 15 of the Atharva-Veda, cosmic speculation and the body of man were made into a formal homology, as well as being described as if a three-dimensional maṇḍala.[1] There a *vrātya* ascetic 'belonging to an unorthodox order'[2] is described as confronting his own divinity as

---

[1] Whitney 1905: 769 comments that the Cūlikā-Upaniṣad "reckons the *vrātya* as one among the many forms in which Bráhman is celebrated in AV., mentioning in the same verse with *vrātya* (celebrated in AV. xv.) also the *brahmacārin* and the *skambha* and the *palita*."

[2] Heesterman 1962: 36, on the other hand, concluded that the *vrātyas* were "authentic Vedic Aryan ... predecessor[s] of the dīkṣita."

'Ekavrātya, the sole Vrātya' (Kramrisch 1981: 472, 486). In Stella Kramrisch's retelling, "[t]he transfiguration of the Vrātya has three phases: the birth of the god, the vision of that god, and the building of his monument" (Kramrisch 1981: 89). She describes the 'Sole Vrātya' as "a choreographed monument of deity built up by the words of hymns," having "a *maṇḍala* for a pattern" (Kramrisch 1981: 95, 93): "He moves out on his vehicle, the mind, first toward the east, then toward the south, toward the west, and finally toward the north.... [He] incorporates into his presence the four directions of the extended universe" (Kramrisch 1981: 93).

Kramrisch saw this vision of the *vrātya* ascetic—already in the early first millennium B.C.—as a forecast of her dictum that the Hindu temple of a much later period could be described as a 'monument of manifestation' (Kramrisch 1946: passim), characterizing what the *vrātya* saw as the "lord of the space-time universe, himself the central pillar of a four-sided pyramid" (Kramrisch 1981: 96). Yet such a 'vision' did not then constitute architecture nor represent a developed practice.

Of several versions of the origin of the universe in the Vedas, "the simplest is that the creator built the universe with timber, as a carpenter builds a house" (Encyclopædia Britannica on-line; Brown 1942, 1965). Indeed the rituals surrounding the making of Vedic shelters provide a vocabulary for wood and reed construction (Renou 1998) and suggest the presence of a cosmography (Bodewitz 1979) by having central and cardinal orientations, but do not define a 'generative tool' (Bafna 2000: 45) for architecture, as may maṇḍalas of a later period.

In the building of altars (Staal 1984), bricks were laid to form an orthogonal frame, and altered to make a variety of shapes to suit different ritual purposes. Perhaps the grid of later maṇḍalas has one source in the piled bricks of such sacrificial surfaces. We have few texts to suggest this. We do, however, have quite early texts, Śulba-Sūtras (Datta 1932), of ca. the third-fourth centuries B.C., that provide the geometric construction, using cords to draw circles, needed to locate the square and cardinal orientation essential for the plot of a sacrificial altar (Apte 1926; Bag 1971) (Illustration 1). These geometric manuals scrupulously avoid interpretation, yet we know that their function was in part to assure that an altar would conform as a homologue to an oriented and therefore square universe (Menon 1932: 94–95).

It is in fact only in the time of Varāhamihira's Bṛhat-Saṃhitā, written in the sixth century A.D., that the use of something like a *vāstupuruṣamaṇḍala* to plan cities and buildings was first designated, in his chapter 53 'On Architecture.'[3] A distinction must be made between a diagram as a ritual tool or a 'constructional device' (Mosteller 1988) for architecture; Varāhamihira, however, had compiled in this text many earlier layers of knowledge as well as contemporaneous practice, as he had also assembled rival systems of astronomy in his Sūryasiddhānta.[4] As he introduced his project (53.1), "[t]o gratify clever astrologers, I now proceed to compose a work on the art of building, such as it has been transmitted from the Creator to our days, through an unbroken series of sages." He first invokes a Vedic description of the original act of sacrifice (53.2–3): "There was ... some Being obstructing ... both worlds ... [who] was subdued by the host of gods and hurled down. Of the several parts of his body, each is subjected to the particular deity by which it was attacked. It is that Being of immortal substance, who ... was destined to be the dwelling-house personified [the *vāstupuruṣa*]."[5] He then goes on for a number of verses (53.4–41) to describe a variety of house structures, their class linkage, orientation, storeys, balconies, etc., as if this architecture were an elaboration of the vernacular shelters of Vedic India (Renou 1998).

Only at 53.42 does he introduce the division of the plan into squares to fit the rite of sacrifice and the placement of deities from the older myth (Illustration 2): "In order to divide (the ground-plan of a house) into eighty-one squares, draw ten lines from east to west, and ten others from north to south."[6] He discusses the placement of 45 deities over the body of the *vāstupuruṣa* for 13 verses (53.42–

[3] I refer to Kern's translation throughout.

[4] Kramrisch 1946: 79 comments that the "symbolism of the Vāstupuruṣa-maṇḍala" was "a residue of traditions still known and practiced though no longer realized in all their import."

[5] Kramrisch 1946: 73, 78 makes the important distinction that "Vāstupuruṣa as support of the building ... is described as lying with his face down ... whereas Agni Prajāpati of the Vedic altar lies facing upwards." His head should lie to the north-east.

[6] He does not describe the location of the square required by the geometry of the Śulba-Sūtras.

54),[7] then introduces an alternative practical maṇḍala for construction: "One may also, should one prefer it, divide the area into sixty-four compartments" (53.55).

For the remainder of this chapter (53.57–125) Varāhamihira discusses vulnerable crossings (*marman*), displacement of pillars, and a range of magical associations and consequences still part of traditional wood architectural practice today (Libersat 1988), with the significant dictum that "[t]he householder ... should carefully preserve Brahman, who is stationed in the centre of the dwelling, from injury ..." (53.66).[8]

I take this time to lay out Varāhamihira's order of presentation because it is he who first puts together *vāstu* (building), *puruṣa* ('man,' but as a trace of sacrifice), and *maṇḍala* (diagram), summing up many centuries of speculation on the rituals of building (53.98): "At a period indicated by the astrologer, let the householder go to a piece of ground which has been ploughed, abounds with seed grown up, has served as a resting-place of cows, or has got the approval of the Brahmans." He gives us a sense of the range of caste patrons (53.100): "Then—touching his head, if he be a Brahman; the breast, if a Kshatriya; the thigh, if a Vaiçya; the foot, if a Śûdra—let him draw a line, the first act when a house is to be built ..." and of the important role of a proficient "holder of the measuring line," the architect or Sūtradhāra (53.110): "By the measuring line snapping asunder may be predicted death; by the plug drooping its top, great sickness; by the house-owner and architect falling short in their memory, death." Kern, Varāhamihira's translator, accused him of having "the habit of un-critically copying his authorities" (1872: 292, note 1), and yet he is not merely summing up a millennium of building, but marking a major transition. A new practice of stone construction to make temples to shelter images of deities was just beginning (Meister 1986) and the utility of the *vāstupuruṣamaṇḍala* was about to be given a new life (Meister 1979).

---

[7] Alternative arrangements of deities do exist in other and later texts (Apte/Supekar 1983). Kramrisch 1946: 19–98 best synthesizes the multiple layers of significance laid over the maṇḍala by a variety of sources: sacrificial, zodiacal, chronometric, astronomic, mythological, etc., a palimpsest or mosaic, at best, not ever a whole fabric.

[8] Pāñcarātra diagrams used for worship significantly exchange Viśvarūpa for Brahman (Apte 1987: 143).

Before writing of temples explicitly, however, Varāhamihira provided two chapters (54–55) 'on the exploration of water-springs' and 'culture of trees,' things essential to the establishment of a sacred landscape. Then, in a chapter (56: 1–31) with only 31 verses, he provided a brief 'description of various temples,' which he begins (56.1): "Having made great water reservoirs and laid out gardens, let one build a temple, to heighten one's reputation and merit." "The gods used to haunt those spots which by nature or artifice are furnished with water and pleasure-gardens" (56.3), he writes, then describes these in loving detail (56.4–8). He comments that the soils he had indicated "when treating of house-building ... are likewise recommended to persons of the different classes, when they wish to erect temples" (56.9), and then, in a significant verse, he specifies (56.10): "Let the area of a temple always be divided into sixty-four squares, while it is highly commendable to place the middle door in one of the four cardinal points."[9] It is this dictum that seems to define a new millennium of *vāstupuruṣamaṇḍala*s, to be used in practice (Illustration 3) as well as ritual.

Most remarkable to me, at the time of Varāhamihira's writing in the sixth century, is how few stone temples—and how experimental their architecture—had by then been built (Meister 1981a). Varāhamihira was on the forward cusp of a new, even 'modern,' architecture meant to shelter newly manifest images (Meister 1990).

The remainder of Varāhamihira's chapter is a listing of 'twenty kinds of shrines' (56.17), with varied plans, storeys, turrets, and dormer windows that probably existed not in stone but in wood.[10] As he casually concluded (56.31): "Herewith are the characteristics of temples described in compendious form.... Of the voluminous works by Manu, etc., have I, in writing this chapter, only taken notice in as much as I remembered."

The distinction between a proportional system, which the ritual *vāstupuruṣamaṇḍala* is for the universe, and a constructional device, such as Varāhamihira stipulates for the temple, was drawn some time ago (Panofsky 1955).[11] "The notion that magical diagrams called

---

[9] Bafna 2000: 38 is not correct in stating that Varāhamihira's chapter on temples "does not even mention the diagrams."

[10] At least one engineer (Pramar 1985) has attempted to analyze and apply a maṇḍala designed for wooden structures to the building of stone temples.

[11] Panofsky distinguishes between a theory of proportions and a practical system of construction.

mandalas," according to one recent analysis (Bafna 2000: 26), "underlie most traditional Hindu [I would prefer Indic] architectural production has become well entrenched within current thought.... [F]ew scholars have attempted to describe the precise manner in which the mandala could have acted as a generative diagram." Stella Kramrisch, whose 'The Hindu Temple' (1946) had collected a wide body of references to the Śāstric texts on the building of temples that followed Varāhamihira's, had in fact concluded that "the Vāstumaṇḍala is the metaphysical plan of the temple primarily; its cosmological and magical implications are derived from it" (Kramrisch 1946: 37, note 40).

The attempt at the literal mapping of the *vāstupuruṣamaṇḍala* onto buildings by modern architects, both Western (Volwahsen 1969: 44) and Indian (Kagal 1986; Correa 1996), or the recent resurgence of 'Shilpa Shastrins' orienting houses as an Indian astrological equivalent of Chinese *feng shui* (for example, Rao 1995), however, are no test to the use of *vāstumaṇḍala*s as a constructional tool in the past (Meister 1997). Bafna 2000: 31 has put it another way: "[W]hat connection could be posited within diagrams associated with a marginal religious cult [he is referring to Tantrism] and those associated with a practical profession [architecture]?" Yet it is precisely about the division of the plan that Varāhamihira is most explicit and practical (53.42): "[D]raw ten lines from east to west, and ten others from north to south." He is writing about a constructional device related to a proportioning system.

Kramrisch herself was unsure how such a device might have worked (Kramrisch 1946: 58): "The Vāstumaṇḍala is a prognostication, a forecast and 'tonic' of the contents that will be built up in the temple; it is in a literal sense, its programme. This does not imply an identity of the actual plan of the temple, with the maṇḍala." While she found some relationship between the simplified 16-square grid in the Matsya-Purāṇa (Kramrisch 1946: 228), "here, it seems to have been suggested by the simplicity of the shrine; its plain, thick walls, without buttresses, belong to small structural temples in central India of the Gupta Age ...," of later temples she had little doubt: "When the great temples were built, after the ninth century and which still stand, the drawing of the Vāstupuruṣamaṇḍala had become an architectural rite without necessarily coinciding with the laying out of the ground plan of the Prāsāda." Her conclusion was not so different from one scholar's recent attempt to compare square Tantric painted maṇḍalas to the elaborated ground plan of a temple in Orissa, "[i]f we were to accept that the mandala was typically used as a design tool, then actual built examples must show evidence of planning based on the mandala" (Bafna 2000: 38).

It is, of course, this sort of evidence, collected in the field, that has gradually been accumulating over the past half century (Meister 1979, 1985; Pichard 1995; Thakur 1996).[12] Buildings have perhaps proved more reliable than texts as historical documents recording the methodologies that built them (Meister 1989). This is in part because of the multiple uses over time to which the *vāstupuruṣamaṇḍala* was put—ritual, astrological, meditational, devotional, but also constructional.[13]

Referring to the Pauṣkara-Saṃhitā, Apte 1987: 129 comments that "*Mandala* worship, in those days was not a part of the temple ritual only, but often maintained its independent existence like the sacrificial institution (*Yajna*). And for that ritual ... a special *pandal* used to be erected on a chosen site—may be on a mountain or in a forest or by the side of a hermitage or on the bank of a river or inside temple premises" (Pauṣkara-Saṃhitā 2.4–5). This is not so much different from the shelter set up for the ritual painting of *dhūlicitra* in Kerala—a form of '*bhaumika citra*' or 'earth painting' (Jones 1981: 71): "[T]he ceremonial drawing in powders may also be performed at night in an appropriate space within the precincts of a Nambūtiri Brāhmaṇa household or in a palace of a Sāmanta or Kshatriya ruling family. The designated area ... is traditionally covered by a canopy constructed of four slim areca logs, wrapped in new unbleached cloth, supported by pillars of the same wood, similarly wrapped, which form the boundaries of the sacred drawing." The image of the goddess or another deity is built up in coloured powders, then destroyed through ecstatic dance.

A small but significant side current of stone temple architecture that may reflect such temporary pandals are the thin-walled *maṇḍapikā* shrines set up as funereal memorials in Central India

---

[12] See also, however, my cautionary review (Meister 1999).

[13] A recent review (Bafna 2000: 47) is correct to conclude that we must "look upon the *Vāstupuruṣamaṇḍala* as an idea that has been constantly redefined and exploited through history" but his caveat that "what we have made of it now is merely a recently constructed understanding" may best be applied to himself.

from the sixth to tenth centuries A.D. (Meister 1978).[14] These stand in sharp contrast to the thick-walled "temples ... of the Gupta age" (Kramrisch 1946: 228), their inner sancta only twice in width the thickness of their walls. Those, at the very beginning of the stone tradition, measured their inner sacred space by the demands of the maṇḍala, not their walls by the efficiencies of stone (Illustration 3 A).

Actual physical yantras or metal maṇḍala plaques are buried in the foundation of structures as tools to sanctify the building. As the label to two such metal plaques recently on display in the American Museum of Natural History, New York, put it (Huyler 1999), "Yantra are specific mandala created to attract Divine Energy of a deity into a sacred space. Made of metal or stone, yantra are buried beneath a temple's inner sanctum during construction." Such yantras are also drawn at significant points of the plan in late Orissan practice (Boner 1975), but should not be confused with the *vāstupuruṣamaṇḍala* as a whole.[15]

To look for the application of the *vāstupuruṣamaṇḍala* introduced by Varāhamihira as a constructional tool or planning device in the sixth century, it is necessary to measure standing temples. Bafna 2000: 41–42 is mistaken in claiming "a troubling lack of corroborating evidence from surviving built structures." There have been both 'detailed studies of individual plans' as well as what he calls 'comparative morphological studies' that go well beyond imposing a 'constraining orthogonality' (Meister 1982, 1983a; Thakur 1990).

From my own experience, however, certain procedures are important (Meister 1979, 1999). The square Gupta temples of Kramrisch's reference—Sanchi 17, Tigawa, Nachna, even Deogarh—use thick masonry walls to surround an inner sanctum ca. half the width of the whole (Meister/Dhaky/Deva 1988). Early seventh-century shrines in Orissa (Illustration 3 A) with developed *latina nāgara* superstructures and a cross-plan with closed doorways on

[14] An inscription on the seventh-century *maṇḍapikā* shrine at Mahuā refers to a 'stone *maṇḍapikā*' set up in honour of a local ruler's deceased parents.

[15] "The square grid would then simply be an instrument—a yantra—used for the depiction of the *vāstu* deities" (Bafna 2000: 45). Bafna's reference to "yantras embedded within the traditional drawings of temple plans," however, begs the issue that no such drawings survive before the modern period.

three walls,[16] precisely fit a constructing grid of 64 squares when measured at the root of their wall mouldings (the *khura* hoof of the *vedībandha*)—that is, where the maṇḍala could be drawn on the stone foundation that formed the floor level of the sanctum. These shrines well fit Varāhamihira's dictum to let "the area of a temple always be divided into sixty-four squares" and "to place the middle door in one of the four cardinal points" (56.10).

In my own fieldwork (Meister 1979) I first began to measure temple plans thinking they would only confirm Kramrisch's intuition that the *vāstumaṇḍala*s specified by Varāhamihira and by later texts "had become an architectural rite," as temples became more elaborate after the ninth century, "without necessarily coinciding with the laying out of the ground plan" (Kramrisch 1946: 228). However, directly measuring the mouldings of a group of seventh- and eighth-century temples in Madhya Pradesh—in particular the seventh-century *nāgara* temple at Mahuā—first gave me evidence that architects of this region and in this period were using a new procedure (Illustration 3 B). Standing above two levels of a stone foundation, the sanctum walls of this Śiva temple measured ca. 556 cm from corner to corner (ca. 114 cm for *karṇa* and *bhadra* piers; 57 cm for intermediate *pratiratha*s) at the *khura* hoof of the *vedībandha* mouldings, which was the floor level of the sanctum. The inner space of the sanctum measured ca. 228 cm in width.

These measurements embody a new paradigm for both the concept and construction of the multiplying wall offsets that distinguish *nāgara* temples in this period (Illustration 3 C). Central *bhadra*s on the outer walls project the measure of the *brahmasthāna*, flanking *pratiratha* offsets mark the dimensions of the inner sanctum. Such a system I found also rigorously applied to other temples in the Gwalior region (Meister 1979). Such a use of the maṇḍala was new, practical, and expanded the maṇḍala's meaning to the temple, as a physical expression of its plan.[17]

As a test of the 'constraining orthogonality,' as Bafna 2000: 41 put it, I also measured and analyzed rectangular temples in this region and century, as well as those beginning to experiment with

---

[16] Kramrisch 1946: 271 interprets *ṣaḍaśra* to be this type: "[T]he ground plan ... has six faces, for each of its three sides has a central buttress which is set off from the wall...."

[17] Sinha 2000 has extended this analysis of the '*bhadra* cluster' to *vesara* temples in the Deccan.

octagonal and turned-square plans (Meister 1982, 1983a, 1983b, 1984). In both cases, the maṇḍala continued to control the width of walls, location of corners, and to project sanctum and *brahmasthāna* dimensions through the walls as measured offsets (Illustration 6).

Not all temples across all of India yield similar results, but increasingly regional understandings and misunderstandings of this system of planning become clearer, as more temples have been adequately measured and analyzed (Meister 1985; Pichard 1995; Thakur 1996). In South India, for example, use of an odd-numbered grid, centring the sanctum on a square, made rings of expansion possible (Illustration 4). In the north, separate sacred spaces might overlap (Illustration 5).

Bafna 2000: 41 confuses the role of measure and proportion in his conclusion that such variation makes of the *vāstumaṇḍala* "not so much a constructional aid as a tool for the designer, one that was used to control the proportions of the design rather than its measure." Measure in the Indian context was relative, determined by the height or hand of the donor, architect, or image; proportion *was* the 'constructional aid' (Meister 1985).

He also, it seems to me, is wrong to conclude that "the *Vāstupuruṣamaṇḍala* cannot be rotated without losing all its significance" (Bafna 2000: 41). Rotating plans superimpose one turned square on the other, moving toward the circle (Illustration 7) that constitutes a maṇḍala's pre-existent form (and which surrounds the square gated palaces in the painted maṇḍalas of Bafna's article).[18]

Kramrisch 1946: 62, while pointing out that "earlier texts ... do not record circular Vāstus" reported that "Utpala, the tenth century commentator of the 'Bṛhat Saṃhitā' describes in detail the construction of circular sites.... This appears a development around the principal Vāstu, which is and must remain square...." She also cited Agni-Purāṇa 93.40: "In the middle of the six sided, three sided, and circular plan, should be the square." Referring to Vāstuvidyā 7.6 and 10.15, she also observed (Kramrisch 1946: 62, note 105): "as the months advance the Vāstupuruṣa moves ... The spatial order of the 8 directions simultaneously denotes a temporal order; the Vāstu is the time piece.... This rotating Vāstu is called Caravāstu and is

[18] Kramrisch 1946: 41 remarked that the "square symbol of the extended world in its order has precedence over the circle of time, the second ornament."

distinguished from the Sthira-vāstu, whose position is fixed.... Temples are meant to last and are always built [i.e., founded] on the Sthiravāstu."

Experiments with embedded octagons—from the octagonal stone temple at Muṇḍeśvarī and brick temples in Dakṣiṇa Kosala of the seventh century (Meister 1981b, 1984) to the great *miśraka* superstructure of the Chola temple at Gaṅgaikōṇḍacōḷapuram (Pichard 1995)—might suggest that architects at an early period also thought in such terms of their temples (and their construction).

My own work for a period of time focused on measuring and analyzing monuments that could provide test cases for the limits of maṇḍala planning. I had thought that the application of the grid of the maṇḍala and its significance to the proportioning of temples in the seventh and eighth centuries could not explain the variations found in the ninth and tenth. What I discovered, however, in Central India was a shift in construction of the temple that preserved the relation of *bhadra* and *pratiratha*s to sanctum and *brahmasthāna* while pulling the bulk of the temple within the grid (Illustration 3 D).[19] This *bhadravyāsa* measure allowed the fabric of the temple to be reduced, proportions in the wall to be more balanced, and new plans to emerge (Meister 1979, 1985). That the grid of the maṇḍala could continue to have a practical utility, even in complex and huge temples of the 11th century, as at Khajuraho, was startling (Illustration 5).[20] No longer fixed at the foundation as in earlier shrines (Illustration 3), yet still governing the walls enclosing the inner sanctum, the continuing presence of these proportions in the fabric of these stone monuments is perhaps our strongest surviving evidence for the "notion of a geometrical device with symbolic dimensions underlying all architectural production" (Bafna 2000: 42).[21]

I think Bafna 2000: 43 is right that "[p]ractically speaking, a grid is a cumbersome and complicated tool for the laying out of plans; it

---

[19] Bafna 2000: 41 mistakenly attributes this change to the seventh century instead of the ninth.

[20] "Meister's argument is sophisticated and pursuasive: the grid is only a regulative tool and the very act of embedding it is auspicious.... But in formulating this idea, he seems to have moved a good deal away from the strict orientation and hierarchy of the *Vāstupuruṣamaṇḍala*" (Bafna 2000: 41).

[21] Bafna, however, resolves that the "idea of the governing mandala" ... "is merely a recently constructed understanding" (Bafna 2000: 42, 47).

is extremely susceptible of errors unless checked by diagonals," yet find his alternative—"the centerline system ... still used ... to compute the proportion of statues"—an odd choice (see Mosteller 1991). From the time of the Śulba-Sūtras, the geometry and tools for laying out a plan were known. If the Sūtradhāra was controller of the cord—"let him draw a line, the first act ..." as Varāhamihira 53.100 had put it—he also controlled the geometry that the use of the compass made possible (Illustrations 1, 7). Such geometric construction gives precision; a grid establishes proportion; reference to the *vāstupuruṣamaṇḍala* maintains ritual authority.

Bafna 2000: 39, 41, however, calls such construction "an alternative 'peg-and-string' geometry" and comments that "[t]here are no indications within the literature on the history of Indian mathematics, or within *vāstuśāstra* texts, that there were two separate techniques of geometrical constructions prevalent at any time." Yet the constructive geometry prevalent from the time of the Śulba-Sūtras must itself be seen as the source both of the maṇḍala's 'constraining orthogonality,' in Bafna's terms, and of a certain freedom from it. Bafna 2000: 41 admits, "some *śilpa* manuals specifically record peg-and-string operations to ensure a precisely oriented construction of the square perimeter of the *Vāstupuruṣa-maṇḍala* itself."

My analysis of temples with turned-square plans (Meister 1982, 1983b, 1984, 1989) beginning with the remarkable mid-eighth-century Gargaj Mahādeva temple at Indor in Madhya Pradesh (Illustration 6 B), can demonstrate both the continuing 'orthogonality' of temple planning and its freedom from constraint. Bafna 2000: 41 refers to 'stellate' plans with a 'nonorthogonal profile,' yet the angled buttresses of these temples must be observed as right-angled corners of turned squares[22] (that is, as orthogonality unconstrained).

The ground plan of the Gargaj Mahādeva temple at Indor combines what Kramrisch 1946: 62, using Vāstuvidyā, has identified as *sthiravāstu* and *caravāstu*, marking the temple's functions as both cosmogram and chronogram. On the walls of the temple at Indor, Śiva and his family mark fixed cardinal directions; eight *dikpāla*s,

[22] Previous scholars have often not observed this. Willis 1997: 60, for example, describes Indor as having a "stellate shape" with "square and acute projections" while his plans show obtuse corners rather than right-angled ones.

guardians of the quarters, stand on the intermediate rotating *bhadras*, facing sub-cardinal points (Illustration 6 B).[23]

That architects—from the seventh century in Dakṣiṇa Kosala to 11th- to 13th-century Karnataka, Maharashtra, and 16th-century Rajasthan—took the great trouble to build such complexly constructed turned-square monuments in brick and stone (Illustration 7) must be the best evidence for "some special symbolism associated with the composition."[24] It cannot be in doubt that the constructional mechanism making possible such compositions was the simple geometry of the Śulba-Sūtras—not the grid itself, which is consequent—that had located sacred ground for so many centuries. Perhaps that is what the *vāstupuruṣamaṇḍala* hid. Bafna's comments that "buildings can both provide a structure for an embedded mandala, and also serve to hide it" (Bafna 2000: 46) is valid, but I would reverse his conclusion.[25] It is the building that acts in place of the grid, becoming the maṇḍala. As Kramrisch, citing the Mahābhārata, had pointed out for the palaces of the three worlds the temple mimics, "[t]hey revolved, each on its own level; they were part of a revolving universe" (Kramrisch 1981: 414).

---

[23] This geometry, as with all *prāsādas*, is interrupted by the *prāggrīva* entrance to the interior sanctum.

[24] Bafna 2000: 44, however, calls this "problematic."

[25] "The grid acts *in place of* the building, rather than serving *as the basis of it*" (Bafna 2000: 44).

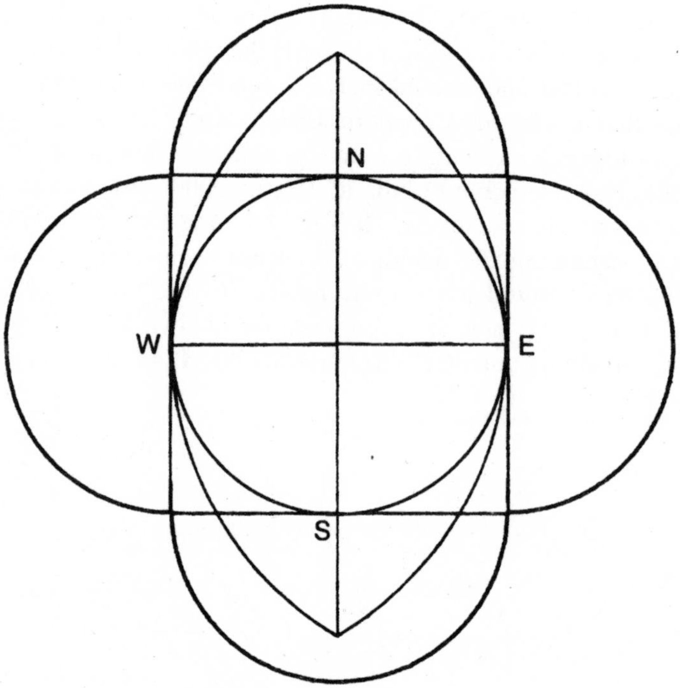

1. The geometric construction of a cardinally oriented square locating an altar as defined in Śulba-Sūtra texts

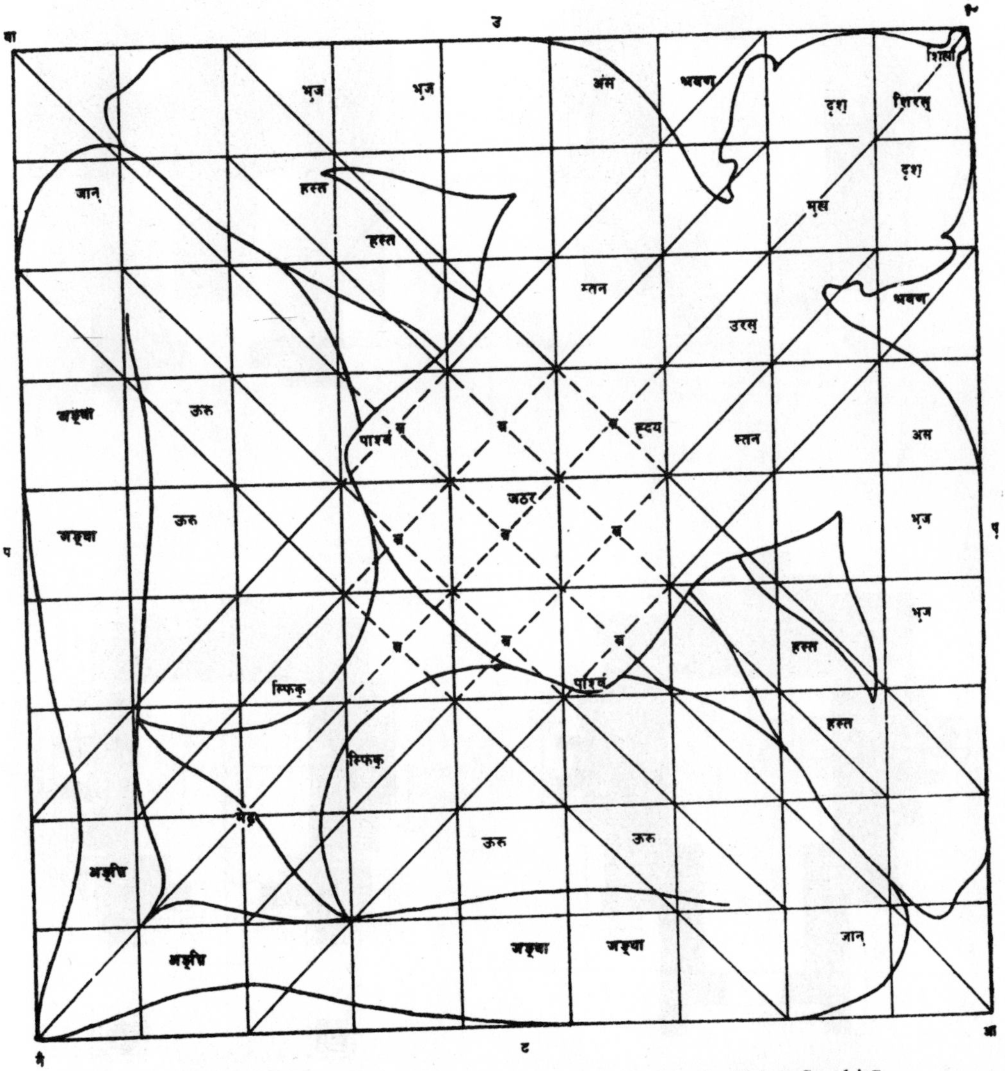

2. Vāstupuruṣamaṇḍala of 81 squares, as described in the Bṛhat-Saṃhitā

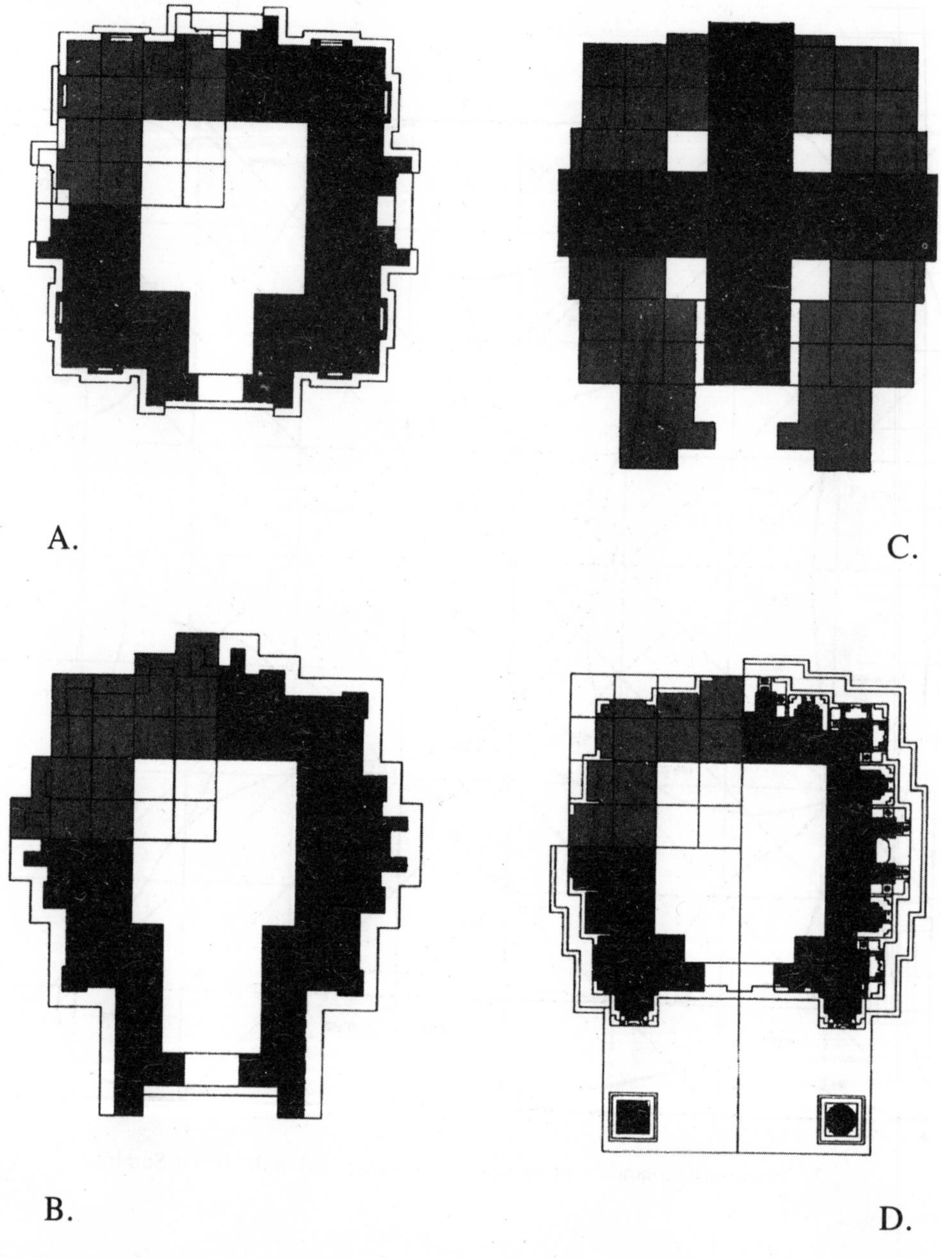

3. Ground plans and constructing maṇḍalas: A. Bharateśvara temple, Bhubaneshwar, Orissa; B. Śiva temple no. 2, Mahuā, Madhya Pradesh; C. Mahādeva temple, Amrol, Madhya Pradesh; D. Naktimātā temple, Bhavanipur, Rajasthan

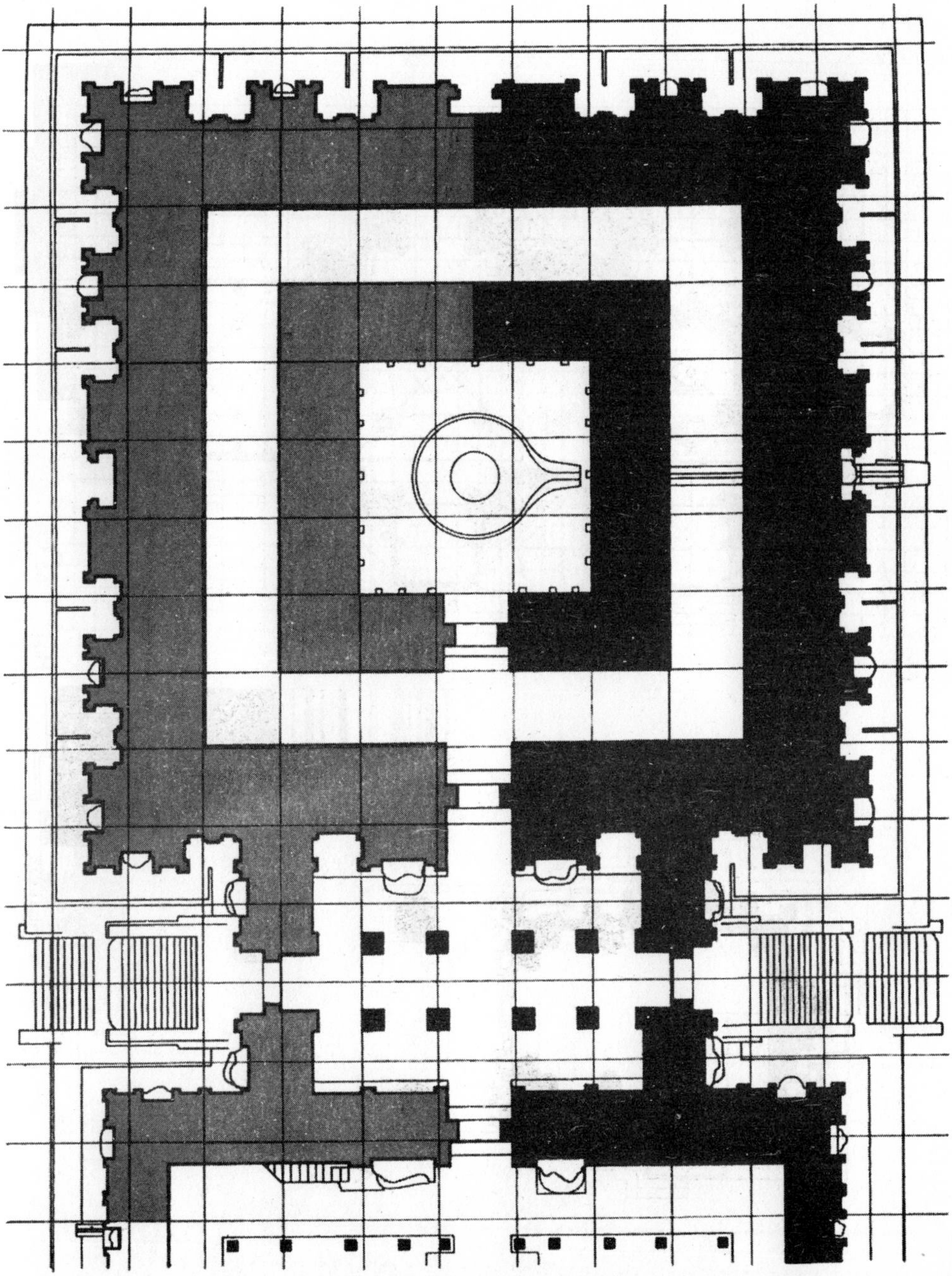

4. Bṛhadīśvara temple, Gaṅgaikōṇḍacōḷapuram, Tamilnadu

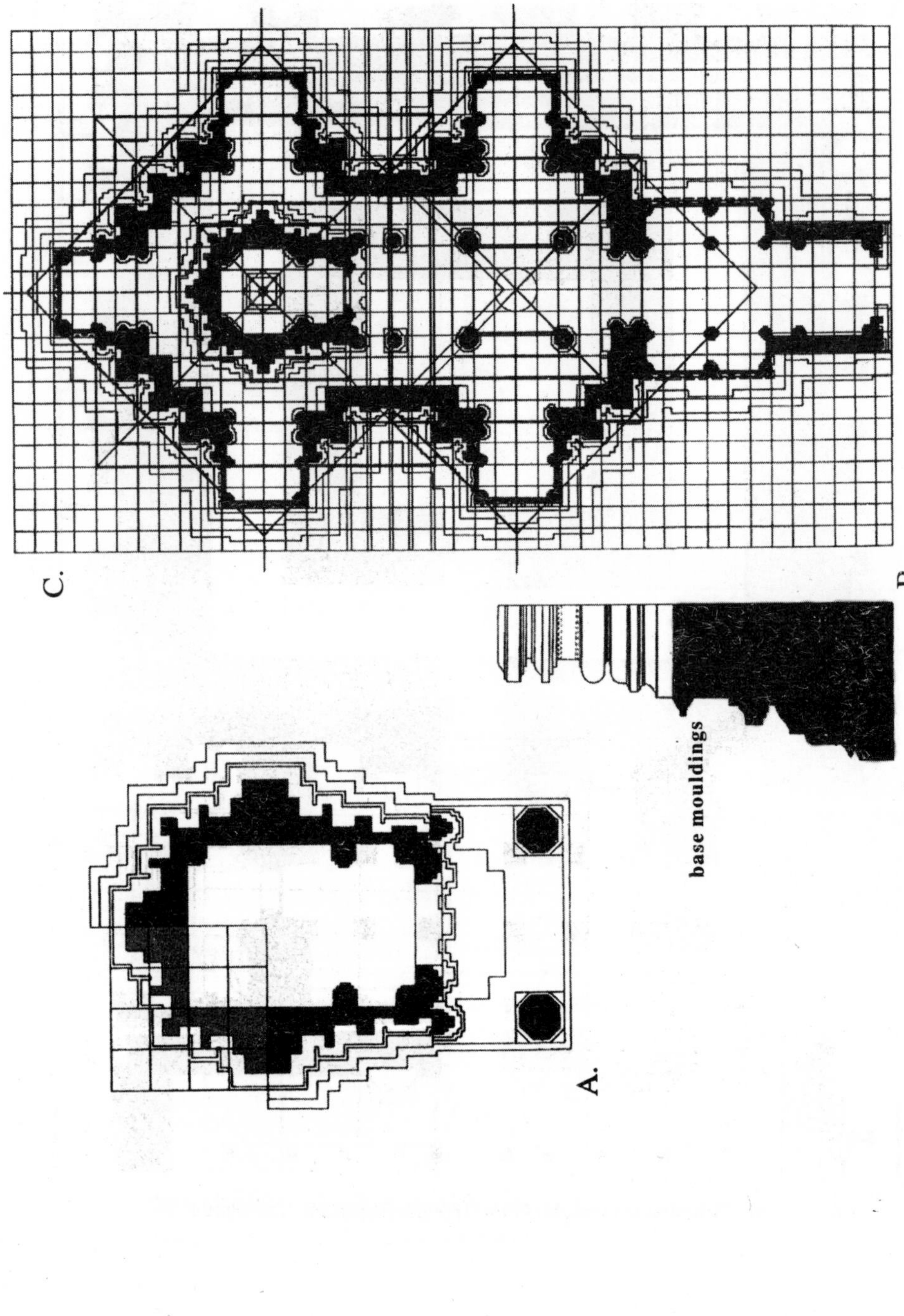

5. Khajuraho, Madhya Pradesh: A. Viśvanātha temple; B. Lakṣmaṇa temple, socle and *vedībandha* mouldings;

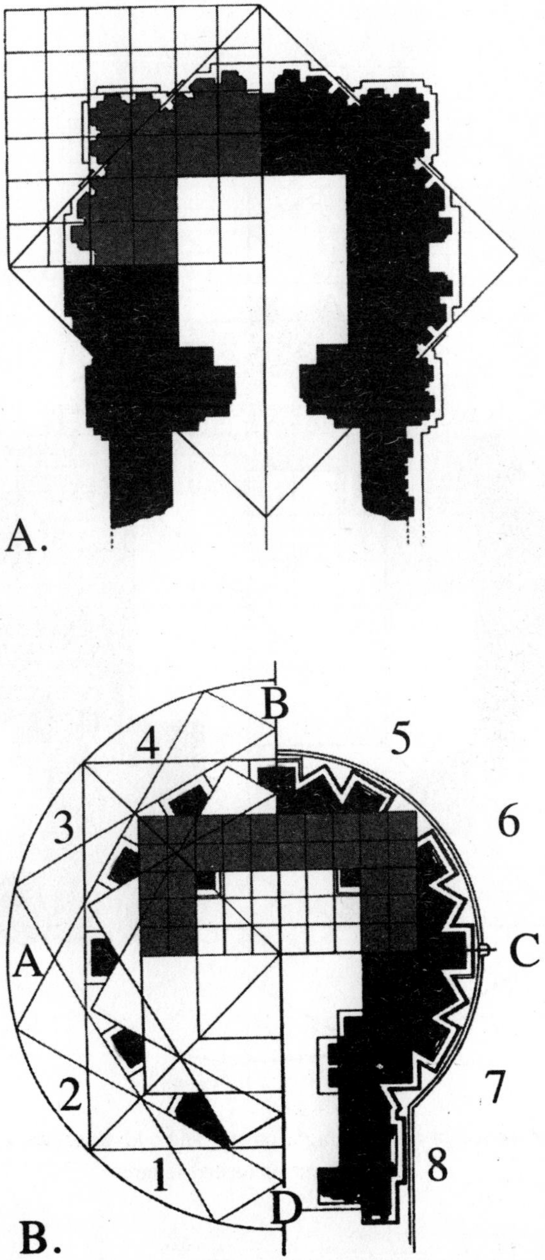

6. A. Śabarī temple, Kharod, Madhya Pradesh; B. Gargaj Mahādeva temple, Indor, Madhya Pradesh

7. Comparison of the use of constructing geometry and odd-numbered grids in plans based on three and six turned squares

COLOUR PLATES

1. A yantra of Guhyakālī

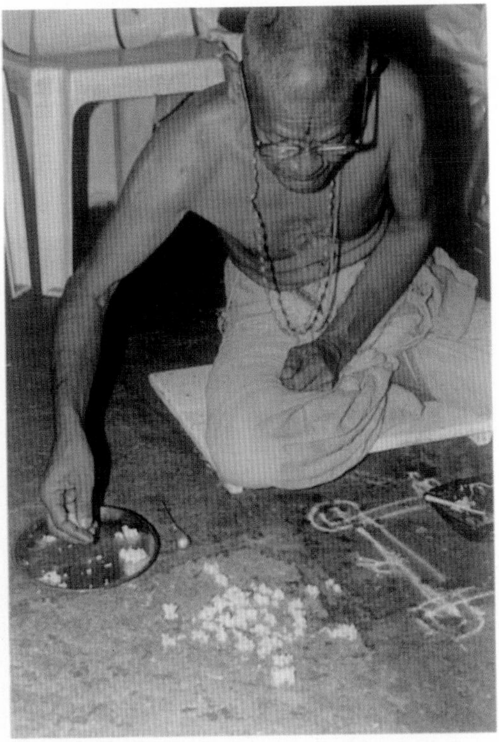

2. The *baliharaṇa of the vaiśvadeva rite*

3. A domestic *śivapañcāyatana*

4. A *rudrapīṭhamahāyantra*

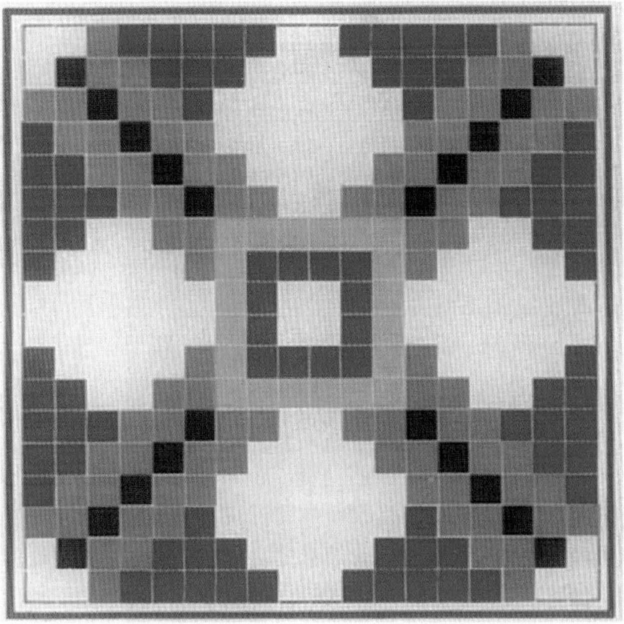

5. A *sarvatobhadra*

6. A *rāmaliṅgatobhadra* with 26 *rāmamudrā*s and 28 *liṅga*s

7. A *caturmudrārāmaliṅgatobhadra* with 4 *rāmamudrā*s and 8 *liṅga*s and a *sarvatobhadra* in the centre

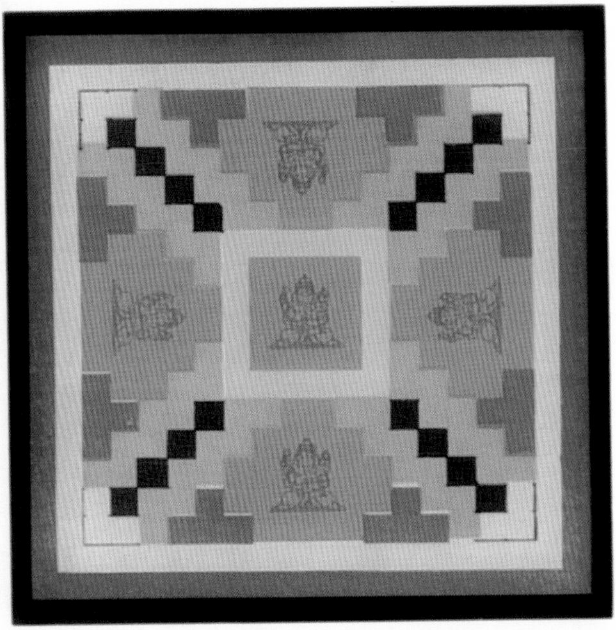

8. A *gaṇeśabhadra* with five icons of Gaṇeśa

9. A *gaṇeśabhadra* with 21 icons of Gaṇeśa

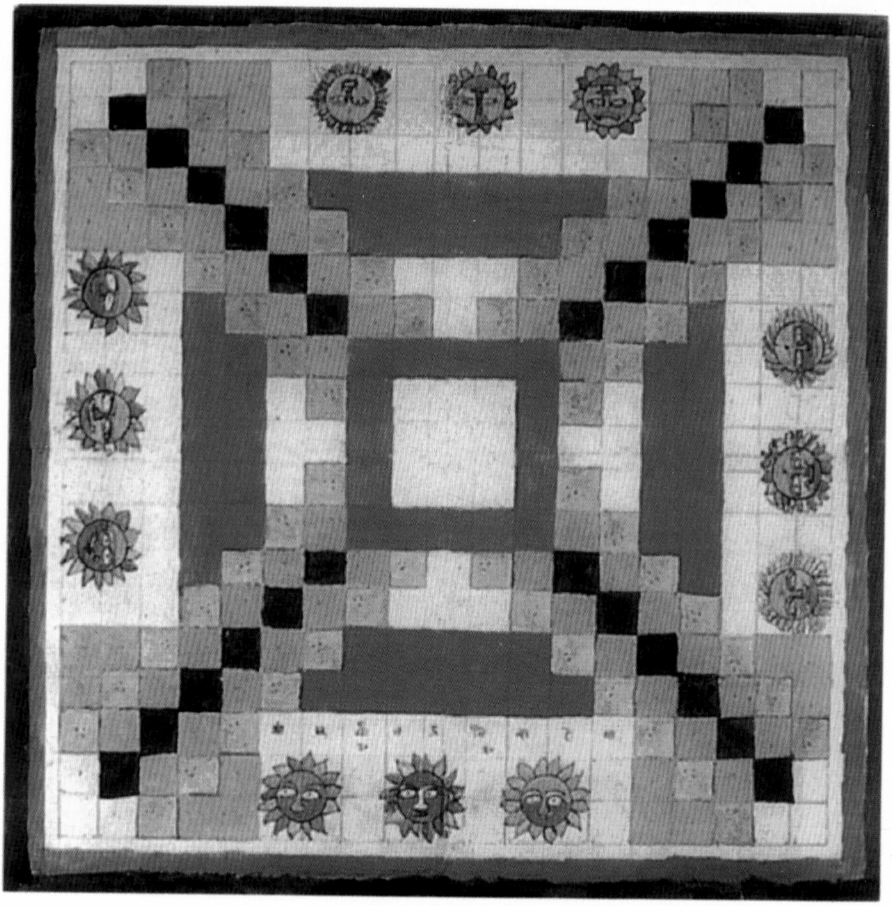

10. A *sūryabhadra* with 12 icons of the sun

11. The construction of a *dvādaśaliṅgatobhadra* with a *sarvatobhadra* in the centre

12. The invocation of deities into areca nuts placed on a *sarvatobhadra*

13. A vessel of plenty placed on a *sarvatobhadra*

14. The *cakrābjamaṇḍala* according to the Pādma-Saṃhitā

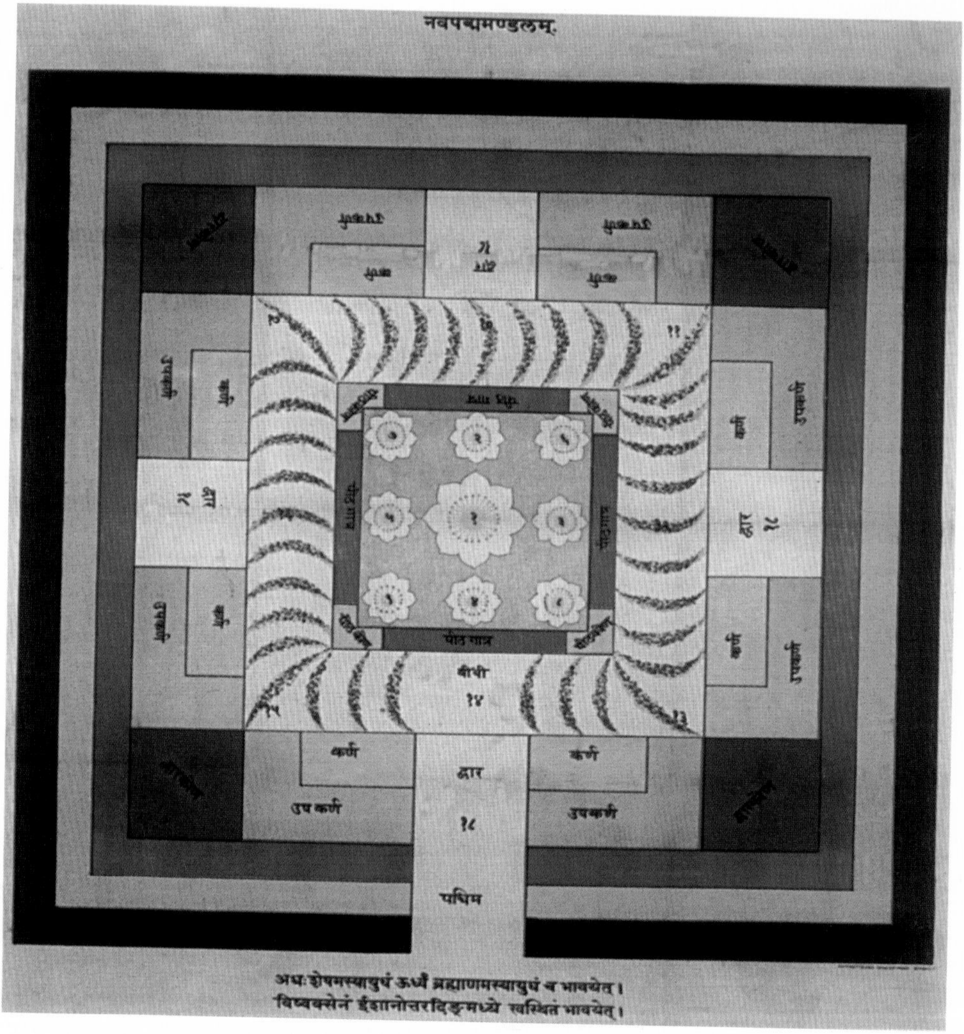

15. The *navapadmamaṇḍala* according to the Jayākhya-Saṃhitā

16. The *śrīmaṇḍala* of the Netratantra following Kṣemarāja's commentary

17. An alternative structure of the *śrīmaṇḍala* of the Netratantra

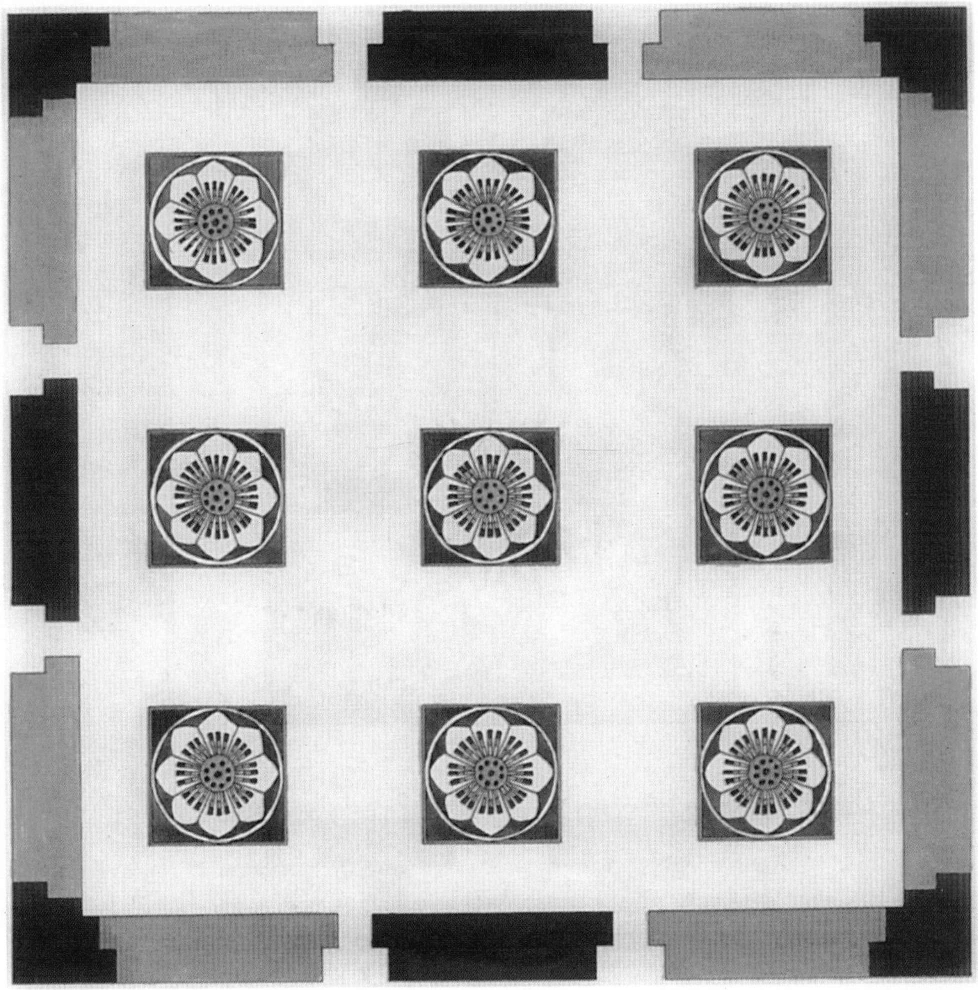

18. The maṇḍala of the nine lotuses *(navanābhamaṇḍala)* according to the Svacchandatantra and Kṣemarāja's commentary

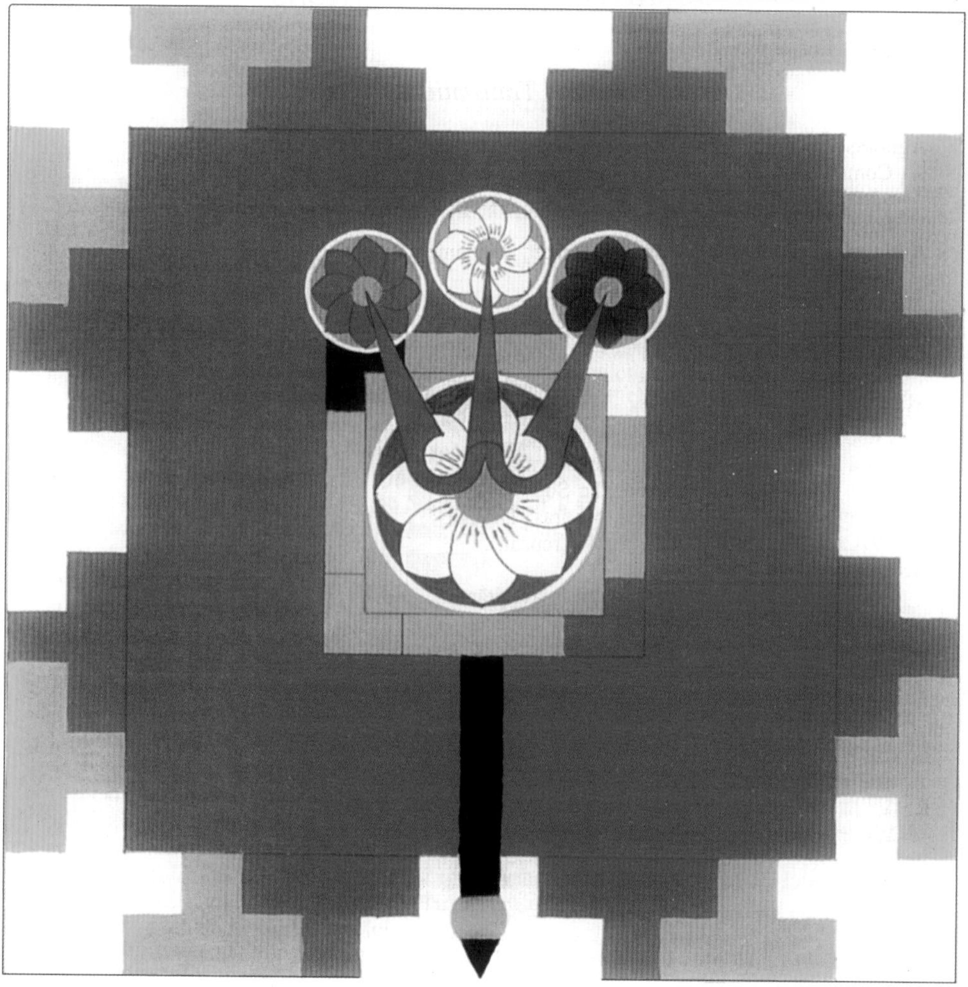

19. A tentative reconstruction of the trident maṇḍala of the Siddhayogeśvarīmata (long recension) according to the Tantrāloka

BIBLIOGRAPHY AND ABBREVIATIONS[1]

Texts and Translations

Aghoraśivācāryapaddhati. Aghoraśivācāryapaddhati (= Kriyākramadyotikā), with Commentary (*Prabhā*) by Nirmalamaṇi. Edited by Rāmaśāstrin and Ambalavānajñānasambandhaparāśaktisvāmin. Cidambaram, 1927 (in *grantha* characters).

Ajitāgama. Édition critique par N.R. Bhatt. 3 volumes. Pondichéry: Institut Français, 1964–1991.

Atharva-Veda
Atharva-Veda Saṁhitā. Translated with a Critical and Exegetical Commentary by W.D. Whitney, revised and brought nearer to completion and edited by C.R. Lanman. 2 volumes. Cambridge, Massachusetts: Harvard University, 1905.

Aniruddha-Saṃhitā. Sree Anirudha Samhita, one of Divyasamhita in Pancharatra. Edited by A. Sreenivasa Iyengar. Mysore, 1956.

Ahirbudhnya-Saṃhitā. Ahirbudhnya-Saṃhitā of the Pāñcarātrāgama. Edited by M.D. Ramanujacharya under the Supervision of F.O. Schrader. Revised by V. Krishnamacharya. 2 volumes. Madras: The Adyar Library and Research Centre, 1916, 1966 (second edition), 1986 (reprint).

ĀR. Ānandarāmāyaṇa
Śrīvālmīkimahāmunikṛtaśatakoṭirāmacaritāntargatam ānandarāmāyaṇam... Rāmatejapāṇḍeyena kṛtayā jyotsnābhidhayā bhāṣāṭīkayā ṭikitam. Edited by Y.K. Dvivedī. Vārāṇasī: Paṇḍitapustakālaya, 1977 (second edition).

Īśānaśivagurudevapaddhati. The îśânasivagurudevapaddhati by îsânaśivagurudevamisra. Edited by T. Gaṇapati Sâstrî. 4 volumes. Trivandrum: Trivandrum University Press, 1920–1925, Delhi: Bharatiya Vidya Prakashan, 1988 (reprint).

Īśvara-Saṃhitā. Īśvarasaṃhitā prativādibhayaṅkarānantācāryais saṃśodhitā. Kāñcī: Sudarśanamudrākṣaraśālā, 1923.

Ṛg-Veda. Die Hymnen des Rigveda. Herausgegeben von Th. Aufrecht. 2 parts. Wiesbaden: Otto Harrassowitz, 1968 (fourth reprint).

Ṛgvedīyabrahmakarmasamuccaya. Atha ṛgvedīyabrahmakarmasamuccayaḥ. Edited by Gaṇeś Śāstrī Śeṇḍye. Puṇe: S.P. Barve Paraśurām, 1979.

Kalyāṇamandirastotra. See Bhaktāmarastotra.

Kālīvilāsa-Tantra. Kâlîvilâsa Tantra. Edited by Pârvatî Charana Tarkatîrtha. London: Luzac & Co., 1917.

Kiraṇavṛtti. Bhaṭṭarāmakaṇṭhaviracitā kiraṇavṛttiḥ. Bhaṭṭa Rāmakaṇṭha's Commentary on the Kiraṇatantra. Volume I: Chapters 1–6: critical edition and annotated translation <by> D. Goodall. Pondichéry: Institut Français de Pondichéry, 1998.

---

[1] I regret that some bibliographical entries pertaining to Brunner's contribution remain incomplete. I was unable to add or confirm names of some editors and/or publishers quoted in her contribution since the books were not accessible to me. The transliteration system from South Indian languages in the references to Brunner's article follows the system she has used in her earlier publications.

Kiraṇāgama. Kiraṇatantra. Edited by T.R. Pañcāpageśaśivācārya and K.M. Subrahmaṇyaśāstrī. Devakoṭṭai: Śivāgamasiddhāntaparipālanasaṅgha, 1932 (in *grantha* characters).

Kubjikā-Upaniṣad. The Kubjikā Upaniṣad. Edited with a translation, introduction, notes and appendices by T. Goudriaan and J.A. Schoterman. Groningen: Egbert Forsten, 1994.

Kulārṇava-Tantra. Kulārṇavatantra. Introduction A. Avalon (Sir J. Woodroffe), Readings M.P. Pandit, Sanskrit Text Tārānātha Vidyāratna. Delhi: Motilal Banarsidass, 1965 (reprint).

Gaṇeśatāpanīya-Upaniṣad. Die Gaṇeśatāpanīya-Upaniṣad. Teil 1: Text und Übersetzung. Teil 2: Anmerkungen. Inauguraldissertation vorgelegt von U. Bergmann (unpublished doctoral dissertation, submitted to Marburg University in 1965).

Caturvargacintāmaṇi II. Chaturvarga Chintāmaṇi by Hemādri. Volume II: Vrata-Khaṇḍa. 2 parts. Part I. Edited by Bharatacandra Śiromaṇi. Part II. Edited by Bharatacandra Śiromaṇi, Yajñeśvara Bhaṭṭācāryya and Kāmākhyānātha Tarkaratna. Calcutta: Gaṇeśa Press, 1978–1879.

Jayākhya-Saṃhitā. Jayākhyasaṃhitā. Critical Edition with an Introduction in Sanskrit, Indices etc. by E. Krishnamacharya. Baroda: Oriental Institute, 1931.

Tantrasadbhāva. A draft edition of selected passages prepared by J. Törzsök based on two manuscripts from the National Archives, Kathmandu (5-1985 and 5-445).

Tantrasāra of Abhinavagupta. Edited with notes by Mukunda Rām Sastri. Bombay: Nirṇaya Sāgar Press, 1918.

TĀ. Tantrāloka (by Abhinavagupta)

The Tantrāloka of Abhinava Gupta, with commentary by Rājānaka Jayaratha. Edited by Mukund Rām Shastri. 12 volumes. Allahabad/Bombay: Venkateshvar Steam Press et al., 1918–1938.

Gnoli, R. 1999. Abhinavagupta: Luce dei tantra, Tantrāloka, a cura di R. Gnoli. Milano: Adelphi.

[Completely revised version of the earlier translation of the Tantrāloka which was published as: Gnoli, R.: Luce delle Sacre Scritture (Tantrāloka). Torino: Unione tipografico-editrice torinense, 1972.]

Silburn, L.† and A. Padoux 1998. Abhinavagupta: La Lumière sur les Tantras, chapitres 1 à 5 du Tantrāloka. Traduits et commentés. Paris: De Boccard.

Devīmāhātmya. Devi Mahatmyam (Glory of the Divine Mother). 700 Mantras on Sri Durga. <Sanskrit Text and> English Translation by Swami Jagadiswarananda. Madras: Sri Ramakrishna Math, no date (fifth impression).

Nāradīya-Saṃhitā. Nāradīya Saṁhitā. Edited by R.P. Chaudhary. Tirupati: Kendriya Sanskrit Vidyapeetha, 1971.

Nityāṣoḍaśikārṇava. (Vāmakeśvaratantrāntargataḥ) nityāṣoḍaśikārṇavaḥ. Śrībhāskararāyonnītasetubandhākhyavyākhyāsahitaḥ. Edited by K.V. Abhyaṃkar. Puṇe: Ānandāśrama, 1973.

Nityotsava. Nityotsava of Umānandanātha [Supplement to Paraśurāma-kalpa-sūtra]. Edited by A.Mahadeva Sastri. Revised and enlarged by Trivikrama Tirtha. Baroda: Oriental Institute, 1977.

Niśvāsa. Niśvāsatattvasaṃhitā. Manuscript 1-227, preserved in the National Archives, Kathmandu (see Goudriaan 1981: 33–35).

NT. Netratantra

NT_1. The Netra Tantram, with commentary (Uddyota) by Kshemarāja. Edited by Madhusudan Kaul. 2 volumes. Bombay: Tatva-Vivechaka Press, 1926–1939.

NT_2. Netratantram with the commentary 'Uddyota' of Kṣemarāja. Edited by V. Dwivedi. Delhi: Parimal Publications, 1985.

Parama-Saṃhitā. Paramasaṁhitā [of the Pāñcharātra]. Edited and translated into English with an introduction by S. Krishnaswami Aiyangar. Baroda: Oriental Institute, 1940.

Parātriṃśikā and laghuvṛtti. La Parātriṃśikālaghuvṛtti de Abhinavagupta. Texte traduit et annoté par A. Padoux. Paris: De Boccard, 1975.

Pādma-Saṃhitā. Pādma Samhitā. Critically edited by S. Padmanabhan. 2 volumes. Madras: Pancaratra Parisodhana Parisad, 1974–1982.

Pārameśvara-Saṃhitā. Śrī Pārameśvara Saṃhitā Śrī Govindācāryaiḥ saṃskṛtā, anekavidhā darśādibhiḥ saṃyojitā ca. Śrīraṅgam: Kodandaramar Sannidhi, 1953.

Puraścaryārṇava. Puraścaryārṇava of His Majesty Shri Pratap Sinh Sah Dev King of Nepal. Edited by M. Jha. Delhi: Chaukhamba Sanskrit Pratishthan, 1985 (reprint).

Pūrva-Kāraṇāgama. Śrīmat-Pūrvakāraṇāgamam. Madras (Çintātripeṭṭai): ÇivañāNa-potayantraçālai, 1922 (*kaliyuga* 5023) (in *grantha* characters).

PauṣS. Pauṣkara-Saṃhitā

PauṣS$_1$. Sree Poushkara Samhita. One of the Three Gems in Pancharatra. Edited by Sampathkumara Ramanuja Muni. Bangalore: A. Srinivasa Aiyangar and M.C. Thirumalachariar, 1934.

PauṣS$_2$. Pauṣkara Saṁhitā. Critically edited <and translated> by P.P. Apte. <Part 1.> Tirupati: Rashtriya Sanskrit Vidyapeetha, 1991.

Pratyabhijñāhṛdaya of Kṣemarāja. Edited by J.C. Chatterji. Srinagar: Archaeological and Research Department, 1911.

Bṛhat-Saṃhitā

Varāhamihira's Bṛhat Saṃhitā with English Translation, Exhaustive Notes and Literary Comments by M. Ramakrishna Bhat. 2 parts. Delhi: Motilal Banarsidass, 1981–1982.

The Bṛhat-Saṅhitâ; or, Complete System of Natural Astrology of Varâha-mihira. Translated from Sanskrit into English by H. Kern. Journal of the Royal Asiatic Society of Great Britain and Ireland, new series, 4. 1870: 430–479; 5. 1871: 45–90, 231–288; 6. 1872: 36–91, 279–338; 7. 1875: 81–134.

BM. Bhadramārtaṇḍa

Atha bṛhajjyotiṣārṇavāntargate ṣaṣṭhe miśraskandhe bhadramārtaṇḍākhyaḥ saptadaśo 'dhyāyaḥ prārabhyate. Bombay: Śrīveṅkaṭeśvar Press, 1933 (second edition; first printed at Aurangabad in 1883 and at Bombay in 1902).

Brahmayāmala. Manuscript 3-370, preserved in the National Archives, Kathmandu (see Goudriaan 1981: 42–44).

Bhaktāmarastotra. Camaktī maṅgalmaya adbhuta-navasmaraṇam. Śrīvarddhamān bhaktāmara, navasmaraṇam, kalyāṇamaṅgala stotram. Edited by Ghāsīlālјī Mahārāj/Madanlālјī Mahārāj/S.D. Gomāṇṭh. Kāṃkarolī: Śrī Hind Kānūn Printing Press, 1943/1944 (third edition).

Bhārgava-Tantra. Bhargava Tantra. Edited by R.P. Chaudhary. Allahabad: Rashtriya Sanskrit Sansthan, 1981.

Mataṅgapārameśvarāgama. Mataṅgapārameśvarāgama, avec le commentaire de Bhaṭṭa Rāmakaṇṭha. Édition critique par N.R. Bhatt. 2 volumes. Pondichéry: Institut Français d'Indologie, 1977–1982.

Manu-Smṛti. Manusmṛti With the Sanskrit Commentary Manvarthamuktāvalī of Kullūka Bhaṭṭa. Edited by J.L. Shastri. Delhi: Motilal Banarsidass, 1983, 1990 (reprint).

Mantramahodadhi. Mantramahodadhiḥ saṭīkaḥ. Bombay: Śrīveṅkaṭeśvar Steam Press, 1910, 1962 (re-edited), 1983 (reprint).

Mayamata. Mayamata, traité sanskrit d'architecture. Édition critique, traduction et notes par B. Dagens. 2 volumes. Pondichéry: Institut Français d'Indologie, 1970–1976.
[English version: Mayamatam: treatise on housing, architecture and iconography. Sanskrit text edited and translated by B. Dagens. 2 volumes. New Delhi: Indira Gandhi National Centre for the Arts and Motilal Banarsidass Publishers Pvt. Ltd., 1994.]

Mālinīvijaya/Mālinīvijayottara
Mālinīvijaya. Sri Mālinīvijayottara Tantram. <Edited> by Madhusūdan Kaul. Bombay: Tatva-Vivechaka Press, 1922.
Mālinīvijayottara. Electronic text prepared by S. Vasudeva, containing his unpublished critical edition of chapters 1–4, 7 and 11–17.[2]

Mṛgendrāgama
Mṛgendrāgama (Edition of *kriyāpāda* and *caryāpāda*). Mṛgendrāgama (*Kriyāpāda* et *Caryāpāda*) avec le commentaire de Bhaṭṭa-Nārāyaṇakaṇṭha. Édition critique par N.R. Bhatt. Pondichéry: Institut Français d'Indologie, 1962.
Mṛgendrāgama (Translation of *kriyāpāda* and *caryāpāda*). Mṛgendrāgama. Section des Rites et Section du Comportement, avec la vṛtti de Bhaṭṭanārāyaṇakaṇṭha. Traduction, Introduction et Notes par H. Brunner. Pondichéry: Institut Français d'Indologie, 1985.

Yantracintāmaṇi. Yantracintāmaṇiḥ of Dāmodara. Critically edited by H.-G. Türstig. Stuttgart: Steiner Verlag, 1988.

YH. Yoginīhṛdaya. See Padoux 1994.

Rauravāgama. Édition critique par N.R. Bhatt. 3 volumes. Pondichéry: Institut Français d'Indologie, 1961–1988.

Lakṣmī-Tantra
Lakṣmī-Tantra. A Pāñcarātra Āgama. Edited with Sanskrit Gloss and Introduction by V. Krishnamacharya. Madras: The Adyar Library and Research Centre, 1959, 1975 (reprint).
Lakṣmī Tantra. A Pāñcarātra Text. Translation and Notes by S. Gupta. Leiden: E.J. Brill, 1972.

Lalitāsahasranāma. Lalitâsahasranâma (of the second part of Brahmâṇdapurâṇa.) With the Commentary Saubhâgya-Bhâskara of Bhâskararâya. Edited by W.L. S'âstrî Faṇs'îkar. Bombay: Nirṇaya Sâgar Press, 1927 (third edition).

Viśvāmitra-Saṃhitā. Viśvāmitra Saṁhitā. Critically edited by U. Shankara Bhatta. Tirupati: Kendriya Sanskrit Vidyapeetha, 1970.

Viṣṇu-Saṃhitā. The Viṣṇu Saṁhitā. Edited by M.M. Gaṇapati Sāstrī. With an Elaborate Introduction by N.P. Unni. Delhi: Nag Publishers, 1991 (revised and enlarged edition; first edition 1925).

Viṣvaksena-Saṃhitā. Viṣvaksena Saṁhitā. Critically edited by L.N. Bhatta. Tirupati: Kendriya Sanskrit Vidyapeetha, 1972.

Vīṇāśikha. The Vīṇāśikhatantra. A Śaiva Tantra of the Left Current. Edited with an introduction and a translation by T. Goudriaan. Delhi: Motilal Banarsidass, 1985.

Vratodyāpanakaumudī. Atha cittapāvanakulābdhisaṃbhava-ghāre-ityupanāmaka-ballāḷasūrīsūnu-śaṃkaraviracitā vratodyāpanakaumudīprārambhaḥ. Bombay: Jñānadarpaṇ Press, no date.

Śabdakalpadruma. See Deva, Raja Radha Kanta 1961.

[2] J. Törzsök would like to express her thanks to S. Vasudeva for making this electronic text available to her.

Śāktānandataraṅgiṇī. Brahmanandagiri's Sakatanandtarangini. Text with Hindi Translation by R.K. Rai. Varanasi: Prachya Prakashan, 1993.

Śāntisāra. Atha śāntisāraprārambhaḥ <dinakarabhaṭṭakṛtaḥ>. Mumbaī: V.V. Goḍbole, 1861.

ŚT. Śāradātilaka

Śāradātilakam of Śrī Lakśmaṇadeśikendra [*sic!*] with Padārthādarśa Commentary by Śrīmad Rāghava Bhaṭṭa. Edited by M. Jha Bkashi. Varanasi: Chaukhambha Sanskrit Sansthan, 1986 (third edition).

Śrītattvacintāmaṇi. Pūrṇānanda's Śrītattvacintāmaṇi. Critically Edited from Original Manuscripts (Chapters I–XVIII) with an original commentary by Bhuvanmohan Sankhyatirtha and (Chapters XIX–XXVI) with Notes by Chintamani Bhattacharya. Introduction by Prabodhchandra Bagchi. Delhi Motilal Banarsidass, 1994 (reprint).

Śrīpraśna-Saṃhitā. Śrīpraśna Samhitā. Edited by S. Padmanabhan with the Foreword of V. Raghavan. Tirupati: Kendriya Sanskrit Vidyapeetha, 1969.

Sanatkumāra-Saṃhitā. Sanatkumāra-Saṃhitā of the Pāñcarātrāgama. Edited by V. Krishnamacharya. Madras: The Adyar Library and Research Centre, 1969.

Sātvata-Saṃhitā

Sātvata-Saṁhitā. With Commentary by Alaśiṅga Bhaṭṭa. Edited by V.V. Dwivedi. Varanasi: Sampurnanand Sanskrit Vishvavidyalaya, 1982.

Hikita, H. 1990. Sāttvata Saṃhitā: An Annotated Translation, Chapter 17 (1). Sōtō-shū kenkyū kiyō 21: 190–137.

Hikita, H. 1991. Sāttvata Saṃhitā: An Annotated Translation, Chapter 10–11. Aichigakuin daigaku zen kenkyūjo kiyō 18–19: 340–294.

Hikita, H. 1992. Sāttvata Saṃhitā: An Annotated Translation, Chapter 17 (2). Sōtō-shū kenkyū kiyō 23: 214–168.

Sātvata-Saṃhitā-Bhāṣya. See Sātvata-Saṃhitā.

Sārdhatriśatikālottarāgama. Sārdhatriśatikālottarāgama avec le commentaire de Bhaṭṭa Rāmakaṇṭha. Édition critique par N.R. Bhatt. Pondichéry: Institut Français d'Indologie, 1979.

Siddhayogeśvarīmata. See Törzsök 1999a and Törzsök forthcoming.

Siddhāntaśekhara. Ubhayavedānti-viśvanāthakṛtaḥ siddhāntaśekharaḥ. Edited by S. Somayājin. Mysore: Tāṇḍavamūrti Mudraṇālaya, 1971.

Siddhāntasārāvali (with Anantaśambhu's commentary). Siddhāntasārāvali of Trilocanaśivācārya with commentary of Anantaśivācārya. Edited by A.A. Ramanathan et al. 6 parts. Government Oriental Manuscripts Library Bulletin (Madras) 17.1: 29–68; 17.2: 1–48; 18.2: 1–64; 19.1: 53–84; 19.2: 1–48; 20.2: 49–71. 1965–1972.

Suprabhedāgama. (No editor accredited.) Madras (Çintatripeṭṭai): ÇivañāNapotayantraçālai, 1929 (*kaliyuga* 5030) (in *grantha* characters).

Sūryasiddhānta by Varāhamihira

Sūrya-Siddhānta: A Text Book of Hindu Astronomy. Translated by E. Burgess. New Haven: American Oriental Society, 1860.

Saundaryalaharī. Saundarya-Laharī of Śrī Śaṃkarācārya. With Commentaries Saubhāgyavardhanī of Kaivalyāśrama, Lakṣmīdharā of Lakṣmīdharācārya, Aruṇāmodinī of Kāmeśvarasūrin. English Translation and Notes by R. Anantakṛṣṇa Śāstrī and K.R. Gāru. Prayogas illustrated with Yantras. Madras: Ganesh & Co., 1957.

SP. Somaśambhupaddhati

SP1, SP2, SP3, SP4. Somaśambhupaddhati. Texte, traduction et notes par H. Brunner-Lachaux. 4 volumes. Pondichéry: Institut Français d'Indologie, 1963–1998.

Spandanirṇaya. The Spandakarikas of Vasugupta. With the Nirnaya by Ksemaraja. Edited by Madhusudan Kaul Shastri. Srinagar: Kashmir Pratap Steam Press, 1925.

SvT. Svacchandatantra

SvT1. The Swacchanda-Tantra, with commentary of Kshemaraja. Edited with notes by Madhusudan Kaul. 6 volumes. Bombay: Nirṇaya-Sagar Press, 1921–1935.

SvT2. Svacchandatantra. Svacchandataṇtram with commentary 'Uddyota' by Kṣemarāja. Edited by V.V. Dwivedi. 2 volumes. Delhi: Parimal Publications, 1985.

Svāyambhuvasūtrasaṃgraha. Electronic text prepared by D. Goodall, based on the Mysore edition of 1937 (edited by Veṅkaṭasubrahmaṇyaśāstrī), with corrections and notes.[3]

Secondary Sources

Abbott, J. 1932. The Keys of Power: A Study of Indian Ritual and Belief. London: Methuen & Co.

Acharya, P.K. 1946. An Encyclopedia of Hindu Architecture. London: Oxford University Press.

Apte, P.P. 1973. Maṇḍalārādhana (Diagram Worship in Āgamas). Journal of the Oriental Institute (Baroda) 22: 501–524.

Apte, P.P. 1975. Maṇḍala-Diagrams (An Artist's Approach). Proceedings of the All-India Oriental Conference, Poona: 367–374.

Apte, P.P. 1986. Vāstu-Puruṣa-Maṇḍala—A Micro-Cosmic Architectural Plan. Seminar on Vaastushastra in Perspective, January 27, 28, 1986, organized by: Pune Construction Engineering Research Foundation, Pune -4. Institute of Engineering (India). Pune Local Centre, Pune -5. Vaastu Vedic Research Foundation, Madras. Maharashtra Chapter, Pune: 1–35.

Apte, P.P. 1987. The Scheme of Mandala-Diagrams and Vāstupuruṣa-Maṇḍala in the Vaiṣṇava Āgama: Structure, Colours, Ritual and Architectural Aspects. In: Vaiṣṇavism in Indian Arts and Culture (Collected Papers of the University Grants Commission National Seminar on 'Impact of Vaiṣṇavism in the Indian Arts'). Edited by R. Parimoo. New Delhi: Books & Books: 127–149.

Apte, P.<P.> 1999. The Introduction to Jayākhya Saṃhitā by Benoytosh Bhattacharyya and Indological Chronology. In: Tantric Buddhism: Centennial Tribute to Dr. Benoytosh Bhattacharyya. Edited by N.N. Bhattacharyya. New Delhi: Manohar: 17–22.

Apte, P.P. and S.G. Supekar 1983. Vāstu-Puruṣa-Maṇḍala in the Pauṣkara-Saṁhitā and Bṛhat-Saṁhitā—A Comparative Study. Bulletin of the Deccan College Research Institute 43: 5–17. [This article also appeared in: Agama and Silpa. Proceedings of the Seminar Held in December, 1981. Edited by K.K.A. Venkatachari. Bombay: Ananthacharya Indological Research Institute, 1984: 132–148.]

---

[3] J. Törzsök would like to express her thanks to D. Goodall for making this text available to her.

Apte, R.N. 1926. Some Points Connected with the Constructive Geometry of Vedic Altars. Annals of the Bhandarkar Institute 7: 1–16.

Apte, V.S. 1957. The Practical Sanskrit-English Dictionary. Revised & Enlarged Edition. Poona: Prasad Prakashan, Kyoto: Rinsen Book Company, 1992 (third reprint).

Arraj, W.J. 1988. The Svacchandatantram: History and Structure of Śaiva Scripture (unpublished doctoral dissertation, submitted to the Department of South Asian Languages and Civilizations, the University of Chicago).

Auer, G. and N. Gutschow 1974. Bhaktapur: Gestalt, Funktionen and religiöse Symbolik einer nepalischen Stadt im vorindustriellen Entwicklungsstadium. Aufgezeichnet und interpretiert von G. Auer and N. Gutschow. Darmstadt: Technische Universität.

Bafna, S. 2000. On the Idea of the Mandala as a Governing Device in Indian Architectural Tradition. Journal of the Society of Architectural Historians 59: 26–49.

Bag, A.K. 1971. The Knowledge of Geometrical Figures, Instruments and Units in the Śulbasūtras. East and West 21: 111–119.

Bahulkar, S. 1979. Concept of Dharmodayā (Chos Ḥbyuṅ). Report of the Japanese Association for Tibetan Studies 25: 13–16.

Banerji, S.C. 1978: Tantra in Bengal: A Study in its Origin, Development and Influence. Calcutta: Naya Prokash.

Bangdel, D. 1999. Manifesting the Maṇḍala: A Study of the Core Iconographic Program of Newar Buddhist Monasteries in Nepal. 3 volumes (unpublished doctoral dissertation, submitted to the Department of History of Art, Ohio State University).

Bäumer, B. 1986. Pañjara et yantra: le diagramme de l'image sacrée. In: Mantras et diagrammes rituels dans l'hindouisme. Table Ronde, Paris 21–22 juin 1984. <Edited by A. Padoux.> Paris: Éditions du Centre national de la recherche scientifique: 49–61.

Beckman, H. 1996. Mantras, Yantras & Fabulous Gems. The Healing secrets of the ancient Vedas. [Hastings:] Balaji Publishing Co.

Begley, W.E. 1973. Viṣṇu's Flaming Wheel: The Iconography of the *Sudarśana-Cakra*. New York: New York University Press.

Béguin, G. 1990. Art ésotérique de l'Himâlaya: Catalogue de la donation Lionel Fournier. Paris: Éditions de la Réunion des musées nationaux.

Bernier, R.M. 1978. Wooden Windows of Nepal—An Illustrated Analysis. Artibus Asiae 39: 251–267.

Bernier, R.M. 1979. The Nepalese Pagoda: Origins and Style. New Delhi: S. Chand & Company Ltd.

Bhandarkar, R.G. 1965. Vaiṣṇavism, Śaivism and Minor Religious Systems. Varanasi: Indological Book House.

Bhattacharyya, T. 1986. The Canons of Indian Art, or, A Study on Vāstuvidyā. Calcutta: Firma K.L. Mukhopadhyay Private Ltd. (third revised and enlarged edition).

Bizot, F. 1981. Notes sur les *yantra* bouddhiques d'indochine. In: Tantric and Taoist Studies in Honour of R.A. Stein. Edited by M. Strickmann. Bruxelles: Institut belge des hautes études chinoises. Volume 1: 155–191.

Bodewitz, H.W. 1979. The Raising of the Central Pillar (Made of Udumbara Wood) of the Sadas Hut by the Udgātṛ, according to Jaiminīya Brāhmaṇa I.70-72. In: Ludwik Sternbach Felicitation Volume. Part 1. Edited by J.P. Sinha. Lucknow: Akhila Bharatiya Sanskrit Parishad: 77–82.

Bolton, N.J. and D.N.G. Macleod 1977. The Geometry of the Śrī-Yantra. Religion: Journal of Religion and Religions 7: 66–85.

Boner, A. 1975. Extracts from the Śilpasāriṇī. In: Studies in Indian Temple Architecture. Papers presented at a Seminar held in Varanasi, 1967. Edited by Pramod Chandra. New Delhi: American Institute of Indian Studies: 57–79.

Bourquin, A. 1884. Brahmakarma ou rites sacrés des Brahmanes, traduit du Sanscrit et annoté. Annales du Musée Guimet 7. Paris: Ernest Leroux.

Brentjes, B. 1981. Die Stadt des Yima: Weltbilder in der Architektur. Leipzig: E.A. Seemann Verlag.

Brooks, D.R. 1990. *The Secret of the Three Cities*: An Introduction to Hindu Śākta Tantrism. Chicago: The University of Chicago Press.

Brooks, D.R. 1992. Auspicious Wisdom: The Texts and Traditions of Śrīvidyā Śākta Tantrism in South India. Albany, New York: State University of New York Press.

Brown, W.N. 1942. The Creation Myth of the Rig Veda. Journal of the American Oriental Society 62: 85–98 (reprinted in Rocher 1978: 20–33).

Brown, W.N. 1965. Theories of Creation in the Rig Veda. Journal of the American Oriental Society 85: 23–34 (reprinted in Rocher 1978: 40–52).

Brunner, H. 1975. Le *sādhaka*, personnage oublié du śivaïsme du Sud. Journal Asiatique 263: 411–443.

Brunner, H. 1977. Importance de la littérature āgamique pour l'étude des religions vivantes de l'Inde. In: Indologica Taurinensia III–IV. Torino: 107–124.

Brunner, H. 1986. Maṇḍala et yantra dans le śivaïsme āgamique: Définition, description, usage rituel. In: Mantras et diagrammes rituels dans l'hindouisme. Table Ronde, Paris 21–22 juin 1984. <Edited by A. Padoux.> Paris: Éditions du Centre national de la recherche scientifique 11–31.

Brunner, H. 1992. Jñāna and Kriyā: Relation between Theory and Practice in the Śaivāgamas. In: Ritual and Speculation in Early Tantrism. Studies in Honor of André Padoux. Edited by T. Goudriaan. Albany, New York: State University of New York Press: 1–59.

Bühnemann, G. 1983. Budha-Kauśika's Rāmarakṣāstotra: A Contribution to the Study of Sanskrit Devotional Poetry. Vienna: Institute for Indology.

Bühnemann, G. 1987. Bhadramaṇḍalas in the Ritual Practice. Wiener Zeitschrift für die Kunde Südasiens 31: 43–73.

Bühnemann, G. 1988a. Pūjā: A Study in Smārta Ritual. Vienna: Institute for Indology.

Bühnemann, G. 1988b. The Worship of Mahāgaṇapati according to the Nityotsava. Wichtrach: Institut für Indologie.

Bühnemann, G. 1992. On Puraścaraṇa: Kulārṇavatantra, Chapter 15. In: Ritual and Speculation in Early Tantrism. Studies in Honor of André Padoux. Edited by T. Goudriaan. Albany, New York: State University of New York Press: 61–106.

Bühnemann, G. 2000–2001. The Iconography of Hindu Tantric Deities. 2 volumes. Volume I: The Pantheon of the Mantramahodadhi. Volume II: The Pantheons of the Prapañcasāra and the Śāradātilaka. Groningen: Egbert Forsten.

Bühnemann, G. 2005. A Note on the Term Smārta and the Smārta Tradition. In: *Kalhāra-Mālikā: Adhyāpak Enamul Haque Abhinandan Grantha* (*Felicitation volume for Enamul Haque*). Edited by G. Bhattacharya. Delhi: Kaveri Books (forthcoming).

Bulcke, C. 1962. Rām-Kathā (utpatti aur vikās). Prayāg: Hindī Pariṣad Prakāśan (second edition).

Bunce, F.W. 2001. The Yantras of Deities and their Numerological Foundations—an Iconographic Consideration. New Delhi: D.K. Printworld (P) Ltd.

Bunce, F.W. 2002. The Iconography of Architectural Plans: A Study of the Influence of Buddhism and Hinduism on Plans of South and Southeast Asia. New Delhi: D.K. Printworld (P) Ltd.

Cairns, G.E. 1992. Man as Microcosm in Tantric Hinduism. New Delhi: Manohar Publications.

Cammann, S. 1969. Islamic and Indian Magic Squares. 2 parts. History of Religions 8: 181–209, 271–299.

Chakravorty Spivak, G. 1999. Moving Devi. In: Devi, The Great Goddess: Female Divinity in South Asian Art. Edited by V. Dehejia. Washington, D.C.: Arthur M. Sackler Gallery: 181–200.

Chattopadhyaya, D. 1973. Lokāyata: A Study in Ancient Indian Materialism. New Delhi: People's Publishing House (third edition).

Chattopadhyaya, S. 1978. Reflections on the Tantras. Delhi: Motilal Banarsidass.

Chawdhri, L.R. 1990. Practicals of Yantras. New Delhi: Sagar Publications (second revised and enlarged edition).

Chawdhri, L.R. 1992. Secrets of Yantra, Mantra and Tantra. New Delhi: Sterling Publishers.

Chenet, F. 1986. De l'efficience psychagogique des *mantras* et des *yantras*. In: Mantras et diagrammes rituels dans l'hindouisme. Table Ronde, Paris 21–22 juin 1984. <Edited by A. Padoux.> Paris: Éditions du Centre national de la recherche scientifique: 65–78.

Coburn, T.B. 1991. Encountering the Goddess: A Translation of the *Devī-Māhātmya* and A Study of Its Interpretation. Albany: State University of New York Press.

Colas, G. 1986. La vision de la divinité dans les diagrammes selon le vishnouisme vaikhānasa. In: Mantras et diagrammes rituels dans l'hindouisme. Table Ronde, Paris 21–22 juin 1984. <Edited by A. Padoux.> Paris: Éditions du Centre national de la recherche scientifique: 83–95.

Conio, C. 1986. Les diagrammes cosmogoniques du Svacchandatantra: Perspectives philosophiques. In: Mantras et diagrammes rituels dans l'hindouisme. Table Ronde, Paris 21–22 juin 1984. <Edited by A. Padoux.> Paris: Éditions du Centre national de la recherche scientifique: 99–113.

Coomaraswamy, A.K. (1927) 1985. History of Indian and Indonesian Art. New York: Dover Publications.

Correa, C. 1996. Charles Correa. London: Thames & Hudson.

Ḍabrāl, L. 1934. Śrīyantra kā svarūp. Kalyāṇ (Gītā Press, Gorakhpur), Śakti *aṅka*: 592–609.

Dakshinaranjan Shastri 1940. Altars, Diagrams, etc. in the Ritual of Ancestor-Worship. Journal of the Indian Society of Oriental Art 8: 166–173.

Dakshinaranjan Shastri 1963: Origin and Development of the Rituals of Ancestor Worship in India. Calcutta: Bookland Private Limited.

Daniélou, A. 1964. Hindu Polytheism. London: Routledge & Kegan Paul.
[Slightly different from: A. Daniélou: Le polythéisme hindou. Paris: Buchet/Chastel, 1960.]

Daniélou, A. 1977. Le temple hindou: Centre magique du monde. Paris: Buchet/Chastel.
[English translation: The Hindu Temple: Deification of Eroticism. Translation by K. Hurry. Rochester, Vermont: Inner Traditions, 2001.]

Datta, B. 1932. The Science of the Śulba: A Study in Early Hindu Geometry. Calcutta: The University of Calcutta.

De Mallmann, M.-Th. 1986. Introduction à l'iconographie du tântrisme bouddhique. Paris: J. Maisonneuve.

Deep, D.K. 1993. Popular Deities, Emblems & Images of Nepal. Jaipur/New Delhi: Nirala Publications.

Dehejia, V. 1986. Yoginī Cult and Temples: A Tantric Tradition. New Delhi: National Museum.

Deva, Raja Radha Kanta 1961. Sabda-Kalpadrum: An Encyclopedic Dictionary of Sanskrit Words. 5 parts. Varanasi: Chowkhamba Sanskrit Series Office.

Devarāj Vidyāvācaspati 1934. Tantra meṃ yantra aur mantra. Kalyāṇ (Gītā Press, Gorakhpur), Śakti *aṅka*: 387–397.

Dietrich, A. 1998. Tantric Healing in the Kathmandu Valley: A comparative study of Hindu and Buddhist spiritual healing traditions in urban Nepalese society. Delhi: Book Faith India.

Drège, J.-P. 1999–2000. Les premières impressions des *dhāraṇī* de Mahāpratisarā. Cahiers d'Extrême-Asie 11: 25–44.

Dyczkowski, M.S.G. 1988. The Canon of the Śaivāgama and the Kubjikā Tantras of the Western Kaula Tradition: Albany, New York: State University of New York Press.

Dyczkowski, M.S.G. 2001. The Cult of the Goddess Kubjikā: A Preliminary Comparative Textual and Anthropological Survey of a Secret Newar Kaula Goddess. Stuttgart: Franz Steiner Verlag.

Elder, G.R. 1978. The Saṃpuṭa Tantra: Edition and Translation, Chapters I–IV (unpublished doctoral dissertation, submitted to the Faculty of Philosophy, Columbia University).

Eliade, M. 1969. Yoga: Immortality and Freedom. Princeton, New Jersey: Princeton University Press (second edition with corrections and additional bibliographical notes).

English, E. 2002. Vajrayoginī: Her Visualizations, Rituals, & Forms. A Study of the Cult of Vajrayoginī in India. Somerville, Massachusetts: Wisdom Publications.

Fonseca, R. 1986. Constructive Geometry and the Śrī-Cakra Diagram. Religion 16: 33–49.

Gaborieau, G. 1993. Des dieux dans toutes les directions: Conception indienne de l'espace et classification des dieux. In: Classer les dieux? Des panthéons en Asie du Sud. Classifying Gods? Pantheons in South Asia. Études réunies par V. Bouillier et G. Toffin. Paris: Collection Puruṣārtha: 23–42.

Gaeffke, P. 1987. Hindu Maṇḍalas. In: The Encyclopedia of Religion. Editor in Chief: M. Eliade. Volume 9. New York: MacMillan Publishing Company: 153–155.

Gail, A.J. 1984–1988. Tempel in Nepal. 2 volumes. Graz: Akademische Druck- und Verlagsanstalt.

Garzilli, E. 2000. Flowers of Consciousness in Tantric Texts: The Sacred Lotus. In: Pandanus (2000): Natural Symbolism in Indian Literatures. Edited by J. Vacek. Prague: Signeta: 73–102.

Ghoshal Sastri, S.N. 1983. Elements of Indian Aesthetics (in three Volumes). Volume II: Two Streams of Indian Arts (in four parts). Part IV: Primitive Arts, Crafts and Ālpanā (accompanied with three separate parts). Varanasi: Chaukhambha Orientalia.

Gode, P.K. 1947. History of the raṅgavallī (rāṅgoḷī) art between c. A.D. 50 and 1900. Annals of the Bhandarkar Oriental Research Institute 28: 226–246. [Reprinted in: Studies in Indian Cultural History by P.K. Gode. Volume 3. Poona: Bhandarkar Oriental Research Institute, 1969: 87–102.]

Gonda, J. 1977. Medieval Religious Literature in Sanskrit. Wiesbaden: Otto Harrassowitz.

Gonda, J. 1980. Vedic Ritual: The Non-Solemn Rites. Leiden: E.J. Brill.

Goodall, D. 2000. Problems of Name and Lineage: Relationships between South Indian authors of the Śaiva Siddhānta. Journal of the Royal Asiatic Society. Series 3. 10: 205–216.

Goudriaan, T. 1978. Māyā Divine and Human: A study of magic and its religious foundation in Sanskrit texts, with particular attention to a fragment on Viṣṇu's māyā preserved in Bali. Delhi: Motilal Banarsidass.

Goudriaan, T. and S. Gupta 1981. Hindu Tantric and Śākta Literature. Wiesbaden: Otto Harrassowitz.

Granoff, P. 2000. Other People's Rituals: Ritual Eclecticism in Early Medieval Indian Religious [*sic!*]. Journal of Indian Philosophy 28: 399–424.

Granoff, P. 2001. My Rituals and My Gods: Ritual Exclusiveness in Medieval India. Journal of Indian Philosophy 29: 109–134.

Guptā, A. 1984. Ānanda-Rāmāyaṇa kā sāṃskṛtik adhyayan. Dillī: Eastern Book Linkers.

Gupta, S. 1976. Viṣvaksena the Divine Protector. Wiener Zeitschrift für die Kunde Südasiens 20: 75–89.

Gupta, S. 1988. The Maṇḍala as an Image of Man. In: Indian Ritual and Its Exegesis. Oxford University Papers on India, volume 2/2. Edited by R.F. Gombrich. Delhi: Oxford University Press: 32–41.

Gupta, S./D.J. Hoens/T. Goudriaan 1979. Hindu Tantrism. Leiden: E.J. Brill.

Gutschow, N. 1982. Stadtraum und Ritual der newarischen Städte im Kāṭhmāṇḍu-Tal: Eine architekturanthropologische Untersuchung. Stuttgart: W. Kohlhammer.

Gutschow, N. 1997. The Nepalese Caitya: 1500 Years of Buddhist Votive Architecture in the Kathmandu Valley. Stuttgart/London: Edition Axel Menges.

Gutschow, N. and B. Kölver 1975. Ordered Space: Concepts and Functions in a Town of Nepal. Wiesbaden: Franz Steiner GmbH.

Gutschow, N./B. Kölver/I.Shresthacarya 1987. Newar Towns and Buildings: An Illustrated Dictionary Newārī – English. Sankt Augustin: VGH Wissenschafts-verlag.

Havell [Chandra] 1964.
Havell, E.B.: The Art Heritage of India. Comprising Indian Sculpture and Painting and Ideals of Indian Art. Revised Edition with Notes by Pramod Chandra. Bombay: D.B. Taraporevala Songs & Co.

Heesterman, J.C. 1962. Vrātya and Sacrifice. Indo-Iranian Journal 6: 1–37.

Heilijgers-Seelen, D. 1990. The Doctrine of the Ṣaṭcakra according to the Kubjikā-mata. In: The Sanskrit Tradition and Tantrism. Panels of the VIIth World Sanskrit Conference, Kern Institute, Leiden: August 23–29, 1987. Edited by T. Goudriaan. Leiden: E.J. Brill: 56–65.

Heilijgers-Seelen, D. 1994. The System of Five Cakras in *Kubjikāmatatantra* 14-16. Groningen: Egbert Forsten.

Hikita, H. 1990, 1991, 1992. See Sātvata-Saṃhitā.

Hooykaas, C. 1980. Drawings of Balinese Sorcery, published with a Commentary. Leiden: E.J. Brill.

Huyler, S.P. 1999. Meeting God: Elements of Hindu Devotion. New Haven: Yale University Press.

Jain, J. 1997. Ganga Devi: Tradition and Expression in Mithila Paintings. Middletown, New Jersey: Grantha Corporation.

Jhavery, M.B. 1944. Comparative and Critical Study of Mantrasastra (With Special Treatment of Jain Mantravada), Being the Introduction to Sri Bhairava Padmavati Kalpa. Ahmedabad: Sarabhai Manilal Nawab.

Johari, H. 1986. Tools for Tantra. Rochester, Vermont: Destiny Books.

Jones, C.R. 1981. Dhūlicitra: Historical Perspectives on Art and Ritual. In: Kalādarśana: American Studies in the Art of India. Edited by J.G. Williams. New Delhi: Oxford & IBH Publishing Co.: 69–75.

Joshi, H.R. 1981. Shatkon. Rolamba (Tri-monthly research journal, Joshi Research Institute, Lalitpur, Nepal) 1: 2–4.

Jung, C.G. 1950. Über Mandalasymbolik. In: Gestaltungen des Unbewussten. Zürich: Rascher Verlag: 187–235.
[English translation: Concerning Mandala Symbolism. In: The Archetypes and the Collective Unconscious. The Collected Works of C.G. Jung, volume 9, part 1. London: Routledge & Kegan Paul, 1953 (second edition): 355ff.]

Jung, C.G. 1964. Die Mandalasymbolik. In: Traumsymbole des Individuationsprozesses. Olten/Freiburg im Breisgau: Walter-Verlag: 103ff.

Kagal, C. (ed.) 1986. Vistara: The Architecture of India. Catalogue of the Exhibition. Bombay: Festival of India.

Kahrs, E. 1998. Indian semantic analysis. The 'nirvacana' tradition. Cambridge: Cambridge University Press.

Kane, P.V. 1968–1977. History of Dharmaśāstra (Ancient and Mediaeval Religious and Civil Law in India). 5 volumes. Poona: Bhandarkar Oriental Research Institute (second edition).

Kenoyer, J.M. 1998. Ancient Cities of the Indus Valley Civilization. Karachi: Oxford University Press.

Khan, H. 1987. Charles Correa. Singapore: Concept Media Pte Ltd (completely revised edition of the first edition 1984).

Khanna, M. 1979. Yantra: The Tantric Symbol of Cosmic Unity. London: Thames and Hudson.

Khanna, M. 1986. The Concept and Liturgy of the Śrīcakra based on Śivānanda's Trilogy (unpublished doctoral dissertation, submitted to Wolfson College, Oxford University).

Khanna, M. 1987. Yantra. In: The Encyclopedia of Religion. Editor in Chief: M. Eliade. Volume 15. New York: MacMillan Publishing Company: 500–502.

Khurrana, P. 2000. Healing through Yantra. New Delhi: Crest Publishers.

Kölver, B. 1992a. Some Examples of Syncretism in Nepal. In: Aspects of Nepalese Traditions. Edited by B. Kölver. Stuttgart: Franz Steiner Verlag: 209–222.

Kölver, B. 1992b. Das Symbol *evaṃ*. Studien zur Indologie und Iranistik 16: 101–107.

Kölver, B. 1996. Constructing Pagodas according to Traditional Nepalese Drawings. Berlin: Akademie Verlag.

Kölver, U. and I. Shresthacarya 1994. A Dictionary of Contemporary Newari. Newari – English. Bonn: VGH Wissenschaftsverlag.

Kossak, S.M. and J.C. Singer 1998. Sacred Visions: Early Paintings from Central Tibet. New York: The Metropolitan Museum of Art.

Kramrisch, S. 1946. The Hindu Temple. 2 volumes. Calcutta: University of Calcutta Press.

Kramrisch, S. 1981. The Presence of Śiva. Princeton: Princeton University Press.

Kreijger, H.E. 1999. Kathmandu Valley Painting: The Jucker Collection. London: Serindia Publications.

Kulaichev, A.P. 1984. *Śrīyantra* and its Mathematical Properties. Indian Journal of History of Science 19: 279–292.

Kulaichev, A.P. and D.M. Ramendic 1989. *Śrīyantra*—The Ancient Instrument to Control the Psychophysiological State of Man. Indian Journal of History of Science 24: 137–149.

Kulkarni, R.P. 1979. Vāstupadamaṇḍala. Journal of the Oriental Institute (Baroda) 28: 107–138.

L'Hernault, F. 1987. Darasuram: epigraphical study, étude architecturale, étude iconographique. With the collaboration of P.R. Srinivasan and J. Dumarçay. Tome 1 – texte. Paris: Publications de l'École Française d'Extrême Orient.

Leidy, D.P. and R.A.F. Thurman 1997. Mandala: The Architecture of Enlightenment. New York: Asia Society Galleries and Tibet House.

Lessing, F.D. and A. Wayman 1978. Introduction to the Buddhist Tantric Systems. Translated from MKHAS GRUB RJE'S Rgyud sde spyiḥi rnam par gźag pa rgyas par brjod With Original Text and Annotation. Delhi: Motilal Banarsidass (second edition).

Levy, R.I. 1990. Mesocosm: Hinduism and the Organization of a Traditional Newar City in Nepal. Berkeley: The University of California Press.

Libersat, M. 1988. Architects and Architecture in Kerala. In Meister 1988: 96–102.

Liebert, G. 1976. Iconographic Dictionary of the Indian Religions: Hinduism – Buddhism – Jainism. Leiden: E.J. Brill.

Lienhard, S. 1997. Martial Art and Poetics: Some More Observations on *Citrakāvya*. In: Lex et Litterae: Studies in Honour of Professor Oscar Botto. Edited by S. Lienhard and I. Piovano. Torino: Edizioni dell'Orso: 343–359.

Macdonald, A.W. and A. Vergati Stahl 1979. Newar Art: Nepalese Art during the Malla Period. Warminster: Aris & Phillips Ltd.

Matsubara, M. 1994. Pāñcarātra Saṃhitās & Early Vaiṣṇava Theology. With a Translation and Critical Notes from Chapters on Theology in the Ahirbudhnya Saṃhitā. Delhi: Motilal Banarsidass.

Mayrhofer, M. 1986–2001. Etymologisches Wörterbuch des Altindoarischen. 3 volumes. Heidelberg: Universitätsverlag C. Winter.

McGee, M. 1987. Feasting and fasting: The vrata tradition and its significance for Hindu women (unpublished doctoral dissertation, submitted to the Faculty of Harvard Divinity School, Harvard University).

Meisezahl, R.O. 1974. Śmaśānavidhi des Lūyī: Textkritik nach der tibetischen Version des Kommentars Lūyipādābhisamayavṛtti Sambarodaya nāma von Tathāgatavajra. Zentralasiatische Studien 8: 9–178.

Meister, M.W. 1978. Construction and Conception: Maṇḍapikā Shrines of Central India. East and West. New Series 26: 409–418.

Meister, M.W. 1979. Maṇḍala and Practice in Nāgara Architecture in North India. Journal of the American Oriental Society 99: 204–219.

Meister, M.W. 1981a. Darrā and the Early Gupta Tradition. In: Chhavi-2. Rai Krishnadasa Felicitation Volume. Edited by A. Krishna. Banaras: Bharat Kala Bhavan: 192–205.

Meister, M.W. 1981b. Muṇḍeśvarī: Ambiguity and Certainty in the Analysis of a Temple Plan. In: Kalādarśana: American Studies in the Art of India. Edited by J.G. Williams. New Delhi: Oxford & IBH Publishing Co.: 77–89.

Meister, M.W. 1982. Analysis of Temple Plans: Indor. Artibus Asiae 43: 302–320.

Meister, M.W. 1983a. Geometry and Measure in Indian Temple Plans: Rectangular Temples. Artibus Asiae 44: 266–296.

Meister, M.W. 1983b. The Udayeśvara Temple Plan. In: Śrīnidhiḥ: Perspectives in Indian Archaeology, Art and Culture. Edited by K.V. Raman et al. Madras: New Era Publications: 85–93.

Meister, M.W. 1984. Śiva's Forts in Central India: Temples in Dakṣiṇa Kosala and Their "Dæmonic" Plans. In: Discourses on Śiva. Proceedings of a Symposium on the Nature of Religious Imagery. Edited by M.W. Meister. Philadelphia: University of Pennsylvania Press: 119–142.

Meister, M.W. 1985. Measurement and Proportion in Hindu Temple Architecture. Interdisciplinary Science Reviews 10: 248–258.

Meister, M.W. 1986. On the Development of a Morphology for a Symbolic Architecture: India. Res Anthropology and Aesthetics 12: 33–50.

Meister, M.W. (ed.) 1988. Making Things in South Asia: The Role of Artist and Craftsman. Philadelphia: Department of South Asia Regional Studies.

Meister, M.W. 1989. Reading Monuments and Seeing Texts. In: Shastric Traditions in Indian Arts. Edited by A.L. Dallapiccola. 2 volumes. Stuttgart: Steiner Verlag: volume 1: 167–173; volume 2: 94–108 & plates 81–88.

Meister, M.W. 1990. De- and Re-constructing the Indian Temple. Art Journal 49: 395–400.

Meister, M.W. 1997. Reassessing the Text. In: Contemporary Architecture and City Form: The South Asian Paradigm. Edited by F. Ameen. Bombay: Marg Publications: 88–100.

Meister, M.W. 1999. Review of L.S. Thakur: The Architectural Heritage of Himachal Pradesh: Origin and Development of Temple Styles. The Indian Historical Review 26: 187–191.

Meister, M.W./M.A. Dhaky/K. Deva (eds.) 1988. Encylopædia of Indian Temple Architecture. Volume 2/1: North India: Foundations of North Indian Style. Princeton: Princeton University Press.

Menon, C.P.S. 1932. Early Astronomy and Cosmology: A Reconstruction of the Earliest Cosmic System. London: George Allen & Unwin Ltd.

Michael, T. 1986. Le śrī-cakra dans la Saundarya-Laharī. In: Mantras et diagrammes rituels dans l'hindouisme. Table Ronde, Paris 21–22 juin 1984. <Edited by A. Padoux.> Paris: Éditions du Centre national de la recherche scientifique: 127–137.

Michaels, A. 1996. Goddess of the Secret: Guhyeśvarī in Nepal and Her Festival. In: Wild Goddesses in India and Nepal. Proceedings of an International Symposium Berne and Zurich, November 1994. Edited by A. Michaels / C. Vogelsanger / A. Wilke. Bern: Peter Lang: 303–342.

Miśra, J. 1959. A Yantra of the Tāntrikas. Journal of the Bihar and Orissa Research Society 45: 482–488.

Mitra, H. 1958. Gaṇapati. Visva-Bharati Annals 8: 1–120.

Mookerjee, A. 1971. Tantra Asana: A Way to Self-Realization. Basel / Paris / New York: Ravi Kumar.

Mori, M. 1997. The Vajrāvalī of Abhayākaragupta: A Critical Study, Sanskrit Edition of Selected Chapters and Complete Tibetan Version (unpublished doctoral dissertation, submitted to the School of Oriental and African Studies, University of London).

Mosteller, J.F. 1988. Texts and Craftsmen at Work. In Meister 1988: 24–33.

Mosteller, J.F. 1991. The Measure of Form: A New Approach for the Study of Indian Sculpture. New Delhi: Abhinav Publications.

Mus, P. (1935) 1998. Barabuḍur: Sketch of a History of Buddhism based on Archaeological Criticism of the Texts. Translated from the French by A.W. Macdonald. New Delhi: Sterling Publishers Private Limited.
[Translation of: Mus, P.: Barabuḍur: Esquisse d'une histoire du bouddhisme fondée sur la critique archéologique des textes. Hanoi: Impr. d'Extrême-Orient, 1935. 2 volumes (published in one volume, New York: Arno Press, 1978 and Paris: Arma Artis, 1990)].

Nath, R. 1975–1976. Depiction of a Tantric Symbol in Mughal Architecture. Journal of the Indian Society of Oriental Art. New Series 7: 73–85.

Padmaja, V.T. 1985. Yantra Worship in the Śākta Centres of Gujarat. Journal of the Oriental Institute (Baroda) 34: 173–179.

Padoux, A. 1974. Introduction: *Mantra* et *yantra-maṇḍala*. In: G. Tucci: Théorie et Pratique du Mandala. Traduit de l'italien par H.J. Maxwell. Paris: Fayard: 1–8.

Padoux, A. 1977. Un terme technique du *mantraśāstra* : *vidarbha*. Journal Asiatique 265: 345–349.

Padoux, A. 1986 (ed.). Mantras et diagrammes rituels dans l'hindouisme. Table Ronde, Paris 21–22 juin 1984. Paris: Éditions du Centre national de la recherche scientifique.

Padoux, A. 1986–1992. Mantric Practices and the Nature of Mantric Utterances. The Journal of Oriental Research 56–62: 65–76.

Padoux, A. 1987a. Cakras. In: The Encyclopedia of Religion. Editor in Chief: M. Eliade. Volume 3. New York: MacMillan Publishing Company: 4–5.

Padoux, A. 1987b. Tantrism. In: The Encyclopedia of Religion. Editor in Chief: M. Eliade. Volume 14. New York: MacMillan Publishing Company: 272–274.

Padoux, A. 1990a. Vāc. The Conception of the Word in Selected Hindu Tantras. Translated by J. Gonthier. Albany, New York: State University of New York Press.

Padoux, A. 1990b. The Body in Tantric Ritual: The Case of the Mudrās. In: The Sanskrit Tradition and Tantrism. Panels of the VIIth World Sanskrit Conference, Kern Institute, Leiden: August 23–29, 1987. Edited by T. Goudriaan. Leiden: E.J. Brill: 66–75.

Padoux, A. 1994. Le cœur de la Yoginī. Yoginīhṛdaya, avec le commentaire Dīpikā d'Amṛtānanda. Paris: De Boccard.

Pal, P. 1974–1978. The Arts of Nepal. 2 parts. Leiden: E.J. Brill.

Pal, P. 1992. Himalayan *Mandalas* in the Zimmerman Collection. Orientations 23/2: 36–45.

Pal, P. 1993. Indian Painting: A Catalogue of the Los Angeles County Museum of Art Collection. Los Angeles: Los Angeles County Museum of Art.

Pal, P. 1997. A Collecting Odyssey: Indian, Himalayan, and Southeast Asian Art from the James and Marilynn Alsdorf Collection. New York: Thames and Hudson Ltd.

Panofsky, E. 1955. The History of the Theory of Human Proportions as a Reflection of the History of Styles. In: Meaning in the Visual Arts: Papers in and on Art History. Garden City, New York: Doubleday & Company, Inc.: 55–107.

Parpola, A. 2002. Pre-Proto-Iranians of Afghanistan as Initiators of Śākta Tantrism: On the Scythian/Saka Affiliation of the Dāsas, Nuristanis and Magadhans. Iranica Antiqua 37: 233–322.

Pichard, P. 1995. Tanjavur Bṛhadīśvara: An Architectural Study. New Delhi: Indira Gandhi National Centre for the Arts.

Pott, P.H. (1946) 1966. Yoga and Yantra: Their Interrelation and their Significance for Indian Archaeology. Translated from the Dutch by R. Needham. The Hague: Martinus Nijhoff.
[Translation of: Pott, P.H.: Yoga en yantra in hunne beteekenis voor de Indische archeologie. Leiden: E.J. Brill, 1946.]

Pramar, V.S. 1985. Some Evidence on the Wooden Origins of the Vāstupuruṣamaṇḍala. Artibus Asiae 46: 305–311.

Pranavananda, Swami <1977>. A Treatise on Sricakra. Yenugula Mahal: Sri Swami Pranavananda Trust: no year, approximately 1977.

Pratyagatmananda Saraswati, Swami. The Yantram. Calcutta: Benly Press: no year, 1960?

Pratyagatmananda Saraswati, Swami and J. Woodroffe 1963. Sadhana for Self-Realization (Mantras, Yantras & Tantras). Madras: Ganesh & Co.

Pruscha, C. 1994. Das Observatorium des Jai Singh: Das Yantra von Jaipur. In: Das Bauwerk und die Stadt. The Building and the Town. Aufsätze für / Essays for E.F. Sekler. Herausgegeben von W. Böhm. Wien: Böhlau Verlag: 265–268.

Rabe, M.D. 2000. Secret Yantras and Erotic Display for Hindu Temples. In: Tantra in Practice. Edited by D.G. White. Princeton, New Jersey: Princeton University Press: 434–446.

Raghavan, V. 1956. Yantras or Mechanical Contrivances in Ancient India. Bangalore: The Indian Institute of Culture (second edition, revised and enlarged).

Raghavan, V. (†) 1998. Sanskrit Rāmāyaṇas Other Than Vālmīki's - The Adbhuta, Adhyātma, and Ānanda Rāmāyaṇas. Chennai: Dr. V. Raghavan Centre for Performing Arts.

Rambelli, F. 1991. Re-inscribing *Maṇḍala*: Semiotic Operations on a Word and its Object. Studies in Central and East Asian Religions 4: 1–124.

Rangachari, D.B.K. 1930. The Sri Vaishnava Brahmans. Bulletin of the Madras Government Museum. New Series. General Section 2, 2. Delhi: Gian Publishing House, 1986 (first reprint).

Rao, C.S. 1998. Śrīyantra - A Study of Spherical and Plane Forms. Indian Journal of History of Science 33: 203–227.

Rao, D.M. 1995. Vāstuśilpaśāstra. Bangalore: S.B.S. Publishers.

Rao, S.K.R. 1988. The Yantras. Delhi: Sri Satguru Publications.

Rao, S.K.R. 1988–1990. Maṇḍalas in Temple Worship. 2 volumes. Bangalore: Kalpatharu Research Academy.

Rao, S.K.R. 1988–1992. Pratimā-Kosha. Encyclopaedia of Indian Iconography. 6 volumes. Bangalore: Kalpatharu Research Academy.

Rao, S.K.R. 1990. The Tāntrik Practices in Śrī-Vidyā (with Śrī Śāradā-Chatuśśatī). Bangalore: Kalpatharu Research Academy.

Rao, T.A.G. 1914–1916. Elements of Hindu Iconography. 2 volumes. Madras: Law Printing House.

Rastelli, M. 1999. Philosophisch-theologische Grundanschauungen der Jayākhyasaṃhitā. Mit einer Darstellung des täglichen Rituals. Wien: Verlag der Österreichischen Akademie der Wissenschaften.

Rastelli, M. 2000a. Die fünf Zeiten (*pañca kālas*) in den ältesten Pāñcarātra-Saṃhitās. Wiener Zeitschrift für die Kunde Südasiens 44: 101–134.

Rastelli, M. 2000b. The Religious Practice of the *Sādhaka* According to the Jayākhyasaṃhitā. Indo-Iranian Journal 43: 319–395.

Rastelli, M. 2002. The *āsana* According to the Pārameśvarasaṃhitā or A Method of Writing a Saṃhitā. In: Studies in Hinduism III: Pāñcarātra and Viśiṣṭādvaitavedānta. Edited by G. Oberhammer and M. Rastelli. Wien: Verlag der Österreichischen Akademie der Wissenschaften: 9–32.

Rastelli, M. 2003. Der Tempel als Mythisierung der Transzendenz. In: Mythisierung der Transzendenz als Entwurf ihrer Erfahrung. Arbeitsdokumentation eines Symposions. Herausgegeben von G. Oberhammer und M. Schmücker. Wien: Verlag der Österreichischen Akademie der Wissenschaften: 313–348.

Ray, R.A. 1973. Maṇḍala Symbolism in Tantric Buddhism (unpublished doctoral dissertation, submitted to the Faculty of the Divinity School, University of Chicago).

Reitz, F. 1998. *Pañcāyatana*-Komplexe in Nordindien. Entstehung, Entwicklung und regionale Besonderheiten einer indischen Architekturform (unpublished doctoral dissertation, submitted to the Institut für Indische Philologie und Kunstgeschichte, Freie Universität, Berlin).

Renou, L. 1998. The Vedic House. Translated and edited by M.W. Meister. Res Anthropology and Aesthetics 34: 141–161.

Renou, L. and J. Filliozat 1947–1953. L'Inde classique: Manuel des études indiennes. 2 volumes. Paris: Payot.

Rhie, M.M. and R.A.F. Thurman 1999: Worlds of Transformation: Tibetan Art of Wisdom and Compassion. New York: Tibet House.

Rhodes, N.G./K. Gabrisch/† C.V.P. della Rocchetta 1989. The Coinage of Nepal from the earliest time until 1911. London: Royal Numismatic Society.

Rocher, R. (ed.) 1978. India and Indology. Selected Articles by W. Norman Brown. Delhi: Motilal Banarsidass.

Roşu, A. 1986a. *Mantra* et *yantra* dans la médecine et l'alchimie indiennes. Journal Asiatique 274: 203–268.

Roşu, A. 1986b. *Mantra* et *yantra* dans la médecine et l'alchimie indiennes. In: Mantras et diagrammes rituels dans l'hindouisme. Table Ronde, Paris 21–22 juin 1984. <Edited by A. Padoux.> Paris: Éditions du Centre national de la recherche scientifique: 117–121.

Roşu, A. 1989. Les carrés magiques indiens et l'histoire des idées en Asie. Zeitschrift der Deutschen Morgenländischen Gesellschaft 139: 120–158.

Roy, A.K. 1977. The Dream and the Plan. Marg 4: 25–26.

Roy, M. 1984. The Concept of *Yantra* in the *Samarāṅgaṇa-Sūtradhāra* of Bhoja. Indian Journal of History of Science 19: 118–124.

Sabarathinam, S.P. 1995. Āgamic Treatment of Mahābhūtas in Relation to Maṇḍalas and Arts. In: Prakṛti: The Integral Vision. Volume 3: The Āgamic Tradition and the Arts. Edited by B. Bäumer. New Delhi: D.K. Printworld (P) Ltd.: 47–66.

Sanderson, A. 1986. Maṇḍala and Āgamic Identity in the Trika of Kashmir. In: Mantras et diagrammes rituels dans l'hindouisme. Table Ronde, Paris 21–22 juin 1984. <Edited by A. Padoux.> Paris: Éditions du Centre national de la recherche scientifique: 169–207.

Sanderson, A. 1988. Śaivism and the Tantric Traditions. In: The World's Religions. The Religions of Asia. Edited by F. Hardy. London: Routledge, 1988, 1990 (reprint): 128–172.

Sanderson, A. 1990. The Visualization of the Deities of the Trika. In: L'image divine. Culte et méditation dans l'hindouisme. Edited by A. Padoux. Paris: Éditions du Centre national de la recherche scientifique: 31–88.

Sanderson, A. 2001. History Through Textual Criticism in the Study of Śaivism, the Pañcarātra and the Buddhist Yoginītantras. In: Les Sources et le Temps. Sources and Time. A Colloquium, Pondicherry 11-13 January 1997. Edited by F. Grimal. Pondicherry: Institut Français de Pondichéry: 1–47.

Schneider, U. 1988. Tantra – Endpunkt eines strukturierten Ablaufs? Saeculum 39: 96–104.

Shankaranarayanan, S. 1970. Sri Chakra. Pondicherry: Dipti Publications.

Sharf, R.H. 2001. Visualization and Mandala in Shingon Buddhism. In: Living Images: Japanese Buddhist Icons in Context. Edited by R.H. Sharf and E.H. Sharf. Stanford, California: Stanford University Press: 151–197, 239–251.

Sharma, B.R. 1994. A Brief Note on Yantras and Maṇḍalas. In: Pandit N.R. Bhatt Felicitation Volume. Edited by P.-S. Filliozat/S.P. Narang/C.P. Bhatta. Delhi: Motilal Banarsidass: 419–424.

Shubhakaran, K.T. 1992. Mystical Formulae. Part II. Yantras. New Delhi: Sagar Publications.

Shukla, D.N. 1967. Royal Arts: Yantras and Citras. Lucknow: Vastuvanmaya-Prakasna-Sala 1967 (Student Edition).

Singh, S.K. 2000 (ed.). Mandala Festival. Kathmandu: Nepal Lithographing Co. (P) Ltd.

Sinha, A.J. 2000. Imagining Architects: Creativity in the Religious Monuments of India. Newark: University of Delaware Press.

Sircar, D.C. 1968. Studies in Indian Coins. Delhi: Motilal Banarsidass.

Smith, B.K. 1987. Exorcising the Transcendent: Strategies for Defining Hinduism and Religion. History of Religions 27: 32–55.

Smith, V.A. 1972. Coins of Ancient India: Catalogue of the Coins in the Indian Museum Calcutta. Volume I. Delhi: Indological Book House (reprint).

Snellgrove, D.L. 1959. The Hevajra Tantra: A Critical Study. 2 parts. London: Oxford University Press.

Srinivasan, P.R. 1987. See L'Hernault, F. 1987.

Staal, F. 1984. Agni. The Vedic Ritual of the Fire Altar. 2 volumes. Delhi: Motilal Banarsidass.

Stadtner, D. 1998 (ed.). A India, pórtico do norte. <catalogue of an exhibition> 3 de outubro 1998 – 10 de xaneiro 1999. Santiago de Compostela: Auditorio de Galicia.

Stoddard, H. 1999. Dynamic Structures in Buddhist *Maṇḍalas*. *Apradakṣina* [*sic!*] and Mystic Heat in the Mother *Tantra* Section of the *Anuttarayoga Tantras*. Artibus Asiae 58: 169–213.

Syed, R. 1990. Die Flora Altindiens in Literatur und Kunst (unpublished doctoral dissertation, submitted to the Philosophische Fakultät, Ludwig-Maximilians-Universität, München).

Takashima, J. 1992. *Dīkṣā* in the *Tantrāloka*. The Memoirs of the Institute of Oriental Culture (The University of Tokyo) 119: 45–84.

Taylor, K. 2001. Sir John Woodroffe, Tantra and Bengal: "An Indian Soul in a European Body?" Richmond, Surrey: Curzon Press.

Thakur, L.S. 1990. Application of Vāstupuraṣamaṇḍala [*sic!*] in the Indian Temple Architecture: *An Analysis of the Nāgara Temple Plans of Himachal Pradesh*. Artibus Asiae 50: 263–284.

Thakur, L.S. 1996. The Architectural Heritage of Himachal Pradesh: Origin and Development of Temple Styles. New Delhi: Munshiram Manoharlal Publishers.

Thurston, E. 1912. Omens and Superstitions of Southern India. London: T. Fisher Unwin.

Tillotson, G.H.R. 1987. The Rajput Palaces: The Development of an Architectural Style, 1450–1750. New Haven/London: Yale University Press.

Toffin, G. 1999. Spatial Categories of the Newars of Kathmandu Valley: The Inside – Outside Opposition. In: Himalayan Space: Cultural Horizons and Practices. Edited by B. Bickel and M. Gaenzle. Zürich: Völkerkundemuseum: 33–70.

Toganoo, S.M. 1971. The Symbol-System of Shingon Buddhism (unpublished doctoral dissertation, submitted to the Faculty of Claremont Graduate School, Claremont University).

Törzsök, J. 1999a. 'The Doctrine of Magic Female Spirits:' A Critical Edition of Selected Chapters of the *Siddhayogeśvarīmata(tantra)* with Annotated Translation and Analysis (unpublished doctoral dissertation, submitted to Oxford University).

Törzsök, J. 1999b. Why throw a flower?—Some problems concerning the Samaya initiation (unpublished paper presented at the Tantric seminar held in All Souls College, Oxford, Hilary term 1999).

Törzsök, J. forthcoming. The Siddhayogeśvarīmata. A critical edition and annotated translation.

Tribe, A.H.F. 1994. The Names of Wisdom: A Critical Edition and Annotated Translation of Chapters 1–5 of Vilāsavajra's Commentary on the Nāmasaṃgīti, With Introduction and Textual Notes (unpublished doctoral dissertation, submitted to the Faculty of Oriental Studies, Oxford University).

Tsuda, S. 1990. The Cult of Śmaśāna, the Realities of Tantrism. In: The Sanskrit Tradition and Tantrism. Panels of the VIIth World Sanskrit Conference, Kern Institute, Leiden: August 23–29, 1987. Edited by T. Goudriaan. Leiden: E.J. Brill: 96–108.

Tucci, G. 1949. Tibetan Painted Scrolls. 2 volumes. Roma: La Libreria Dello Stato.

Tucci, G. (1949) 1961. The Theory and Practice of the Maṇḍala. *With special reference to the modern psychology of the subconscious. Translated from the Italian by* A.H. Brodrick. London: Rider & Company.
[Translation of: Tucci, G.: Teoria e pratica del mandala, con particolare riguardo alla moderna psicologia de profondo. Roma: Astrolabio, 1949.]

Ugaz-Ortiz, J. 1986. Triangle and Triad, and their Relation to 'Heart' in the Śivaism of Kāśmīr and Śaktism. Orientalia Lovaniensia Periodica 17: 209–231.

Untracht, O. 1997. Traditional Jewelry of India. London: Thames and Hudson Ltd.

Urban, H.B. 1999. The Extreme Orient: The Construction of 'Tantrism' as a Category in the Orientalist Imagination. Religion 29: 123–146.

Vatsyayan, K. 1983. The Square and the Circle of the Indian Arts. New Delhi: Roli Books International.

Verardi, G. 1994. *Homa* and Other Fire Rituals in Gandhāra. Napoli: Istituto universitario orientale.

Vergati, A. 1982. A Sketch-Book of Newar Iconography. Printed as an appendix in: Lokesh Chandra: Buddhist Iconography in Nepalese Sketch-Books. New Delhi: Jayyed Press, 1984.

Vergati, A. 1986. Quelques remarques sur l'usage du maṇḍala et du yantra dans la vallée de Kathmandu, Népal. In: Mantras et diagrammes rituels dans l'hindouisme. Table Ronde, Paris 21–22 juin 1984. <Edited by A. Padoux.> Paris: Éditions du Centre national de la recherche scientifique: 37–45.

Volwahsen, A. 1969. Living Architecture: Indian. New York: Grosset & Dunlap.

Volwahsen, A. 2001. Cosmic Architecture in India: The Astronomical Monuments of Maharaja Jai Singh II. Munich: Prestel.

Wayman, A. 1973. The Buddhist Tantras: Light on Indo-Tibetan Esotericism. New York: Samuel Weiser.

Wayman, A. 1974. The Ritual in Tantric Buddhism of the Disciple's Entrance into the Maṇḍala. Studia Missionalia 23: 41–57.

Wayman, A. 1999. The *Maṇḍa* and the *-la* of the Term *Maṇḍala*. In: Tantric Buddhism: Centennial Tribute to Dr. Benoytosh Bhattacharyya. Edited by N.N. Bhattacharyya. New Delhi: Manohar: 23–30.

Wegner, G.M. 1992. Invocation of Nāsaḥdyaḥ. In: Aspects of Nepalese Traditions. Edited by B. Kölver. Stuttgart: Franz Steiner Verlag: 125–134.

Wheatley, P. 1971. The Pivot of the Four Quarters: a Preliminary Enquiry into the Origins and Character of the Ancient Chinese City. Edinburgh: Edinburgh University Press.

White, D.G. 1998. Transformations in the Art of Love: Kāmakalā Practices in Hindu Tantric and Kaula Traditions. History of Religions 38: 172–198.

Wilke, A. 2005. Mental Journeys, Cosmic Geography, and Intermediary Space: *śrīcakra* and *śrīcakrapūjā*. In: Sacred Geography of Hindu Goddesses. Festschrift to David Kinsley. Edited by R.P.B. Singh (forthcoming).

Willis, M.D. 1997. Temples of Gopakṣetra: A Regional History of Architecture and Sculpture in Central India AD 600–900. London: British Museum Press.

Witzel, M. 1992. Meaningful Ritual: Vedic, Medieval, and Contemporary Concepts in the Nepalese Agnihotra Ritual. In: Ritual, State and History in South Asia: Essays in Honour of J.C. Heesterman. Edited by A.W. van den Hoek / D.H.A. Kolff / M.S. Oort. Leiden: Brill: 774–827.

Woodroffe, J. 1914. Principles of Tantra: The Tantra-Tattva of Śrīyukta Śiva Candra Vidyārṇava Bhattacārya [*sic!*] Mahodaya. 2 volumes. London: Luzac & Co.

Woodroffe, J. 1956. Introduction to Tantra Śāstra. Madras: Ganesh & Co. (third edition).

Zanen, M. 1986. The Goddess Vajrayoginī and the kingdom of Sankhu (Nepal). Puruṣārtha 10: 125–166.

Zimmer, H. (1926) 1984. Artistic Form and Yoga in the Sacred Images of India. Translated from the German and edited by G. Chapple and J.B. Lawson in collaboration with J.M. McKnight. Princeton, New Jersey: Princeton University Press.
[Translation of: Zimmer, H.: Kunstform und Yoga im indischen Kultbild. Berlin: Frankfurter Verlags-Anstalt, 1926.]

INDEX